Foundation Web Design

Sham Bhangal
Tomasz Jankowski

DESIGNER TO DESIGNER™

Foundation Web Design

© 2003 friends of ED

First Printed March 2003

Trademark Acknowledgements

friends of ED has endeavored to provide trademark information about all the companies and products mentioned in this book by the appropriate use of capitals. However, friends of ED cannot guarantee the accuracy of this information.

Published by friends of ED

Arden House, Warwick Road,
Acocks Green, Birmingham.
B27 6BH. UK.
Printed in USA

ISBN 1-904344-16-x

Foundation Web Design

Credits

Authors Sham Bhangal Tomasz Jankowski	**Editors** Matthew Knight Alan McCann
Technical Reviewers Sally Cruikshank Leon Cych Cath O'Flynn Vibha Roy	**Project Manager** Jenni Harvey **Graphic Editors** Ty Bhogal Matt Clark Paul Grove
Proof Readers Simon Collins Jenni Harvey Jo Crichton	**Author Agents** Gaynor Riopedre Chris Matterface
Index Simon Collins Jo Crichton	**Development** Ben Renow-Clarke
Cover Design Katy Freer	**Original Concept** Andy Corsham
Managing Editor Sonia Mullineux	

Sham Bhangal

Sham found himself working with friends Of ED after being mislead into thinking he was applying for a Flash web design position for an internet start-up (remember those?). This misunderstanding was soon forgotten, and this is the 15th book he has contributed to so far. He would like to point out that he has moved on from wearing black leather and looking sullen, but has run out of the cute 'Young Sham' pictures seen in the aforementioned other books.

Sham lives in Somerset, England, with his partner Karen.

Tomasz Jankowski

Tomasz Jankowski is an award-winning Polish designer/ photographer, with seven years' experience in graphic design and four years' experience in web design and new media technologies. Four years ago he started his personal project, Mondo (www.mondo.com.pl), which features as the case study in this book. Professionally, Tomasz focuses on designing corporate web sites and presentations using HTML and Flash technology, and in 2000 he was showcased alongside other top designers in friends of ED's New Masters of Flash.

He currently lives in the city of Kalisz, Poland.

12 Introducing Flash 359

Appendix A: Getting Your Site Online 385

Appendix B: Debugging 397

Appendix C: HTML Events 403

Appendix D: Layers 409

Index 415

Welcome

Hello and welcome to the book that will take you through everything you need to know about web design. We believe that what we've achieved in this book is unique, and that the mix of topics that you need to know about gives you an unrivalled introduction to the otherwise complex and confusing world of web design.

By the end of the book, you'll have a broad and practical understanding of web design. More importantly, you'll know how it all fits together. You won't know how to create brilliant graphics, but have no idea how to make them appear in a pop-up window, nor will you create a brilliant website that suddenly looks like it's been hit by a large quantity of explosives when viewed on another platform or another browser.

You'll also have seen inside of a top-level professional site in our Case Study. Watch out for the Case Study headings in the book for more information, but suffice to say that – by the end of the book – you'll have created a site originally created by the award-winning Polish designer Tomasz Jankowski. More on this in the next chapter but take a look at the screenshot for a sneak preview.

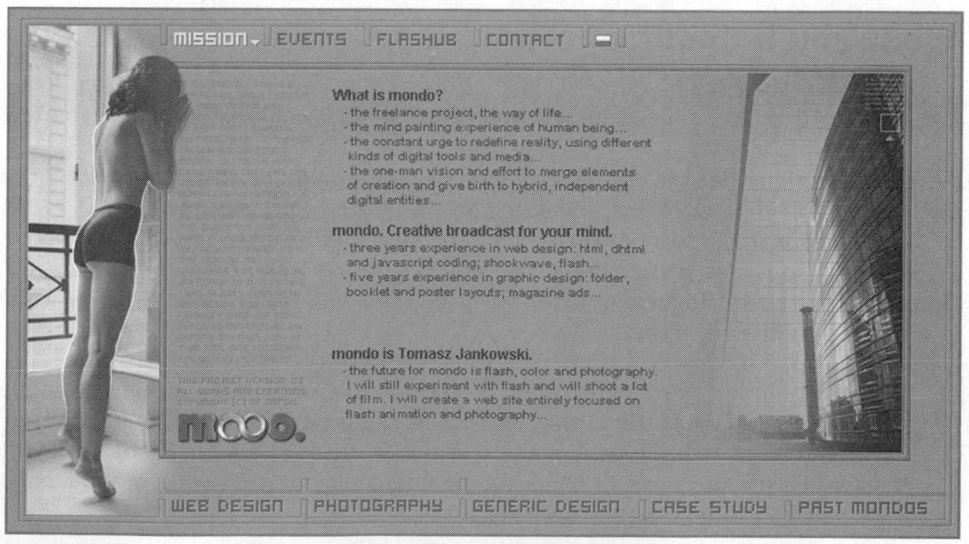

How to use this book

This book follows the standard friends of ED Foundation structure of building up a case study site as you progress through the book. To get the maximum benefit, then, you are recommended to read right the way through the book, from start to end. There's nothing to stop you going straight for certain chapters on certain subjects, but unless you've got a project deadline breathing down your neck, you'll probably get more out of the experience by seeing your knowledge gradually build up and fit together.

We're covering a lot of ground, and we've had to make sure that we only include material that's relevant and important - so even if you feel like you might not need to know about a certain topic, give it a try, and you may well be surprised. In a few cases, we've encountered information that, while highly useful, is not absolutely vital, and this has been placed in the Appendices at the back of the book.

Because we're covering so many different topics – image-editing, scripting, HTML, CSS – you're inevitably going to find some chapters more difficult than others. Which chapters you find easy and which you find hard are going to vary depending on your skills and experience. The beauty of this book is that, even if you do find certain chapters difficult, you'll be able to see what you've learned put into practice immediately, and there are never more than two consecutive chapters on the same subject, so you'll soon move onto something different.

If you're looking for some specific information, or get lost, your best friend is the lovingly prepared index at the back of your book. The Mondo website case study used throughout this book is divided into separate tutorials for indexing purposes, there are entries for standalone tutorials, and of course pointers to definitions of key terms.

What you'll need

Not much, apart from yourself and your imagination. We'll be using a plain text editor for most of the time, so PC users will need to find Notepad, and Mac users TextEdit (or SimpleText for OS9 users).

It'll be useful if you have the most recent versions of the Internet Explorer and Netscape Navigator browsers on your machines, and at the time of going to press, these are 6 (5 for Mac) and 7 respectively. As we'll be learning, part of successful design involves testing to make sure that your site works on both browsers, so it is worth acquiring both: you can do this from the many free CDs from magazines and web service providers floating around, or by downloading them from http://microsoft.com/downloads and www.netscape.com respectively.

We'll also be using Adobe Photoshop or Macromedia Fireworks for our image editing chapters. If you've got access to either of these, that's great (they're occasionally slightly different in the way that they do things, and when that happens, we've split the exercises into two). If not, then either take a look around the free CDs on your desk, or go to www.macromedia.com/ fireworks or www.adobe.com/photoshop and download fully functioning trial versions.

The final chapter of this book is an introduction to the exciting world of Macromedia Flash – you don't have to complete the exercises to follow along, but to get the full benefit, it might be worth getting a trial version of the software from www.macromedia.com/flash.

Conventions

We want this book to be as clear and easy to use as possible, so we've introduced a number of layout styles that we've used throughout.

- We'll use different styles to emphasize things that appear on the screen, KEYSTROKES and also hyperlinks.

- If we introduce a new **important term** then this will be in bold.

> *If there's something you shouldn't miss, it will be highlighted it like this! When you see the bubble, pay attention.*

- When we want you to click on a menu, and then through subsequent sub-menus we will indicate to like so: File > New. This would translate to:

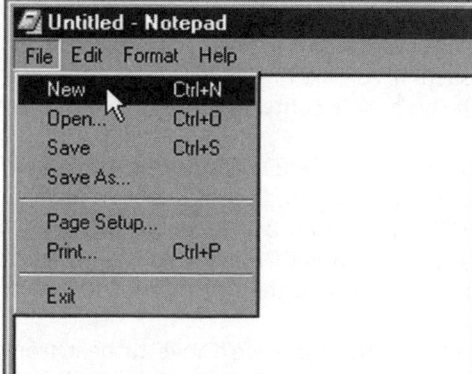

- If there's a practical exercise for you to follow then it'll be headed:

Like this, in a bubble

1. Then the steps that you have to follow will be numbered.

2. Follow them through, checking the screenshots and diagrams for more hints.

Further explanation of the steps may appear indented like so.

3.   When you get to the end, you can stop.

■   When we use code, we use a `courier font` to denote this. Sometimes, we want to highlight the code you need to add in a block of code you've already entered, so we make it **bold**. Finally, when a line of code that *doesn't* need a carriage return added to it automatically scrolls onto the next line, we add a ➡ character to make sure you don't go pressing that ENTER key and potentially break your script...

Download Files

This book is based on practical exercises, and not esoteric description. If you go to www.friendsofed.com/fwd, then you'll find completed versions of all the chapter exercises, as well as chapter-by-chapter versions of the case study files, so that you can save yourselves some typing by downloading starting documents and check your files against ours if things start to go wrong.

To view the Mondo Case Study source files exactly as they looked originally, you'll need to have a couple of fonts created by miniml.com's Craig Kroeger installed, and these are also available from www.friendsofed.com/fwd. (If you load these files in Photoshop 7, you will be asked whether it can update the font layers for vector support, as a result of a new feature in Photoshop 7 – OK this, and everything will work as intended.)

Support – we're here to help

At friends of ED, we aim for the purchase of a book to be the start of a relationship that helps you, and not simply the end of a transaction. As part of this belief, we offer fast and free technical support. If you encounter any problems with this book's contents, please don't hesitate to get in touch.

You can do this by emailing support@friendsofED.com, quoting the last for digits of the ISBN in the subject of the e-mail (that's 416x). Even if our dedicated support team are unable to solve your problem immediately, your queries will be passed onto the people who put the book together, the editors and authors, to solve. All foED authors help with the support on their books, and will either directly mail people with answers, or (more usually) send their response to an editor to pass on.

The relationship doesn't stop there, though – we'd love to hear from you: what books you'd like us to publish in the future, how we can make even better books, and what your favorite Star Wars film is. In order to let you talk to us and to each other, and to ask more general questions not directly related to the book content, we've set up a forum for this book at: www.friendsofed.com/fwd/support

Do drop by and let us know how you're doing. For news about new friends of ED books, sample chapters, author interviews, and more, try www.friendsofED.com.

Foundation Flash MX Applications provides a solid introduction to the exciting world of Flash applications, the popular way of presenting visually rich interfaces to useful data and services.

Photoshop Elements 2 may be Photoshop 7's younger, cheaper, sibling, but with our Tips & Tricks book we uncover some of its powerful hidden secrets.

Flash MX does video...we all know that, but see just what is possible when some of the hottest designers around get creative in Flash MX Video Creativity.

Who would have thoughts you could get your hands on a full color book covering five pieces of software for under $10? It's just 9.9 cents per fresh idea in 99 Phenomenal Digital Photo Tricks.

In case you missed them, January bought you...Flash MX Components Most Wanted, Photoshop Elements 2 Face Makeovers and Foundation Swift 3D

Introducing Web Design

What this chapter will do

This chapter will show you the process of web design in outline, using the completed files from the example site for this book, the *Mondo* site by Tomasz Jankowski. We'll look at all the components that make this and other sites work, and look at the sort of applications and workflows that went into their creation.

You'll soon have a firm grounding in how web design works, what tools you will need and what processes you will work through in your time as a web designer. We'll specifically cover:

- Designing for the Web
- Browsers
- Web creation tools
- The components of a web site
- Website usability and navigation

What you'll have learned by the end of this chapter

You will already be aware of what web pages look like by using the web previously. This chapter will have shown you the other side of the mirror; *what a website looks like from the designer's point of view*. You'll have seen how the site is built up and which files do what, and how they are all created.

Rather than try to explain what this book will do, it is probably better to tell you what this book will *not do* and what it *is not*:

- This isn't one of those big thick web reference books, but hey, you can tell that just by looking at it!

- It's not one of those beginner's web design books that spends the early chapters looking at web design from the user's point of view. We're going to assume you are already a competent web user, and already have a view of what your favorite sites are, and why. This assumes you're looking to create and design websites from the off.

- Lastly, we won't be following a beginner's case study site that we cooked up specifically for the book, and neither will we take the easy way out by just pointing vaguely at successful websites currently on the Web as examples (that no-one involved with the book actually took any part in designing). Instead we'll use a commercially proven site, originally designed for the Web, and not just for this book.

> The case study site in Foundation Web Design was originally designed by Tomasz Jankowski, the acclaimed Polish designer first featured in friends of ED's landmark New Masters of Flash book – but more on this later!

What this book *will* be presenting is a design-centric view for beginners. We took a long hard look at the world of the Web and tried to cram in all the core information that you need to be able to create a website that holds its own in the wide wide world of the World Wide Web.

The trouble with web design is that there are four fairly hefty subjects you need to know, each of which is probably a whole book in itself:

- **HTML** – the easy to use code that makes up what we know as a web page.

- **Web Graphics** – the images that spice up your design – from full color photos to interface elements, buttons and animations.

- **JavaScript** – the scripting language that allows you to enhance the user's experience, generate effects, open pop-up windows and more.

- **CSS** – the technology that allows you to control the presentation of entire sites in just a few lines of code.

The cool thing about these big subjects is that you spend 80% of your time just using 20% of each, so those are the parts we will be looking at in this book; the bits you *need* to create standard websites. That's better than teaching you how to write *beginner* websites, because that would teach you the easy parts rather than the stuff you really need.

It does, however, mean that the chapters are *not* graded from easy to hard as the book moves along, something that you should be aware of from the start. We're covering the topics *in the order you need to know them* rather than confusing you by ordering them any other way. This means for example that we'll be exploring some JavaScript fairly early on (**Chapter 3**) but this will allow us to build on this in later chapters and keep our case study example as interesting and as realistic as possible.

Yeah, I know, a simple enough idea. Not many people do it in books, though, so we thought we'd better point it out.

How web design works

The best thing about designing for the Web is that web design in principle is a lot less complicated than you might think.

A website is stored remotely on a server – this is a computer which answers requests from other computers to see the web pages – it then serves them up. The information is transmitted to your computer and you use a browser (such as Internet Explorer or Netscape Navigator) to decode the information and display the website.

Take a look at this in action, with a 'randomly selected' website...

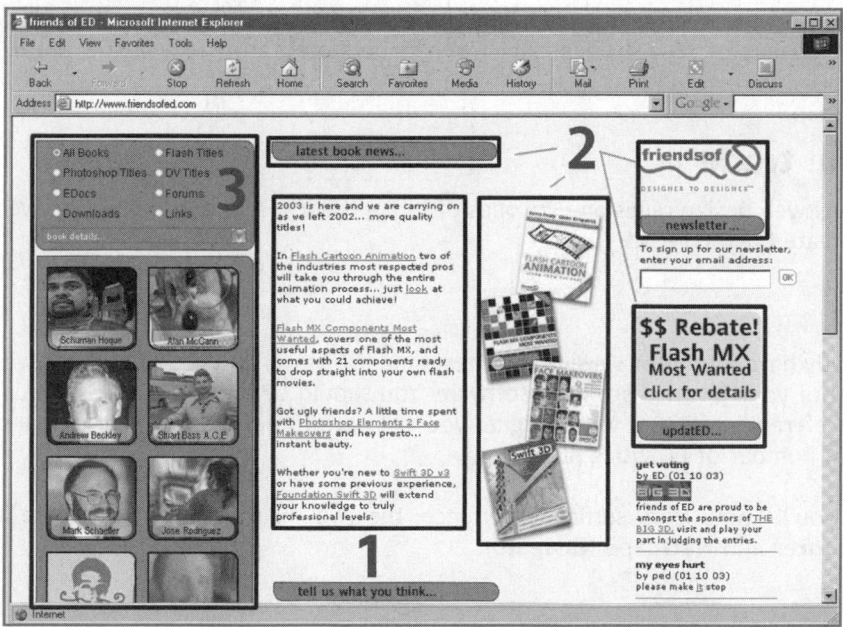

The friends of ED homepage is made up of three main interface elements:

1.   The first is text; this text can appear in a range of fonts and formats, and also include hyperlinks – which take you to new pages in this site or another site.

2. The second element is graphics; we've only highlighted some examples but all the buttons and headings, as well as the foED logo and the 'Rebate' ad are graphics – images which are composited into the page by your browser.

3. The third is Flash – an animation technology we'll be seeing towards the end of the book. As well as graphics your page can include other visual elements that, as in this case, can be made to integrate seamlessly into the page design. In this example, the Flash sidebar is used to generate an animated gallery of foED authors.

This is how it works. A web page is made up of HTML code, which your browser decodes into the page you see.

HTML stands for **HyperText Markup Language**. The HTML code contains any text you include as well as formatting and layout information. Some text, as you see above, has special properties, such as the hyperlinks that will take you to different parts of the site.

In addition to the text-based content, the HTML also includes references to other files, such as graphics, sound files or Flash. Since the text-only HTML cannot contain these more complex kinds of information, these files exist separately on your server, and the HTML code tells your browser where to find them and where to put them on the page.

The end result is a mixture of text, graphics and other elements that looks seamless but is actually made up of maybe dozens of separate files which might be stored anywhere in the world, from Canada to Singapore.

Tools of the trade

At a basic level web design relies on two kinds of tool – the tool you use to view the Web and the tool you use to create for the Web.

The browser

You will already have a tool for viewing websites – the browser – and you're probably very used to the look and feel of your favorite browsing software. You should be aware though that not everyone will share your preference and as a web designer you will have to design sites that look and feel right on the maximum number of browsing platforms.

As I expect you'll know from surfing experience, the two main browsers out there are **Microsoft Internet Explorer** and **Netscape Navigator**.

> *Once you've got the 'big two' under your belt, another type of browser to get used to looking your designs with is a text only browser such as* **Lynx** *(www.trill-home.com/lynx.html). Such browsers ignore any images, and show the pages as text only. They are useful for seeing if your pages are suitable for the sight impaired, something that is fast becoming a legal requirement in many countries and/or clients (particularly government and public information sites). We'll look more at accessibility issues a little later in the chapter.*

Internet Explorer is by far the most common browser (about 90% of all browsers), and therefore should be your main testing browser. Netscape Navigator is much less common (about 5%) although this figure is still high enough to mean that you have to make sure all your pages also work on Netscape.

For the examples we will look at, you don't necessarily need the most recent browser, but we recommend that you are using:

- Netscape Navigator 6 or higher (at the time of writing the current version is version 7)

- Microsoft Internet Explorer 5 or higher (at the time of writing the current version for PCs is 6, and for Macs is 5)

We won't go into the issues of what went on before those versions, and why there are all sorts of major compatibility issues before these magic revisions, but will say that if you have at least these versions, then you should be good to go.

> *If you are unsure of your current browser version, you can go to* Help > About Netscape *or* Help > About Internet Explorer. *In many versions, this information is also displayed on the splash screen. You can get newer versions of these browsers from* www.microsoft.com *and* www.netscape.com *respectively, or from the wide range of magazine and internet provider CD-ROMs that come bundled with these most essential tools.*

Web creation software

You've probably been surfing the Web for ages, but as you now start on your journey towards *creating* professional looking sites of your own, you'll need to be aware of the wide range of tools you can use to design, author and edit on the Web.

Maybe your choices here might be budget dependent, or down to ease of use or personal choice, but in Foundation Web Design, we'll try to cater for the most basic software you might have. For creating HTML and CSS code, this is a simple text editor like **TextEdit** (**SimpleText** for OS 9 folks) or **Notepad**. For image editing and web graphics we will be using the most popular choices for this task – **Adobe Photoshop** and **Macromedia Fireworks**.

We will also be using **Netscape Composer**, the free web page editing package which comes bundled with their browser to give you a taste of WYSIWYG (What You See Is What You Get) visual editing, where you create and edit pages that appear just how they will appear in the browser.

Many web designers use a professional HTML editor / web page designer tool such as Macromedia Dreamweaver or Microsoft FrontPage. These are not necessary for the solid foundation that this book seeks to offer in HTML, JavaScript and CSS, but you may well wish to consider obtaining one of them in the future, as they can speed your workflow, and - in the case of Dreamweaver – add the potential for some exciting and easy use of databases, a subject slightly outside of the scope of this book.

The Foundation Web Design Case Study

As we've already touched upon, we're going to be following through a professionally designed (and award-winning) site example.

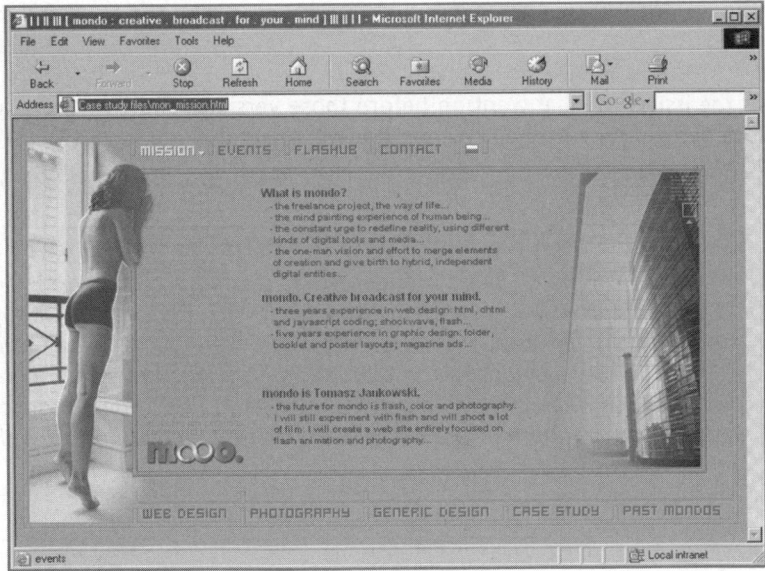

This is a previous iteration of Tomasz Jankowski's stunning homesite at www.mondo.pl. His designerly mix of graphics, interface elements and cutting edge layout is ideal for our purposes, and will help us showcase all the most important aspects of great web design. In each chapter, we'll work towards building our site up, putting into practice everything we've learned.

Site concept

Every designer has his or her own way of defining what the look and feel of the site will be. Sometimes it involves looking at other sites for inspiration, or it can involve looking at other design disciplines such as magazines, films, posters, or whatever. It can even involve no preconception, just doodling whatever comes into your mind's eye. You almost certainly have design ideas already in you, although you might not necessarily have the skills to realize these ideas and get them onto the Web – which is where we come in.

There are many ways your site can come together. You can start building your site around textual content, adding links and pictures later, or you can go for a very visual design where a graphic interface is your starting point and text comes later. *Foundation Web Design* will equip you for all possible workflows.

You've probably seen sites that consist almost entirely of graphics, and might even have wondered how designers go about weaving all these individual graphic elements into one seamless whole. The answer is that professional graphics products like Photoshop and Fireworks give you the ability to create whole web interfaces, which you can then divide up into smaller individual images (called **slicing**). These packages even generate the necessary HTML which you use to piece the graphics together. We'll be covering this most design-friendly of workflows later in the book.

> *In the earlier parts of the book, we'll concentrate on building from the ground up, moving onto the creation of more advanced graphics-based interfaces after* **Chapter 6**.

Preliminary views of what the site will look like take many forms, from Photoshop images built up with photographs, hand drawn or scanned images, to something as simple as a few sketches. In any case, these are called **storyboards**, and not only do they define what the site will look like, but also what it *does*.

In the example of our case study site, the whole thing was originally designed in Photoshop. Not only were the graphics built up to show what the final site would look like; they were also used to form the final graphics themselves.

Constructing your storyboards so that they also become the final graphics themselves is a well-known trick in the industry; no work goes unused in the final design, and it allows you to create sites quicker, but it is also a trick that takes practice.

In the real world, you would only do a set of storyboards to this high standard for one page until the client thinks it is a good idea; the rest of the pages could just be sketches until the go ahead to do a full site development is given.

> *Don't be disappointed if it takes several attempts before a final page design emerges; this is one of the realities of design. It never works out like on the TV where the first idea is a maverick long shot, but is the one that works!*

For now, let's take a look at all the files that make up our case study site...

Final site files

For this section, you will need the `mondo_assets.zip` file. When you unzip this, you will see *loads* of files:

> *Don't be daunted by the sheer volume of files. The number of files involved depends on the number of pages and also the number of individual graphics, icons and buttons used. Because of this, some small sites have tons of files and vice versa.*

As well as there being loads of files, there are also a few different *types* of file and we've begun to discuss this already. Let's take a journey through the different parts which will make up our case study, learning a little bit more about web design technologies as we go...

HTML

You can see the individual web pages by double clicking on any of the HTML icons. The page here is what you will see if you double - click `mon_news.html`.

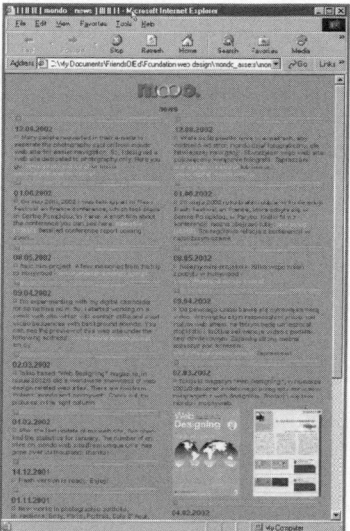

Although the next few steps can be done using Internet Explorer, you will get more out of using Netscape Navigator. It is a paradox of web design that although Internet Explorer is the most commonly used browser, Netscape Navigator is actually the better choice for seeing a web page from a designer's eye view...

You can see the raw HTML file by selecting View > Source (Internet Explorer) or View > Page Source (Netscape Navigator).

As you can see, it's a text file, and quite a complicated looking one at that! It consists of things called **tags** (the things that start and end in < and > respectively). Some of these are longer than others. As mentioned earlier HTML is a fairly easy to understand language – and you can guess fairly easily what the `<img>` tag does, or what `<title>` refers to. The information between the tags simply tells you things like 'what the title of the page is' or 'where to find the image'.

They are all doing fundamentally the same thing though, and that is to give the browser *instructions on how to build up the page*, and this brings us neatly onto the graphics...

Graphic assets

You can see how graphics are added into the mix if you select View > Page Info (Netscape Navigator only).

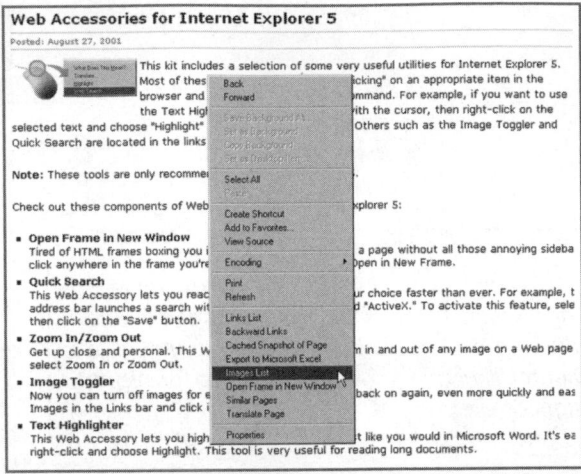

> If you have Internet Explorer 5 there is a cool add-in for this version called **Web Accessories** – which adds more than a few neat functions to your right-click context menu. These include Images List and Links List, which together form an IE version of Page Info.

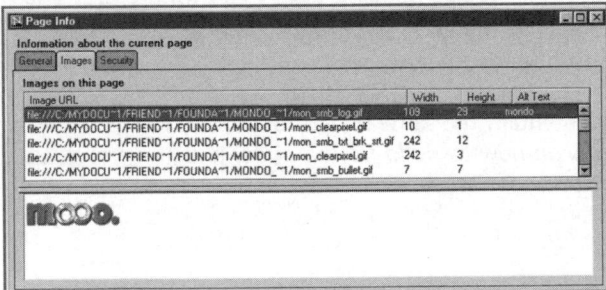

Sticking with Netscape as an example, click on the Images tab. This window shows a column called Image URL and this shows the locations of all the separate images that make up the web page. If you highlight any of the image URL lines, the corresponding graphic file will be shown in the bottom panel.

It's like I said earlier. The HTML doesn't *contain* the graphics, but it tells the browser where to find them. The HTML is a bit like an instruction pamphlet that tells you how to build a model car. All the bits are separate when you open the box, but the instructions on how to put them all together to create a 1:72 scale model of an F1 racing car are close to hand. It's the same with a web page.

The HTML document is the instructions, and the parts are all the other files. If the browser reads (or **parses** to use the technical term) the HTML in order tag by tag and follows the instructions these supply, the page is built up piece by piece. The individual parts (graphics etc) are not part of the instructions, but where to find them is.

In professional web design, each graphic will also have been manipulated in a number of ways to make it more suitable for the Web. These manipulations can include:

- Reducing file size by **optimizing** the graphic, a process that reduces information in the image that will not be missed by the user, but will tend to mean the image will download faster.

- Combining a series of static images to create an animated sequence (rather like a flipbook animation).

- Adding special effects such as transparency, so the image has no background.

The HTML file actually contains something else as well as the HTML; it contains **scripts**.

Scripts

Scripts can be written in a number of languages, but one of the most common for standard web design is **JavaScript**. Scripts tell the web page what to *do* once it is assembled, and can allow you to interact with a page, or allow the designer to control aspects of the visitor's experience, from altering parts of the page *on the fly* to generating pop-up windows.

We'll cover JavaScript further in **Chapter 3**, and then in even more detail later on in the book. We're covering this early as part of our commitment to telling you what you need to know in the order you need to know it.

Not only is JavaScript a key technology but it's a remarkably designer-friendly language, relatively easy to learn and use, where you can get maximum results from minimum typing!

Cascading Style Sheets

Apart from the HTML file (and associated scripts) and the graphics, there is one other important file; the CSS file. This contains global formatting instructions for the whole site, relating to typography, colors, links, and even precise layout of the page.

You can open these with a simple text editor because - like the HTML files - they are text only. Here's a view of one of them in Windows Notepad:

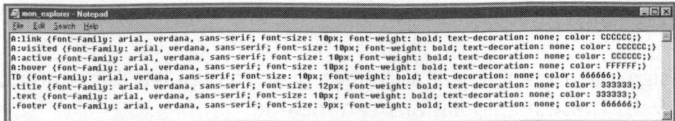

As you can see, this looks a little dense, but not to worry, it's really very simple (if a bit repetitive). We'll learn more about CSS in its own dedicated chapter later on (**Chapter 4**) but for now you just need to know that CSS provides the Style Sheet that our HTML pages conform to.

Navigation

When you click on a link (in this site, links will highlight when you mouse over them) what happens is that the HTML contains a tag that again points to an external file. In this case, the file is not a graphic, CSS or other file that is needed to make up part of the page, but is instead *another HTML file*. The browser will load this file up, and the new page defined by it will be built up, as was the previous one.

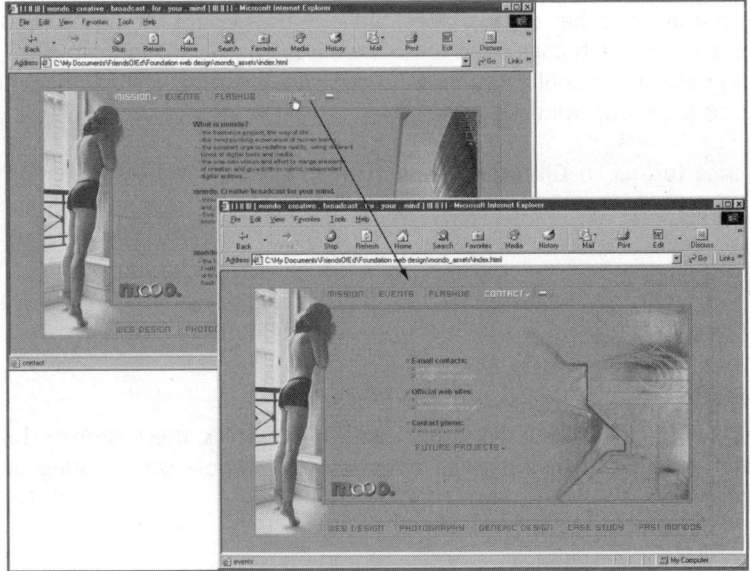

Although navigation is one of the best things about the Web, and you can be just one click away from any bit of information anywhere in the world, the actual design of the basic links is one of the easiest things about web pages.

Of course if you think about it, navigating from one page to the next, and using links to find information is really what the Web is all about. This raises one final issue for this introductory chapter, and that is the question of how **usable** your site is.

Design vs. Usability

One of the most important considerations when defining your site is **usability**, and this will be one of your issues when you define your conceptual site design and storyboards.

Usability has different aspects, these include:

1.   **Prior knowledge**. This relates to how much the user needs to know before they can begin to become familiar with your site and how to use it. Generally, the less prior knowledge the user needs, the better, although when your audience is very specific (such as a medical site for surgeons, say), you can safely assume quite a lot.

2.   **Familiarization**. This is how fast a user can see how your site works, and how quickly they can begin to use it. Many sites where usability is a prime concern use the concept of predictability: everything is where you'd expect it to be. Although many successful sites do this, there is also the often-conflicting issue of design flair; designers like to create original sites, and this makes them non-standard.

3.   **Efficiency**. This relates to how quickly the user can get their required tasks done once they are familiar with your site. There is an unofficial rule of thumb that any page on a site should be accessible from any other by no more than two mouse clicks (the 'Two Click rule').

4.   **Fault prevention and recovery**. This relates to how easy it is for the user to make mistakes or become confused, and once they do, how easy is it for them to get help and/or recover. Sign posting help links next to any parts of your site that may confuse is always a good idea.

5.   **Experience**. This is a measure of how a user would rate your site. It includes issues such as how much they liked it, and whether they will come back again. This doesn't always correspond to how usable the site was because some sites are not about 'how fast can I go', but *entertainment* value.

6.   **Accessibility**. This is a measure of how useful the site is to extreme ends of the cross-section of users. If your site can serve a blind person as well as it can serve a sighted person, and can also serve someone using a mouse-less palm top computer, then you are big on accessibility. Accessibility is fast becoming a legal imperative in public information sites.

In general, the points above have different weightings for different types of site, and this always relates to the **purpose** of the site itself.

The two sides of the coin...

Some sites are there to provide information and so the user would visit on a data gathering or fact-finding mission. This means that **3** might be by far the most important point, with **1**, **2**, and **4** being of lesser importance.

A good example of an information site is www.scambusters.org, an e-zine dedicated to revealing the most popular internet scams. People who go to this site may want to get clued up about Identity Theft or the World Trade Center scams, or just to get some information about all the bad people out there, so the site uses a very basic scheme that is content led.

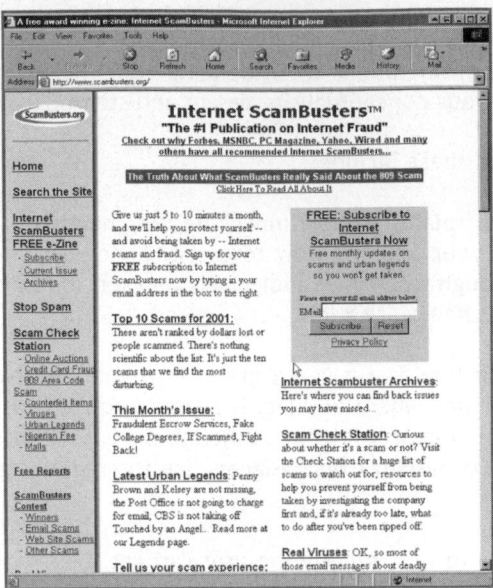

How can we arrange the site so that the user can get to the relevant information quickly?
A common factor to notice here is the use of links; users tend to search for a link that describes what they are looking for rather than the surrounding text. By making all your main title headings into obvious links, you can get the user to look at them first.

Another common feature here is the way that the site uses a *metaphor* to increase the speed of familiarisation. By looking like a newspaper, something that all users will already be used to, the site not only makes it obvious what to expect, it also subtly suggests that this is an up to the minute news site.

Finally, the site design contains no surprises or anything that would give a low specification computer any problems. The homogeneity of the design makes it easy (or at least, easier) for palm tops and other potentially non-standard hardware to have very few issues with it.

This lo-fi design ethos is consistent with a content led site that wants to be compatible with as many users as possible.

Other sites are there to provide entertainment, so point **5** is actually the main goal, and the others are some way behind. Where you are providing an online cartoon series, the issue of whether the user liked viewing episode 1 enough to see episode 2 is of primary importance; a totally efficient site that takes you to something you did not actually enjoy is not useful. Have a look at http://pi.canongate.net/life_of_pi.htm, a promotional web site for the book *The Life of Pi*.

Here, you stay at the site to see what will happen next; the whole thing is a series of puzzles, experimentation, and exploration. In a strict sense, the site is totally unusable, but that ignores the fact that it is also both novel and fun, and that's why you carry on!

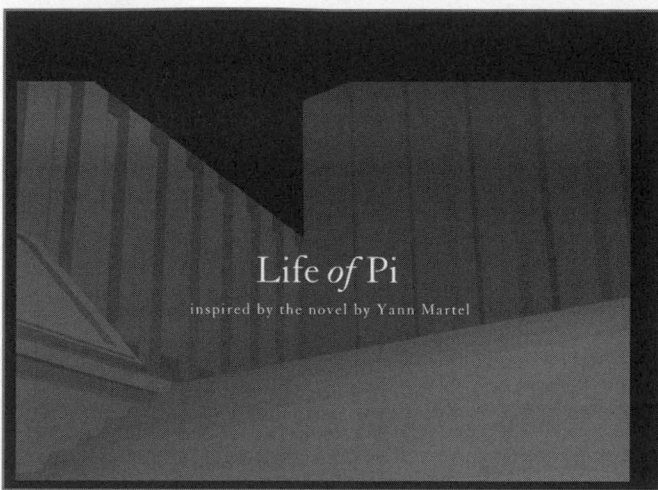

By far the best way of learning usability for the beginner is to bear in mind the six points above when browsing the Web, picking out the way popular sites achieve them. There are also a large number of usability sources available on the net.

> *One of the best places to read up on real world usability for the web is* www.usability.gov. *It is run by the US National Cancer Institute, and is dedicated to providing usability and accessibility tips for web designers. Better than most books on the subject, it even has a walk through of a typical site design, which is useful for the beginner to pick up tips and tricks.*

As a designer, you always have to know what the purpose of the site is before you can start to think about its usability. Although this is a common sense conclusion to make from all of the above, experience shows that it is not always that clear cut; the client is not always forthcoming with the relevant information, which is:

- **What** is the aim of the site?
- **Who** is it aimed at, and does this group include anyone who might have special requirements?

So, how does this final section relate to our case study site?

The Mondo site

The Mondo site is there as an online flyer to promote the work of a designer. It has to have a cool designerly look about it that makes the potential client say 'we like this stuff, we want one like it'.

Despite the designed look, it also has to have a navigation that looks as if Tom recognises the issues with usability, and it also has to allow the client to get an overview of what is on offer quickly and efficiently.

Finally, for folks who have simply dropped by to see what is up in Tom's world, they want to be entertained by some cool and interesting content.

> *Small text is one of those common designer idiosyncrasies that you either love or hate. The Mondo site and other design houses use it often in their portfolio/homesites because it avoids needing a scrollbar, and results in either compact site pages or lots of empty space. Some usability experts hate it, and have put small text in the list of don't dos. Obviously, this is one of those issues that come back to purpose. There is no right or wrong, it's simply a case of whether it is compatible with the site aim and the target audience.*

The site is therefore part way between the *clear text/clear links/no surprises* 100% usable site, and the *idiosyncratic/novel/requires thought to use* designer site. Good website to use as a book project then!

We'll be following the Mondo site throughout the book, starting properly in **Chapter 3**, by which time we'll have learned enough of the basics to really get to grips with building the structure of our site. In the next chapter, we'll turn our attention to the bread and butter of web designing – HTML…

HTML

What this chapter will do

This chapter is going to cover a fair bit of ground in that, by the time you've finished it, you'll have a firm grasp of all the major HTML tags that you'll see in use on the Web. Don't worry, though - we'll give you examples to work through so that you see everything that we talk about in action. HTML was designed to be simple, and we've kept it that way.

To this end, this chapter is divided into three main sections. We'll start by setting up a basic HTML file, and then take a look at the structure of an HTML file. After that, we can really get our hands messy, so we'll run through an exercise that shows us the common tags that we can use to format text. We'll finish up by seeing how to include graphics and links in our pages.

This chapter will show you how to create HTML files that:

- Use formatted text
- Include graphics
- Link to other pages

What you will have learned by the end of this chapter

By the end of this chapter, you will be able to recognise and understand the structure of HTML documents. You will have learned how to build web pages that include formatted text, links, and graphics - and be more than ready for the exciting potential unlocked by the following chapters.

In this chapter, we'll take a hands-on approach. We won't spend ages explaining in-depth intricacies of HTML; we'll just do it, and explain as we go along. You could just get a copy of a visual web page creation program like **Dreamweaver** or **FrontPage** at this stage, and use them to create HTML for you. The problem with this approach is that you don't learn about the HTML that these programs produce, so you won't be able to understand what's going on, and how to tweak it.

It also makes things much more difficult for you when you start looking at other web technologies later, so the **hand-coding** route we're going to take here stays true to the core doctrine of the Foundation series of books by giving you a rock-solid basis on which to build.

HTML authoring requires nothing but the basic text editor installed with your operating system - that's **Notepad** for PC users, and **TextEdit** for Mac users (or **SimpleText** for folks using OS9). Notepad should be in the Start > Programs > Accessories folder, and if you have a Mac, TextEdit and SimpleText are found with the rest of your accessories.

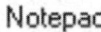

Notepad

TextEdit

Although HTML is text-based, it uses its own file extension to distinguish it from other files. HTML files, as you've probably seen, end with the extension `.html`*.*

Be aware that, whereas you can open most files by double-clicking them, your HTML files will be different. If you double-click an HTML file, it will be opened *for viewing* in your default browser. To open it *for editing*, either use File > Open in your text editor, or (PC) right-click the file and Open With > Notepad/(Mac) CTRL-click, and select Open.

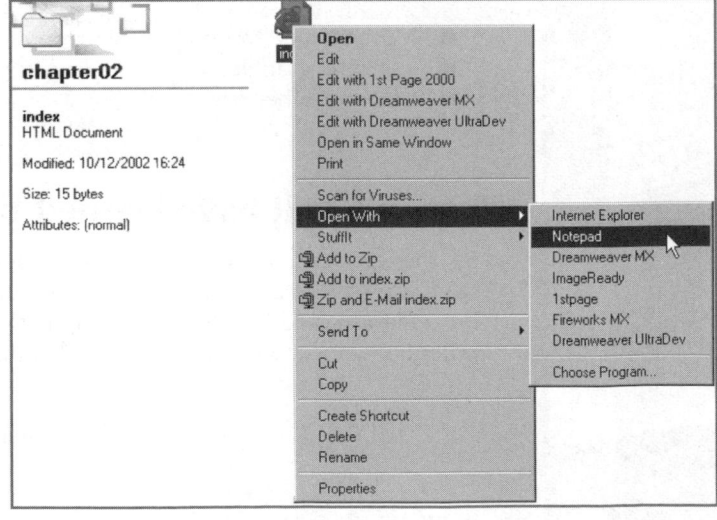

Creating a basic HTML file

OK, let's get to work.

1. The first thing we probably need to do is set up a folder to put our work into, so create one called `chapter02`.

2. Next, open your text editor or word processor and enter the following in a blank file:

    ```
    <html>
    </html>
    ```

    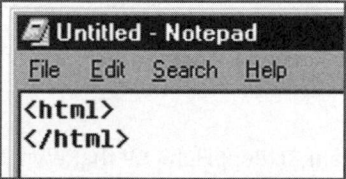

3. Now save this as a plain text document called `index.html` in your `chapter02` folder.

    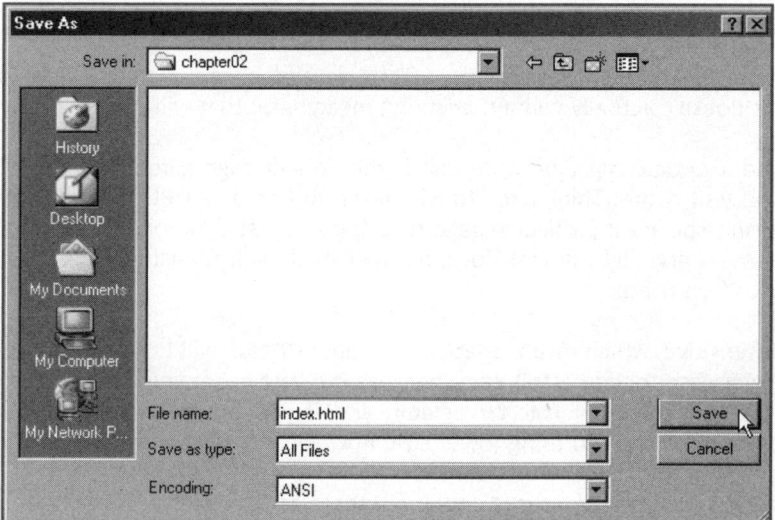

4. If you make sure the Save as type box contains All Files, you'll be able to make sure the program doesn't automatically add a `.txt` extension by mistake. If you end up with a file called `index.html.txt`, it will be recognized as a text file and you'll have to rename it. You can tell if your file is saved correctly by checking if the icon for the file looks like a web page icon: for my computer (where Internet Explorer is the main browser) the file looks like the image over the page:

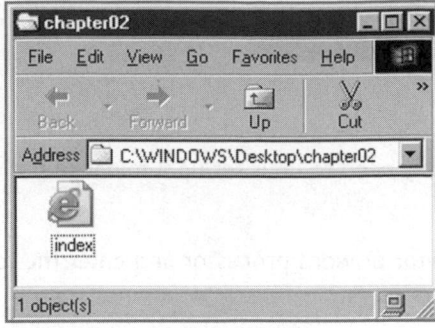

5. To see this file in your default browser, simply double-click it, and you should see a blank white screen in the browser.

So what does that get us? A blank screen! Huh? All that work for a screen full of nothing? Well, if you've got a blank screen, you have proved that you can create HTML files and your browser recognizes them as such, which is a small step, but very important.

So why did we get a blank page, and why did we call it index.html?

- We saw a blank screen because the HTML we added earlier simply tells the browser 'this is HTML'. It doesn't actually contain anything meaningful that will appear in the window just yet.

- We called it index.html because that is the default page name that the browser will head to when you visit a site. Think back to whenever you enter a URL such as www.friendsofed.com. This doesn't specify a particular page to display, it just asks for the default homepage of that site. Browsers actually will look for a number of default filenames, and index.html is one of the most often used.

HTML is case-insensitive, which means that <html> and <HTML> will both work in the same way. We're going to use lower case for our HTML tags, because it is fast becoming the standard convention. Most HTML editors use lower case HTML by default, and if you move up to XHTML, you'll find that it demands lower case for tags, so using lower case now will pay dividends later.

You can also add as many blank spaces and line returns as you want in HTML: the browser will ignore these, and adding them can make your HTML a lot easier for you to read. The following three examples will all have the same effect, but we'll be using the final version:

> *Don't worry – we'll be telling you what the* <head> *and* <body> *tags do in a moment...*

Version 1:

```
<HTML><HEAD></HEAD><BODY></BODY></HTML>
```

Version 2:

```
<HTML>
<HEAD>
</HEAD>
<BODY>
</BODY>
</HTML>
```

Version 3:

```
<html>

<head>
</head>

<body>
</body>

</html>
```

Add the last version to your index.html file, and we have built our basic HTML file. All HTML files have this basic structure.

The structure of an HTML file

The <html> tag simply denotes the start of a HTML document, and the </html> tag denotes the end. Within a HTML file, there are two parts: the **head** and **body**. Both contain formatting tags, but they work on different parts of the web page. The <html>, <head>, and <body> tags are sometimes referred to as the **structure tags**, because they define the different parts of a HTML document:

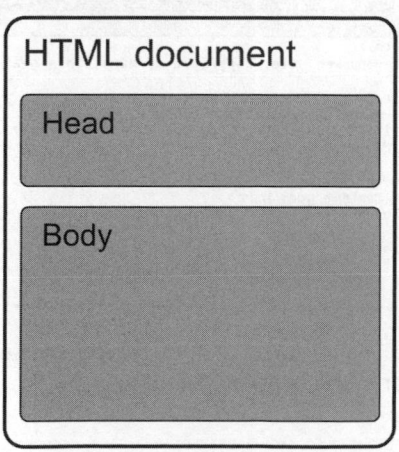

The head

The head part of the HTML document tells the browser things about the overall document itself. It's like the cover of a book. The first thing the cover will tell you is the title and the author, plus some blurb about what the book is actually about. More subtly, it also tells the bookshop stuff like which shelf to put the book on (the shelving category), and other information (in the form of barcodes) that is not meant for us, but for the shop's stock-tracking computer systems.

So the cover tells you a lot of things about the contents of the book, without actually being part of the main text of the book. It also tells other people or systems, stuff that isn't meant for you directly, but which allows you to find the book easily. For a web page, the 'shelving category' and 'barcodes' relate to a number of things, including search engines and HTML validation applications.

Only a select few tags are allowed to exist in the head part of the HTML document. The most important of these is the ability to add scripts. We will touch on this in the next chapter when we look at **JavaScript**. The easiest to understand are the `<title>` and `</title>` tags. Anything you add between these tags will be taken to be the web page title. Add the following line to your HTML:

```
<html>
    <!---my web site, copyright my name, this year--->

    <head>
    <! document definitions go here>
        <title>My web page, hope you like it!</title>
    </head>

    <body>
        <! Content goes here>
    </body>

</html>
```

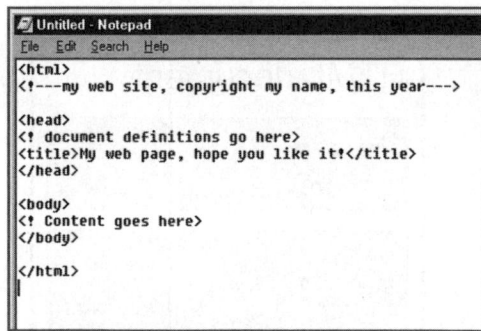

Save the file and then view it in your browser. Although you will see the same blank browser window, you should see your title appear in the browser title bar:

The body

The `<body>` and `</body>` tags tell the browser 'this is the main content of the page'. This is where much of the stuff you see on a web page usually lives, so in our metaphor, it'd be the actual text of the book.

We're going to add some sample gobbledegook for the moment, so add the following text to your HTML:

```
<html>
    <!---my web site, copyright my name, this year--->

<head>
    <! document definitions go here>
    <title>My web page, hope you like it!</title>
</head>

<body>
    Lorem ipsum dolor sit amet, consectetuer adipiscing elit, sed diam
    nonummy nibh euismod tincidunt ut laoreet dolore magna aliquam erat
    volutpat. Ut wisi enim ad minim veniam, quis nostrud exerci tation
    ullamcorper suscipit lobortis nisl ut aliquip ex ea commodo conse-
    quat.
</body>

</html>
```

Save, load in a browser, and you'll see the blank space finally change to the text seen below:

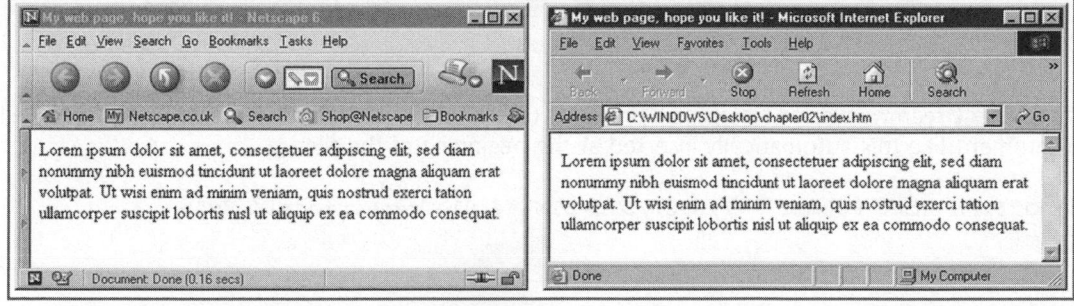

Notice that if you resize the browser window, the text will also change to fill the new available space. That's a cool trick, but also one of the biggest issues with web design over print-based design. In web design, you don't know how big the window that shows your page will be, and this can change the look and layout of your design.

We will look at this in much more detail as we build our own web page in the book project (where we will be using **tables** and other HTML features to limit the effects of the browser on our page layouts).

Comments

There is one additional basic tag that you need to know about, the **comment**. The comment tag is ignored by the browser and is used to insert a comment in the HTML source code. You can use comments to explain your code, which can help you when you edit the source code at a later date:

```
<!comment goes here>
```

Anything between the `<!` and `>` is ignored by the browser. Add the comment lines shown below to your document:

```
<html>
        <!---my web site, copyright my name, this year--->

        <head>
                <! document definitions go here>
        </head>

        <body>
                <! Content goes here>
        </body>

</html>
```

Save your file and view it in a browser, making sure that you still see a blank browser window.

> The comment tag is the only tag that is allowed to exist outside the `<html>` and `</html>` *tags*.

DOCTYPE

If you use Dreamweaver or Netscape Composer (more on this later in this chapter), you may well see a comment like this automatically inserted at the beginning of the file:

```
<!DOCTYPE html PUBLIC "-//W3C//DTD HTML 4.01 Transitional//EN">
<html>
...
...
</html>
```

There are several different versions of HTML, and this line allows other applications to check the HTML in the file. We won't need this line for a while, so we won't bother adding it to our file for the moment.

Meta tags

We can also add some **meta tags** to our `<head>`. They're called **meta tags** because they won't appear on the web page, but are used to identify it. They are most often used by search engines to catalog your page, so you can make your page a lot easier to find by adding them.

Add the following between your `<head>` tags:

```
<head>
        <title>My web page, hope you like it!</title>
        <meta name="author" CONTENT="Sham B">
        <meta name ="description" CONTENT="My first web page">
        <meta name ="keywords" CONTENT="Sham B, homepage, Foundation Web
        ➡Design">
</head>
```

The `<meta>` tag is a new type of tag, one that includes **attributes**.

When we are doing simple things like formatting text, all the information that the browser needs to know is already included:

- The formatting we want to perform is defined by the tag name (such as `<BR>` for "add a line break here").

- What we want to format is implied by the positions of the tags (for example: `<strong>`*Make me bold*`</strong>` *but leave me as normal text*)

When we want to specify something to do with the tag itself, we can't provide information in either of these ways, so we include it within the tag itself as extra information, and this information is called an **attribute** of the tag. Usually, the attribute also needs to be assigned a value, and we express this value inside quotes. A typical tag with a single attribute that we want to make equal to a value will be written like this:

```
<tagName attribute = "value">
```

For our meta tags, the *tagName* is *meta* and the attributes we are setting are **author**, **description** and **keywords**.

The `author` field is self-explanatory, but the other two may need some explaining:

- The **description** is a bit like the book blurb on a book's back cover: it describes why you may want to visit the site. If seen, many search engines will print this information next to the search result corresponding to your site. If you don't add this meta tag, the search engine will usually simply show the first paragraph of text it sees in your HTML, which may be not very descriptive!

- The **keywords** are words that will be used by search engines to match people's searches to your page. For example, if you were to create a website that taught beginners HTML, you might choose the keywords *HTML, HTML primer, HTML-Primer, HTMLprimer, web design, webdesign, Dreamweaver*, and so on. Notice that we are not just limiting ourselves with simple keywords such as 'web design' but are listing all the possible spellings of each keyword, and also related keywords such as *Dreamweaver*. The better your keywords, the more people will actually find your site, so think carefully about these.

Now we have our text, let's see about giving it some formatting. The first thing is to remember what we said earlier about HTML ignoring spaces and carriage returns. For example, if you tried to make the text a little different by splitting the main text into two sentences separated by a blank line, you might try this:

```
<body>

Lorem ipsum dolor sit amet consectetuer adipiscing elit, sed diam nonummy
nibh euismod tincidunt ut laoreet dolore magna aliquam erat volutpat.

Ut wisi enim ad minim veniam, quis nostrud exerci tation ullamcorper
suscipit lobortis nisl ut aliquip ex ea commodo consequat.

</body>
```

Unfortunately, if you try doing this, and viewing it in a browser, you'll see that nothing has changed. As we said earlier, the browser will ignore any line breaks in your text, and it will also ignore multiple spaces (it will keep the first space, but ignore all subsequent ones). To add headings, additional spaces (also called 'whitespace'), and line breaks/indentation to the page, we need to define them implicitly using HTML tags.

Line breaks

To add a line break in our text, we use the `<br>` (break) tag, which you need to add as shown in the `<body>` section, and then save and test the HTML file:

```
<body>

Lorem ipsum dolor sit amet
        <br>
consectetuer adipiscing elit, sed diam nonummy nibh euismod tincidunt ut
laoreet dolore magna aliquam erat volutpat.
        <br>
        <br>
Ut wisi enim ad minim veniam, quis nostrud exerci tation ullamcorper
suscipit lobortis nisl ut aliquip ex ea commodo consequat.

</body>
```

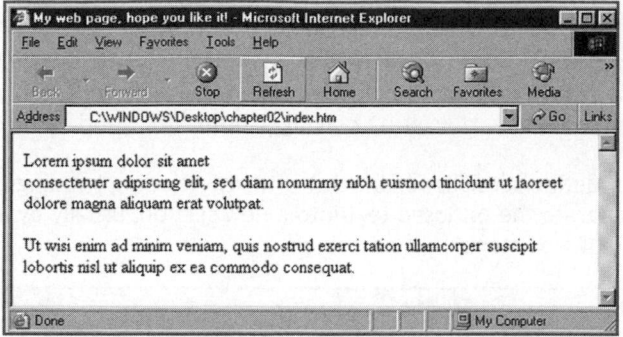

Notice that a single <br> gives you a new line, and two give you a new line plus a line of whitespace. Also, feel free to add line returns in your text file with each <br> tag to give you a feel for how it will look – these will be ignored, as we found earlier.

Now what about our indents? To add additional spaces in text, we use a special symbol to represent a space, and it goes by the rather catchy name of ** **. Not something that exactly trickles off the tongue, but it actually stands for **n**on-**b**reaking-**sp**ace, and the **&** is there to signify that the **nbsp** is part of a **control code** (used to give formatting instructions to the browser), rather than the plain text nbsp. Add the following to give us our indents:

```
<body>

Lorem ipsum dolor sit amet
<br>
  consectetuer adipiscing elit, sed diam nonummy nibh euismod
tincidunt ut laoreet dolore magna aliquam erat volutpat.
<br>
<br>
  Ut wisi enim ad minim veniam, quis nostrud exerci tation
ullamcorper suscipit lobortis nisl ut aliquip ex ea commodo consequat.

</body>
```

Actually, you'd probably use the <p> tag to separate out paragraphs in reality. Now that you've tried out a couple of tags, this leads us nicely into the next exercise…

Inline and Block tags

We'll now take a look at the features available in HTML to format text. We will look at two types of tag that allow us to do this, **inline tags** and **block tags**. Inline tags are concerned with how text will appear: they change the appearance of text itself by making it **bold,** *italic* and so on.

Block tags are used to define sections (or blocks) of text, including headings, lists and paragraphs. All block level tags will separate the enclosed text into a new section, usually by adding a line break at the start of the block so that text starts on a new line.

> *There's a more advanced way of formatting text, using CSS, and we'll show you this in* **Chapter 3.** *What we'll show you here is enough to give you the basics that you'll need to understand before moving onto CSS.*

Using inline tags

What we're going to do here is go through a small example. If you can see what each tag does, you're much more likely to remember them.

1. Open up Notepad, TextEdit or SimpleText. You'll want to be testing this file a fair bit as we go through, so save it somewhere easy to find, and make sure that you've saved it with a `.html` extension.

2. First thing is to add a heading. You can see the heading sizes available to us below: heading 1 is the largest and heading 6 is the smallest, with heading 4 the same size as plain text.

This is heading 1

This is heading 2

This is heading 3

This is plain text for comparison

This is heading 4

This is heading 5

This is heading 6

We use the tags <hn></hn> where *n* is the number of the heading you want to use, so add an opening and a closing <body> tag, and then:

<h2>friends of ED's Foundation Web Design</h2>

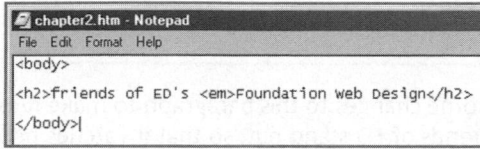

Heading 6 can be too small to make out clearly on some monitors, because not only is it small, but it is also in bold. This can close up the hole in letters like 'o' and 'e', making them difficult to make out.

3. Save your file, and then test it (by double-clicking on it) to check that our heading has come up. As we work through the rest of the exercise, remember that you need to save your file for the changes to appear in your browser.

4. We need some way of distinguishing the title of the book, so it's time to meet the emphasis tag. Add <em></em> around the Foundation Web Design text, and test again (if your browser is still open, just Refresh the page).

Using <i></i>would have the same effect here, but using <em> allows us to change the way we emphasize text with our style sheets in the next chapter.

5. The <p></p> tags allow you to define a block of text as a paragraph, usually with a line of whitespace at the top and bottom. Add one of these now, after the title, and add this text into it: *friends of ED is a bunch of really cool people, devoted to helping you break your creative boundaries.* Test it again. (This is really a block tag that belongs in the next section, but our text is going to get messy without it here so we'll sneak this one in.)

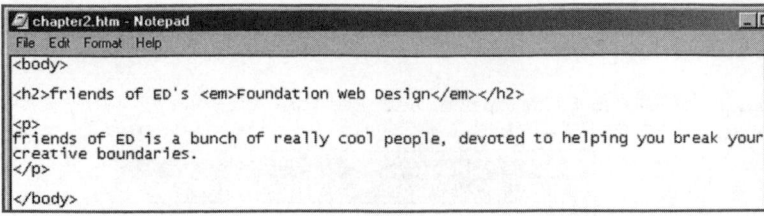

```
chapter2.htm - Notepad
File  Edit  Format  Help
<body>

<h2>friends of ED's <em>Foundation Web Design</em></h2>

<p>
friends of ED is a bunch of really cool people, devoted to helping you break your
creative boundaries.
</p>

</body>
```

6. We can now make some changes to this paragraph to make it look a little less like dull text. First, we want to make friends of ED stand out, so that it catches people's eyes. The `<big>` tag makes text slightly bigger than the default size, so add `<big></big>` tags around the *friends of ED* text.

> # friends of ED's *Foundation Web Design*
>
> **friends of ED** is a bunch of really cool people, devoted to helping you break your creative boundaries.

7. We want to make 'friends of ED' stand out even more, so we'll make it bold as well. Like the `<i>` tag, people used to use `<b>` for this, but using `<strong>` is much more flexible when we come to do other things later, so add some `<strong></strong>` tags around the friends of ED text.

```
<p>
<big><strong>friends of ED</strong></big> is
you break your creative boundaries.
</p>
```

8. Now, I thought that saying 'friends of ED' were a bunch of really cool people was OK, but it's probably a little bit less informative than people might want. I'm not going to remove it for the moment, though, so add `<small></small>` tags around the *is a bunch of really cool people* text to make it smaller, and then add `<strike></strike>` tags to put a line through the text. This option isn't used that often, but it can be useful if you're working on a site with someone else and want to let them know that you're removing text.

> # friends of ED's *Foundation Web Design*
>
> **friends of ED** is ~~a bunch of really cool people~~, devoted to helping you break your creative boundaries.

9. To replace the text that we've put a line through, add *a small publishing company* just after the closing `</small tag>` and before the comma. The last thing we want to do with this line is to make the *break your creative boundaries* phrase stand out a little. Add `<em>` tags, as we did earlier, and then add `<u><ul>` tags to underline it as well.

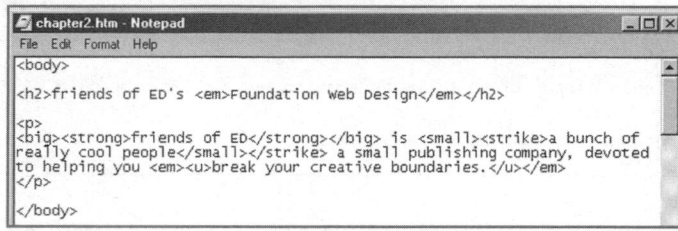

friends of ED's *Foundation Web Design*

friends of ED is ~~a bunch of really cool people~~ a small publishing company, devoted to helping you *break your creative boundaries.*

```
chapter2.htm - Notepad
File  Edit  Format  Help
<body>

<h2>friends of ED's <em>Foundation Web Design</em></h2>

<p>
<big><strong>friends of ED</strong></big> is <small><strike>a bunch of
really cool people</small></strike> a small publishing company, devoted
to helping you <em><u>break your creative boundaries.</u></em>
</p>

</body>
```

10. Test your file to make sure everything is working as it should, and we'll move on to add some block tags.

Using block tags

Most of the tags we've used so far (with the exception of `<p>`) have been inline tags that change the text itself rather than block tags that change the position of a block of text. We're now going to use a couple of block tags.

1. First, we're going to add a quotation from a reader after the text we've just added, so add a couple of carriage returns after the last paragraph to your text document, and add `<blockquote>` `</blockquote>`. This tag is used whenever quoting an external source, and adds a right and left margin to the text black, as well as adding whitespace above and below it.

2. Add the text `"I just got the book you recommended and Jeez it's good. You all are way better than any of the other books" - a reader` between the tags (we promise we're not making that up!).

helping you *break your creative boundaries.*

"I just got the book you recommended and
better than any of the other books" - a rea

The `<blockquote>` *tag is the only way to indent text in HTML, so it's also used as a common way of adding indented paragraphs in HTML. You don't need to use this trick when you know CSS, so wait until the next chapter to find out how to indent paragraphs rather than getting into bad habits here...*

3. We're still a little short on details about the book, so we want to create a list of what this book will allow you to do before the details about friends of ED and the customer quote. Just after the title, add a new set of `<p>` tags, and enter the text *Foundation Web Design will show you:*

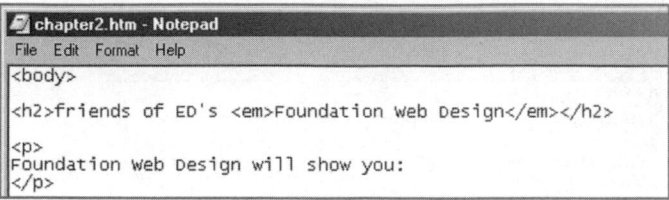

4. There are two types of list: **unordered** (which uses bullet points), and **ordered** (which uses numbers). We're going to start off by using an ordered list, so add a set of `<ol></ol>` tags on the next line after the text we've just added. This will create the ordered list:

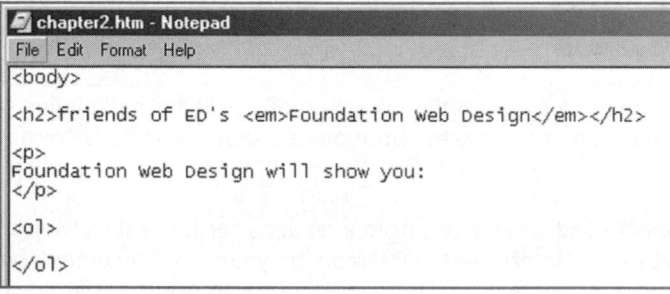

5. Each item in the list must then be enclosed by the **List item** tag `<li>`, so in between the `<ol></ol>` tags, add something like the following, save, and test:

```
<li>How to use HTML to get a site up and running</li>
<li>How to use CSS to make formatting text easy</li>
<li>How to optimize your images for use on the web</li>
```

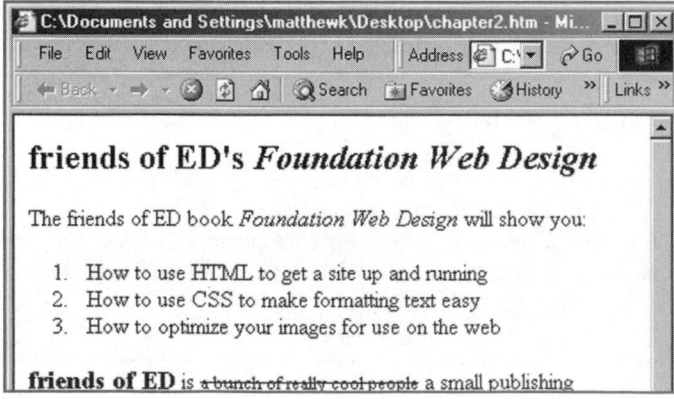

6. What if you wanted to use something instead of numbers to order the list by? The `<ol>` tag has an attribute *type* that allows you to define what the entries will be ordered by. Replace your `<ol>` tag with `<ol type = "a">`, and you should find that our list is now ordered abc instead of 123. If you want this list to use capital numbers, then simply capitalize the "a".

```
chapter2.htm - Notepad
File  Edit  Format  Help
<p>
Foundation Web Design will show you:
<ol type = "a">
<li>How to use HTML to get a site up and running</li>
<li>How to use CSS to make formatting text easy</li>
<li>How to optimize your images for use on the web</li>
</ol>
```

You could also specify Roman numerals with `<ol type = "i">` *(or* `"I"` *for upper case numerals).*

7. It would be good to add a few more details to some of our listed points, and HTML allows us to add another list into our existing list without any problems. We'll use an unordered list for this, so add `<ul></ul>` after the first point in our existing list:

```
chapter2.htm - Notepad
File  Edit  Format  Help

<p>
Foundation Web Desig
<ol type = "a">
<li>How to use HTML
<ul>

</ul
<li>How to use CSS t
<li>How to optimize
</ol>
```

8. Now add a few points, enclosing each with the list item tag `<li>`, save, and test:

friends of ED's *Foundation Web Design*

Foundation Web Design will show you:

    a. How to use HTML to get a site up and running
        o How to change the appearance of text with inline tags
        o How to format blocks of text with block tags
    b. How to use CSS to make formatting text easy
    c. How to optimize your images for use on the web

```
chapter2.htm - Notepad
File  Edit  Format  Help

<p>
Foundation Web Design will show you:
<ol type = "a">
<li>How to use HTML to get a site up and running</li>
<ul>
<li>How to change the appearance of text with inline tags</li>
<li>How to format blocks of text with block tags</li>
</ul
<li>How to use CSS to make formatting text easy</li>
```

9. Just as we changed from numbers to letters with our ordered list earlier, we can change the appearance of the bullets in our unordered list. There are three options – circle (hollow dot), bullet (filled dot), or square. Try changing your `<ul>` tag to `<ul type = "square">`, saving, and testing.

> Foundation Web Design will show you:
>
> a. How to use HTML to get a site up and running
>   - How to change the appearance of text with inline tags
>   - How to format blocks of text with block tags
> b. How to use CSS to make formatting text easy
> c. How to optimize your images for use on the web

Finishing touches

We're almost done, but a contact address at the bottom would be useful.

1. Just before the final `</body>` tag, add a new set of `<p>` tags. Add *friends of ED*, and wrap this in `<big>` and `<strong>` tags as we did before:

```
<p>
<big><strong>friendsofED</strong></big>
</p>

</body>

</html>
```

2. gotoAndPlay is a Flash ActionScript command often used to start Flash movies running, and friends of ED has used it as a slogan to suggest that we try to make sure that our readers have fun while they create their web projects. Add *.gotoAndPlay* after the *friends of ED text*, and wrap it in `<small>` tags.

3. The *y* of the word play seems to stick out a bit, so we can use the superscript tags to lift *.gotoAndPlay* up. Wrap `<sup></sup>` tags around *.gotoAndPlay*, save, and test.

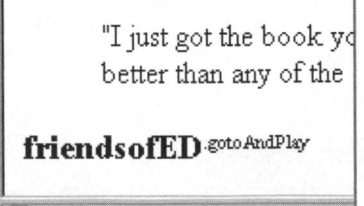

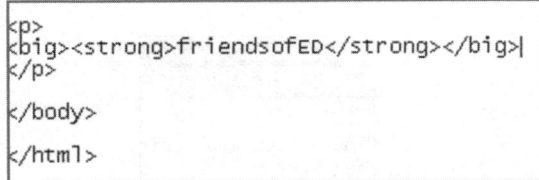

The `<sub>` tag does exactly the opposite, and sinks the text below the line that it's on.

4. As a final touch, wrap .*gotoAndPlay* in <tt> tags. <tt> stands for teletype, or a mono-spaced font (such as courier) where each letter takes up exactly the same amount of space. This is useful for displaying code listings, or tabulated columns of currency values that need to line up. Here, it makes the text look like the code it's supposed to be.

5. The <address> tag is used to denote the address of the web site author. It will start with a line break and is rendered in italics. You should think carefully before including your **full** postal address here - life is bad enough with e-mail spam without opening yourself up to the real world variety! In the case of friends of ED, though, our address is freely available, so just before the closing </small> tag, add:

<address>Arden House, 1102 Warwick Road, Acocks Green, Birmingham, UK,
➡ *B27 6BH</address>*

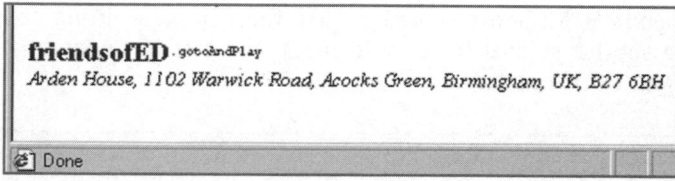

6. It'd be nice to justify the address to the right, wouldn't it? We can use an align attribute in the division tag to left align, right align, center align and justify text. Wrap the whole last section of text in <div align = "right"></div> tags.

```
<html>

<body>

<h2>friends of ED's <em>Foundation Web Design</em></h2>

<p>
Foundation Web Design will show you:
<ol type = "a">
<li>How to use HTML to get a site up and running</li>
     <ul type = "square">
     <li>How to change the appearance of text with inline tags</li>
     <li>How to format blocks of text with block tags</li>
     </ul>
<li>How to use CSS to make formatting text easy</li>
<li>How to optimize your images for use on the web</li>
</ol>
</p>


<p>
<big><strong>friends of ED</strong></big> is <small><strike>a bunch of
really cool people</strike></small> a small publishing company, devoted to
helping you <em><u>break your creative boundaries.</u></em>
</p>
```

continues overleaf

```
<blockquote>"I just got the book you recommended and Jeez it's good. You
all are way better than any of the other books" - a reader</blockquote>

<p>
<div align = "right">
<big><strong>friendsofED</strong></big><small><sup><tt>.gotoAndPlay</tt></
sup>
<address>Arden House, 1102 Warwick Road, Acocks Green, Birmingham, UK,
B27 6BH</address></small>
</div>
</p>


</body>
```

7. Save, check your HTML looks something like the complete listing above (notice how we've indented the sub-list so that it's easy to read), and test it. Congratulations: you're now fully fluent in HTML text formatting.

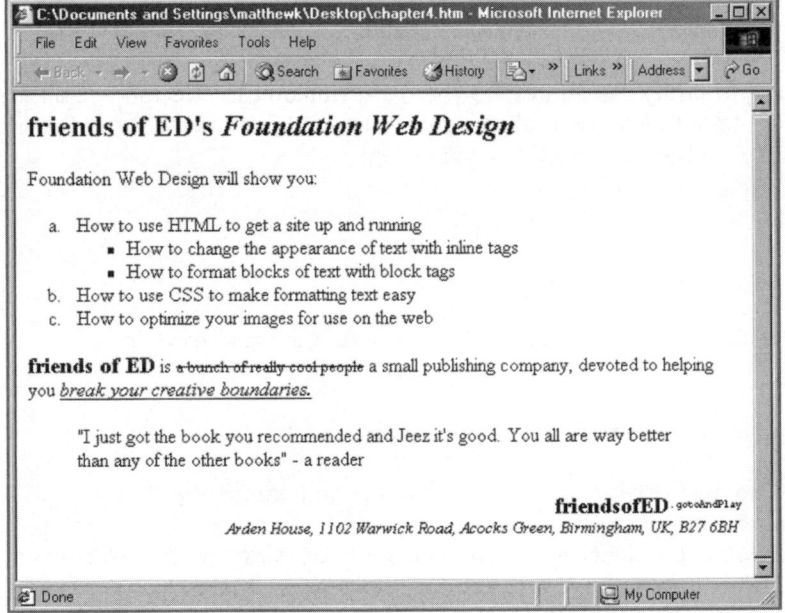

The <font> tag

Before the Cascading Style Sheets (CSS) we'll look at in the next chapter became common, web designers used the <font> tag to define different fonts, and their size and color. If you view the source HTML of many websites (using View > Source in Internet Explorer or View > Page Source in Netscape Navigator), you'll see this used quite frequently.

We really don't recommend that you use this tag, as it will make your web design work much harder in the long run. For a start, it doesn't give as much control over defining font face and size as CSS does. It also makes it much more difficult to change pages - supposing you used <font> instead of <h1> to create your titles, and then wanted to change the heading style. Instead of just changing one setting in your Cascading Style Sheet, you'll have to change every single place where you've used the `<font>` tag.

The `<font>` tag works like this:

```
<font color = "#hex" , face = "fontList", size = "size");
```

The **color** can be either a hexadecimal number such as `#FF0000`, or a plain text color name such as `"teal"` (for more on these, see **Chapter 6**).

The **face** attribute sets the font. The user has to have the font installed for this to work, so most people define a list of font choices, and the browser will use the first font in the list that it can find. The last font in the list should therefore be one of the three fonts that every browser can find: *sans*, *sans-serif* and *mono*.

size can be a reference to a pre-defined font size from 1 to 7, or a size relative to the default font size. The starting size for unmodified text is the default (3), so given default text at the start (the normal case) you can only go from +4 (giving 7) to -2 (giving 1). Obviously, you can go further if you are at anything other than size 3 as your starting point, so in this case you can go from -6 (assuming your starting point is 7) to +6 (giving 1).

So, the following font tag will display our text in grey mono text that is a little larger than normal:

```
<html>

<body>
     <font color="#666666" size="+1" face="Courier New, Courier,
        ➥ mono">hello!</font>
</body>

</html>
```

> *The default web font is usually serif, but the* `<font>` *attribute allows you to change this by using the* `<basefont>` *tag – for example,* `<basefont face = "Ariel, Helvetica, sans-serif" color = "#505050">`*. This doesn't work with some other tags, notably tables in some browsers, though this can be fixed by adding another* `<basefont>` *tag where the original tag doesn't seem to be having any effect.*

Using Netscape Composer

The formatting of text can be a little daunting using just HTML hand-coding, so it's a good place to use an editor of some kind. Perhaps the safest bet is to use Netscape Composer, which comes free with Netscape Navigator. This is a much better bet than competitors in the free HTML editor arena like FrontPage Express, as it respects the HTML you enter and doesn't mess around with your tags like they do (although it will sometimes remove the whitespace and indentations that you add to your code).

1. Start up the Netscape Navigator browser. Select File > New > Composer Page, and a blank Composer window will open up. (If you want to edit the page currently being displayed in *Navigator,* select File > Edit Page.)

2. This shows a blank screen, but it's actually a bit more than that; *Composer* has created the HTML to create a blank screen. You can see this if you hit the <HTML> Source tab at the bottom.

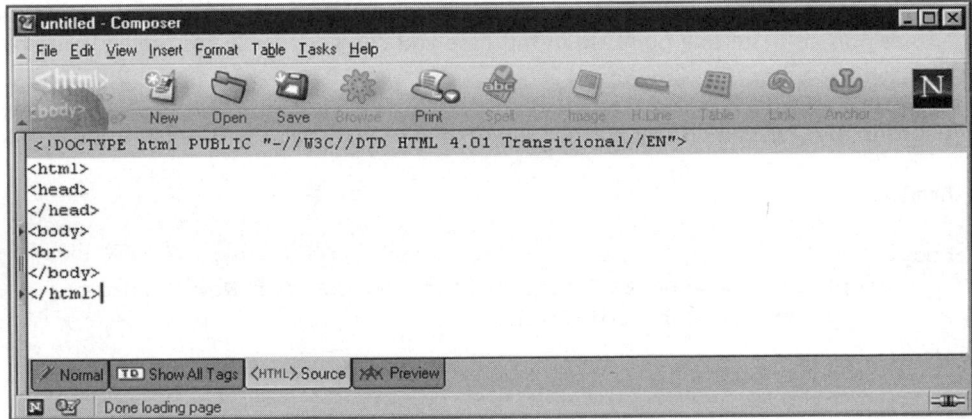

3. To work in what-you-see-is-what-you-get code, make sure the Normal tab at the bottom of the window is selected.

4. You can now edit just as if you were in a word processor with the icons at the top of the window, and the drop-down menu to the left of them.

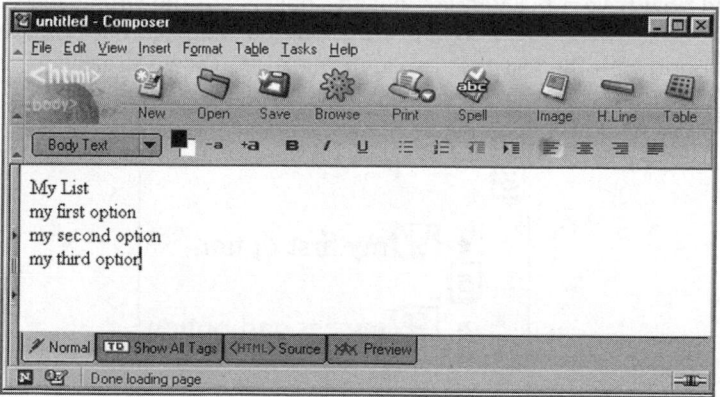

foreground color

heading +/-

bold/italic/underline

bulleted list

indent/outdent

background color

numbered list

align left/center/right/justify

Body Text
✓ Body Text
Paragraph
Heading 1
Heading 2
Heading 3
Heading 4
Heading 5
Heading 6
Address
Preformat
Blockquote

5. To select an option that isn't shown on either of these menus, you can select Format > Text Style to choose from the full list of available formatting options.

6. Notice that you can switch quickly between the NORMAL and <HTML> Source modes simply by hitting the appropriate tabs at the bottom of the Composer window, and this is a cool way of seeing the relationship between the formatted text and the underlying HTML that Composer is creating.

> *Netscape isn't very good at maintaining spaces added to HTML to make the code readable, so large HTML files can start to look unintelligible...*

7. Switch back to the **Normal** tab at the bottom of the window to get into visual editing mode, and enter some text as shown:

8. Highlight the text 'My List' and select Heading 2 from the drop-down, turning the text into a heading. (You could do the same thing by selecting Format > Paragraph > Heading 2.)

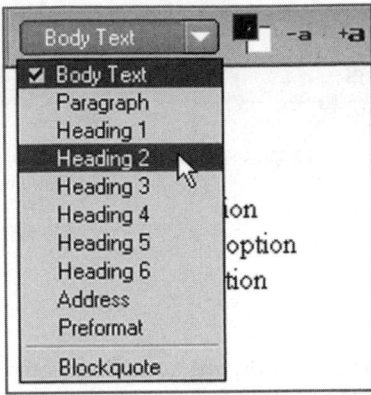

9. Highlight the remaining text and hit the Bulleted list icon just to the right of the underline button.

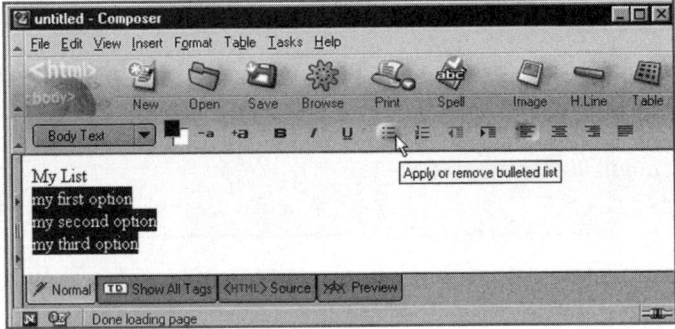

10. We should now have a bulleted list, but the bullets are the wrong style. Select Show All Tags from the tabs at the bottom left-hand corner of the window. Your display should now look like the screenshot, with the tags that make up the HTML shown visually:

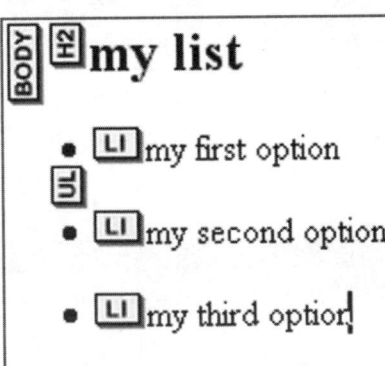

11. To change our list, we need to work with the `<ul>` tag. Double-click on it, and this will bring up the List Properties window. Select Solid Circle from the Bullet Style drop-down, and select Solid Circle.

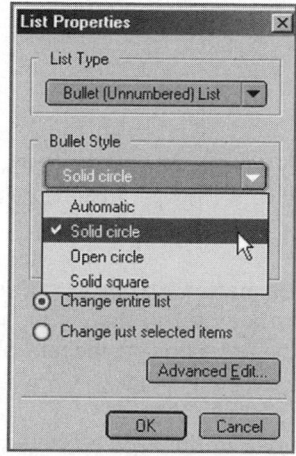

12. Finished! You can check the HTML by clicking the <HTML> Source tab, and the best way to view the final page is by selecting File > Browse Page. You will be prompted to save the page and give it a HTML title, if you have not done so already.

> *Composer only allows you to view the page in Navigator, so if you want to view it in Internet Explorer, you will have to go to the* `.html` *file and open it in Internet Explorer.*

We'll be coming back to use Composer at several points throughout the book, but if you're impatient to check out the features that we haven't shown you, go to Help > Help and Support Center, and select Creating Web Pages from the Help Contents sidebar.

Using tags to refer to other elements

Web pages are not **just** HTML, but also consist of graphics, and other files. As well as rendering the text and formatting it, the HTML contains the code that pulls all these items together and puts them in the appropriate places. We'll finish this chapter by taking a look at adding graphics and links to other pages into our pages.

Graphics

To add a **graphic**, you simply add a tag that specifies the graphic to insert. The HTML doesn't contain the graphic itself, only a **reference** to where the graphic can be found. Thus, when the browser comes to render the final web page, it uses the tag reference to find the graphic on your website or computer, and inserts it in the page.

We're going to use a picture of my trusty pencil sharpener; the file was imported from my camcorder as a TIFF file. We'll see more about preparing images in **Chapter 6**, but I cropped the image, changed the colors to make it a little more eye-catching, and converted it to a JPEG. This bought the file size down from 900KB to 3KB!

The tag to embed an image is the `<img>` tag. The main attribute is the `source` or `src`. This points to the location of the graphic file itself and is required for obvious reasons – the browser has to know where to find this picture.

It is also good manners to add the **alternative text** or `alt`. This text appears if the graphic is not found, not yet displayed, or the browser has been set to show no graphics. It is used by audio screen readers for the blind and partially sighted. The most obvious benefit of including alt text is that it appears as a tooltip when you hover your mouse over the image.

The `carOptimized.jpg` file is included in the source files for the book, so grab it and place it in the `chapter02` folder that we created earlier. Now create the following HTML, saving it as `car_sharpener.html`:

```
<html>

<head>
      <title>pencil sharpener</title>
</head>

<body>

      <img src="carOptimized.jpg" alt="my pencil sharpener!">

</body>

</html>
```

If you view this HTML in a browser, you will see something like this:

It would be better if the image was centered instead of in the corner. This is where we get to use all the text formatting tags we've just learned about, because text formatting can also be used for aligning graphics, as the following changes show. Add the bold code to center the image and add a caption:

```
<html>

<head>
 <title>pencil sharpener</title>
</head>
```

```
<body>

        <div align="center">

                <br><br><br>

                <img src="carOptimized.jpg" alt="my pencil sharpener!">
                <br>

                <h3>
                        My pencil sharpener
                </h3>

        </div>

    </body>

    </html>
```

Links

The Web is nothing without the ability to link to other sites. With both images and links, the link is defined as an attribute for a tag. The only thing that really changes is the particular tag you end up using. As we've just seen, if we're linking to a graphic that forms part of our web page, we use something like this:

```
<img src="carOptimized.jpg">
```

For a link to a new page, we do essentially the same thing, except this time we use the `<a>` or **hyperlink anchor** tag, and the attribute we have to use is `href` or the **hyper-link reference**.

The following HTML will turn the text 'sharpener' in the sentence 'link to my pencil sharpener' into a link to the web page we created in the last section, `car_sharpener.html`. Save this HTML in the same folder as the last page, and call it `link_example.html`.

```
<html>

<head>
 <title>link example</title>
</head>

<body>
     <br><br>
     Link to my pencil <a href="pencil_sharpener.html"> sharpener</a>

</body>

</html>
```

Test, and you should see the following simple page. Hitting the link text will take you to the pencil sharpener page.

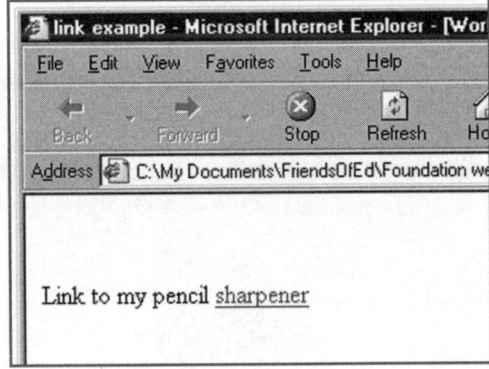

Because HTML treats graphics and text in much the same way, we can make our pencil-sharpening car a link back to `link_example.html` by simply adding an `<a>` tag around the `<img>` tag that calls up the image. Add the lines shown in bold to `pencil_sharpener.html`:

```
<html>

<head>
 <title>pencil sharpener</title>
</head>

<body>

     <div align="center">

             <br><br><br>
```

```
<a href="link_example.html">
        <img src="carOptimized.jpg" alt="my pencil sharpener!">
</a>
<br>

<h3>
        My pencil sharpener
</h3>

        </div>

</body>

</html>
```

You will now see an outline around the image, and this signifies it has become a link back to link_example.html. Click it and see!

> There is only really one thing to bear in mind when defining your links, and that is the difference between an **absolute** and **relative** link. A relative link starts from where the current file is. This is why I asked you to make sure that link_example.html *and* pencil_sharpener.html were in the same folder. You can also specify an absolute link, which gives the full path to a file.

We will look at this issue a bit more by example, when we start to build our web pages, but for now let's move onto the next chapter to look at HTML's sophisticated older brother, JavaScript.

JavaScript

What this chapter will do

This chapter introduces the reasons why we need something in addition to HTML to build most pages. It will then introduce the basics of JavaScript, including:

- An introduction to the object-oriented approach to scripting, and how to use this in JavaScript
- Using JavaScript to create dialog boxes and status text
- Using JavaScript to open, close, and customize browser windows

Crucially, we'll also take a first practical look at our case study, the award-winning Mondo site by designer Tomasz Jankowski, and sketch out the basic structure of our project, learning a few things about navigation and site planning in the process.

What you will have learned by the end of this chapter

By the end of this chapter, you will have learned the importance of JavaScript, and how it addresses the shortcomings in HTML's ability to control and customize the browser window. You will also have created the foundations of the Mondo website which we'll be building on in future chapters.

We have seen that HTML stands for HyperText Markup Language. We know that **Hypertext** is referring to the fact that you can jump from page to page via links, and **Markup** means that HTML is just a way of formatting a web page's elements (text, graphics, and other media).

HTML provides basic navigation facilities and a system of tags that specify the appearance of your web page. This is all cool, but there are a lot of things that HTML *doesn't* allow you to do:

- It doesn't allow much in the way of **interactivity** beyond simple links.

- It doesn't allow you any control of the browser, leaving you without any control of your site's immediate environment (for example, you can't open new browser windows).

- It doesn't let your web page ask questions like 'what kind of browser am I being viewed on?' and 'what is the size of the screen?'. Knowing these and other facts can help you control how your site appears for different viewers.

- It doesn't allow your web page to make decisions. This stops your web page doing many useful things - such as deciding whether the user has entered a valid e-mail, or has filled in all the fields in a form, or has all the features installed needed to view your web page properly.

To fix all of these shortfalls you need to use a separate language that co-exists with your HTML, and this language is **JavaScript**.

JavaScript 101

JavaScript was introduced way back in 1995 as a part of Netscape Navigator 2.0, and has also been adopted in Internet Explorer under Microsoft's implementation, which is called *JScript*. Although there are some differences between these two dialects, there is no real implication for basic web design, given that Internet Explorer recognises the parts of JavaScript in common use.

It does, however, mean that it is much more important that you test your web pages in both Internet Explorer and Netscape Navigator when you are using script as well as HTML. Although the two browsers tend to conform to the same HTML standards, they are actually being driven by *different* scripting standards, something to always bear in mind.

> *When we refer to JavaScript in this book, we will stick to the bits of the language that both Netscape and Microsoft understand.*

JavaScript is based on a fairly recent style of programming languages called *object-oriented* or 'OO' for short. We will look at the implications of this when we come to investigate the **Document Object Model**, and we will also revisit *The Making of Tron*, because I think it's a great film (no, really).

> Incidentally, JavaScript is <u>not related</u> to the more powerful language <u>Java</u>. If anything, the similarity in names is purely a clever marketing tactic on the part of the folks who created JavaScript!

JavaScript is usually either included as part of your HTML document, or may be included as a separate file that the HTML refers to (in the same way as the graphic in the last chapter). When a browser sees JavaScript, all it does is change 'read and parse HTML' to 'read and execute JavaScript'. In both cases, the tools you need to create your scripts are exactly the same as the tools you need to create HTML: a browser and a text editor.

Many applications (such as Dreamweaver) are able to generate script for us. Just as with HTML, in the last chapter, this will not only leave you short against industry standards, it will leave you with nothing to build on in the future, and in a heap of trouble when things start to go wrong. Other books may put JavaScript at the end of the book as an optional chapter, but we think it's pretty mandatory. It's also easier than a lot of people make out...

A bit about Scary Code Stuff and why you shouldn't worry!

OK, so some of you might be thinking "scripting?! ... I want to be a designer, not a beardy programmer!" Granted, JavaScript is a little more like code than the user-friendly HTML but don't run for the hills just yet. Although JavaScript is a scripting language, it's only as complicated as you want to make it.

You can use JavaScript to create games and all sorts of fun but complicated stuff, but for basic browser control, you don't need to know anything about variables and expressions and all that. In this chapter, all we will be doing is working with simple generic statements that you can just learn off by heart if you don't quite understand them.

Adding comments to JavaScript

One JavaScript feature worth mentioning now is the **comment**. Last chapter, we saw that comments in HTML must take the form:

```
<!comment goes here>
```

It would be nice if both JavaScript and HTML used the same syntax for a comment, but unfortunately, they don't. Furthermore, you cannot use the HTML form outlined above in a `<script>` section, as the browser will only expect comments in JavaScript format and will throw errors if it meets anything else.

If you want to add a comment inside the `<script language = "JavaScript">` ... `</script>` tags, you must either:

1. Precede your comment with //:

```
<html>

<head>
        <script language = "JavaScript">

                // write some text to the current web page
                document.write("This text is generated by JavaScript!");

        </script>

<body>
</body>

</html>
```

2. Or enclose your comment with /* comment */: (this allows you to have multiple lines of text in your comment)

```
<html>

<head>
        <script language = "JavaScript">

                /*
                This is a simple test script to
                write some text to the current
                HTML document...
                */

                document.write("This text is generated by JavaScript!");

        </script>

<body>
</body>

</html>
```

Note that the comment does not need the ; at the end like the other JavaScript lines need. This is because it isn't strictly a JavaScript line; the browser simply ignores everything after a line containing a // or between the /*...*/.

We haven't added any comments into the scripts in this chapter because it saves an awful lot of typing, and there is plenty of explanation of the code in the main text anyway, but it's a good idea to comment your code as much as possible when you start writing your own stuff.

Now that we know how and where to insert JavaScript in our HTML pages, it's time to take a closer look at the language itself, and for this, we have to know something about the **Document Object Model**, or DOM for short...

Objects and the object-oriented world view

Years ago, I was watching a TV program about the making of the film *Tron*, where the main character finds himself sucked into a computer. They interviewed the movie set designer about how he had visualized this computer virtual world, and something he said struck me. A rough paraphrase of what he said was:

> *If you shoot a story in the real world, and you need a trashcan in an office scene, all you do is go to the store and buy one. If you want to create a virtual world using computer graphics, you can assume nothing about what we take for granted. A computer knows nothing about real trashcans, so you have to define everything; how big, what shape, what color, how it moves, how heavy, how gravity affects it when you throw it... everything!*

Tron was a good bit of fiction, but the trashcan problem is not fictional. It's a real problem for programmers; how do you define real things on a computer? There are several ways to do this, but in general they all do the same thing; they reduce real things to bits of **structured information**. Computers know nothing about reality, but they can deal with information, or **data**, as long as it is well ordered and consistent. One of the most popular ways to do this is the object-oriented process. This describes everything as an **object**, and each object is described with **properties**, and made to do things with **methods**.

In term of our Tron trashcan, the object is `trashcan`, and the properties might include:

`name`	The name of the trashcan we are describing
`color`	The color of the trashcan
`material`	The material that the bin is made of
`cubic capacity`	The maximum amount of trash the trashcan can hold
`base diameter`	The diameter of the bottom of the bin
`mouth diameter`	The diameter of the top hole of the bin

You will of course see all sorts of additional properties that we might want to add. For example, a trashcan can be many other things as well as the small and neat variety that exist under office desks. The more properties we add to our object, the better described the object becomes. We are stopping at a few basic properties just to show the way the theory works for now.

To describe an individual trashcan (or in computer speak, an **instance** of a trashcan) we give it values for all the properties. For example, to describe the trashcan I have under my home-office desk, I could define it as follows:

```
name              ShamsTrashcan
color             silver
material          fishnetSteel
```

This defines our trashcan in a uniform way. The computer knows that a trashcan is an object with a certain cubic capacity, colors, and so on. It still doesn't know what a trashcan is and how it works though.

The first of these issues, "what a trashcan is," is a strange question, because a computer doesn't have to know, for reasons we will look at in a moment. The second issue, "how it works," is more important. We define this by another feature of objects called **methods**. My dictionary defines the word method as "a way of doing something, especially an ordered set of procedures."

For a trashcan instance, `tronCan`, that we wanted to model in our new film, *Tron 2*, what methods would we need to add? Well, the hero might want to search the trashcan for a crucial bit of virtual paper in an important scene. To allow the virtual hero to do this, he would have to be able to view the contents of the trashcan. This implies that our trashcan object would have to have a list of items that it contains.

> We've named the trashcan instance `tronCan` because the name has to be descriptive, but must contain no spaces (if you use a space between `tron` and `Can`, then the parser will assume that it is two objects, not one). Using `tron_can` is another way round, but is not used so often.

Remember, the virtual hero can't take the easy option and just look inside the trashcan with his eyes (as we do in reality) *because the trashcan doesn't actually exist!* Instead we need to view the computer model as **data**, and use code to manipulate this data.

Whenever another object is thrown into the bin, that object should be added to the list. We could define a method that does this called `addTrash`. When any other object falls through the top hole of the bin, the `addTrash` method would add that object to the list of things the bin contains. We also need to specify what we have just thrown into the bin, and which bin we are throwing it into. To specify the first thing, we use something called **dot notation**. Assuming that the bin has a name property of `tronCan`, then to add something to it we do this:

```
tronCan.addTrash
```

Dot notation is a way of moving through the object-based structure we have set up. First, we state the instance we want to work with (`tronCan`) followed by what we want to do with it (`addTrash`).

We still don't know what we are throwing away. To specify this, we add an **argument** to the method. An argument is data we can pass to the method that we want it to work with. In this case, it refers to the name of the thing we want to trash.

```
tronCan.addTrash(tronPen)
```

In some cases (one of which we will see almost immediately), you don't actually need any arguments, because what the method needs to do is obvious. Here, our hero has a virtual pen that has just run out of virtual ink, so he has decided to drop it into the `tronCan` instance.

OK, back to our original problem: the fact that our hero needs to search through this bin. To empty our bin we would define a new method, `emptyTrash`. In most operating systems, the virtual trashcan simply empties its contents, to be lost forever, so we have no arguments. We would therefore have something like this:

```
tronCan.emptyTrash()
```

The thing is, our script requires the hero to empty the trashcan onto the desk so he can pick through the contents in full view of the audience, so our method also needs to be able to handle the following version:

```
tronCan.emptyTrash(desktop)
```

In this case, the list of rubbish inside the bin will transfer itself into the desktop object, which defines what is sitting on top of the desk.

By now maybe you're thinking, 'yes, I see all this, but it all seems a little longwinded and I can see no real advantage!'. The cool thing about objects is that they are **general** and **reusable**. When we define a general object that defines trashcans, we can define it so that it covers all trashcans, so we can say `tronCan.emptyTrash`, but also `myotherCan.emptyTrash` and each will use the same method of `emptyTrash()`.

We can do the same for other things that are more variable, such as the actors themselves. The hero may be just one instance of another object called `actor`, and have a property `sex` set to `male`. The heroine may be another instance of the same object, but has (amongst other things) the property `sex` set to `female`. For both actors though, the method `walkTo` will be fundamentally the same, as will the methods `grimace` and `collisionTest`.

The other cool thing is that objects can be defined by other lower-level objects. For example, the trashcan, hero and heroine all act differently, but they also have some identical low-level behaviours. They all follow the same basic rules of physics, and will fall or bounce based on these rules. So they all have a common set of properties/methods that define these sorts of things, such as the properties `mass` and `elasticity`, and the methods `drop` and `bounce`.

So we could have:

```
redTrashCan.drop();
hero.drop();
```

...so that both a red trash can and the hero can be made to fall until they collide with a solid surface. It gets even more interlinked, because the `drop()` method will probably simply consist of calls to further methods, such as `collisionTest()`(to see when we hit the surface) and `bounce()`(following the collision).

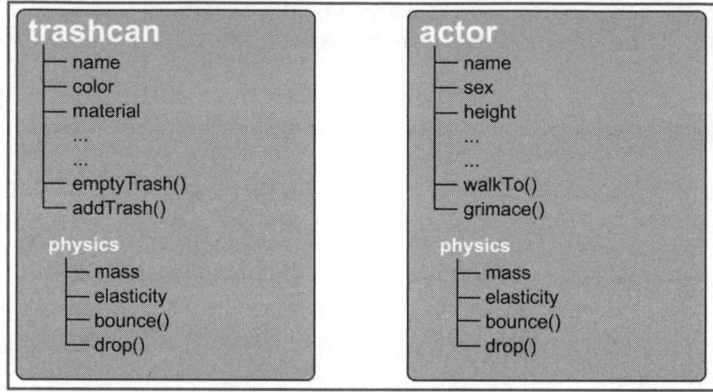

If we drew pictures of the trashcan and actor objects (or rather, the data that defines them, because that is all that really exists; the final movie will simply be a visual representation of this data), we would see something like the diagrams shown. The `trashcan` object has its own set of properties and methods, as does the `actor` object. Both also contain a lower - level object called `physics`, and both the trashcan and actor conform to its methods and have its properties. Physics makes real things in the real world act, well, realistically, and we are modeling the same thing in our virtual objects by creating a common object to represent real-world physics.

So the way we would build up our virtual computer-generated film set would be to first define the low-level objects, such as `physics`, which defines how everything moves and reacts, and then add this object as a base for other, more complicated objects. We reuse the low-level objects to make more complicated ones.

We can build a new object for example, called `crowd`, which consists of a large number of `actor` objects, plus a few properties that define an individual crowd instance (such as `population`, `disposition`...). We could define a large angry crowd by setting `population` to `1000` and `disposition` to `angry`, which would probably also make all the actor objects in the crowd `grimace()`.

Unlike the `trashcan` and `actor` objects, `physics` is not actually something real, but is rather a set of rules corresponding to the laws of nature. An object doesn't have to have a solid physical equivalent - if you can assign properties and methods to something, then you can make a virtual representation of that, and re-create it on a computer.

You might be starting to understand what we said earlier - that we don't have to define what a trashcan actually *is* to the computer. In writing the methods and properties of each object, we imply what a trashcan is in the code and data. The computer doesn't know what a trashcan is, because it follows these instructions blindly, but it looks as if it does because the code makes it act as if it is using the trashcan in a sensible way. When you play a flight simulator game, your computer has no idea what a F-14 Tomcat is, but that doesn't matter; it will just blindly follow the rules for modelling a F-14 that the programming team set up in the code.

The browser is exactly the same as the trashcan. When we say 'browser window' we certainly don't mean a thing of wood and glass. A browser button isn't a real button made of plastic and copper, and the HTML file we see inside the window is called a 'document' but there is no paper to be seen, so what do we really mean?

We are referring to **objects**. This distinction is not apparent when we are using a browser to surf the Web, as we can assume a window is a thing you look out of, and a button is something you click, in the same way as when we watch *Tron* we can assume all the simulated trashcans are real and the lightcycles are real motorbikes.

When we want to control the browser through code, it's a different matter: we have to start thinking about the **Window**, **Document** and all the buttons on the browser interface in terms of what they really are: **objects**, **properties** and **methods**, and all objects are the same as far as code is concerned. When we control the window, we don't look at it based on what it looks like, but through its properties and methods. We do exactly the same for the document, even though it is a totally different object. This means that our code for controlling the two objects will also look very similar, even though the end results may be totally different.

Object-oriented systems used to describe things like the browser are very common, because you can visually see the objects and the properties that define them on your computer screen. There's a one-to-one relationship between objects and parts of the interface in GUI design; there will be a scrollbar object that controls the scrollbar and a textfield object that controls all the input text boxes, for example. Because a good part of web design is about designing and/or working with GUIs, the object-oriented approach is something you will see often.

Now we can see how an object-oriented approach could be used to model a virtual version of an everyday object such as a trashcan, let's turn that knowledge to the browser. If all this seems a bit new and confusing to you, don't worry – we're about to see this in practice, which should make things a lot clearer.

The DOM

So how do we describe the browser as a series of objects? Well, just like the trashcan, we can make up a good object model simply by looking at it and seeing what the objects that make it work might be:

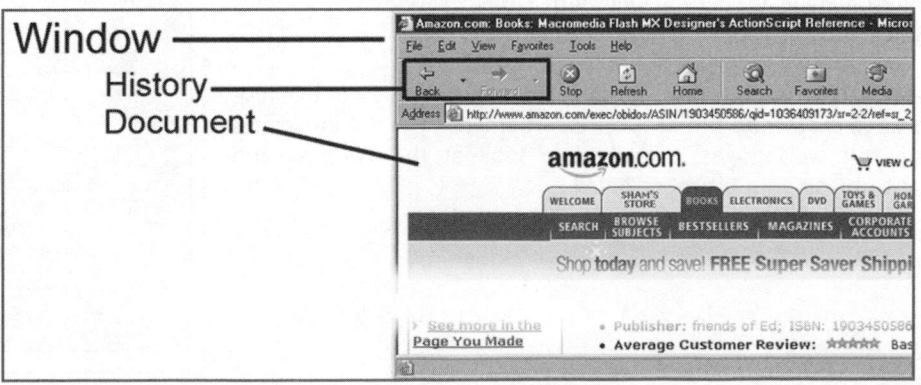

The top level object is the **Window**. This includes the browser window and associated toolbars, scrollbars and status bar.

Contained inside the Window is our **Document**, so it follows that the Document object is part of the Window object, or in dot notation (which is simply a way of showing the path through the objects), you access the document with:

    window.document

This tells us that the window contains an object called `document`, and we want to access it. This is much like paths you use in your operating system - if `window` was a folder that contained a file called `document.doc`, you would access it with `window/document.doc`. If you think of the dot as very much the same as the `/` in a file path, you won't be far wrong; both are ways of representing a **path** to a **resource**.

The `document` contains methods and properties that allow us to change the 'HTML document' (a.k.a. the web page).

Finally, amongst the buttons of the Window are the forward and back buttons that allow you to move back and forward through the list of pages that you have visited. There needs to be a set of data that defines this list of web pages, and this is the **History** object. Again, the History is part of the Window, so you access it with:

    window.history

Notice how similar the browser History is to the list of trashed items we defined for our Tron trashcan: the trashcan contained a list of objects thrown into it, while the History is a list of visited pages. You empty things from the trashcan in the same way as you move back through the history; reading the list sequentially. In the case of the trashcan, you take the last thing in the list, remove it from the trashcan and do something else with it (like put it on the desk to search through). In the history, you take the last URL and make the browser display it.

We will look at the History object in later chapters, but will concern ourselves with the two most important objects for now, `window` and `document`. This hierarchy of objects is a simple object model that defines how the environment containing the HTML document is represented, hence the name **Document Object Model**. It is actually a very small subset of the full JavaScript DOM.

The DOM used through JavaScript is important to web design because it allows us to customize the browser environment so that it integrates well with our web pages. Let's have a look at the Window and Document objects in a bit more detail.

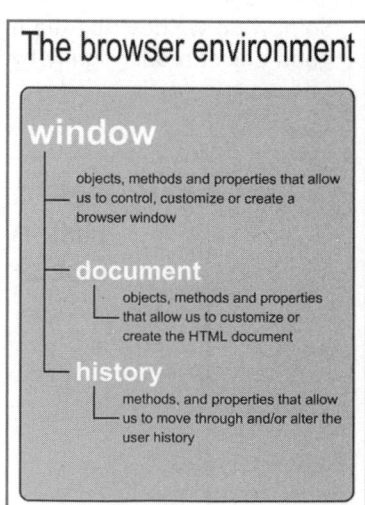

The browser environment

window
— objects, methods and properties that allow us to control, customize or create a browser window

— **document**
— objects, methods and properties that allow us to customize or create the HTML document

— **history**
— methods, and properties that allow us to move through and/or alter the user history

Window

The Window object contains one or more HTML documents (we will see how a window can have more than one HTML document when we look at **frames** in **Chapter 11**). There are several things that the methods and properties of the Window object allow us to do:

- Open and close windows, as well as customizing any new windows we create, so that they fit in better with the HTML documents that they will contain.

- Decide which of the open windows we choose to place in front (or 'in focus').

- Create warning, input and information dialog boxes.

- Control the status text (the text that appears at the bottom left of the browser window).

Dialog boxes and status text

The browser Window is able to generate dialog boxes as shown below. The first JavaScript listing we looked at earlier created an *alert* window using the `window.alert()` method. You can recreate it again with the following simple HTML:

```
<html>

<head>
    <script language = "JavaScript" >
    window.alert("Welcome to my site!");
    </script>
</head>

<body>
</body>

</html>
```

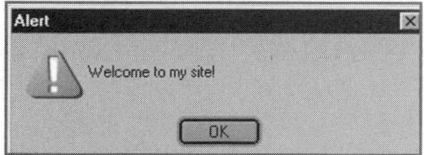

The alert box is used to bring something to the attention of the user, but it can be a little overwhelming as it stops everything until the user clicks OK. The status bar at the bottom of the window is a more subtle way to use the window to present messages (and, more importantly, has much less of the irritation factor of the alert box!).

The default status message of the window is a property called `defaultStatus`, so the way to change it using dot notation is `window.defaultStatus`. The following code does this:

```
<html>

<head>
    <script language = "JavaScript" >

            window.defaultStatus = 'Welcome to my site!';

</script>
</head>

<body>
</body>

</html>
```

If you view this in a browser you will see our welcoming message at the bottom left of the window:

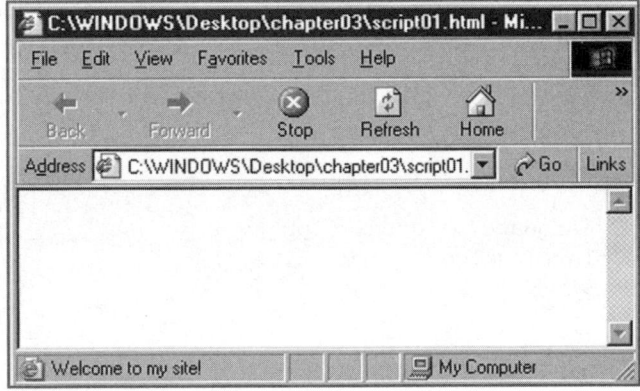

Notice that this time we are changing a **property** rather than using a **method**.

Opening, closing, and customizing windows

The real meat of the Window object is the two methods `window.open()` and `window.close()`. These allow you to open new pop-up and browser windows.

Opening a browser window

To open a new browser window, we use the `window.open()` method. The syntax looks like this:

```
window.open(location, name, options) ;
```

- *location* is the name of the document you want to load into the new window.
- *name* is the name that you want to give to the window. This name can be used by HTML to change the content of the newly created window. This is optional but it's a good idea to always add it, because it allows you to differentiate between multiple windows.

- *options* is an optional series of values that define the look of the window. For example, you can make the new window appear as a pop-up or as a standard browser window by changing some or all of the options.

Create the following HTML, saving it as `newWindow.html` in your `chapter03` folder;

```
<html>

<head>
      <title>.:: I am a new window ::.</title>
</head>

<body>
      <div align = "Center">
             <br><br>
             <h2>I have been opened by the parent window</h2>
      </div>
</body>

</html>
```

If you view this in a browser you will see something like this:

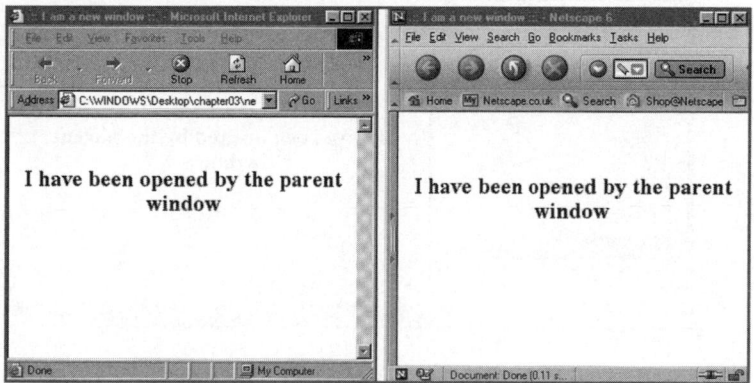

There's nothing new in this HTML; all it does is display some centered Heading 2 text. Close this window, create the following HTML and save it as `mainWindow.html` in the same directory:

```
<html>

<head>
      <title>.:: original window ::.</title>

      <script language = "JavaScript" >
             window.open('newWindow.html', 'popup');
      </script>
</head>
```

```
<body>
        <div align = "center">
                <br><br>
                <h2>I am the original window</h2>
        </div>
</body>

</html>
```

The body of this HTML does almost the same thing; it simply displays some centered Heading 2 text. The difference here is that there is a line of JavaScript that uses `window.open()` to open our file `newWindow.html` in a new browser window instance `newWin`.

Notice that the name field of `window.open()` (in this case, `popup`) is **not** the name JavaScript recognises the new window as. This is the name that HTML will recognise the window as, so it is still useful, and we will see this when we come to look at the Document object.

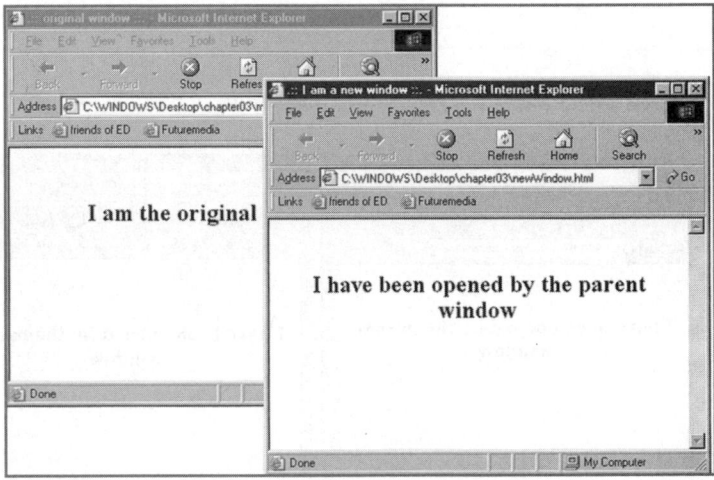

As soon as this file is displayed, a new window is opened displaying `newWindow.html`. The new window gets focus, which means that it appears in front as the selected window. Sometimes you don't want this to happen, and another method of the window object, `window.blur()` allows us to do this. Although `blur` and `focus` may imply some effect, they actually refer to 'the window in front that is taking input' (the window in focus) and 'the window that is sent to the back and is grayed out' (the blurred window or windows) Add the following to the `<script>` part of `mainWindow.html`:

```
<script language = "JavaScript" >
        newWin=window.open('newWindow.html', 'popup');
        newWin.blur();
</script>
```

Close all the browser windows except one, and view the amended document in the browser window that remains.

So what have we done here and what happens? The `window.open` method is now equated to something else called `newWin`. Why? Well, the name of the window (`popup`) is an **attribute** value known to HTML, but (rather confusingly) is not a name that JavaScript can use. To allow JavaScript to refer to the window, you have to give the new window an **instance name**, and this is what `newWin` is.

We can then use this instance name to apply methods to the newly created window.

> *Rather than use the general name* `window` *that means 'the window that this code appears in', we have to use a different name for the* `blur()` *method because we want it to act on a window other than the one the code is in. This can be* `newWin`, `mylilPopup`, *or any name different from the other windows.*

To make the original window focused, add the following line:

```
<script language = "JavaScript" >
      newWin=window.open('newWindow.html', 'popup');
      newWin.blur();
      window.focus();
</script>
```

You should now see the original window keep its focus as the new window is created. Notice that this time we have used `window.focus()` to tell the browser *focus the current window*, where *current* means the window this code appears in.

> *Depending how you send* `mainWindow.html` *to the browser, you may end up getting slightly different results. The best way to test the script is by simply double clicking on* `mainWindow.html` *and letting your default browser open it.*

Now we've got a new window created, we can use the *options* part of window.open() to customize our new window. We can change the following parts of the new window's **chrome** (chrome is a web designer term for the areas of the window that are not part of the central document area):

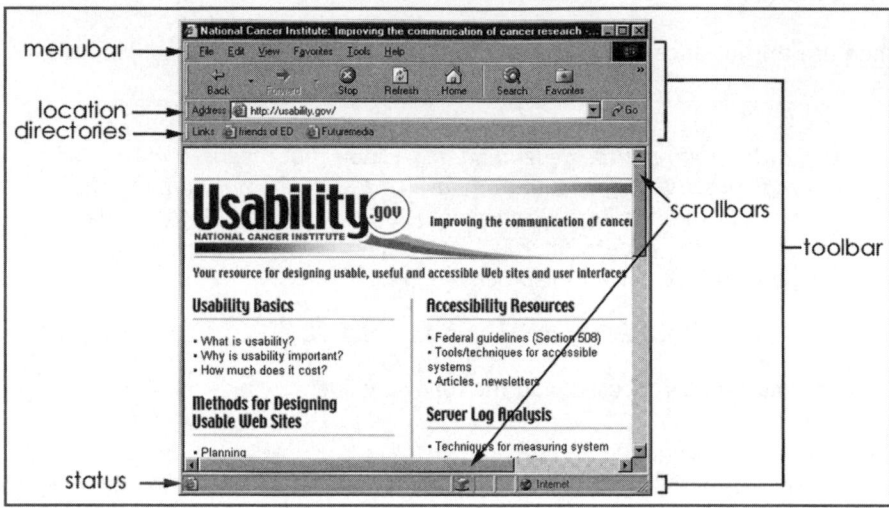

This is done by adding the titles above followed by an instruction to enable them or not in the form of a yes or no. The options are given in a list, separated by commas, and set to either yes or no (you can also use 0 and 1).

The following change to mainWindow.html will create a new browser window with the minimum chrome at the top, but with scrollbars and a status bar:

```
<script language = "JavaScript" >
    newWin=window.open('newWindow.html', 'popup', 'menubar=no,
        ➥location=no, directories=no, status=yes,
        ➥scrollbars=yes');
</script>
```

Close all browser windows except one, and view the modified mainWindow.html in it:

As you will have noticed from the previous example but one, omitting the options altogether makes the browser open a new window with all the options set. Also worth noting is that you cannot alter the options of the first browser window, because it is already open.

In general, once you start entering options, you only need to specify the options you want to appear. Any options that you want set to no can be simply omitted. The following line would open a window containing only the status bar:

```
newWin=window.open('newWindow.html', 'popup', 'status=yes');
```

This rule isn't always followed for all options when using certain browsers, so be sure to check that the resulting new window looks the same in both Netscape Navigator and Microsoft Explorer. If in doubt, use the full list of options, setting each to 'yes' or 'no' explicitly.

Why open a new window?

Showing pages in a new window rather than allowing them to overwrite the current page is a useful trick for certain types of page:

- **Microsites** are small sites that consist of a small number of pages, and which are separate from, but related to the main site. They are usually opened in a new window to differentiate them from the main page. Think of them as supplementary magazines folded into a weekend newspaper; something that is part of the main content, but meant to be read separately. Some companies like to use microsites for each of their products, with the main site representing the company itself.

- **Large images** are sometimes opened in their own window, because this gives the user the option of carrying on looking at the main site while they wait for the image to appear in a new window.

- When you give the user the option to follow links to other sites, it is sometimes useful to open the new sites in their own window, because this practice also keeps your site on the user's screen. Be careful with this, because the user may get a little sick of all the windows that your site is opening! There are ways round this, and we will look at these when we look at opening new documents in an existing window.

More options

You can also add some more options that define how the new window will behave:

- `resizable` defines whether you want the window to be resizable. If you select `yes`, the user will be able to resize the window by click-dragging a window edge.

- `width` and `height` defines the width and height of the window, and you need to specify this as a number of pixels. If you don't specify either, the window will usually be about the same size as the window that opened this window. Some browsers will open a window sized to fit around the HTML document if this will result in a smaller window.

> *There are security limits as to how small a window JavaScript is allowed to open. A very small window could appear invisible or be otherwise difficult to find, and this window could remain undetected whilst it gets up to all sort of mischief. The smallest allowable value is set at 100 for both height and width.*

The following line would create a resizable new window with the menubar and scrollbars showing (though some browsers will hide scrollbars until the document no longer fits, and they're needed), with the window initially appearing at a size of 400x400 pixels:

```
newWin=window.open('newWindow.html', 'popup', 'menubar=yes,
    ➡ scrollbars=yes, height=400, width=400, resizable=yes');
```

There are a number of types of web page that appear much neater if they appear in a window of a particular size, and which you would use the `height`, `width` and `resizable` options for. The most common use is for pages containing multimedia, such as Flash sites and video streams. These usually appear in small fixed size pop-up windows because Flash sites are sometimes small in height and width and would get lost in a large window, and also because – as we noted with image files above – some of these assets are large and take a while to download.

Adverts sometimes open in windows with no chrome at all ('pop-up' windows), because the user will want to do one of only two things: click on them or (most usually) simply close them. Another more controversial reason that advert pop-ups are popular is that you can get more advertising on a site in this way than if you just stuck to banner adverts in the main window.

Linking to new windows

So we're now able to navigate to new windows using JavaScript. Usually, however, you would want to open a window when the user asks for it to open, not immediately as we have here. We have already seen the easiest way to do this, adding a script to an `<a>` anchor tag so it launches from a link.

Change the `mainWindow.html` file so that it looks like this:

```
<html>

<head>
    <title>.:: original window ::.</title>
</head>

<body>
    <br><br>This <a href="javascript:newWin=window.open
➥           ('newWindow.html', 'popup', 'menubar=yes,
            scrollbars=yes,
➥           height=400, width=400, resizable=yes');">link</a> will
            open
➥                   a new window with newWindow.html inside it...

</body>

</html>
```

We have changed the word 'link' in the text to a hyperlink.

This <u>link</u> will open a new window with newWindow.html inside it...

The `<a>` tag that does this uses a JavaScript instruction as its `href` attribute, so that when the link is clicked, this JavaScript line is executed:

```
newWin=window.open('newWindow.html', 'popup', 'menubar=yes,
➥   scrollbars=yes, height=400, width=400, resizable=yes');
```

It works, but something odd happens. If you look at the original window now, the address bar looks like a bomb has hit it on most browsers (Mac Explorer users might miss out on this one, but you still need your site to work for everyone else, so read on...):

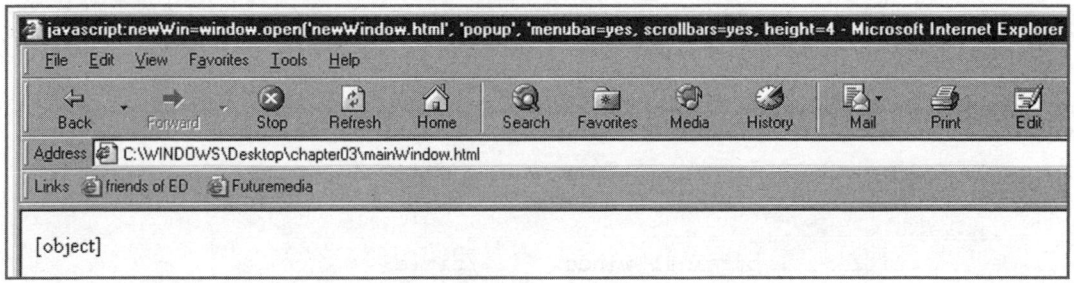

Not only has the original HTML disappeared to be replaced by the cryptic `[object]` (Explorer) or `[object Window]` (Netscape), but the window title will change to our line of JavaScript.

The reason for this is that the `href` in an `<a>` link is **always** used to modify the HTML page it appears on. If you use JavaScript as the `href`, the browser will send the output from the last JavaScript line it sees in the `href` to the current window as HTML text. The output of `window.open()` is a new window object, and expressed as HTML text, this is the short text description we see.

To stop this happening, we need to add a new line at the end of our script that returns nothing that can be written to the HTML. Nothing in JavaScript goes by the funky name `void 0`. This isn't usually a lot of use, but we can use it here. By adding it as the last line in our `href` script, we preserve the original HTML. Add the new line shown:

```
<html>

<head>
      <title>.:: original window ::.</title>
</head>

<body>
      <br><br>This <a href="javascript:newWin=window.open
                         ➡ ('newWindow.html', 'popup', 'menubar=yes,
                         ➡ scrollbars=yes, height=400, width=400,
                         ➡ resizable=yes');
                         void 0;">link</a> will open a new window
                         ➡ called 'popup' with newWindow.html inside it...

</body>

</html>
```

Multiple windows

Matters can get a little more interesting when you want to open multiple new windows, or you want several links to open documents into the same window. The following addition creates a second link that will open a new window with `mainWindow.html` in it. If you click on both links you will end up with two new windows:

> This link will open a new window called 'popup' with newWindow.html inside it...
>
> This link will open **another** window called 'popup2' with mainWindow.html (this page) inside it...

```
<html>

<head>
      <title>.:: original window ::.</title>
</head>

<body>
```

```
                    <br><br>This
                        <a href="javascript:newWin = window.open('newWindow.html',
                            ➡ 'popup', 'menubar=yes, scrollbars=yes, height=400,
                            ➡ width=400, resizable=yes'); void 0; ">link</a>
                            ➡ will open a new window called 'popup'
                            ➡ with newWindow.html inside it...

                    <br><br>This <a href="javascript:newWin2 = window.open
                            ➡ ('mainWindow.html', 'popup2', 'menubar=yes,
                            ➡ scrollbars=yes, height=400, width=400,
                            ➡ resizable=yes');
                            void 0; ">link</a> will open <b>another</b>
                            ➡ window called 'popup2' with mainWindow.html
                            ➡ (this page) inside it...

        </body>

        </html>
```

Notice that:

- the instance names of the two windows are different (newWin and newWin2). If we made these two the same (or just omitted them), the windows would do exactly the same thing, but JavaScript would not be able to reference them later, so we could not easily close them individually later.

- two of the three windows that you will end up with if you click on both links have the same title (as defined in the head). The title is not actually important to either the HTML or JavaScript, so you can give them the title you want, even if this is the same in more than one case.

- the name attribute of the two windows is different (popup and popup2). If you change the second window name to the same as the first, you will see that only one new window is created. Sometimes you want this to happen, because it minimizes the number of separate windows that your web page creates.

Finally, you can create a third standard HTML link that uses one of the newly created windows;

```
        <html>

        <head>
            <title>.:: original window ::.</title>
        </head>

        <body>
            <br><br>This <a href="javascript:newWin = window.open
                            ➡        ('newWindow.html', 'popup',
                            ➡        'menubar=yes, scrollbars=yes,
                            ➡        height=400, width=400,
                            ➡        resizable=yes');
                            void 0; ">link</a> will open a new
```

```
                                                window with newWindow.html
                                          ➡    inside it...

                <br><br>This <a href="javascript:newWin2 = window.open
                                          ➡    ('mainWindow.html', 'popup2',
                                          ➡    'menubar=yes,
                                          ➡    scrollbars=yes, height=400,
                                          ➡    width=400, resizable=yes');
                                          ➡    void 0; ">link</a> will open
                                          ➡    <b>another</b> window with
                                          ➡    mainWindow.html (this page) inside
                                          ➡    it...

                <br><br>This <a href = "mainWindow.html", target = "popup">link</a>
                                          ➡ will replace the content in the window
                                          ➡ 'popup' (if it already exists),
                                          ➡ or create it (if it doesn't).

        </body>

        </html>
```

The new link is a pure HTML link using the standard <a> tag with no JavaScript. Notice how the third link creates a new standard window (with all options enabled) if you click on this new link first. If this is the case, then the new window will not have a JavaScript instance name, which reduces the options for controlling it from any other window except itself. This can be a problem for more advanced sites, where you may want the ability to selectively close all new windows created, and do it from the main page. The third link also changes the window 'popup' if it already exists (i.e. the top link is selected before this one).

> *You can use JavaScript buttons, which we'll take a look at in the calculator example in* **Chapter 8**, *instead of text links.*

Closing windows

As you can see from this, creating windows gives you more options for inter-page navigation than just following links in a single browser window. By creating custom windows, you can create a much more professional - looking site, although this stops being the case if you open too many additional windows! The only thing we need to look at now is how to close a window.

JavaScript is not allowed to close a window it has not opened itself without first prompting the user to ask if it is okay to do this (this happens in most but not all browsers). This is to prevent a JavaScript programmer creating bad joke code that goes around closing everyone's browsers on the first of April or whatever. Most users will say *no* to any scary-looking prompt that they don't understand, so it's considered bad design to write code that tries to close a window requiring a prompt.

When you are working with mutiple windows, you can use the following general window object names to make life easier.

- `self` or `window` for the current window (or 'the window this line of code is inside')

- `parent` for the window that opened the current window

To close the current window, you simply use the lines:

```
window.close();
```

or

```
self.close();
```

To close a particular window, you use

```
myName.close();
```

where `myName` is the JavaScript instance name of the window (in the examples above, this would be either `newWin` or `newWin2`, and not `popup` or `popup2`).

Change the body of `mainWindow.html`, adding the new link shown below:

```
<html>

<head>
    <title>.:: original window ::.</title>
</head>

<body>
    <br><br>This <a href="javascript:newWin = window.open
                    ➥ ('newWindow.html', 'popup', 'menubar=yes,
                    ➥ scrollbars=yes, height=400, width=400,
                    ➥ resizable=yes'); void 0;">link</a>
                    ➥ will open a new window with newWindow.html
                    ➥ inside it...

    <br><br>This <a href="javascript:newWin2 = window.open
                    ➥('mainWindow.html', 'popup2', 'menubar=yes,
                    ➥scrollbars=yes, height=400, width=400,
                    ➥resizable=yes'); void 0; ">link</a>
```

```
                             ➥ will open <b>another</b> window with
                             ➥ mainWindow.html (this page) inside it...

                    <br><br>This <a href = "mainWindow.html", target =
                    ➥"popup">link</a> will replace the content in the
                    ➥ window 'popup' (if it already exists), or
                    ➥ create it (if it doesn't).

                    <br><br><a href = "javascript:self.close();">close</a>

        </body>

        </html>
```

Because the window will close itself, we don't need the `void 0` on the last line, because there is no document left to corrupt once the window is closed. When you view this page, you will see a new close link:

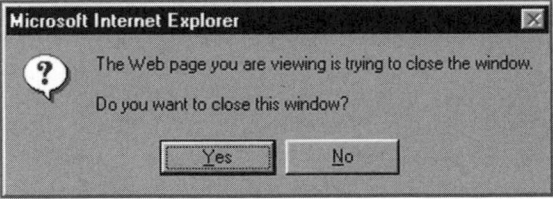

This link will do one of two things:

- If you view the page in Internet Explorer, and click the close link as the first thing, you will see the following prompt:

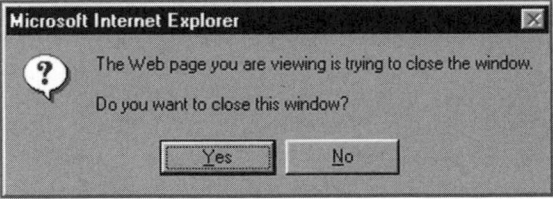

Most users would say *'what the heck is that?'* and click No at this point, so your window will stay open. Some versions of Netscape Navigator will close the window without a prompt, which isn't strictly correct, so you shouldn't assume future versions of this browser would do the same.

- If you hit the second link down, and then click the close link that appears in the resulting pop-up, the window will close with no problems. This is because JavaScript created the pop-up, so the rules say JavaScript is allowed to close it again.

Being able to close a window through code is useful, because it allows you to close a window automatically when it is no longer needed, without leaving it up to the user. A lot of advert pop-ups do this when you are tempted enough to follow their links. They tend to open a new window for the product site, and then close themselves.

We will look at fine-tuning the Window object in **Chapter 7**, when we look at creating windows that can move around, or pop up in a particular place. We will also look at cool features like turning the status bar area into a ticker tape display, but for now, we have learnt that there are more options to navigation than keeping your entire site in a single window.

Opening your own browser windows also allows you to specify the size of your window area, something that can ruin some web pages if you have no control over it, with important content getting hidden in windows that are too small, or pages containing small video streams getting lost in a big browser window.

Document

The Document object represents the HTML document inside the window. Although you can control most things to do with the document's appearance using HTML formatting, you can alter it after the document has been displayed using JavaScript, or use JavaScript to customize or create a page whilst it is being parsed.

This feature of HTML and JavaScript confuses a lot of beginners to web design; if there are things that you can do to the page in HTML (such as set the page background color) that you can also do with JavaScript, which do you use?

There are only two combinations of any use:

- Use HTML to set the page's initial appearance, but then use JavaScript to change parts of the page after this. This allows you to create interactive pages that can change themselves based on what the user does. We can't really look at this feature of JavaScript in great detail (which incidentally, also goes by the general name **DHTML** or Dynamic HTML) until we know more about **variables**, **Cascading Style Sheets** and **events**, but we'll have a look at a simple example that doesn't use any of them for now.

- Use JavaScript to optionally add or modify parts of a new web page as it is being opened. This allows you to create customized or dynamic pages whose initial appearance can vary depending on conditions set up by JavaScript. For instance, a page that changes depending on which browser you're using – our case study example uses slightly different Cascading Style Sheets for each browser to overcome a slight difference in the way the two browsers display the same Style Sheet.

Path to the Document object

Because the Document object is contained inside the Window object, we refer to it with the dot path:

```
window.document
```

You can omit the window part of the path if you are referring to the current document, but it is usually better to keep it in at this stage (a bit more legibility for not a lot of extra typing).

Dynamically altering an HTML document

There are a number of basic properties that the document has, and these include:

- document.fgColor - the foreground color of the document, and the color that default text will appear in.
- document.lastModified - this property contains the date that this document was last modified, and is often useful to put at the bottom of your site's home page.
- document.linkcolor - the color of links that have not yet been visited.
- document.vLinkColor - the color of visited links document.title - the title of the HTML document, as appears in the title bar of the browser window.

In your chapter03 folder, create a new HTML document called colors.html and add the following to it:

```
<html>

<head>
    <title>colors</title>
</head>

<body>
    <div align = "Center"><br><br>

        <h3>click on a color...</h3><br>

        <a href="javascript:window.document.bgColor = '#FFFF00'; void
                  ➥ 0;">
        yellow</a>
          

        <a href = "javascript:window.document.bgColor = '#FF00FF';
                  ➥ void 0;">
        magenta</a>
          

        <a href = "javascript:window.document.bgColor = '#00FFFF';
                  ➥ void 0;">
        cyan </a>
          
```

```
        </div>

    </body>

    </html>
```

This code will create the following centered text using the included HTML formatting tags:

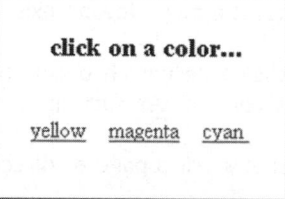

When you click on the yellow link, the following JavaScript code will be executed and the background will turn yellow:

```
window.document.bgColor = '#FFFF00';
void 0;
```

This changes the background color property `bgColor` of `window.document`, the document in the current window. This will cause the background color of the rendered page to change interactively. Finally, the first line will send the color value to `self.document` unless we add a `void 0` so that it instead sends nothing, hence line 2.

> We'll be looking at color and hexadecimal codes like `#FFFF00` in detail in **Chapter 6.**

As we saw earlier, `window.document` can also be written as `self.document`. I personally always use `self` for the windows I create with JavaScript, so that I know I can always close a window I've referred to with `self` with JavaScript without occasioning one of those nasty prompt windows we saw earlier.

The Case Study – Navigation

Now it's finally time to put all this into action. We've covered enough on HTML and JavaScript to start to create the basic structure of our Mondo case study. In this extensive first instalment, we'll:

- Add a 'Work in Progress' page
- Create the basic site structure via placeholder pages, and test it locally

Rules of Navigation

One of the biggest concerns with web design is making sure that the user is able to travel between pages of your site quickly and intuitively. There are many different ways to achieve this, but what follows are perhaps the four most important considerations.

The 'three-click' rule

The three-click rule states that *a user should take no more than three clicks to go from any one page in your site to any other*. If the user does not get to somewhere they would like to be within this limit, many will assume they are either lost or that the page doesn't exist.

Where you cannot meet the three-click rule (which occurs particularly in e-commerce sites with many product lines), there are other things you can use such as:

- a 'site map' page (which is usually just a page of direct links, structured to show the general site layout)
- a search box or a drop-down menu

What you should always avoid doing is creating massive pages in order to meet the three-click rule; a three-click path that requires the user to be constantly using the scrollbar to actually find the links on a massive page layout is not really conforming to the intent behind the rule!

The 'unwanted page' concept

The user must never follow links to end up at a page that they did not want, or did not expect. Sites like Amazon certainly don't follow the three-click rule, but you are always sure that your path through the site is vaguely related and every page is requested and not a dead 'I didn't ask for that!' page.

Just like a real bookshop, Amazon allows the visitor to browse through lots of related information about a potential purchase (reviews, what previous purchasers of this book also bought, related book links, other books by the same author, etc).

Although you may not have realised that these pages exist when you start, you are introduced to them in a way that keeps them in context of what you might sensibly want to do next.

In all cases though, *it is important that the user never has to go through pages they don't want to see to access pages they do want to see*. A common-sense design point perhaps, but it's amazing how many sites don't follow it!

Consistency of controls

The user will not be able to get close to the last two ideals if the site doesn't make the navigation buttons and links obvious. The easiest way to do this is using the standard browser link text and big clunky buttons that could not possibly be mistaken for anything else.

More importantly, it's a good idea to *make sure that each page has a basic and consistent subset of the site navigation in it so that the user never feels lost*, and can always:

- Go back to the home page immediately from any other page
- Skip to the main section pages immediately from any other page
- Access a site map from any page

Maintain credibility

Let's face it; the average web surfer is hardened to all those banners, misdirection and unwanted pop-ups thrown at them. There comes a point when they will lose interest from the nag factor and just go elsewhere. You may not be able to do much about that (given that advertising revenue is one of the things that keeps the Web free), but you can make sure that your site will not compound the issue by:

- Avoiding leaving too many opened pop-ups floating around following a typical user visit
- Making sure that the content-to-advertising ratio will always be sufficient to keep the user interested, and creating more/less pages within the navigation to meet this if necessary

The users should always be able to trust that a link will do what it says, and the site should not do anything that destroys this trust to the extent that they are driven away. This is certainly a new and emerging design constraint, but your awareness of it may make the client think twice.

> *There are of course many things that can kill credibility straight away, and dishonest navigation is the tip of the iceberg:*
>
> - *Many would think twice about visiting most sites that come up in a search engine with what looks like a free URL.. It's certainly the biggest no-no for an up-and-coming web designer looking for customers!*
> - *A large amount of broken links or out-of-date content is another more obvious issue that implies an ineffective (or non-existent) organization behind the site.*
> - *Finally, any business site that doesn't include at least a postal address as well as the normal e-mail contact address will put off a significant number of customers, many of whom are now web-savvy enough to recognise the difference between real customer service and an e-mail-only black hole. Surprisingly, one of the top five e-commerce sites doesn't realise this, and doesn't include a postal address or phone number.*

Defining the Navigation

There are a number of different types of site, but they all have one thing in common; a starting HTML page, usually called `index.html`. As mentioned earlier, this is the HTML document the browser will look for first. In short, this page (usually index.html, but sometimes home.html or default.html) is the **default web page**, and is assumed whenever the URL doesn't otherwise specify a page, e.g. www.friendsofed.com.

In many cases, `index.html` is simply the home page of your site, but websites are becoming increasingly slick, and one of the things that you'll find now is that `index.html` may be a **gateway** to a number of other sites, which may include:

- A standard HTML site which will work on all browsers
- A slightly slicker site which uses more up-to-date HTML, using features that some browsers may not support (such as **frames**, which are discussed in **Chapter 11**)
- Browser-specific HTML sites, such as separate sites for Internet Explorer and Netscape Navigator
- Localized versions of the site, which may include separate sites for different geographic areas (North America, Europe, etc) or different language versions
- A high-bandwidth HTML site
- A site using non-HTML technology, such as Macromedia Flash

> *As well as providing a more interactive, animation-heavy site, Flash is increasingly used to replace the high-bandwidth HTML site option. We'll be learning more about Flash as a web design tool in* **Chapter 12**.

We have chosen the Mondo site as an example for this book because it addresses many of these issues. For a start, Mondo is required to cater for two languages; English and Polish (Tom is based in Poland, but has a large US and Western Europe audience). Secondly, Mondo has an optional Flash site. Let's see how Tom solved this.

`index.html` is not being used in Mondo as simply a home page, but is a gateway to two different sites: an HTML version, and a Flash version. As well as catering for the English-speaking audience, the Mondo site also contains Polish language translations for each page, and these appear as pop-ups.

> *Having the completed site to hand is obviously an advantage here because we can cheat and look forward, so feel free to look at the complete site and pick out how everything has ended up!*

Designing the gateway navigation options

It is always a good idea to start off with a sketch.

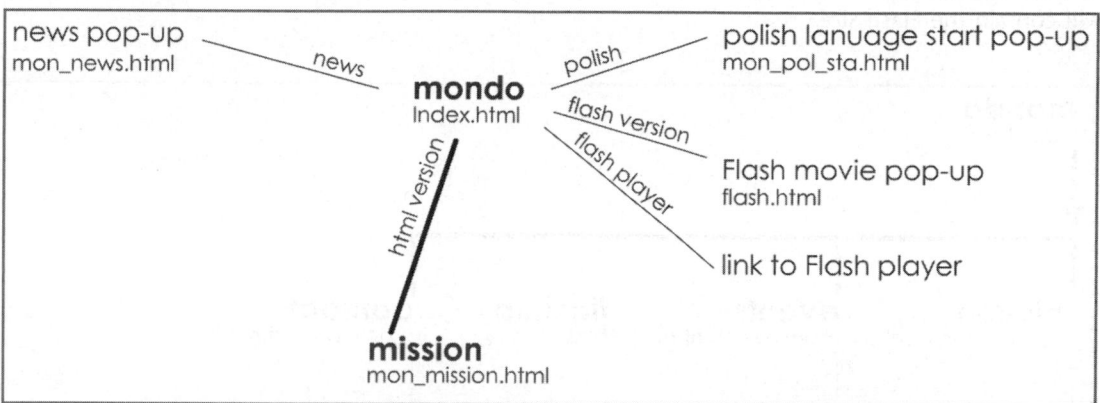

The thin lines represent any link that doesn't change the current page (they will usually signify a pop-up or a page opened in a new browser window). There are three pop-ups; one for Mondo news, one for the Polish translation and one for the Flash version of the site. Because the Flash version of the site also requires the free Flash plug-in to be present, there is also a link to a location where the user can get it.

The thick lines represent links that will change the current page. If we select the link 'html version', we go to the first page of the HTML site proper, `mon_mission.html`.

Notice that Tom has gone for a news pop-up at the gateway. This is placed very early in the site because many users simply want to see if there have been any changes to the site since their last visit. By allowing them to go straight to a news section (which will have links to any new material) you cater directly for the repeat visitor. Not only do they see only the new stuff, they don't need to have to go through any 'seen that one before' unwanted pages to get to it.

Although this is a large number of pop-ups, remember that most users will not need to open all three.

Designing the site sections

Once we get to the Mission page `mon_mission.html`, we are into the HTML site itself. We will have a number of different section pages, including the Mission, Events and Contact pages.

We don't really need to link back to our gateway page, `index.html`, but the user could conceivably want to move on to the Flash version of the site after viewing the HTML site, so we will also add a link to go to the Flash site.

Below is a sketch showing what we want pictorially. Once the user has moved to the mission page from the Mondo page, they should be able to move between the mission, events and contact pages, irrespective of their current page. Also shown are the Polish translation pop-ups and the Flash pop-up (flashub) that will contain the Flash site.

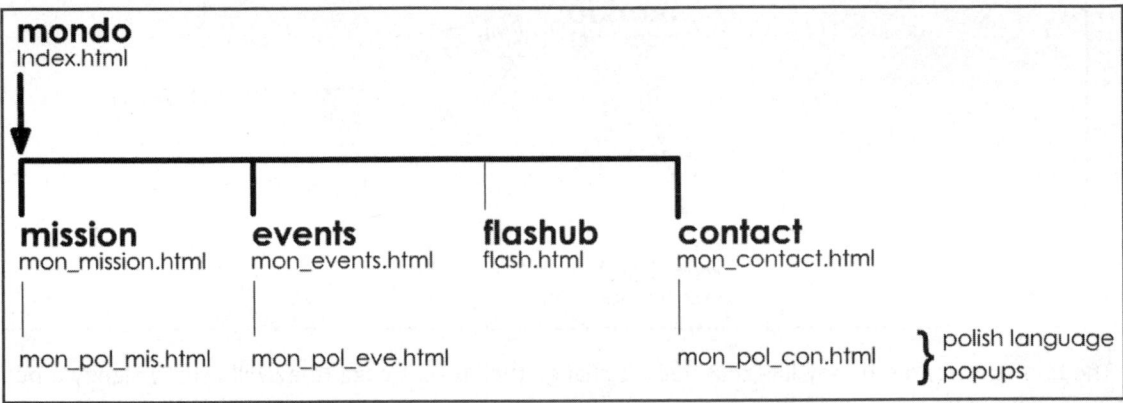

Adding the sub-navigation options

As well as our section pages discussed above, we will most likely need lower sub-pages. There are actually three distinct ways of forming links, and these are the **star**, **sequential** and **tree** methods:

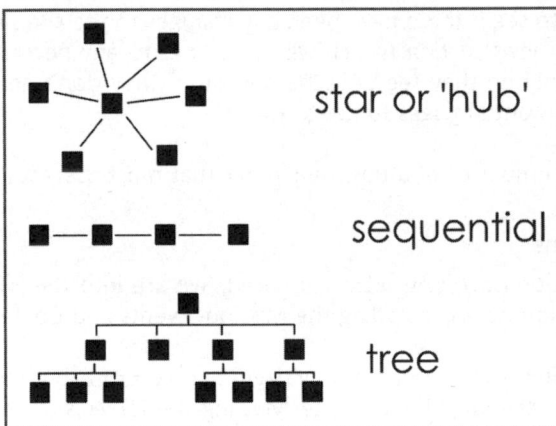

The star-connected site consists of a central or 'hub' page (again, usually index.html) with all the other pages coming directly from it. It's particularly popular with small sites, and most sites' 'links' pages are actually a star, with the page being a hub to other related home pages.

Then there are sequential sites, where you have to go through each page in order, much like you do with a book. This is used most often with online forms and shopping (where you have to complete each page in order), slideshows or narrative-based sites.

The most popular is probably the tree structure:

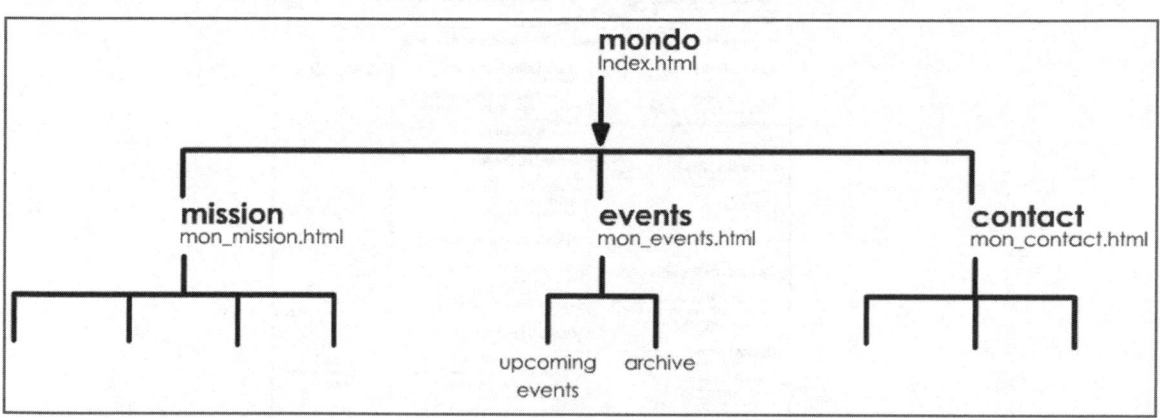

This creates further pages (sub-pages) coming from each of the site sections, so that the final navigation sketch looks like an upside-down tree. It's a cool concept because it maintains a good ordering system; as long as the sub-pages coming from the events section are related to 'events' (in the sketch above, the two sub-pages to the events section could be 'upcoming events' and 'archived events' for example), an intuitive set of links is quickly built up. Another advantage of the tree structure is that it is easy to set up, and it is equally easy to add new pages later. It is therefore the way many small sites are set up.

The big disadvantage of the tree structure is although it is easy to go forward through the navigation, it is difficult to go *back*. For example, getting from the 'upcoming events' sub-page to a mission sub-page would require you to use three clicks, which is one more than would get you to 'upcoming events' from the mondo page. *The back-path is always the longest path, and will exceed the three-click rule very quickly in a tree structure.* In fact, the sketch above shows the largest depth of the tree (two levels) you can create that maintains the three-click rule in both the forward and backwards paths.

There are things you can do that get over the failings in the standard tree structure, such as designing the index page so that it shows the subject matter of the sub-pages as well as the main pages, making it much harder for the user to get lost. Essentially, what you need to do is build the index.html page so that the tree structure is actually implicit in the layout and design. www.usability.gov does just this, and does it rather well, as you can see from the screenshot on the next page.

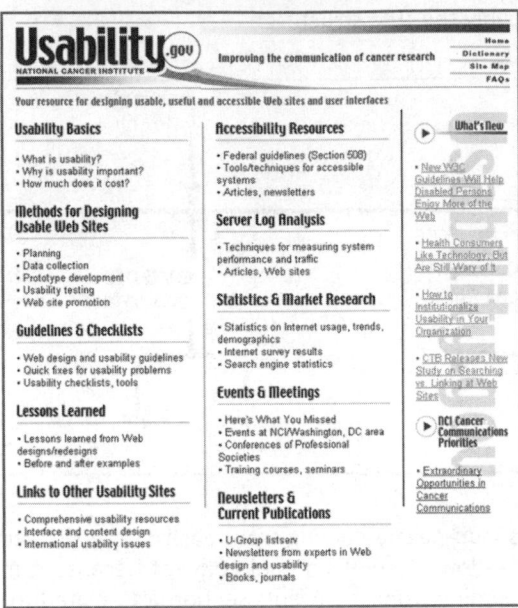

We know from this that if we click on the Lessons Learned page, the sub-pages will include one that shows before and after examples; the tree structure of the site is obvious right at the start, rather than forcing us to explore the site navigation tree (by exploring the links) before we know what it is.

> *You can also create a 'site map' page that does exactly the same thing (shows all the navigation links in the site on one page, arranged to reflect the site structure), but remember that you will waste one of your precious three clicks by doing it that way!*

The Mondo site chooses a slightly more devious option, and one that seems initially simple, but actually requires a lot of forethought; all the main sections and sub pages are available all the time.

There are five sub-pages, web design, photography, general design, case study and past mondos. Rather than associate them with any of the main pages, Tom has simply created a 'sub-navigation' menu that includes the sub-pages on every page. This means that all the main and sub-pages are available from any other page via a single click. Effectively, what we have done is to make all the sub-pages as accessible as subject pages by putting them all at the same level in the tree, but the user will still able to differentiate between the two levels of page because we will present the two sets of links separately.

Implementation

To start the ball rolling on our site, we will first create a **skeleton site**. This includes a number of simple text-only, content - free pages called **placeholders**. Placeholders are cool because they allow you (amongst other things) to check the basic navigation of your site without having to spend any time building the content or graphics associated with each page.

Rather than describe how this works, it is far better simply to show the individual pages.

Creating the default page, index.html

1. Create a new folder on your hard drive and call it mondoSkeleton.

2. Open your preferred text editor and enter the following HTML:

```
<html>
<head>
<title>gateway</title>
</head>

<body>
<h2>gateway placeholder</h2>
<hr>
<p>polish help</p>
<p>HTML version</p>
<p>Flash version Flash plug-in</p>
<p>news</p>
<hr>
</body>

</html>
```

3. Save the file as index.html in the new folder you created.

   This simply creates the following page:

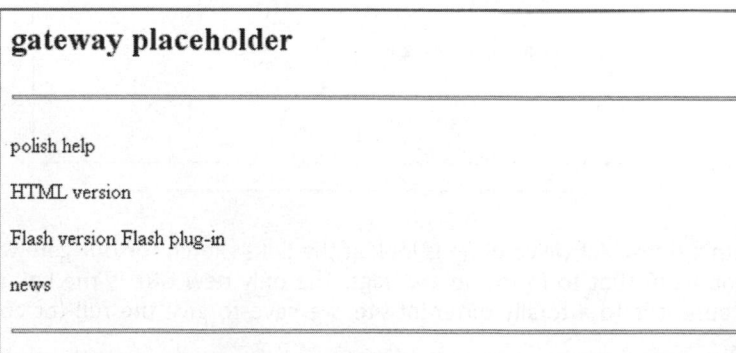

89

There's nothing really new here, except the `<hr>` tag. This creates the two horizontal rules. The text between the lines represents all the links that our sketches describe. Right now though, they're just plain text, but we can easily change all that with a few anchor tags.

4. Change the `<body>` section so that it now reads as follows;

```
<body>
<h2> gateway placeholder</h2>
<hr>
<p> <a href="javascript:polWin=window.open('mon_pol_sta.html',
➡'polishPopup', 'menubar=no, scrollbars=no, width=550, height=300,
➡resizable=no');void 0;">polish help</a> </p>
<p> <a href = "mon_mission.html">HTML version</a> </p>
<p>
<a href="javascript:flashWin=window.open('flash.html', 'flashPopup',
➡'menubar=no, scrollbars=no, width=800, height=600, resizable=no');void
➡0;">Flash version</a>
<a href =
➡"http://www.macromedia.com/shockwave/download/download.cgi?P1_Prod_Version
➡=ShockwaveFlash">Flash plug-in</a>
</p>
<p> <a href="javascript:newsWin=window.open('mon_news.html', 'newsPopup',
➡'menubar=no, scrollbars=yes, width=550, height=300, resizable=no');void
➡0;">news</a> </p>
<hr>
</body>

</html>>
```

---

gateway placeholder

---

polish help

HTML version

Flash version Flash plug-in

news

Again, nothing new. All we've done is look at the links sketch for our gateway page, and taken the information from that to form the `<a>` tags. The only new URL is the link to the Flash download page; because it is to a totally different site, we have to give the full (or absolute) URL, including the http://.

5. If you test the page now, you will see that apart from the 'gateway placeholder' text, everything is now a link.

    Clicking on any of the links will give you a page not found error though, because we haven't yet created the other placeholders! The pop-ups don't contain any content yet for the same reason.

    Notice though, how I have used the `href="javascript"` attribute to open three *different* windows for the three pages-in-pop-ups that can be accessed from this page.

Creating the page placeholders

Creating the other placeholders is much the same process; look at the sketches and build a basic page containing the same link information. We will walk through the skeleton page for the mission page, `mon_mission.html`.

> Because the pages are essentially the same, I have created a skeleton template page, `pageTemplate.html`, which you can use as a starting point to save typing.

1. The placeholder page for `mon_mission.html` looks like this:

    ---

    mission placeholder

    ---

    mission events flashub contact polish help

    web design photography generic design case study past mondos

    ---

2. Replicate the code below in your own file and save it in the `mondoSkeleton` folder:

```
<html>
<head>
<title>mission</title>
</head>

<body>
<h2>mission placeholder</h2>
<hr>
```

```
<!—Top menu—>
<p>
mission  
<a href = "mon_events.html">events</a>  
<a href="javascript:flashWin=window.open('flash.html', 'flashPopup',
➡'menubar=no, scrollbars=no, width=800, height=600, resizable=no');void
➡0;">flashub</a>  
<a href = "mon_contact.html">contact</a>  
<a href="javascript:polWin=window.open('mon_pol_mis.html', 'polPopup',
➡'menubar=no, scrollbars=no, width=550, height=300, resizable=no');
➡polWin.focus(); void 0;">polish help</a> </p>
</p>

<!—Content area—>
<br><br><br><br>

<!— sub-menu—>
<p>
<a href = "mon_webdes.html">web design</a>  
<a href = "mon_photo.html">photography </a>  
<a href = "mon_generic.html">generic design </a>  
<a href = "mon_casestud.html">case study </a>  
<a href = "mon_past.html">past mondos</a>
</p>
<hr>
</body>

</html>
```

3. The only thing that needs to change for the other pages is the page <title>, the <h2> text, the name of the Polish language pop-up corresponding to the link Polish help, and each page shouldn't link to itself (which is why the link to mission in this page is not a link text but instead plain text).

4. You can either have a look at my versions of the placeholder pages, or create your own using pageTemplate.html. The latter is strongly recommended, because it is good practice in creating basic linked web pages.

5. If you are creating the placeholders of the sub-pages, you will need to use the same pages as our example. They are:

    ■   web design: save it as mon_webdes.html
    ■   photography: save it as mon_phtoto.html
    ■   generic design: save it as mon_generic.html
    ■   case study: save it as mon_casestud.html
    ■   past mondos: save it as mon_past.html

Notice again how I have managed the pop-ups. Because I have kept the same name for the pop-ups between this and the last page, clicking on the Polish help or flashub will use the same windows from `index.html` if they are already open. If the user wants the Polish language translation, for every page, then it's likely that they want to read it immediately after they click the link for it, so I have put the pop-up in front with `polWin.focus()` (although the popup will still come up with a cannot find server error because we haven't yet defined the content we want to show in the placeholders).

The skeleton site should now work for all links except those that create a pop-up (because we haven't created placeholders for them yet). Notice that even at this early stage, we are already forming an impression of how usable the navigation of the final site will be. Getting this sort of feedback at an early stage is crucial, because it costs no time to change a few links around now. this will not be the case later, when you may have to totally redesign the page graphics and rearrange the content to do the same thing later on in the design process!

Creating the pop-up placeholders

1. We have to create a number of HTML files to go in our pop-ups. Here's a list of everything we need, and suggested names for the HTML files:

    Polish help pop-ups

`index` page:	`mon_pol_sta.html`
`mission` page:	`mon_pol_mis.html`
`events` page:	`mon_pol_eve.html`
`contact` page:	`mon_pol_con.html`
`web design` page:	`mon_pol_webdes.html`
`photography` page:	`mon_pol_photo.html`
`generic design` page:	`mon_pol_generic.html`
`case study`:	`mon_pol_casestud.html`
`past mondos`:	`mon_pol_past.html`

    We also need a placeholder for the Flash version of our site and the news pop-up, and we will call these `flash.html` and `mon_news.html` respectively.

2. To create the Polish pop-up placeholders, all we really need is a basic page like this:

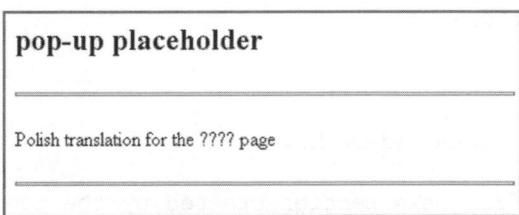

```
<html>
<head>
<title>Polish translation</title>
</head>
```

```
<body>
<h2>pop-up placeholder</h2>
<hr>
<p> Polish translation for the ???? page.</p>
<hr>
</body>

</html>
```

3. This file is saved as popupTemplate.html, and you can modify it for each of the pop-ups we need. All you need to do is change the text that reads "???? page" to the name of the page that creates it. For example, to create mon_pol_mis.html, you would put mission page.

Flash site and news pop-up placeholders

1. The Flash pop-up placeholder flash.html is just the following simple file:

```
<html>
<head>
<title>Flash Mondo Site</title>
</head>

<body>
<h2>pop-up placeholder</h2>
<hr>
<p>Placeholder for Flash version of site.</p>
<hr>
</body>

</html>
```

2. The news pop-up mon_news.html is the equally simple:

```
<html>
<head>
<title>news</title>
</head>

<body>
<h2>mondo news placeholder</h2>
<hr>
<p>Placeholder for news section created by the index page.</p>

<!—Lots of breaks to make page bigger than window—>
<!—and force scrollbar to become active—>
<br><br><br><br><br><br><br>
<br><br><br><br><br><br><br>
```

```
<hr>
</body>

</html>
```

3. There! Finished. OK, that's not really a step, but doesn't it feel good!

You should now be able to check all the navigation links of our site. As mentioned before, a skeleton site allows you to check the navigation of your site and its general link usability *before you actually design the pages themselves*. This saves a lot of time later on because your site is better defined at the start.

As always, a bit of planning before work starts is always a good thing, but most people skip this step if it is seen as *extra* work. That's actually a very important issue when you are designing in a commercial environment; you don't get paid for extra work, and if you do, it may make you look more expensive on the initial work estimate. The cool thing about a site of placeholder pages is that you can replace any placeholder with the final or 'work in progress' version and *immediately test the page within the overall site design*.

Summary

Well, we've now taken our first steps towards our site, by adding a little HTML and creating some basic pop-ups with JavaScript. In the next chapter, we'll cover Cascading Style Sheets, the one-stop solution to all your web formatting needs. And once you're fully primed up on CSS, we'll instantly apply what we've learned to our Mondo case study.

Cascading Style Sheets

What this chapter will do

This chapter gets deeper into text formatting, showing you how you can use CSS to easily change style settings for your web pages, and gain close control of:

- Font sizes and styles
- Blocks of text including positioning, and varying the whitespace surrounding the text blocks
- Page attributes, like margins and whitespace padding

What you'll have learned by the end of this chapter

By the end of this chapter you will have a general understanding of what CSS is and how it relates to HTML, as well as a knowledge of what you can and cannot define when working with typography on the Web. This will enable you to build up a general look and feel for your site using styles.

After having read the first four chapters of this book, you will have gained a useful insight into what underpins web design in terms of the underlying technologies and core coding skills that define a typical web page (HTML, CSS, and JavaScript). You're well equipped to go on and learn how to add graphics and interactivity to your site in the rest of the book.

Introducing CSS

It's hard to change HTML formatting. For example, if all your titles needed to be in the style heading 1, and you later decided they were better off as heading 2, you would have to go through your pages and change all the `<h1>` tags to `<h2>`. Surely it would be better if we could simply change the heading 1 setting to be smaller – you can do this with most Desktop Publishing applications, so why not HTML?

HTML defines what the separate parts of your plain text are, so that you can say 'this is a paragraph', or 'this is bold text'. It doesn't give you any detailed control, such as being able to specify 'a paragraph should be separated by the previous text by one blank line' or 'when I define italic text, look for a true italic font, but if you don't find one, generate an oblique one electronically, based on the normal font'.

This is a big problem, because it doesn't allow you anywhere near the level of layout and typographical control that most print-based graphic designers have come to expect. We need something other than HTML to have that sort of control.

It would be very difficult to change the way HTML worked so that it gave more control over typography and layout, whilst at the same time maintaining compatibility with older sites. Instead, a new system called **Cascading Style Sheets (CSS)** has been added.

For example, if you did not like the way the `<p>` (paragraph) tag left only one line of white space between it and the content above it, CSS allows you to simply change the definition of what `<p>` does. This is called changing the **style** of the tag, and you can do this with almost any tag. That's a powerful addition, because it allows you to change the way HTML tags will format your text and graphics in a way that makes your final page easier to build up.

> *An additional advantage is that a Cascading Style Sheet can be separate from your HTML, just referenced or 'included' the same way images are. All your HTML pages for a site can use the same Style Sheet, so you can change the appearance of several pages just by altering one Style Sheet.*

You can begin to see the functional relationship between HTML and CSS: HTML defines what each part of your website is with things like 'this is a link to an image, and you should place it here', or 'this is bold text'. CSS then acts as a *specification* that tells the browser what each tag should actually do, so you can say things like 'when you actually place the image, put a 10 pixel border all around it'.

> *Rather than see CSS as functionally separate from HTML, it is better to see it as part of the overall formatting and typography control of your web page.*

Like JavaScript, CSS is one of those subjects that turns many HTML designers off because (a) it doesn't look like HTML, so it 'must be hard' and (b) it's probably cool, but you need loads of stuff to get it to work, right? Well, actually, no. If you understood the last chapter, you'll actually find learning CSS easier than HTML. Like HTML, you can get big thick books on CSS, and I really can't tell you who buys them, because there's not that much to know!

A Style Sheet consists of *rules* that define how your page will look. We'll be building up a set of simple rules in the next section. In the rest of the chapter, we will define:

- Typography for the Web
- Font justification, spacing, color and style
- Overall page attributes (such as background color and margins)
- Changes to individual HTML tags

Our first Style Sheet

1. Create a new folder called chapter05. Create a new HTML document called CSS01.html using Notepad, TextEdit or SimpleText, and save it in your new folder.

2. In your text file, add the following:

```
<html>

<head>

</head>

<body>
      <h2>Style Sheets</h2>
      <p>
            In this example, we will see how this boring bit of HTML can
            be changed to something more funky with the application of
            simple CSS rules that alter:
      </p>
      <ul>
            <li>The default font and page attributes</li>
            <li>The default formatting of the HTML tags used in this
                  ➥ page</li>
      </ul>
</body>

</html>
```

3. If you view this file in a browser (just double-click on the file you've just created) you'll get the rather drab web page you can see in the screenshot.

Style Sheets

In this example, we will see how this boring bit of HTML can be changed to something more funky with the application of simple CSS rules that alter:

- The default font and page attributes
- The default formatting of the HTML tags used in this page

HTML is nothing if not consistent, and we add a Style Sheet in much the same way as we add JavaScript; we can either link to a separate file (a **linked** Style Sheet), place the CSS in the head of the HTML page itself (an **embedded** Style Sheet) or use it within tags (**inline rules**, in the same way that we added JavaScript to links in **Chapter 3**).

4. For simplicity's sake, we'll use the second option here. Style Sheets go inside a `<style>` ... `</style>` tag, so add the following tags to the head of your file:

```
<head>
<style>

</style>
</head>
```

We're now going to go away and have a look at how to create rules before coming back to add some of these in between our `<style>` tags.

Creating rules

A rule looks like:

```
selector { declaration }
```

The **selector** is the HTML tag that you want to redefine, and the **declaration** is a list of the changes you want to make to the tag. Each change consists of a **property** and the **value** that you want to define. If you want to add one change, your rule would look something like this:

```
selector { property: value }
```

... but if you wanted to make several changes, you would have this:

```
selector { property1: value1; property2: value2; property3: value3 }
```

A better way to arrange your declaration is with one property-value pair per line like this:

```
selector    {

                      property1: value1;
                      property2: value2;
```

```
property3: value3;
}
```

Our first Style Sheet ... part 2

5. Add the following in between your `<style>` ... `</style>` tags. Don't worry too much about the properties and values we're setting here; we'll be coming back to examine these in greater detail later in this chapter.

```
<style>

BODY {
        font-family: Verdana, Arial, Helvetica, sans-serif;
        background-color: #FFCC00;
        margin: 10px 50px;
        }

</style>
```

6. Save this, and test it as before. You should see something like the screenshot (but with some orange, rather than the gray you see here). You should see:

- A different font
- Left and right margins of 50 pixels
- A smaller 10-pixel margin at the top and bottom
- A pale orange background color

Style Sheets

In this example, we will see how this boring bit of HTML can be changed to something more funky with the application of simple CSS rules that alter:

- The default font and page attributes
- The default formatting of the HTML tags used in this page

Inheritance

What we have just done is redefine the page appearance. We have added margins, a new default font, and a new default background color. We have done this by changing the attributes of a single tag, `<body>`.

Changing the rules for this tag has changed what all the other tags do. This is because style sheet rules use **inheritance**, and this relates to how the tags are embedded. If you make a change to a tag on the outside of an embedded set of tags, all the tags on the inside will reflect the changes.

In general, embedding looks something like this:

```
<body>
     <block tag>
             <inline tag>some text</inline tag>
     </block tag>
</body>
```

Any change to `<body>` will cause every other tag to inherit the same changes because `<body>` encloses all tags that can affect formatting. So, changes to `<body>` affect the whole page, and you can treat the `<body>` tag as the one that sets overall web page properties.

The previously mentioned big thick books on CSS take the long route of actually knowing about all the rules of inheritance, but that's not really what CSS is all about; it's meant to be simple! Inheritance confuses a lot of people, but in reality, you don't usually even have to think about it if you remember to design with the following rules:

- Define your page Style by defining rules for `<body>`, just as you would define certain starting values when opening a new graphics file or word processor document (size, type, and so on...).
- Design your basic page in pure HTML: don't add any attributes that change appearance.
- After writing the HTML, view your page in a browser, identify the block level tags that could do with tweaking, and add rules to make those changes.
- Look at the page in the browser again, identify the inline tags that need altering, and make rules for the changes.
- Finally, step back and look at the finished site, identifying any parts of it where you could have done with more typographical or layout control than CSS allows. Where this happens, consider adding bitmaps instead of pure text (we'll show you how to do this in a moment).

> *Another common early mistake to make is that this concept of inheritance rippling down the levels of embedded tags is what the Cascading part of Cascading Style Sheets means. It isn't, and we will see what Cascading actually refers to when we look at using multiple Cascading Style Sheets at the end of the chapter.*

Our first Style Sheet ... part 3

We've set the general page margins and font, so let's start tweaking the block level tags. Again, don't worry about the individual properties and values we're setting: we'll be listing those for you in a moment. The aim here is to show you *how* CSS works:

7. Add the bold code to your text file:

```
<style>

BODY {
```

```
                      font-family: Verdana, Arial, Helvetica, sans-serif;
                      background-color: #FFCC00;
                      margin: 10px 50px;
                      }

H2                    {
                      background-color: #FF9900;
                      font-size: xx-large;
                      font-weight: 100;
                      font-style: oblique;
                      color: #FFFFCC;
                      text-indent: 2%;
                      white-space: nowrap;
                      line-height: 120%;
                      }

</style>
```

> The line **white-space: nowrap;** *actually controls whether our text wraps to the browser window. Normally, text wraps, but sometimes you don't want that to happen because it might make your layout look ugly. You might prefer the heading to never wrap so that it always limits itself to one line (and the extra text is hidden until the user resizes the browser window bigger). Try resizing the browser to something really thin with and without the* white-space: nowrap; *to see what the difference is.*

8. Save, and test in your browser. You should see that the <h2> tag has a different background color, size, and weight (the amount of 'boldness'). You should also notice that it is slightly indented, and we have stopped it from wrapping, as well as changing the line height (which affects how far the background color will go).

> *Notice that we haven't changed the font, or defined the margins for* <h2> *because these are inherited from the <body> tag that encloses it.*

Style Sheets

In this example, we will see how this boring bit of HTML can be changed to something more funky with the application of simple CSS rules that alter:

- The default font and page attributes
- The default formatting of the HTML tags used in this page

9. The <p> (paragraph) tag that we've used for the text that comes after our heading and before the bullets inherits settings from the <body> tag because it is enclosed by it. It doesn't inherit from the <h2> tag because it isn't enclosed by it. Indenting the title seemed to work well, so let's indent our <p> text by a slightly larger amount than the <h2> text to make the two seem linked. Add the following bold line:

```
H2      {
        background-color: #FF9900;
        font-size: xx-large;
        font-weight: 100;
        font-style: oblique;
        color: #FFFFCC;
        text-indent: 2%;
        white-space: nowrap;
        line-height: 120%;
        }

P       { margin-left: 5% }

</style>
```

10. Save and test again, and you should see the effect of the indenting:

11. Now we need to indent the list tag <ul> a bit more, so add the bold code just after the last code we added:

```
P       { margin-left: 5% }

UL      { margin-left: 10% }

</style>
```

12. Save your file as CSS02.html, and test it.

13. The last item is to make some changes to individual HTML tags. We're going to change a link, so make the word example a link by enclosing it with an <a> ... </a> tag:

```
<p>
        In this <a href = "http://www.friendsofed.com">example</a>, we
        will see how this boring bit of HTML can be changed to
        something more funky with the application of simple CSS rules
        that change:
</p>
```

14. Save and test as usual. The link appears correctly, but doesn't look integrated into our overall page style. Let's change the color to the same orange as we've used for the title, and make it a little bolder by adding the following at the end of our style sheet:

```
P       { margin-left: 5% }

UL      { margin-left: 10% }

A       {
        color: #DD7000;
        font-weight: bolder;
        text-decoration: none;
        }

</style>
```

> *Setting* text decoration *to* none *means that the normal underlining for links is suppressed. Again, I haven't needed to define anything already inherited by this tag: I looked at the last screenshot and thought 'the font face seems alright, so I don't have to define that again'.*

15. Save and test, and you should see the new link style.

Relative text size

One thing to note before we move on is a hidden feature that I have been designing into this layout. If you select View > Text Size in your browser and change it from the default (which is Medium for Internet Explorer or 100% for Netscape Navigator), the whole page text will change (you will also have to select View > Reload on Netscape Navigator).

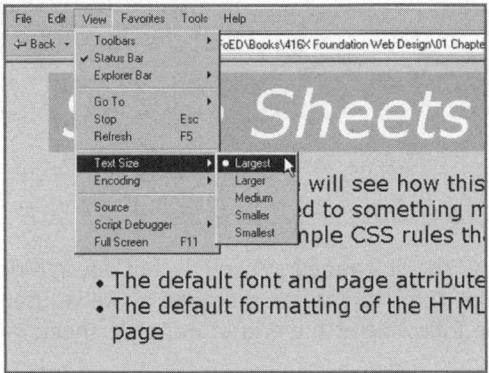

This is because I have set **relative** text sizes in my style sheet: xx-large, for example, rather than 7. It's also possible because I have made sure that all my HTML is structural. By not using any HTML that defines absolute values such as 'use this font' or 'use this color', I have allowed all my page style information to be in the Style Sheet. This makes it easy to change my design at this stage, particularly if the HTML was big and complicated. It also allows the user to configure the text to their own preferences in their browsers. I've used percentages rather than pixel values for some of the other settings for the same reasons.

Our first Style Sheet ... the final part

The only real place you're likely to want more typographical control than HTML/CSS allows you is in titles. Suppose we wanted our title text to look like this:

You can't really do this using CSS or HTML because we're using a font called Century Gothic rather than the fonts normally available to the browser, and we have a rounded shape that isn't compatible with either HTML or CSS, both of which prefer box shaped formatting cells.

What we can do is insert this text as a bitmap. You would do this for all sorts of reasons, such as logo design, where you might want to make your text follow a curve, or use complex text effects like glowing metallic text, none of which can be done with CSS. Let's do this, and also change the bullet points of our list to something more in keeping with our design.

16. Copy `style.gif` and `arrow.gif` from your **Chapter 4** source files to the same folder as `CSS02.html`.

17. In the `<body>` part of the HTML file, delete the `<h2>` ... `</h2>` text and add the `<img>` tag.

```
<body>

<img src = "style.gif" alt="Title: style sheets">
    <p>
        In this <a href = "#">example</a>, we will see how this boring
        bit of HTML can be changed to something more funky via the
        application of simple CSS rules that change:
    </p>
```

18. Save the file as `CSS03.html`, and test it.

19. This causes a problem: we cannot allow the user to scale the text anymore, because the bitmap text will not scale like text. We have to give the main text an **absolute** size that can't be changed, so change the BODY rule declaration like this:

```
BODY {
            font-family: Verdana, Arial, Helvetica, sans-serif;
            background-color: #FFCC00;
            margin: 10px 50px;
            font-size: 14px;
            }
```

20. To change the bullet point to a little arrow graphic, change the UL declaration like this:

```
UL            {
            margin-left: 10%;
            list-style-image: url(arrow.gif);
            }
```

21. Save and test, and our first CSS is finished.

Accessibility

Notice how we have had to change our text from **relative** to **absolute** as soon as we start to add graphics. As soon as we start adding elements that rely on precise sizes such as bitmaps, we have to fix things like text size to make it all fit into place.

Although allowing the user to restrict text may seem to be a minor deal, consider the following users:
- A partially sighted person who needs a 21-inch screen and sites to allow him to change the default text to very large sizes before he can read it.
- A person with a palm computer and a very small but sharp TFT screen, whose browser needs to be able to set the default font to a very small size.

This is one of the challenges facing web designers when deciding how much control we give the user. If we give them total control, our designs can start to look generic, but if we fine-tune our designs, we have to take some of this control away from the user. Being able to design both types of site and make them look good is one of the most important qualifications of the web designer of tomorrow.

On that sobering note, let's see the difference between the default and what we ended up with. The browser default looks like this:

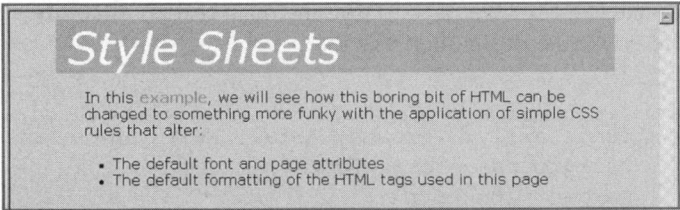

...the configurable 'accessibility' version looks like this:

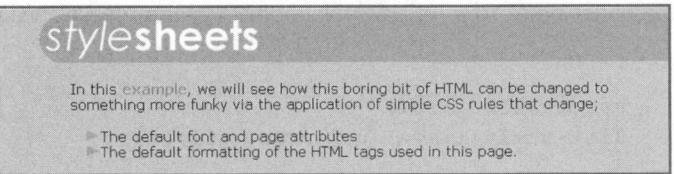

...and the fixed 'designer' version looks like this:

Ask yourself which of these you would be most likely to read if you stumbled across it on the Web. We have become so accustomed to good use of typography and layout that we ignore it when it's present, but refuse to read the text when it isn't.

Now that we have a good idea of what CSS can (and can't) do, let's step back and look at the two main areas where CSS rules can help our designs: **typography** and **layout**.

Using CSS for typography

To start with, we will look at changing the default font with a CSS declaration for the BODY tag. The basic set of properties that relate to typography are listed below. If you don't include any of them, then the browser default is assumed.

```
BODY {
            font-family: font list;
            font-size: size;
            font-style: style;
            line-height: height;
            font-weight: weight;
            color: #color;
            text-decoration: decoration;
            }
```

Let's have a look at each of the above properties in detail. Use Notepad, TextEdit or SimpleText to create an HTML file called typo.html with the following HTML and CSS in it. The CSS won't do very much as it stands because it defines the normal browser default CSS, so you won't see any difference until you tweak it after the relevant section and see the effect on the text.

```
<html>

<head>
<style>

BODY {
      font-family: serif;
      font-size: medium;
      font-style: normal;
      line-height: normal;
      font-weight: normal;
      color: #000000;
      text-decoration: none;
      }

</style>
</head>

<body>
      The quick brown fox jumps over the lazy dog.
</body>

</html>
```

The font face and family

The default browser font face is usually Times or Times New Roman. In general, these fonts are both part of a generic font family called **serif**, and this can be any font with serifs. A 'serif' is the name for the little 'feet' that you see on certain characters within this font family

T Times
T Times New Roman

Serif fonts remain readable even when you squash the characters together by reducing the spacing between them, and they are therefore used widely in books and newspapers. Unfortunately, from a web design perspective, serif fonts suffer from two big disadvantages.

Firstly, the use of serifs can show up the limitations of computer displays, especially for smaller text sizes because all those subtle curves have to be rendered using blocky pixels, causing 'staircasing' (or to give it its official name, aliasing). A character free of all the fussy curves suffers considerably less, as you can see in the screenshot.

T T

Secondly, computer screens are harder to read than print, and research suggests that a serif font is less readable on a computer screen than other, simpler typefaces (particularly for low-resolution screens or small text).

The best alternative font family is **sans-serif** ('without serifs'). Many popular sites that use lots of small or closely spaced text tend to use this font in preference to the default serif font. For examples of sites that use sans-serif fonts because the design incorporates lots of small text, take a look at www.google.com, and our very own www.friendsofed.com.

Sans-serif is also a much more modern font and is great for giving a modern, airy feel to a site. There are a number of fonts in the sans-serif family that are either particularly easy to read or look better on screen, and these include Verdana and Trebuchet.

verdana   trebuchet
VERDANA   TREBUCHET

The final font family is the **monospaced** font. This font family consists of characters that are all the same width, so the letter i takes just as much space as the letter w. This font is useful wherever you want columns of text to line up. Monospaced fonts are also used whenever you are showing code listings, and because of the association with all things computerized, monospaced fonts are sometimes used in designs aiming for a techno feel. The most popular monospaced fonts are Courier, and the slightly lighter Courier New.

courier   courier new

COURIER   COURIER NEW

You can see here how the two columns line up, something that doesn't occur with the sans-serif fonts above (and doesn't happen with serif fonts either).

Cursive fonts are those that appear to be handwritten. A typical (and fairly over-used) cursive font is Comic Sans:

comic sans

Finally, there is the **Fantasy** font family. This font family includes all decorative fonts. They are not really designed for use in blocks of text, but rather as decorative banners or in logo design. A typical font used as the default fantasy face is Jokerman.

Jokerman

Opinion is divided in the design fraternity on whether the fantasy font family is any use, given that it is used infrequently, and you never really know which font will be displayed. Most designers tend to just use a bitmap that includes an image of the actual banner they want, because this makes sure that the designer knows exactly what the banner will look like.

The bad news with all these fonts is that, because a web site can only use fonts installed on the user's operating system, you can only *suggest* named fonts. As with the <font> tag we saw in the last chapter, you should give a *list* of alternatives in case the first choice is not available. You should always end with a generic font family in case the user has none of your choices installed: this will be one of the five named above: serif, sans-serif, mono, cursive or fantasy. If none of your suggested specific fonts are found, and you don't suggest a font family at the end of the list, the browser will usually just use the default font, and this will usually be serif.

The font for each of these font families will be very similar for all browsers (most browsers actually install one of each font family as part of the browser install). Note though, that the cursive and fantasy font families have a nasty habit of becoming deleted by some hands-on people who like to tinker with their operating system and tend to delete any fonts that they are unlikely to ever use, so some of us more careful designers don't count on them being available.

There are technologies available to embed fonts into a web page (or rather, link a font file to the HTML in the same way images are linked) so that they are always available to all users, but this hasn't taken off, partly because both Internet Explorer and Netscape Navigator use their own way of doing this, and partly because the technology to allow embedded fonts is not widespread enough to be commonplace on both of the big two browsers.

We would recommend against using embedded fonts until a single specification emerges, to make sure that you don't end up designing to a standard that disappears (as those who used the set of free fonts Microsoft made available for Web use found out when Microsoft discontinued them!).

The following are some default lists that you can try using in your `typo.html` file before using in your designs:

```
font-family: Arial, Helvetica, sans-serif;
```

This is the normal list you should use if you want a sans-serif font. Arial and Helvetica are the most common sans-serif fonts found on the PC and Mac respectively, and if in the unlikely event that neither are available, the browser default for sans-serif is used as a last measure.

```
font-family: Verdana, Arial, Helvetica, sans-serif;
```

This is a better list for sans-serif, because Verdana tends to look (and read) better on a screen than Arial and Helvetica, particularly for small text. It is closely related to the large Humanist family of sans-serif fonts.

```
font-family: Trebuchet, Arial, Helvetica, sans-serif;
```

Trebuchet is generally seen as a font with more personality than either Arial or Helvetica, and can look better in certain designs - particularly in italic, bold, and large font sizes. It is related to the very modern Futura series of fonts.

```
font-family: "Times New Roman", Times, serif;
```

This is the standard list you should define when you want a serif font. Whenever you define a font name with spaces in it, you should enclose it with " " to avoid confusing the browser, as we have done here with "Times New Roman".

```
font-family: Georgia, "Times New Roman", Times, serif;
```

Georgia is a slightly more decorated font than Times and Times New Roman, and you may want to use this in preference when you want to give a slightly more retro or classical feel. Georgia is known as a transitional font style, the oldest type of fonts still in common use today as the default font face for large text areas.

```
        font-family: "Courier New", Courier, mono;
or
        font-family: Courier, "Courier New", mono;
```

There is not much choice when using a monospaced typeface. You get Courier or Courier New. The only real decision is which one to make first choice. As noted earlier, Courier New is slightly lighter than Courier, so your choice should be based on which one looks better within the overall page design.

> *Note that if your computer doesn't have Verdana, Trebuchet or Georgia installed, you may not see any changes when adding certain lists.*

Many designers become dismayed when they realize how few fonts they have available to play with when designing for the Web, but you should bear in mind that:

- Good page typography involves using as few fonts as possible, but creating variation using different styles and weights of the same font.
- In general, you only really need two fonts for standard text passages (one for titles and one for the main text) or three for technical writing (one for titles, one for the main text and one for specialised text such as code listings).
- Screens are generally much poorer at showing text than print because print is three to six times finer. On a screen, it can be very difficult to differentiate between closely related fonts. It is very difficult to differentiate between Times and Times New Roman at the default browser text sizes, for example. This means that the ability to specify only broad font families is not really as much of an issue for the Web as it would be for print. (Remember in the last exercise that the only time we wanted to specify specific fonts was in title text, and you can always use the 'shove it in as a bitmap instead' trick.)

The font size

As well as the face, you can also define the font size in several measurements; some of which are **absolute** (like pixel size), and some that are **relative** to something else (like a percentage of the browser default font size). As we've seen in the earlier example, choosing an absolute measurement makes it impossible for the user to change font sizes, whereas using relative measurements leaves this option open.

Be aware that the CSS definition is designed to be general, and some units of measure relate to printing the web pages rather than displaying them on a screen. Print-based designers are used to specifying font sizes in things like points (one point = 1/72 of an inch), inches, picas (one pica = 12pts) and other measurements that don't really make sense for screen or 'compared to browser default' based measurements.

Many designers who have read up on font terminology prefer to stick with the print world and use point measures. However, all browsers will eventually have to convert the measurements to absolute pixel measures so that they can be rendered to the screen The bad news is that both the PC and Mac use different conversions, so your text will appear at different sizes on the two machines, even though you might be patting yourself on the back, and thinking you're a cool clued-up web designer who creates pages to print-based accuracy!

This means that you should only use print based measurements for 'printer friendly' versions of your page, and browser specific measurements for the normal 'as seen on a screen' page. (You can do this quite easily by using two Style Sheets, and don't have to design two HTML web pages.)

The following are the size options available to you:

> *We'd recommend that you change the font-family back to serif to test the size options, as it makes it easier to assess the changes.*

Browser default sizes

`font size: xx-small` **or** `x-small` **or** `small` **or** `medium` **or** `large` **or** `x-large` **or** `xx-large;`

Because these values are specific to each browser, they will differ slightly between any two browsers. The browser default is usually *medium*. Using these values allows the user to change font sizes using View > Text Size on their browser.

Browser default increment step sizes

`font-size: smaller;` **or** `font-size: larger;`

You can specify `smaller` or `larger` as the font size, and this has the effect of increasing or decreasing the current text size (for example, one bigger than `large` is `x-large`). You would normally use this with block or inline tags rather than the `<body>` tag. Again, the user can change the sizes you specify with View > Text Size.

Percent (%)

`font-size: 90%;`

Selecting percent gives greater control than the above options (you can specify to the nearest 1%), but remember that the scale is still arbitrary, based on the browser defaults. If you use this with the `<body>` tag, the % is based on the default browser font (the medium size). If you specify it as part of a body or inline tag, it will be taken to mean 'as a percentage of what the text size is now'.

> *% seems to work well for all positive values, and certainly for the range of values you would be expected to use (about 10%-1000%).*

Pixels (px)

```
font-size: 16px;
```

Selecting px specifies font sizes in terms of absolute pixels. This measurement gives you the maximum control for normal web design, although it makes your design less flexible and both less future proof and more hardware reliant: a 12 pixel high section of text is readable on my 1024x768 laptop screen, but requires squinting on my 1600x1200 development machines. It also fixes the text size, and the end user cannot easily customise the page for their purposes, creating accessibility issues.

Despite all that, this is the only accurate measurement to use when you want to specify font sizes in terms of other bitmap-based graphics, which are always specified in pixels.

Print based sizes (pt, in, cm, mm, pc, em, ex)

```
font-size: 16pt;
```

Selecting the listed measurements will give you measurements in points, inches, centimetres, millimetres, picas, ems or exs respectively. These measurements may seem absolute, but they are actually relative to the browser's interpretation of real measurements. There is no defined correspondence between an inch and a general monitor screen. If I draw a one inch square on my computer, it will only be a one inch square for everyone else with the same monitor as mine, set at the same resolution.

These measurements only make sense for web pages that you expect to be printed, and should be used with Style Sheets of 'printer friendly' versions of web pages. Rather than mix the different measurements, it is best to choose one and stick to it.

> *You may want to try printing the pages when you test the print-based measurements.*

The font style

The font style allows you to swap between the **normal**, **italic** and **oblique** versions of your selected font. For example, if the font face being used is...

```
font-style: normal;
```

The browser will look for the font Times Normal or Times Roman ('Roman' being an alternative to 'Normal' in font naming). Similarly, for...

```
font-style: italic;
font-style: oblique;
```

...the browser will look for Times italic or Times oblique.

> *The italic font is usually a better bet than an oblique, given that an oblique is usually simply a slanted version of the Roman font. The italic is most likely to be a completely redesigned font, based on the Roman, but changed by hand where slanting causes the font to become less readable.*

The font line-height

The line-height is measured in the same units as seen in the font `size` property. To get a feel for this property, it's not such a good idea to use the `<body>` tag, because you cannot easily see the line-height (if you set the background color to something other than white to see the line-height, the background color will be applied to the whole page).

Instead, create a new HTML file. Save it as `typo02.html`, and enter the following:

```
<html>

<head>
<style>

P       {
        font-family: serif;
        background-color: #C0C0C0;
        font-size: medium;
        line-height: normal;
        }

</style>
</head>

<body>
        <p>The quick brown fox jumps over the lazy dog.</p>
</body>

</html>
```

Here, the background color is only inherited by the area of the page actually underneath the text, and you can see the line-height because it is colored as #C0C0C0 (a gray) rather than white. If you view this HTML in a browser, you will see something like this:

The quick brown fox jumps over the lazy dog.

You can see the line-height this time; it's the grey area. Notice that if you change the `font-size` property, the line-height will also change, as long as you keep the `line-height` equal to `normal`. Try this to see what I mean:

```
font-size: large;
line-height: normal;
```

If you change line-height to a percentage value greater than 100%, you'll see the line spacing increase:

```
font-size: medium;
line-height: 140%;
```

The quick brown fox jumps over the lazy dog.

The quick brown fox jumps
over the lazy dog.

If you change the line-height to a percentage value less than 100%, you will see the line spacing get less than the font height, and this may cause the text lines to overlap:

```
font-size: medium;
line-height: 20%;
```

The quick brown fox jumps over the lazy dog.

The quick brown fox
jumps over the lazy dog.

In general, unless you are trying to produce some grungy text effects, or oversized banner backgrounds for titles (as we did in the worked example earlier) the line-height has few uses, and you should leave it at the default. Also, spacing is usually controlled by the space between lines (or **leading**, pronounced to rhyme with bedding) and this is a paragraph level property rather than a typeface level one.

The font-weight

The font-weight is a cool feature that allows you to change the amount of boldness of the font. The browser usually creates the level of boldness electronically, based on the standard and (if it can find them) bold/light versions of the font. The font-weight property can take three sets of values: specific values, relative values, and numerical values.

Return to typo.html *to test out these values.*

Specific or relative bold values

```
font-weight: normal or bold or bolder or lighter;
```

You can set the weight to either normal or bold to set specific values, or bolder and lighter to set the weight relative to the current value.

Numerical Values

```
font-weight: anywhere from 100 to 900;
```

You can set the weight to any of the standard weight values (100, 200, 300, 400, 500, 600, 700, 800, 900), where `400` = 'normal' (or 'Roman'), and `700` = 'bold'.

You should only really use 800 and 900 with sans-serif fonts, because serif fonts can start to look ugly if you attempt to go beyond the bold value, whereas sans-serif fonts are usually available in 'super bold' weights (or **Black** and **Ultra** to use the correct terminology).

Note that the light values (below 400) are not usually rendered as such with current browsers and most fonts, and you may well just see the 'normal' weight.

The font color

The font color is simply a hexadecimal value representing the color of the font. Try adding the orange we used earlier:

```
color: #DD7000;
```

See **Chapter 6** for more details on finding the hexadecimal code for the color you want.

The text-decoration

The font decoration refers to the ability to add effects like underlining or strikethrough:

None	Text appears like this.
Underline	<u>Text appears like this.</u>
Overline	Text appears like this.
line-through	~~Text appears like this.~~

Other possible decorations (such as `blink`) are possible, but don't show on many current browsers. Try these examples: (note that combining decorations is possible)

```
text-decoration: underline;
text-decoration: underline overline;
```

Layout with CSS

Although most new web designers immediately look to changing the appearance of text with things like the font face, there is also a lot you can do with page layout, another one of those things that we all see in printed material, but never really notice (until it's badly done of course!).

When using word processing or desktop publishing, designers are used to close control of things like margins and line-spacing, and this can aid the readability of a page: the eye can move down a page easier when reading pages where sections are well laid out and the ratio of text to whitespace is sufficient for the page to feel balanced and well proportioned.

People tend to 'scan' pages rather than read them when they are not sure whether the information will be relevant or not, and this is particularly true for web design, where a search engine query can result in 50+ sites that may or may not have the required answers. Setting up pages that contain related information in well-defined blocks, with clear titles and links is important to the overall usefulness of the site. Your site may have the cleverest and most usable navigation system, but if the end information isn't itself usable and well presented, then you might as well not bother.

The most important issue when defining the layout of a page is being able to define margins and a border for each text section. These are called the 'box' properties - when considering top, bottom, left and right margins and padding, the shapes you end up with all form various boxes around the text.

These properties are traditionally only applied to <body> (to set up the overall page margins, and so on) and the block level tags. You don't normally apply them to inline tags, because they can instead inherit their properties from the block level tags (such as the paragraph tag, <p>) that enclose them.

Before we start, we could do with an example file to play with. The following HTML file is a good way of testing the effects of our Style changes. Either create a file in a text editor, call it layout01.html, and add the following, or take the file of the same name from your source files:

```
<html>
<head>
<style>

</style>
</head>

<body>
    <p>
            Lorem ipsum dolor sit amet, consectetuer adipiscing elit,
            sed diam nonummy nibh euismod tincidunt ut laoreet dolore
            magna aliquam erat volutpat. Ut wisi enim ad minim veniam,
            quis nostrud exerci tation ullamcorper suscipit lobortis
    </p>
    <p>

            nisl ut aliquip ex ea commodo consequat. Duis autem vel
            eum iriure dolor in hendrerit in vulputate velit esse molestie
            consequat, vel illum dolore eu feugiat nulla facilisis at vero
            eros et accumsan et iusto odio dignissim qui blandit praesent
```

```
                luptatum zzril delenit augue duis dolore te feugait nulla facilisi.
                </p>

        This is some plain text outside the paragraph block tags for comparison.


        </body>
        </html>
```

Boxes

Both the `<body>` and block level tags have a number of properties, that allow us to define a box with an inner padding whitespace area and an outer margin whitespace area. The box looks like this:

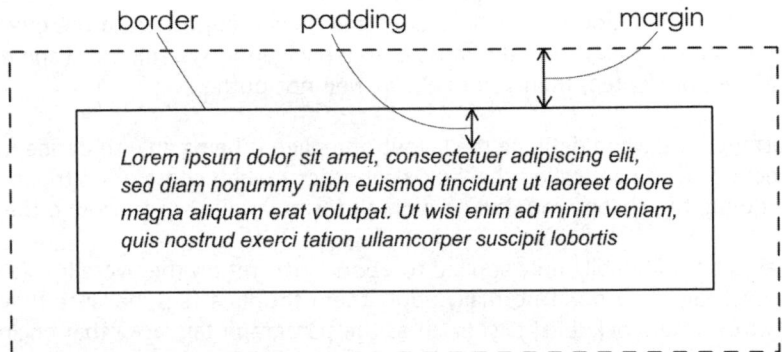

We can define three useful properties:

- **Border**: we can choose to make the box visible by giving it border properties.
- **Padding**: the distance from the text to the inner edge of the box.
- **Margin**: this is the distance between the outer edges of the box and the next item in the web page.

Remember, the web page itself is also a box, so in real life, you have overall layouts that can get quite complicated.

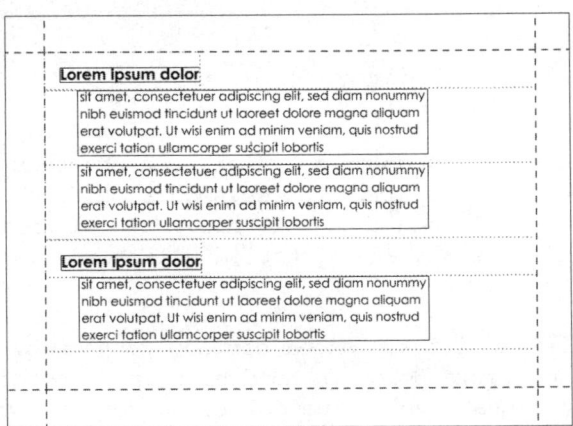

The page in the screenshot has been given margins, and the title and paragraph sections have unequal top, bottom, left and right margins to define their positions relative to each other, making for a precisely defined layout.

> *Some of you may be wondering how we could use this sort of layout with graphics. Well, we really need to get to grips with* **tables** *before we can mix the two effectively, and we will start looking at tables in the next chapter.*

Defining the box

Defining the box is easy if you assume that all your margin and padding settings are the same size, so we will do that to start with. Remember our three properties:

- margin
- padding
- border

Margin and padding are very similar, and by default, they will both be set to zero. The units of measurement for providing values have the same options as the font size property we saw earlier:

- Percent (of the browser window), 20% for example
- Absolute pixel measurement, 15px for example
- Print-based measure (pt, in, cm, mm, pc, em, ex), 15pt for example

Add the following declaration to layout01.html:

```
<style>

P     {
      background-color: #F0E000;
      margin: 10%;
      padding: 30px;
      }

</style>
```

> *I have given the box for the paragraph tag a yellow background (#F0E000) so that you can see it - a white box on a white background would confuse the issue!*

This style change gives you this:

> Lorem ipsum dolor sit amet, consectetuer adipiscing elit, sed
> diam nonummy nibh euismod tincidunt ut laoreet dolore
> magna aliquam erat volutpat. Ut wisi enim ad minim veniam,
> quis nostrud exerci tation ullamcorper suscipit lobortis

> nisl ut aliquip ex ea commodo consequat. Duis autem vel eum
> iriure dolor in hendrerit in vulputate velit esse molestie
> consequat, vel illum dolore eu feugiat nulla facilisis at vero
> eros et accumsan et iusto odio dignissim qui blandit praesent
> luptatum zzril delenit augue duis dolore te feugait nulla facilisi.

This is some plain text outside the paragraph block tags for comparison.

I have given the paragraph tag a margin of 10%. This is relative to the browser window, so you will find that the boxes have a floating size; if you resize the browser window, the boxes will also change. The padding value is defined in absolute pixels however, so it always stays the same.

The text at the end shows a fault in our settings - the text outside the paragraphs doesn't have any margins. We can fix this by giving our overall page a set of margins. Add the bold code:

```
<style>

BODY { margin: 10% }

P     {
      background-color: #F0E000;
      margin: 10%;
      padding: 30px;
      }
</style>
```

This time, we have a margin around the whole page rather than just the paragraphs. Notice that the margin values add together, so the total left margin is now 10% + 10%.

> *You may not be able to see the bottom page margin because of the effects of the scrollbar. In practice, you tend not to need a bottom margin for web pages because of this.*

You can also add different margins for each side of the box. Instead of a single value, you define the values in the order top right bottom left (in other words, 'start from the top edge and work clockwise round the box'). The same applies to padding, as shown if you change the paragraph declaration like this:

```
P     {
      background-color: #F0E000;
      margin: 10%;
      padding: 5px 20px 30px 20px;
      }
```

Border property

The border property simply draws a pattern around the box. You have a number of options to choose from; **style**, **width** and **color**. You write the rule in the form:

```
border: style width #color;
```

The style can be either **dotted**, **dashed**, **solid**, **double**, **groove**, **ridge**, **inset** or **outset**, and the width can be either a percentage (of the browser window), pixels, or any of the print-based measurements. It can also be the browser values **thin**, **medium** or **thick**. Border is one of those properties that you just need to mess about with to get a feel for the different graphical effects, particularly the style and width.

Add a box to the paragraph declaration as shown (you can also get rid of the background color now that we can see the box border), which will give you a thin black outline around the paragraph boxes. Add the other possible values of style and width if you feel like experimenting.

```
P     {
      margin: 10%;
      padding: 30px;
      border: solid thin #000000;
      }
```

> Lorem ipsum dolor sit amet, consectetuer adipiscing elit, sed diam nonummy nibh euismod tincidunt ut laoreet dolore magna aliquam erat volutpat. Ut wisi enim ad minim veniam, quis nostrud exerci tation ullamcorper suscipit lobortis

> nisl ut aliquip ex ea commodo consequat. Duis autem vel eum iriure dolor in hendrerit in vulputate velit esse molestie consequat, vel illum dolore eu feugiat nulla facilisis at vero eros et accumsan et iusto odio dignissim qui blandit praesent luptatum zzril delenit augue duis dolore te feugait nulla facilisi.

This is some plain text outside the paragraph block tags for comparison.

External CSS

So far, we've only used an embedded Style Sheet, but now is the time to try using an external Style Sheet. When defining your website, it's best to set up a dummy page that includes all the tags that you're likely to use. Using this page, you can then define an embedded Style Sheet, testing how the page looks in both Internet Explorer and Netscape Navigator as you go along. This is exactly what we've done earlier in this chapter, and we can now extract the styles and place them in an external Style Sheet.

1. Open up our old friend CSS02.html, and check that your Style Sheet looks like this:

```
<html>

<head>
<style>
BODY {
        font-family: Verdana, Arial, Helvetica, sans-serif;
        background-color: #FFCC00;
        margin: 10px 50px;
        }

H2      {
        background-color: #FF9900;
        font-size: xx-large;
        font-weight: 100;
        font-style: oblique;
        color: #FFFFCC;
        text-indent: 2%;
        white-space: nowrap;
        line-height: 120%;
        }

P { margin-left: 5% }

UL { margin-left: 10% }

A       {
        color: #DD7000;
        font-weight: bolder;
        text-decoration: none;
        }

</style>
</head>
```

2. The first thing to do is copy the Style Declarations. In your text editor, highlight all the text inside (but not including) the <style> ... </style> tags, and copy the block.

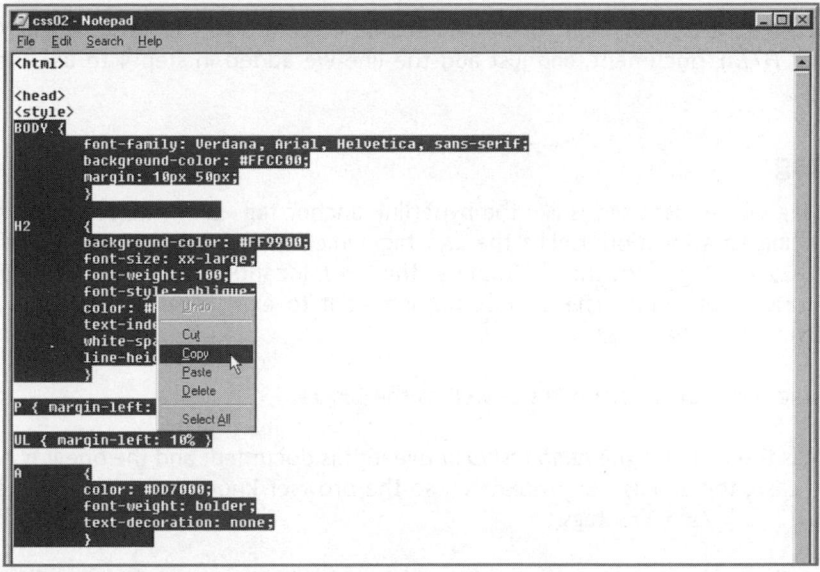

3. Open another text editor (you want both documents open at the same time, so go to the Start menu and open another instance of Notepad if that's what you're using). Copy the text into the new file, and save it as a plain text called `site.css`.

4. We now have a separate file containing our Style Declarations, and this file is called a **linked Style Sheet**. Well, actually, it's just a Style Sheet at the moment, and we need to link it. Back in the original file, delete everything between the `<style>` ... `</style>` tags, including the tags themselves, and add the following line in their place:

```
<head>

<link href="site.css" rel="stylesheet" type="text/css">

</head>
```

5. Save the original `css02.html` file as `cssLinked.html`. You should now have a `cssLinked.html` file and a `site.css` file in the same directory.

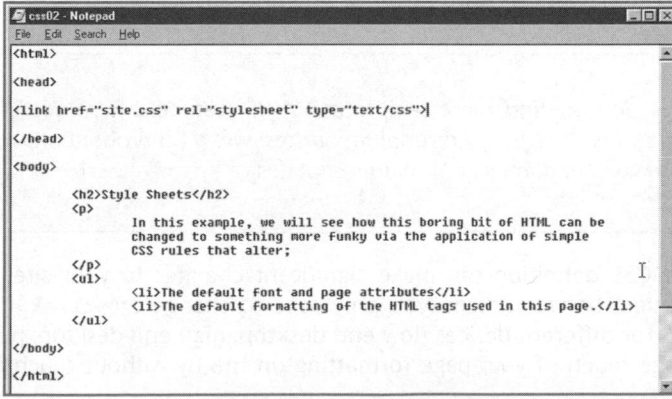

Test `cssLinked.html`, and you should see all of your styles come through. You can now make another HTML document, and just add the line we added in step **4** to use the same Style Sheet settings.

The <link> tag

The `<link>` tag we've just used is like the hyperlink anchor tag `<a>` in that it has a Hyperlink reference attribute pointing to a location. Unlike the `<a>` tag, which is used to form a navigation link to the new location, the `<link>` tag loads the file found at the `href` location into the HTML document itself, at the point the `<link>` was found. The `<link>` tag is meant to exist within the `<head>` part of the HTML document rather than the `<body>`.

The `<link>` tag has 2 other attributes as well as the `href`:

- `rel` tells the browser the *relationship* between this document and the one it is being asked to load. In our case, the `rel` is "stylesheet", so the browser knows to enclose the text in `site.css` in `<style>` ... `</style>` tags.

- `type` tells the browser how to treat the document it sees. "`text/css`" tells the browser "*this is a plain text document, formatted as a CSS*".

So what does this do? When the browser loads `cssLinked`, it sees the `<link>` and loads the contents of `site.css` in place of the tag. So now you're going "Aw, that just puts us in the position we were in before we started all this dumb copy-paste business! What a waste!"

Well, no. This means that you can now link to your Style Sheet from all the pages of your site. This has a number of advantages, including the fact that once your site is finished, you can make site-wide style changes simply by changing *one* document; `site.css`. It means that you have slightly less to download (and a quicker site as a result) – if you have a large CSS file, it will load from the Web for the first page, but then from the browser cache for subsequent pages, preventing the user from downloading a new CSS file for each page.

It also means that you don't have to link to your own CSS Style Sheet. Assuming that you have used only CSS to set up your styles (and if you have written your HTML the way we've shown you so far then you should have), you can simply download one of the many cool ready-written CSS files on the Web, and use it as a ready-made style template. You can even change the overall look and feel of your site every month simply by changing to a new CSS, with no work on your part. Cool!

> How do you find these templates? Well, just do a web search for "CSS templates" or try my personal favourites: www.bluerobot.com/web/layouts and www.endamcg.com/main/templates.

More subtly, each CSS definition can make significant changes to your site, and you will not have to change much to select between them (you only have to change the `<link>` `href`). A website that can select the best CSS for different devices (low end desktop, high end desktop, pocket PC, and so on) means that you can change much of your page formatting on the fly without touching the actual content. This is a feature that will become more important as technology erodes the standard desktop PC or Mac as the standard means of browsing the Web.

All this can happen because you have separated your site **content structure** (which is in the HTML) from your site **layout definition** (which is in the CSS document).

The deal with 'cascading'

There may be times, when an odd page needs additional styles added that are not in the `.css` file. This can also happen when you are using someone else's Style Sheet, but want to tweak a few settings.

This is where the *Cascading* part of Cascading Style Sheet comes in. The rule to remember is that the browser will always act on the last linked CSS definition it sees. The first definition it sees is its own internal default. If you don't change anything, then the browser will use only that. If, however, you link to Styles of your own, your definitions will overwrite any of the defaults. If you load a *second* Style Sheet like this:

```
<link href="site.css" rel="stylesheet" type="text/css">
<link href="page.css" rel="stylesheet" type="text/css">
```

The `site.css` file will define general and overall site styles, but where you want to tweak those styles to something more specific for the particular page, you can then load a second CSS that is more specific. If `site.css` specified page margins of 50 pixels for the whole site, but the current page was actually a pop-up, and you wanted no margins, `page.css` could redefine the `<body>` tag to have margins of zero pixels.

Cascading doesn't stop there, however, because *embedded* CSS has priority over *linked* CSS. So you could also do this:

```
<link href="site.css" rel="stylesheet" type="text/css">

<style>
        <!-- style declarations specific to this page go here -->
</style>
```

This time, the page specific styles are defined at the top of the page. If this page required smaller than normal site text, you could define it in the page HTML itself. That's cool, because then you can have a hierarchy of rules; general site wide rules go in a single linked CSS document, and will change rarely once defined, because when there is the odd problem, you can simply tweak the odd rule local to the page.

> As you can see above, you can also use `<!-- … -->` tags to add comments to CSS.

There is one last place that CSS can be placed and that is within specific tags themselves. We would recommend that you don't use this type of CSS because you lose the major advantage of CSS (the fact that you separate page structure and content from style).

As an example, though, suppose you wanted a particular paragraph to contain red text because it was an important warning. You could add a STYLE attribute to the second <p> tag to declare a rule like this:

```
<html>
<head>
</head>

<body>
    <p>
            This is normal text
    </p>
    <p STYLE = "color: #FF0000; font-weight: bolder">
            This is a warning
    </p>
    <p>
            This is normal text again
    </p>
</body>
</html>
```

This would be treated in the same way as the following declaration:

```
P      {
       color: #FF000;
       font-weight: bolder;
       }
```

If you test this HTML you will see this; only the middle text is red and bold:

This is normal text

This is a warning

This is normal text again

CSS declarations that are inside the tag are called **inline CSS**. As we said at the start, this is not recommended, and there is a much better way of doing this - by using a **class declaration**. A class declaration (also called a **custom style**) allows you to add style rules to only some tags, rather than all of them. A class declaration is just like a normal selector, except that you do not name a tag as the selector, but your own custom style name, preceded by a full stop. Assuming we wanted to call our custom style .warning, the HTML would be changed to this:

```
<html>
<head>
<style>

.warning    {
             font-weight: bolder;
```

```
                color: #FF0000;
    }

</style>
</head>

<body>
    <p>
            This is normal text
    </p>
    <p CLASS = "warning">
            This is a warning
    </p>
    <p>
            This is normal text again
    </p>
</body>
</html>
```

We now regain all our CSS advantages (we still have a centralised style declaration that is not in the HTML), but keep all the advantages of inline tags (the flexibility to target individual tags with our formatting rules, and leave others). We can also use the .warning style whenever we want in the page in future.

In terms of the cascade, inline and custom declarations will overwrite all other CSS declarations, so they are the highest level of priority.

> NB: Although you can use CSS with Netscape Composer, it only allows you to define per-tag inline CSS, without allowing you to use the slightly cleaner class declarations. We wouldn't recommend using this application with CSS, unless you hand code the CSS as a linked .css file and add a <link> tag in the head.

Note that using class declarations blurs the relationship between CSS and HTML. In the normal case, all your style definitions exist in the <style> ... </style> tags, and this is kept separate from your HTML. As soon as you start using class declarations, you are letting bits of CSS seep into the actual HTML and this is seen by many purists as 'bad structure' because your HTML becomes less general.

For example if you have HTML that makes no references to classes, you can very easily change the look of the page by simply selecting a new Style Sheet, (including ones that were written by someone other than you). If you do refer to classes in your HTML, your new Style Sheet *must* also define these classes, so you become very limited; you have to at the very least modify any Style Sheet that you use, and this loses you *flexibility*.

Class declarations are very useful, however, when you want to use the same tag to look different in different contexts, and on the same page.   Using meaningful names for the classes (such as `.warningText` or `.footnoteSmallText`) also makes it easier for someone else to see what your HTML is actually doing by reading the listing.

Our advice is to use classes only when you absolutely have to, and cannot do it using standard CSS.

The Case Study – Creating a Style Sheet

Now we've finished our comprehensive trip through the world of possibilities Cascading Style Sheets offers, we can start thinking of how to apply them to our Mondo case study website.

We've spent a lot of time in this chapter studying typography, fonts, and such style *decisions*, as well as the mechanics of how to technically achieve them, so let's start by looking in more depth at the typography of our site.

Typography – bitmapped text vs live text.

The Mondo site uses some pretty non-standard fonts. Where they are not available as one of the default browser fonts (remembering that we can only really assume Arial/Helvetica, Times New Roman/Times and Courier New/Courier will be there for all users), we simply place our text in the design as part of the bitmap.

You can see this being done on a number of pages:

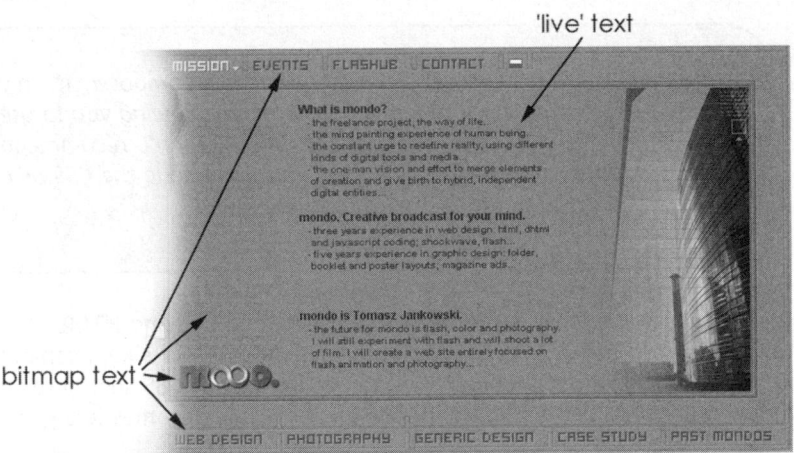

- For example, in the final version of the mission page shown, there's a lot of typography that uses non-standard fonts. The site can do this because these fonts have been added as part of the *image* files rather than as true (or 'live') text.

That's a cool solution for occasional text, such as our menu links, logos and background text, but you can't use it for *all* of your text. Reasons for this include:

- Bitmap text takes longer to be downloaded, because it's composed of image files. Closely typed text requires high quality image files to keep it readable, and that means that they have to be large in KB size as well. Live text, on the other hand, is one of the most file size efficient ways of presenting text, so it's the preferable option for long passages of text.

- Bitmap text is fiddly to edit. When we want to update our text, the fact that it is embedded in the bitmaps means that we have to change our graphics just to change the text. This can be a very laborious process. Many image editing programs don't support any real word processing features when you add text, so you will have to add all your paragraph formatting, spell checking, and all the other stuff we are used to leaving to the computer to take care of. That makes for a very fiddly, error prone process!

- Some people use browsers set to show only text (there are options to do this in each main browser) or maybe they have the Lynx browser we mentioned in **Chapter 1**. If you have placed all your content text in the graphics, they will see nothing!

You can see in the picture that the main text is live text, and the bitmap text is either incidental or there isn't much of it, and it isn't prone to change.

So by choosing trade-off between bitmap and live text carefully, we can always convince the user that we are using all sorts of exotic fonts, whereas the live text portions are only really using the three default fonts!

The Mondo site has been designed with compact pages. The advantage of this is that we don't have to use the scrollbar to see most of the main pages. It also has a disadvantage in that our live text is closely integrated with the graphics, and its size has to be controlled to pixel accuracy by our Style Sheets. Let's create that now...

The Mondo Style Sheet

1. Open up a new text document in your preferred editor and save it as `mon_style.css` in the `mondoSkeleton` folder we created in the last chapter.

2. Let's start with our BODY. Define the font family and our background color as dark gray.

```
BODY {
        font-family: arial, verdana, helvetica, sans-serif;
        background-color: #999999;
        }
```

3. Now our links. You'll notice this is a bit more than our previous listing for A{}. We're specifying different style attributes for each 'state'. This means your links can look different when rolled over, clicked or 'already visited'. HTML can do this also but it is unreliable and can be easily overridden by each user's individual preferences:

```
A:link {
        font-size: 10px; font-weight: bold;
        text-decoration: none; color: #CCCCCC;
        }
```

```
A:visited {
            font-size: 10px; font-weight: bold;
            text-decoration: none; color: #CCCCCC;
            }
A:active {
            font-size: 10px; font-weight: bold;
            text-decoration: none; color: #CCCCCC;
            }
A:hover {
            font-size: 10px; font-weight: bold;
            text-decoration: none; color: #FFFFFF;
            }
```

> *Note that you must always follow this ordering, link, visited, active, hover, for the styles to be read and implemented properly. You can remember it as **Lo**V**e A**nd **H**ate.*

4. Finally, we define a few style classes, `.title` (for our text titles), `.text` (our site normal text) and `.footer` (a smaller than normal style for minor text):

```
.title {
            font-size: 12px; font-weight: bold;
            text-decoration: none; color: #333333;
            }
.text {
            font-size: 10px; font-weight: bold;
            text-decoration: none; color: #333333;
            }
.footer {
            font-size: 9px; font-weight: bold;
            text-decoration: none; color: #666666;
            }
```

5. You can test this Style Sheet by creating the following HTML (save it in the folder `mondoSkeleton` as `test_style.html`):

```
<html>

<head>
<title>CSS test</title>
<link href="mon_style.css" rel="stylesheet" type="text/css">
</head>

<body>
<span CLASS = "title">This is title text</span><br>
<span CLASS = "text">This is normal text</span>, <a href = "#">and this is
```

```
link text.</a><br>
<span CLASS = "footer">Finally, this is footer text.</span>
<br><br>
</body>

</html>
```

In the `<head>`, we call the Style Sheet `mon_style.css`.

The `<span>` tag is something we haven't met before, but it's a very easy tag to understand, so it needs no real introduction; it does *nothing*. The reason that is very useful is that you can use it to:

- Define a style that isn't associated with any of the normal tags. Because `<span>` isn't associated with much of anything, you can define any style you want with

```
SPAN {
    add whatever rules you want here;
    }
```

- Use classes where you want no default. For example, if you wanted a title that was simply bold text, you might not want to use a `<h1>` tag, because it has quite a big bit of whitespace around it by default. By using span instead, the only style changes that occur are the ones you explicitly define for the class (i.e make the text bold), and no odd defaults associated with the `<h1>` tag will creep in.

6. Here's what you will see if you open `test_style.html` in your browser:

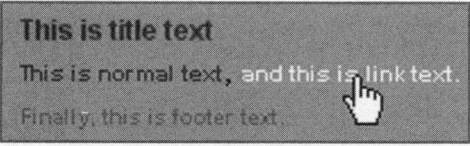

Our new CSS file will make sure that the live text always takes the same amount of room, and doesn't overrun its allotted space in the design for *any* of the pages of our lush new site:

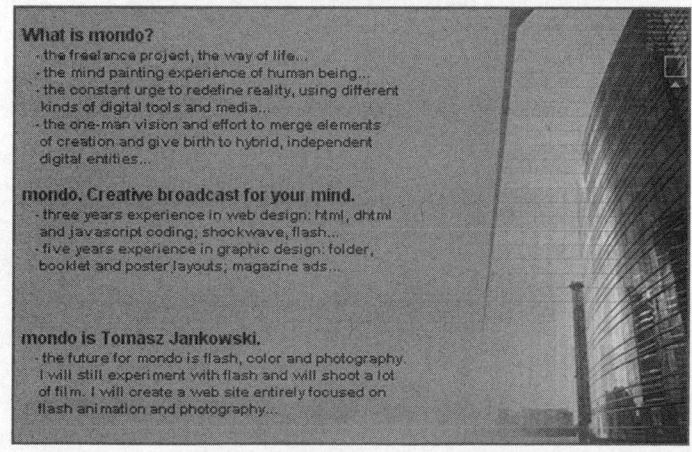

Layout Tables

What this chapter will do

This chapter will look at using **tables** to add additional levels of formatting to your web pages. We will:

- Create tables from scratch
- Show you how to effectively plan tables
- Show you how to use tables for site layout

What you'll have learned by the end of this chapter

By the end of this chapter, you will have a good understanding of how to use tables in web design, and will be able to plan and code tables. This will prepare you nicely for the use of tables to display **sliced images** later on in the book.

Tables are usually associated with the sort of thing we all did in science class, but - as we will see in this chapter - they are much more than that in web design...

Degrees Celsius	Degrees Fahrenheit
30	86
25	77
20	68
15	59
10	50
5	41
0	32

So far, we've covered how to format your web pages using HTML and CSS, but as soon as you look at most websites that contain a lot of content, you'll realise they're using something more – something which can format the entire **layout** of your site rather than just your text. A good example of this is the Amazon site (www.amazon.com):

> If you have your browser open, head over to amazon.com – *we're going to take a look at some specific examples.*

There's a few tricks used in this site that we have already covered:

- The site seems to be using some pretty tight text layout in the menu at the top, but they're actually using *images* with text in them, because neither HTML nor CSS can provide the level of control needed. We looked at this in the last chapter.

- The page uses titles that don't look anything like the default `<h1>` to `<h6>` tags. They are using CSS to redefine these tags, creating titles that use *color* rather than size to differentiate the text sections, and this allows them to cram more text into a limited space.

- The page text conforms to user choices of text sizing (View > Text Size). We now know that they are doing this by using relative text sizes in their CSS. Obviously, Amazon is paying attention to site accessibility.

- One of Amazon's successful features is the ability to browse lots of information about the stuff on offer. Lots of links (all using the <a> tag) allow you to read reviews, view sample pages of books and listen to sampler tracks for audio CDs.

- The site uses pop-up windows, which are using the simple JavaScript we looked at in **Chapter 3** to control the appearance of new browser windows.

But there are a few things here that we don't know how to do yet:

- First off, the site is arranged in three columns. The one on the left is for navigation, the right one has adverts and personalised links, and the main text is in the center.

- Secondly, the way the site reacts when we resize the browser is a little odd. The first and third columns stay the same width, but the central one changes to fit the new browser window.

- Finally, the text seems to be able to co-exist with the graphics in ways we haven't looked at reproducing yet.

Zoom into Detail with the HP PS850 Digital Camera

Designed with the look and feel of a traditional SLR camera, the HP PhotoSmart 850 packs a 4-megapixel sensor, 8x optical and 7x digital zoom (for a 56x total), and a 2-inch LCD screen into a solidly constructed chassis with a classic look.

As you've probably guessed, the additional formatting is being done with **tables**. In the site above, we can't see the table itself because it is drawn with none of its lines showing, but we know it's there because we can see how the content is conforming to it.

row 1, column 1	row 1, column 2
row 2, column 1	row 2, column 2

Tables, often referred to as layout tables, are used to arrange our content on the page. Just like the tables of figures we are used to, they are arranged in **columns** and **rows** – which form **cells**. By specifying different sizes for different columns and rows, and even nesting tables by putting one inside another, we can arrange our web page layout in almost limitless ways. So, to recap, tables are great because:

- They allow you to format text and graphics together effectively.
- They allow you to align multiple elements as if they were a single element by placing them all into a single table cell. Your 'multiple elements' can be anything from a few related pictures and images, up to a whole web page!
- They allow you to force the page to react to changes in the size of the browser window the way you want it to.

> *There is another way to mix graphics and text without using tables called **floating images**, and we will look at that in **Chapter 9**.*

HTML and tables

Designing and coding the basic table

Let's create a bit of HTML that we can play around with and figure how it all works.

1. Make a new folder called `chapter05` and create a new HTML file (in Notepad or your preferred text editor), saving it as `table.html`.

2. Firstly, get the obligatory tags out of the way. Create your `<html>`, `<head>` and `<body>` tags. You also might as well close them too – we'll type our content in the middle:

    ```
    <html>
    <head>

    </head>

    <body>

    <! We'll add our table here in a moment - you don't have to type this in
    by the way :) >

    </body>
    </html>
    ```

3. Now, about that table... Create our table using the `<table>` tag. While you're there, close the tag to save us time later.

    ```
    <table>

    </table>
    ```

    > *It's always a good idea to close your tags as you write them (some code editors even do this for you). When writing HTML, and especially when constructing complex nested tables, it's easy to forget which tags are open and which are closed, so it's an especially good idea when hand-coding tables.*

4. We discussed attributes back in **Chapter 2**, and tables have plenty. For now, add a `border = "1"`
    attribute to our new `<table>` tag.

    ```
    <table border = "1">

    </table>
    ```

5. One of the reasons we've included a border here is so that we can actually *see* the table we're
    designing. It's time for some rows and columns; HTML handles the rows first, using the `<tr>` tag.
    Go ahead and create two rows:

    ```
    <table border = "1">
         <tr>
    <! Columns go here >
         </tr>
         <tr>
    <! Columns go here >
         </tr>
    </table>
    ```

6. The `<td>` tag, or table division, defines our columns. Now, using the `<td>` tag create two cells and
    fill them with some appropriate text.

    ```
    <table border = "1">
         <tr>
                 <td>row 1, column 1</td>
                 <td>row 1, column 2</td>
         </tr>
         <tr>
                 <td>row 2, column 1</td>
                 <td>row 2, column 2</td>
         </tr>
    </table>
    ```

    > *Notice that the indentations I have added in the HTML are crucial in
    > making the table definition readable. When creating tables by hand,
    > it is very important that you add indentation and other white space
    > as necessary, to keep the HTML understandable.*

7.   If you view this in a browser, you will see something like this:

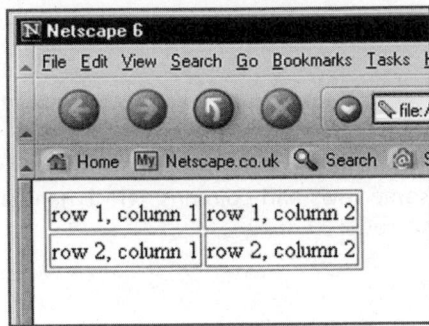

> *Some browsers (particularly Netscape) do not show empty cells. You should therefore always enter something within each <td> ... </td> tag pair. If you actually want to add cells with nothing in them, the trick is to add a blank space :<td> </td>*

8.   Now let's explore the options we have for changing our table's appearance. The first thing we can do is add an unequal number of row cells or columns:

```
<table border="1">
      <tr>
             <td>row 1, column 1</td>
             <td>row 1, column 2</td>
             <td>row 1, column 3</td>
      </tr>
      <tr>
             <td>row 2, column 1</td>
             <td>row 2, column 2</td>
      </tr>
      <tr>
             <td>row3, column1</td>
      </tr>
</table>
```

9.   Test this, and you'll see that the first additional line adds a new table data cell on row one, and the third one gives us an extra row with one cell. Notice that the resulting table is still rectangular - it's just that some of the positions are blank:

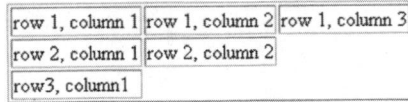

10. Delete the additional lines we just added to get back to the 2x2 table we had before.

11. The table text is a little squashed up within each cell, and we can fix this by adding some **padding** for each cell. The `cellpadding` attribute specifies the amount of space (padding) between the cell border and the cell contents. Change the first `<table>` tag as shown:

```
<table border="1" cellpadding="10">
    <tr>
        <td>row 1, column 1</td>
        <td>row 1, column 2</td>
    </tr>
    <tr>
        <td>row 2, column 1</td>
        <td>row 2, column 2</td>
    </tr>
</table>
```

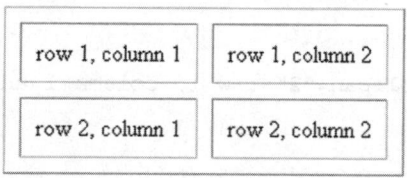

12. As well as the padding within each cell, we can also control the spacing between cells. This isn't something you would normally want to do with tables containing text, although it can be useful when you are using tables to mix text and graphics, as we will see later. Try adding this, and testing:

```
<table border="1" cellpadding="10" cellspacing="10">
```

row 1, column 1	row 1, column 2
row 2, column 1	row 2, column 2

13. Finally, you can also add color. You can set the background color of either the whole table, a row, or a single element by using the `bgcolor` attribute and adding it to the `<table>`, `<tr>` or `<td>` tag.

```
<table border="1" cellpadding="10" cellspacing="10" bgcolor="#606060">
    <tr bgcolor="#A0A0A0">
        <td bgcolor = "#E0E0E0">row 1, column 1</td>
        <td>row 1, column 2</td>
    </tr>
    <tr>
        <td>row 2, column 1</td>
        <td>row 2, column 2</td>
    </tr>
</table>
```

> *We'll be taking a very good look at hexadecimal colors in the next chapter, so use our colors for the moment, and come back and change them when you know how to get exactly what you want...*

14. If you add a `bgcolor` attribute to a combination of table tags, then the innermost `bgcolor` will have priority (i.e. the order of precedence, highest to lowest, is `<td>`, `<tr>`, `<table>`). Test the changes shown above, and you should see this: the first cell (top left) will be colored a light gray (#E0E0E0) explicitly from the `bgcolor` in its `<td>` tag. The first row will be colored a mid gray, but only the top right cell actually becomes this color because of the previous cell color definition. Finally, the rest of the table becomes a dark gray (#606060) through the `<table>` `bgcolor` definition.

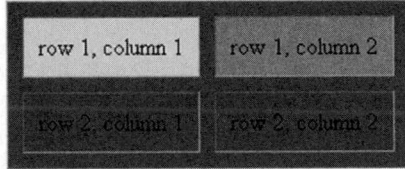

Finally, there are a couple of additional things you can do to create non-standard tables by **spanning cells**. These are cells that are sized to cover more than one row or column.

15. Adding the `colspan` attribute to a `<td>` tag creates a cell that spans columns. The number you equate this attribute to tells the browser how many columns you want to span, in this case two:

```
<table border="1">
     <tr>
            <td colspan="2">row 1, column 1 and 2</td>
     </tr>
     <tr>
            <td>row 2, column 1</td>
            <td>row 2, column 2</td>
     </tr>
</table>
```

row 1, column 1 and 2	
row 2, column 1	row 2, column 2

16. You can also span rows with the `rowspan` attribute in much the same way:

```
<table border="1">
     <tr>
            <td rowspan="2">row 1 and 2, column 1</td>
```

```
                    <td>row 1, column 2</td>
            </tr>
            <tr>
                    <td>row 2, column 2</td>
            </tr>
        </table>
```

| row 1 and 2, column 1 | row 1, column 2 |
| | row 2, column 2 |

Top table tips

If you try creating additional tables using rowspan and colspan, you will quickly realize that they can get a little confusing. The following well-kept secrets of hand-coding tables should help stop the confusion as your tables get bigger...

1. Plan the table

Always sketch the table out first. Graph paper is great if you can get hold of it, otherwise a ruler might be useful (OK, I know, everybody throws them away after they leave college, but just use the spine of the CD you're listening to while you work if you can't find anything else).

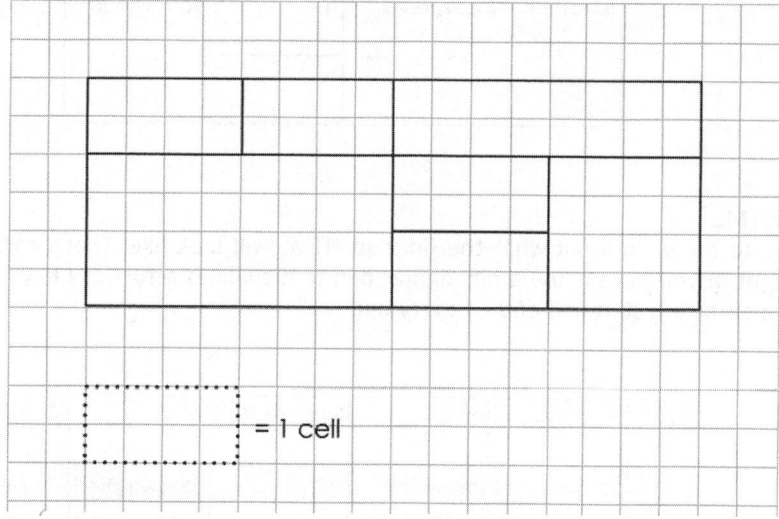

= 1 cell

2. Work out the table order

In a table like this, with cells spanning rows and columns, it's not easy to see in which order you will have to define the cells. Get it wrong and the table won't work, so we need a foolproof way of doing it right every time, given that tables are pretty crucial in web design (some design houses have even been known to test table coding at job interviews!).

HTML will parse the table from left to right, top to bottom. To emulate the way the browser will do this, write td at the *top left hand corner* of every cell:

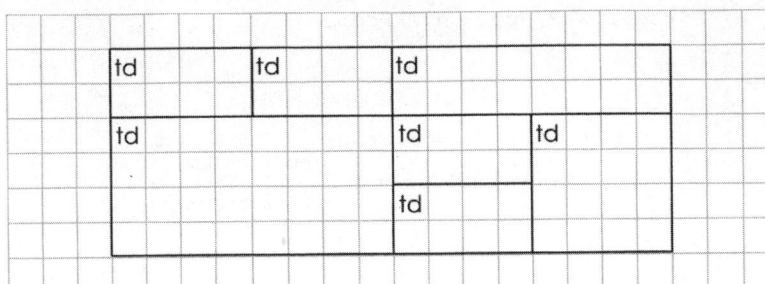

3. Add the span data

The next thing to do is add the span attributes. If a number of rows are spanned, simply count them and add a rowspan = something. If a column is spanned, do the same, this time counting the columns and adding a colspan:

4. Define the HTML

The final thing to do is work out what the finished HTML will look like. That's easily done; simply read from left to right (if you have it, use a highlighter pen to draw lines across as I have done below), putting a tr and /tr pair at the start and end of every line.

Bingo! That's the HTML we need. All that remains to do is to read the information from the table and place it into a HTML document.

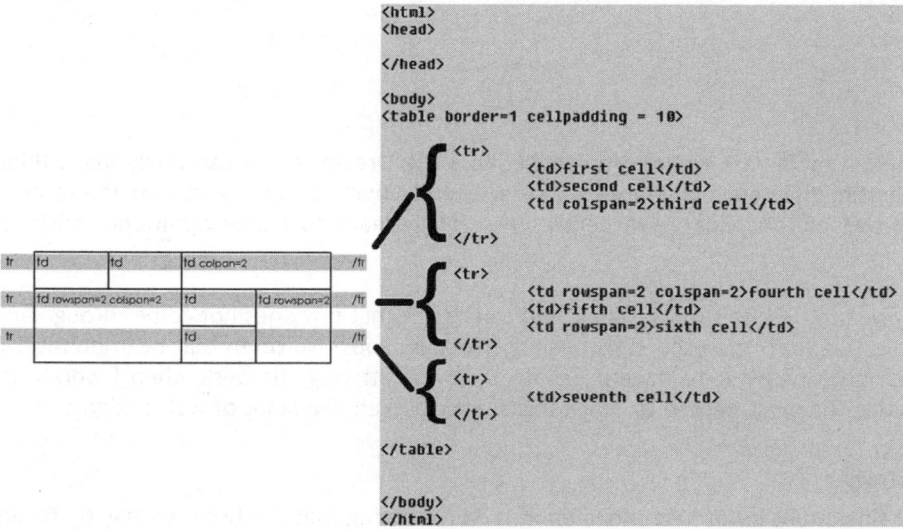

```
<html>
<head>

</head>

<body>
<table border="1" cellpadding = "10">

        <tr>

                <td>first cell</td>
                <td>second cell</td>
                <td colspan="2">third cell</td>

        </tr>

        <tr>

                <td rowspan="2" colspan="2">fourth cell</td>
                <td>fifth cell</td>
                <td rowspan="2">sixth cell</td>
        </tr>

        <tr>

                <td>seventh cell</td>
        </tr>

</table>

</body>
</html>
```

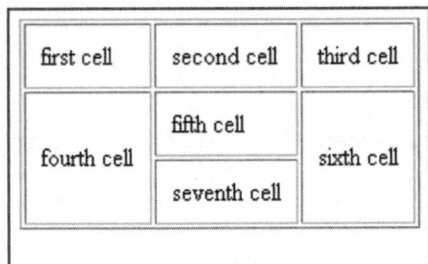

Although tables are where graphical editors like Dreamweaver can really make things easier for you by generating the code for your tables automatically, many web designers use the route we've followed here, with text editor, paper, and pencil. This usually leads to highly optimized HTML that you can quickly modify.

I happen to be one such designer, and can report that this does not come through any particular skill, but by the fact that I have been through the process above so often that I can do most of it without writing much onto paper (and have a lot of CD covers littering the desk when I work!). It doesn't take much practice for most people to reach this seemingly Zen-like state of web design...

The browser

As a final point before we move on, it is worth noting that the browser may try to simplify any table that you define. For example, the table below:

will result in:

The browser will see that you have tried to make the first and fourth cells two spans long, and will realise that it can create essentially the same table if it makes both these cells one span wide. This confuses a lot of table hand-coders, but all the browser is trying to tell you is that your table design could be simpler: the cells will expand to cater for the content you place in them, so there's no reason at all for the first and fourth cells here to be any different in size at this stage.

Table appearances

Let's see if we can create a table of our own: we'll go for the table we started with; the Celsius to Fahrenheit conversion table:

Degrees Celsius	Degrees Fahrenheit
30	86
25	77
20	68
15	59
10	50
5	41
0	32

The basic table HTML itself is pretty straightforward (if a little repetitive):

```
<html>
<head>

</head>

<body>
<table border="1" cellpadding="5">

    <tr>
            <td>Degrees Celsius</td>
            <td>Degrees Fahrenheit</td>
    </tr>

    <tr> <td> 30 </td> <td> 86 </td> </tr>
    <tr> <td> 25 </td> <td> 77 </td> </tr>
    <tr> <td> 20 </td> <td> 68 </td> </tr>
    <tr> <td> 15 </td> <td> 59 </td> </tr>
    <tr> <td> 10 </td> <td> 50 </td> </tr>
    <tr> <td> 5 </td> <td> 41 </td> </tr>
    <tr> <td> 0 </td> <td> 32 </td> </tr>

</table>

</body>
</html>
```

> This file is available from the download site as `degrees.html` *if you want to save yourself some typing.*

Degrees Celsius	Degrees Fahrenheit
30	86
25	77
20	68
15	59
10	50
5	41
0	32

The trouble, of course, is that it's a little ugly, and reminds us all of those awful academic web pages they used to use the Internet for before it all became mainstream (and someone realized that graphic design and web pages might not be unrelated topics). Anyway, when adding formatting to tables, there are two ways to do it: the *hard* way or the *easy* way.

The *hard* way is the way all the old-time web designers still use, where you have to set fonts and background colors for every other cell, and the *easy* way is to use CSS for all your other stuff.

There are a few things to bear in mind when designing text-only tables for the web. Tables on paper are different from tables on a screen. When we draw things like the Celsius-Fahrenheit table in our science notes at school, we draw a table formed from lines. On a screen, that same table scans badly, because the black lines and black text tend to form a mess of information. This is just one of the many places where good design on the printed page doesn't translate directly to the Web.

A lot of designers have noticed this and don't use lines in tables, but instead use **colored cells**. Here's a section from a rather busy real-time share price table to show what I mean (this is in black and white, but you can still see some of the different shades that help make this clear to read) :

			Edit	Alert	Discuss	Chart	Trades	Buy/Sell More...
60 (17:41)	+0.75 (+1.3%) ▲	7.21M	1,825.00	£0.5369	£1076.75			+£96.91 (+9.9%)
			Edit	Alert	Discuss	Chart	Trades	Buy/Sell More...
59.50 (16:34)	0.00 (+0%)	9630	1.00	£0	£0.59			+£0.59 (n/a%)
			Edit	Alert	Discuss [10]	Chart	Trades	Buy/Sell More...
8.25 (16:43)	+0.50 (+6.7%) ▲	1.81M	5,660.00	£0.0791	£452.80			+£5.09 (+1.1%)
			Edit	Alert	Discuss [10]	Chart	Trades	Buy/Sell More...
8.25 (16:43)	+0.50 (+6.7%) ▲	1.81M	11,413.00	£0.085	£913.04			-£57.07 (-5.9%)
			Edit	Alert	Discuss [1]	Chart	Trades	Buy/Sell More...
55 (17:10)	-0.25 (-0.5%) ▼	109.86M	557.00	£1.80	£304.96			-£697.64 (-69.6%)

The designers have used filled cells rather than lines to separate the data. Printed tables in company prospectuses seem to do the same thing nowadays, and that is because line tables may be easy to print or draw, but they're difficult to read when there's lots of information on them.

If you need your text columns to line up (when you are, for example, tabulating figures that will be added), use the `mono` font families so the numbers will line up exactly.

In the HTML below, I have added a Style Sheet to define my table formatting. The CSS defines a style for the table rows via the `<tr>` tag. For the top row only, we need to make the titles stand out a little more that the other rows, so I have added a **class style** definition called `tableHeader` to make the top row stand out a little more.

> Remember, a class definition (such as `.tableHeader`) *has priority over an inline style definition (such as* `tr`) *in the cascade.*

```html
<html>
<head>
<style>
tr {
        background-color: #EDEDED;
        font-family: Arial, Helvetica, sans-serif;
        text-align: center;
}

.tableHeader {
        background-color: #CCCCCC;
        font-family: Arial, Helvetica, sans-serif;
}

</style>
</head>

<body>
<table border="0" cellpadding="5">

        <tr CLASS = tableHeader>
                <td>Degrees Celsius</td>
                <td>Degrees Fahrenheit</td>
        </tr>

        <tr> <td> 30 </td> <td> 86 </td> </tr>
        <tr> <td> 25 </td> <td> 77 </td> </tr>
        <tr> <td> 20 </td> <td> 68 </td> </tr>
        <tr> <td> 15 </td> <td> 59 </td> </tr>
        <tr> <td> 10 </td> <td> 50 </td> </tr>
        <tr> <td> 5 </td> <td> 41 </td> </tr>
        <tr> <td> 0 </td> <td> 32 </td> </tr>

</table>


</body>
</html>
```

Degrees Celsius	Degrees Fahrenheit
30	86
25	77
20	68
15	59
10	50
5	41
0	32

> *Notice that I haven't gone for the usual route of making the top of the table bold or bigger text to make it more prominent (there are actually table tags specifically designed for this, but when using CSS, you don't really need to know about them). Using typography to aid clarity is sometimes all about making the fewest changes to the font and text styles.*

Table sizing and positioning

Once you have got the basic table structure and appearance sorted out, the next big thing to think about is the table size. So far we have had little control over the size of the table (apart from padding), which has been defined by the content we placed inside the cells. The cells simply expand to contain the text we put in them, plus any additional padding we have defined. The table above shows this; the right-hand column is wider than the left-hand one because Fahrenheit is longer than Celsius.

To size the whole table, you can use the **width** and **height** properties of the `<table>` tag. You can express either of these attributes as a % of the available space or as a pixel value (omit the "%"). Change the `<table>` tag in the code above to:

```
table border="0" cellpadding="5" width="40%" height="60%">
```

This will either display the full table, as shown in the first screenshot, or maintain the table at a fixed proportion of the browser window (you can see this in the second screenshot).

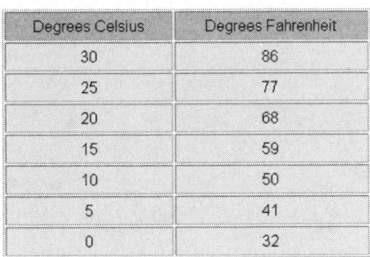

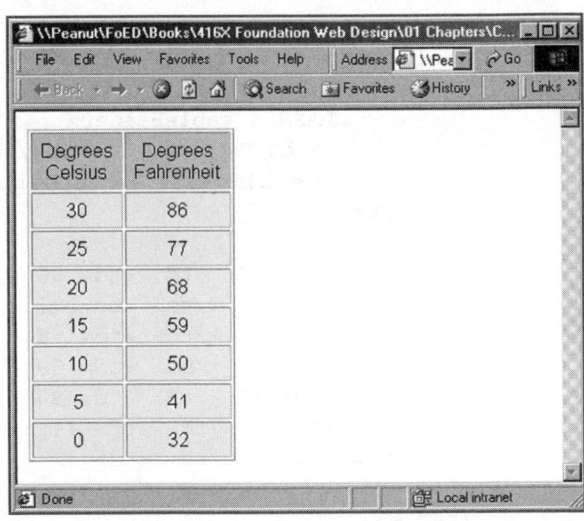

Next, we need to define the width of the columns of cells. The easiest way to do this is to use the `width` and `height` attributes again, but this time applied to the `<td>` tag. For this to work, you should apply it to the topmost cell in every column. You can again add a percentage or absolute pixel value.

Here are the tags for the first row of our table, and these will make the two columns show at equal widths (50% of the total table width):

```
<tr CLASS = tableHeader>
<td width = "50%">Degrees Celsius</td>
<td width = "50%">Degrees Fahrenheit</td>
</tr>
```

Degrees Celsius	Degrees Fahrenheit
30	86
25	77
20	68
15	59
10	50
5	41
0	32

Although setting the height and width of tables with tag attributes is something you are officially recommended to use Cascading Style Sheets for, instead, most designers still use the width attribute, as we have done here, because it is the most direct way to achieve reliable table sizing. It is unlikely that this feature of HTML will disappear, though it is officially deprecated.

Given this conflicting information, the best way to handle tables in practical design is to apply table height and width settings via the `<table>` *and* `<tr>` *height and width attributes, and then apply all other table formatting (color, text alignment, font, margins and other attributes) with CSS.*

Using tables to control site placement

So far we have looked at creating tables to be used in the normal way: for tabulating figures or information into rows and columns.

Tables can also be used to center content in the middle of a page, horizontally and vertically. In this case, the *whole* site is enclosed within a single cell table, and, because one of the features that tables allow us is the ability to center content both horizontally and vertically within a cell, the whole site remains centered within any oversized browser window:

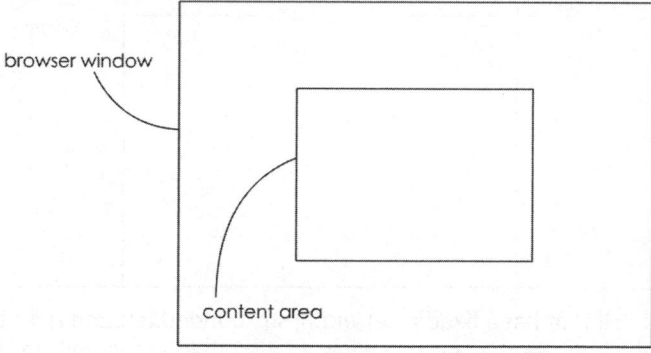

browser window

content area

This is useful when you have a site that will be smaller than the typical browser window, but you don't want to use a separate pop-up to contain it. This is one of those features that many beginners seem to ask about on the newsgroups, thinking it's perhaps some complex JavaScript trick, but it's just a simple table!

You can use tables for a number of other uses, and using variable % and fixed pixel values together in a single table gives you a number of options for controlling how a site will react to changes in the browser window size. Let's have a look at a few examples.

Creating fixed width site layouts

When creating sites with lots of text, the text remains readable as long as the browser width is kept small, but as soon as the user opens a large window (below, right) the resulting long lines of text become difficult to follow. The human eye hates long lines of text (which is why newspapers use columns; consider how difficult a broadsheet newspaper article would be to read if the text went right across the page!):

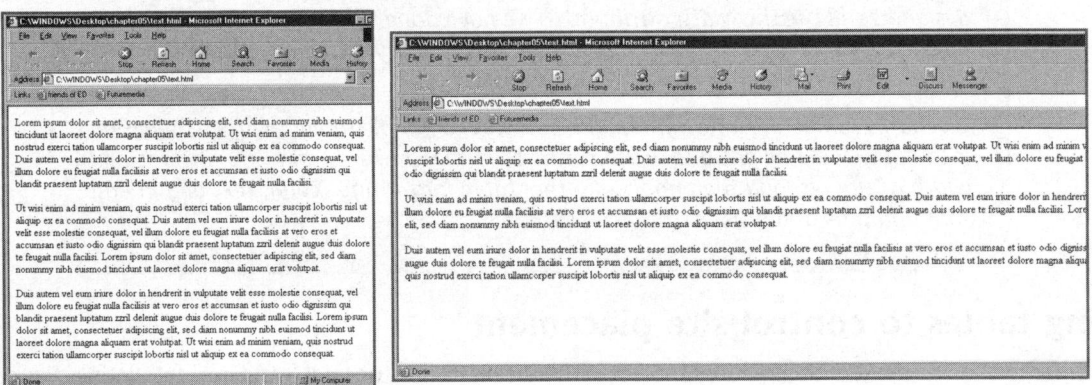

You can fix this by creating a three cell table which scales to 100% of the browser window area as shown:

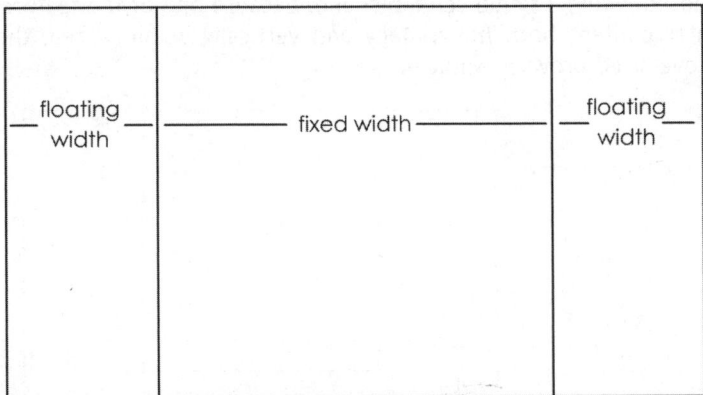

By creating a central cell that has a fixed pixel width, surrounded left and right by cells that have a variable or 'floating' width, you can use the central cell as an area that always will stay the same width for as long as the browser can accommodate that – if it can't, then the central cell will take up the maximum amount of room allowed. This allows you to keep your text at a maximum line length.

A **floating width cell** is a cell that will expand to fill the available space, whereas a **fixed width** cell will try to maintain a minimum width (it will grow no bigger than this width, unless forced to do so by a large graphic that cannot be split over lines to fit like text), and will only grow smaller if the browser window area is reduced to less than this minimum.

The HTML below creates such a table. The `fixedWidth` and `floatingWidth` Style Classes define the attributes of our two types of cell. The fixed width central cell has been given a width of 750 pixels, and a background color of white. The cell will be shown at either the current browser window width, or 750 pixels, whichever is the biggest. The floating width cells are given no width setting, which means that they will resize to the remaining width (if any) after the 750 pixel limit of the central cell is taken up:

```
<html>
<head>
<style>

.fixedWidth {
background-color: #FFFFFF;
                   vertical-align: top;
                   width: 750px;
                   }

.floatingWidth {background-color: #FF0000}

</style>
</head>

<body>
<table width="100%" height="100%" cellspacing="0">
 <tr>
 <td CLASS=floatingWidth> </td>
 <td CLASS = fixedWidth>
     <p>
             Lorem ipsum dolor sit amet, consectetuer adipiscing elit,
             sed diam nonummy nibh euismod tincidunt ut laoreet dolore
             magna aliquam erat volutpat. Ut wisi enim ad minim veniam,
             quis nostrud exerci tation ullamcorper suscipit lobortis
             nisl ut aliquip ex ea commodo consequat. Duis autem vel
             eum iriure dolor in hendrerit in vulputate velit esse
             molestie consequat, vel illum dolore eu feugiat nulla
             facilisis at vero eros et accumsan et iusto odio dignissim
             qui blandit praesent luptatum zzril delenit augue duis
             dolore te feugait nulla facilisi.
     </p>
 </td>
 <td CLASS=floatingWidth> </td>
 </tr>
</table>
</body>
</html>
```

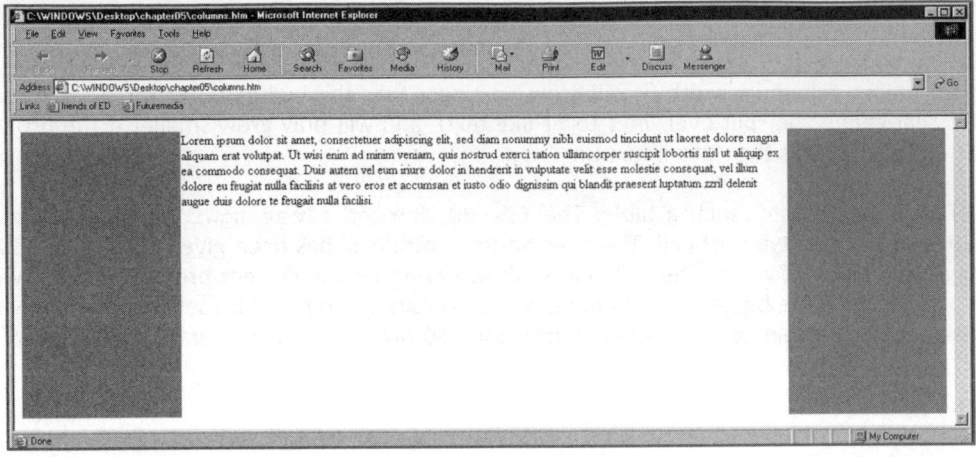

There is a problem here though: the browser window itself has margins and borders around it by default, and this spoils the desired effect, which is a fixed width and centered web page on a colored background. To fix this, add the following additional style declaration for the body tag, which gets rid of any margin/border that the browser may add as part of its default CSS:

```
<style>

BODY {
              margin:0;
              padding:0;
              }

.fixedWidth {
              background-color: #FFFFFF;
              vertical-align: top;
              width: 750px;
              }

.floatingWidth {background-color: #FF0000}

</style>
```

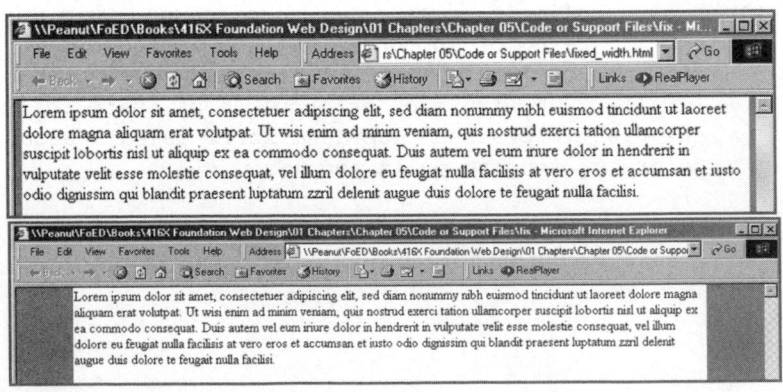

The Amazon site we looked at earlier is actually using a similar trick, using a three-column invisib define the layout.

> If we were going to use this technique in a proper site, the first thing we would do is add in some cell spacing to stop the text from starting on the edge of the red coloring!

Centering in a browser window

A single-celled table that occupies the whole browser window, where the `<table>` width and height attributes are both set to 100%, will allow you to quickly center any single item in the middle of a browser, no matter how much it is resized:

```
<html>

<head>
<style>
.centerSite {
     text-align: center;
     vertical-align: middle;
     height: 100%;
     width: 100%;
     }
</style>
</head>

<body>

<table CLASS = centerSite>
<tr>
<td>

Whatever you place here<br>
Will remain centered in the <br>
browser window...<br>
</td>
</tr>
</table>

</body>

</html>
```

> You can make a CSS class definition as we have here, for any of the table tags.

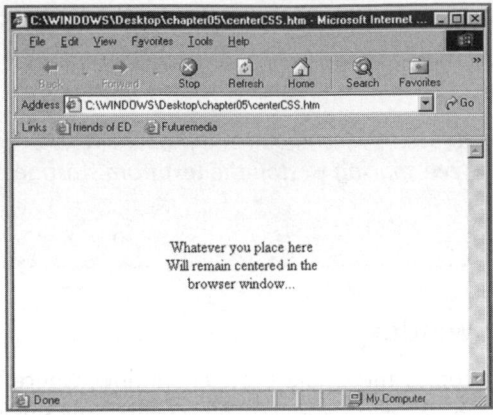

That's a cool trick when your content is a single image, video clip or even Flash movie (see my site, www.futuremedia.org.uk, for an example of the latter), but if your content consists of several elements that you want to have an alignment other than 'centered', it doesn't work well. The text above is center-aligned, but what if we wanted it to be left justified, as text usually is? Well, the answer is to place the content in an **embedded table**:

```
<html>

<head>
<style>
.centerSite {
    text-align: left;
    vertical-align: middle;
    height: 100%;
    width: 100%;
}
</style>
</head>

<body>

<table CLASS = centerSite>
    <tr>
        <td>
            <table><tr><td>

                Whatever you place here<br>
                will be justified according<br>
                to the text-align setting<br>

            </table></tr></td>
        </td>
    </tr>
</table>
```

```
    </body>

    </html>
```

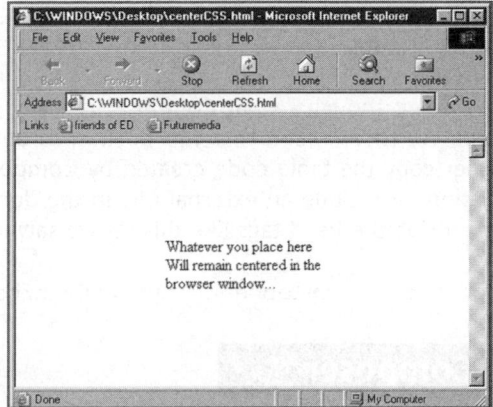

Here, the *outer* table consists of a single cell that is set up to fill the browser window, and this cell has its content set to `center-align`. This alignment makes the *inner* table always centered vertically within the browser, but the content in this table can set to different horizontal alignments, as above.

outer table; fills browser window and centers content

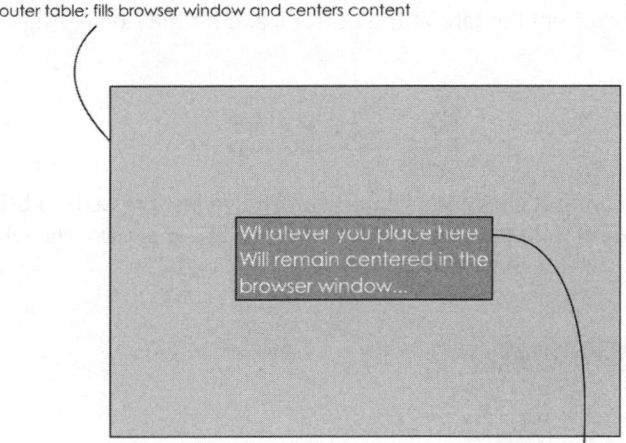

inner table; holds site content in a centered position, which can have its own alignment

Table layouts with Netscape Composer

The tags we have seen so far allow you to build most basic site layouts using tables, but the HTML can start to get a little monotonous as your tables get larger. Now that you have a general understanding of the concepts behind tables, we can take a look at using Netscape Navigator to create them.

It's worth reiterating at this point what we said earlier: although setting the height and width of tables using the `<table>` and `<tr>` tag attributes is still often used (if officially deprecated), using tags for other table formatting is frowned upon, with the use of CSS recommended as an alternative. Composer won't help you in this quest, though, because it doesn't support CSS directly (unlike Dreamweaver).

It's quite easy to add a whole lot of table settings in Composer with tags without even realizing what you're doing – just try formatting the text, and adding color and so on, and then checking the <HTML> Source tab at the bottom of the window – so you need to be careful!

This is getting away from the point, though - what Composer is really good at is allowing you to create tables easily and without pain. We recommend that you do this, as outlined below, without adding any further formatting. Then either copy the table code created by Composer into your text document and add your style sheet information, or include an external CSS in the document by selecting the <HTML> Source tab, and adding a line inside the head tags like this (as we saw in the last chapter):

```
<link href="site.css" rel="stylesheet" type="text/css">
```

Creating tables in Composer

Anyway, enough talking: creating tables in Composer is easy, so this won't take too long.

1. From Netscape Navigator, open a new Composer window (File > New > Composer Page).

2. Select the Normal view from the tabs at the bottom, and hit the Center Align icon from the toolbar at the top.

3. Next, hit the Table icon (just above the center icon you've just pressed) to bring up the Insert Table window. Enter 4 rows and 2 columns, with a width of 75%, as shown. Hit OK when you are done, and you'll see a basic HTML table appear.

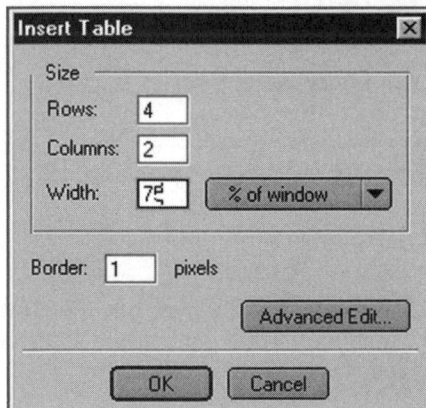
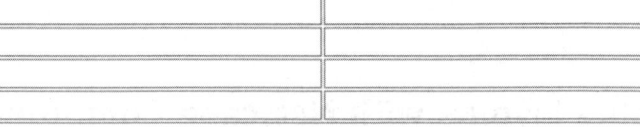

4. Click inside the top left-hand cell, and select Table > Join with Cell to the Right option to create a span. You'll see that here you can also split cells and add rows, columns and cells with this menu.

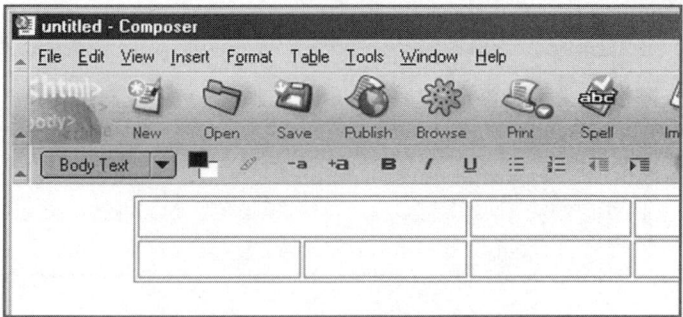

5. Right-click/CTRL-click on the top left cell, and select Table Cell Properties… from the pop-up menu that appears. Select the Table tab. In the Border and Spacing section, set the Border to 0 and Padding to 5.

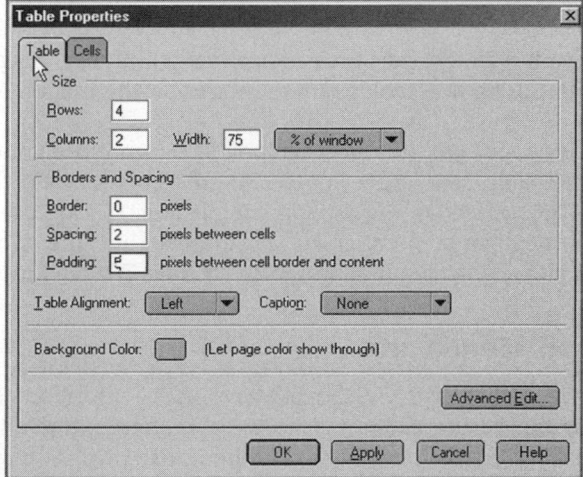

6. When you hit OK, take a look at the Show all Tags tab to see how similar this is to our diagrams earlier, and then go to Preview to see the final table.

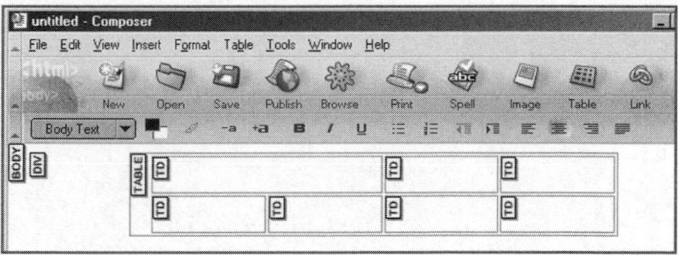

7. You can now click in cells and add text. The table will change its cell dimensions as you add content, and will automatically resize the rows and columns as you type, so that the table constantly takes account of the text changes you make within the table.

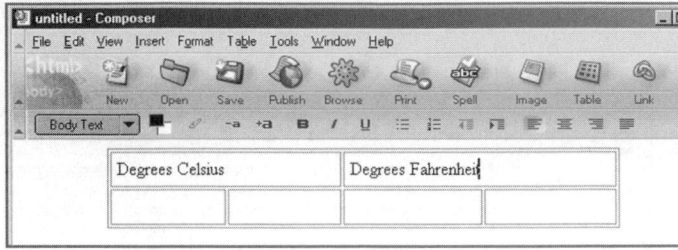

The Case Study – Adding tables

We will be using a combination of tables and CSS to define our site layout. Although you can use CSS to completely replace many tables, there are a large number of situations where tables are easier to setup, including:

- When you really want a table rather than adding margins and padding. When you are tabulating text into complex tables, using true tables is much easier on the brain.

- When you are using *sliced graphics*. We will look at this in more detail in **Chapter 10**, but slicing is simply a way of breaking up a larger image into smaller 'tiles', and the pictures below give you an early idea of how this works on the Mondo site. In short, slicing uses tables to put the slices back together. Using slices has a number of advantages, but the tables created are usually very complicated, and although doing it all in CSS is possible, it would take forever!

Tables in the finished Mondo site

As we mentioned above, tables (and CSS boxes) have uses in positioning as well as the more normal 'tabulated data' kind of table (such as the Celsius vs Fahrenheit example we looked at earlier). Let's see how this works by sneaking a quick peek at the finished site. A typical page in the completed site is this one (it's the file `mon_contact.html` if you want to have a look at it in a browser):

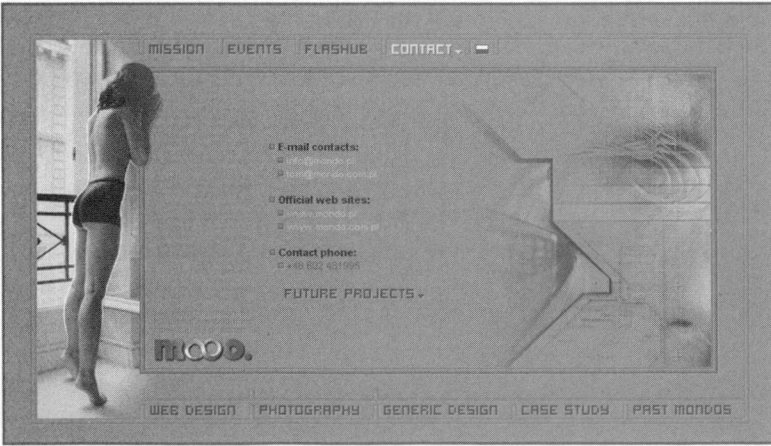

This page has all sorts of HTML tables keeping all those slices and other content areas together, but they are currently not visible. If we alter the HTML so they become visible and obvious, we now see something like this;

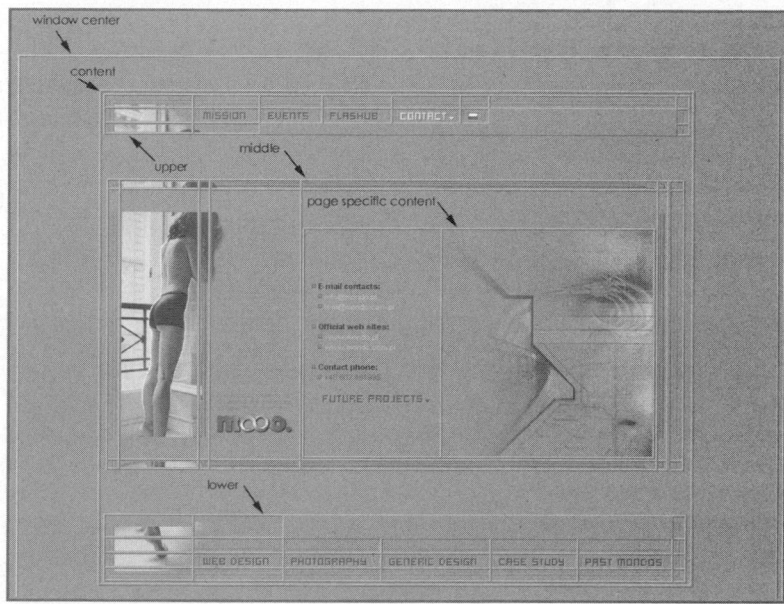

Quite a difference! We can see that the page is actually made of a CSS box and five tables;

There is a table window center that causes another one (content, which is a table to hold all the page content together) to remain centered in the browser.

Inside the table content we have three further tables, upper, middle, and lower. Upper holds together our slices for the top menu, and lower does the same for the bottom menu. The middle table does the same for the slices in the middle, but there is a twist; middle contains a final table inside it that holds the page specific content. The diagram below should make this a bit clearer:

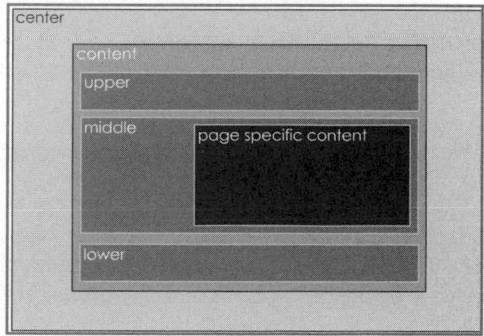

The upper, middle, lower and page specific content tables will be created automatically when we look at **slicing** via Photoshop/Fireworks later in the book. The CSS box center and content are ones we have to create manually, and we will do that in this chapter.

Enhancing the skeleton site

We created a file that is not actually needed in the finished site last chapter, and we may as well remove it now. In your `mondoSkeleton` folder, delete the HTML file `test_style.html` (or move it somewhere else if you would prefer to keep it).

Sketching our new pages

Three important rules of creating CSS/table-based layouts:

> **1** - Sketch it first
> **2** - Sketch it first
> **3** - You guessed it...

Here's what we will be working towards:

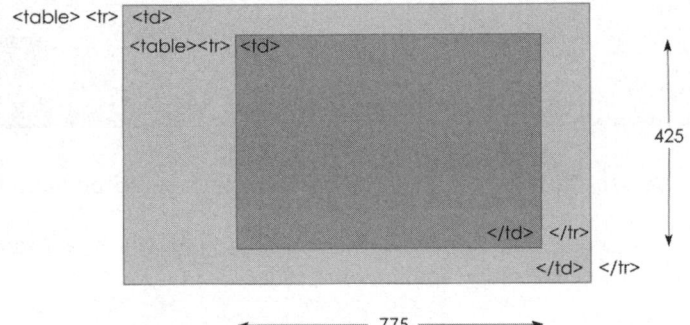

This diagram is much like the earlier sketches we did to form *individual* tables, but we now have to consider *nested* tables. To do that, you are strongly recommended to add *all* the tags rather than just `<tr>` and `<td>`, because the ordering becomes very important.

I have also defined *sizing* information for the inner table here, so that it will go to the specified size (width = 775 pixels, height = 425) even if the table is empty - which is something we know will happen in the skeleton pages.

> *The 775x425 size comes from the requirement for the site to be viewable on an 800x600 screen or better. We can't just go ahead and make the main content 800x600 though, because the browser interface itself (or 'the chrome' if we want to use the web design terminology) takes up some of that room.*

Creating the HTML/CSS

1. Reading the sketch from top left to the bottom right (and putting it inside some HTML that calls up our style sheet, mon_style.css from the last chapter), we get the following code listing:

```html
<html>
<head>
<title>table test</title>
<link href="mon_style.css" rel="stylesheet" type="text/css">
</head>

<body>

<!--TABLE MAIN CENTER - START-->
<table border = "1">
     <tr><td>
          This is the outer table
          <!--TABLE MAIN DIMENSIONS - START-->
          <table border = "1">
               <tr><td>
                         This is the inner table
               </td></tr>
          </table>
          <!--TABLE MAIN DIMENSIONS - END-->
     </td></tr>
</table>
<!--TABLE MAIN CENTER - END-->

</body>
</html>
```

> It's always a good idea to define your basic nested tables in the way shown in this HTML before you start messing about with style sheets or attributes. It's amazing how easily nested tables can end up in the wrong place if you are not careful, because the HTML can start to look very scary very quickly!
>
> Notice also the use of both indentation and commenting to clearly show where each table starts and ends.

2. Save the file as test_table.html in your mondoSkeleton folder (which you have to do if it is to find the mon_style.css file it requires).

3.   Open the file in your browser and you will see this:

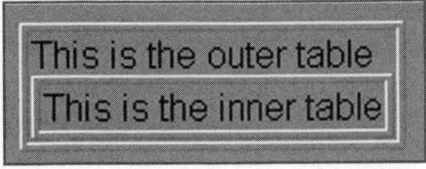

That's all the structural stuff out of the way. All we *should* now have to do is set up some style classes as per the following (don't do it yet):

```
...
...
<!--TABLE MAIN CENTER - START-->
<table CLASS = centerSiteTable>
     <tr><td>
           This is the outer table
           <!--TABLE MAIN DIMENSIONS - START-->
           <table CLASS = mainTable>
                 <tr><td>
...
...
```

... and then set these up in mon_style.css to give us our nice centered central table:

```
.centerSiteTable {
          vertical-align: middle;
          height: 100%;
          width: 100%;
          }
.mainTable{
          height: 425px;
          width: 775px;
          border: thin dashed #666666;
          }
```

Well, we *should,* but certain versions of Netscape Navigator are a bit flaky when it comes to using CSS centering with tables (although Internet Explorer is fine). To maintain compatibility across the board, we therefore have to fall back to using only HTML attributes.

4.   With this in mind, we will use HTML-only tables to make sure we don't break our pages on certain browsers. Add the following attributes to the table tags as shown:

```
...
...
<!--TABLE MAIN CENTER - START-->
<table BORDER="1" CELLPADDING="0" CELLSPACING="0" WIDTH="100%"
HEIGHT="100%" ALIGN="CENTER">
          <tr><td>
```

```
This is the outer table
<!--TABLE MAIN DIMENSIONS - START-->
<table BORDER="1" CELLPADDING="0" CELLSPACING="0" WIDTH="775"
➡  HEIGHT="425" ALIGN="CENTER">
        <tr><td>
```
. . .
. . .

5. If you view test_table.html in both Internet Explorer or Netscape Navigator, you will see the following:

There's a few things wrong here. Firstly, we have a gutter round the edge of the browser window that could do with disappearing, and secondly the text in the tables is a bit too big to go well with any of our site text style classes.

> *There's also the fact that we can see the tables, when in the final site we can't, but we've made them visible for now because we actually want to see what our HTML/CSS does to it.*

6. Save and close test_table.html, and edit mon_style.css, adding the following:

```
BODY {
        font-family: arial, verdana, helvetica, sans-serif;
        background-color: #999999;
        margin:0;
        padding:0;
        }
TD      {
        font-size: 10px; font-weight: bold;
```

continues overleaf

```
                    text-decoration: none; color: 666666;
                    text-align: center;
                    }
A:link {
                    font-size: 10px; font-weight: bold;
                    text-decoration: none; color: #CCCCCC;
                    }
...
...
```

The margin and padding values get rid of our gutter, and the style declarations for the `<td>` tag give us some text that is consistent with the other site typography. Save the CSS file and view `test_table.html` in a browser. You should now see no gutter and the table text will have changed.

7. Now that we know we have got the outer table where we want it, we might as well make it invisible. Open `test_table.html` and set the `border` attribute of the outer table to `0`:

```
...
...
<!--TABLE MAIN CENTER - START-->
<table BORDER="0" CELLPADDING="0" CELLSPACING="0" WIDTH="100%" HEIGHT="100%"
ALIGN="CENTER">
                    <tr><td>
...
...
```

Adding our tables to the skeleton site

1. All we need to do here is move the existing placeholder content into the nested table structure above so that it sits in the inner table. An example of this is shown below for one of our pages (`mon_contact.html`), but note that we have now also used the `<span>` tag to start using our style sheet classes.

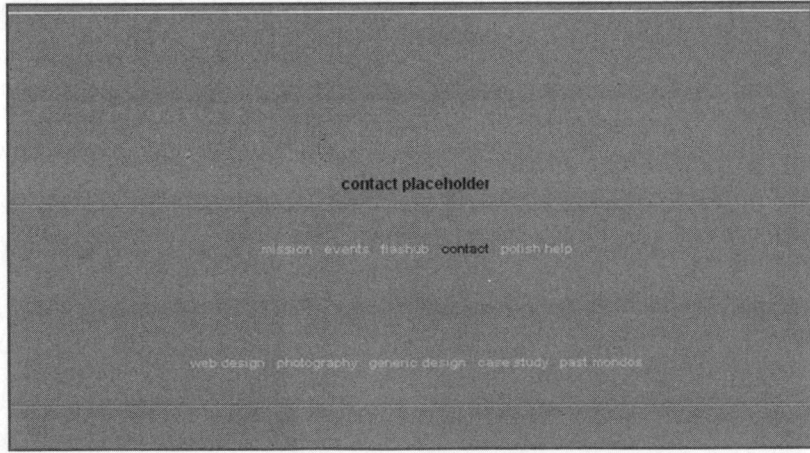

2. Here's the part of mon_contact that we see between the `<body>`...`</body>` tags from last chapter:

```
<body>
<h2>contact placeholder</h2>
<hr>

<!--Top menu-->
<p>
<a href = "mon_mission.html">mission</a>  
<a href = "mon_events.html">events</a>  
<a href = "javascript:flashWin=window.open('flash.html', 'flashPopup',
    ➥ 'menubar=no, scrollbars=no, width=800, height=600,
        ➥ resizable=no');void 0;">flashub</a>  
contact  
<a href="javascript:polWin=window.open('mon_pol_con.html', 'polPopup',
    ➥ 'menubar=no, scrollbars=no, width=550, height=300, resizable=no');
    ➥ polWin.focus(); void 0;">polish help</a> </p>
</p>

<!--Content area-->
<br><br><br><br>

<!-- sub-menu-->
<p>
<a href = "mon_webdes.html">web design</a>  
<a href = "mon_photo.html">photography </a>  
<a href = "mon_generic.html">generic design </a>  
<a href = "mon_casestud.html">case study </a>  
<a href = "mon_past.html">past mondos</a>
</p>
<hr>
</body>
```

The new updated page is simply this same HTML placed in the inner table, plus we have changed:

- the `<h2>` title to `<span CLASS="title">`
- the paragraph `<p>` text so that it is all enclosed by a `<span CLASS="text">`

3. Both of these changes allow our pages to finally start showing the classes we defined in mon_style.css last chapter:

```
<html>
<head>
<title>table test</title>
<link href="mon_style.css" rel="stylesheet" type="text/css">
</head>

<body>
```

continues overleaf

```
        <!--table main center - start-->
        <table border="0" cellpadding="0" cellspacing="0" width="100%"
    ➥ height="100%" align="center">
                <tr><td>
                <!--table main dimensions - start-->
                <table border="1" cellpadding="0" cellspacing="0" width="775"
    ➥ height="425" align="center">
                        <tr><td>

                        <span CLASS="title">contact placeholder</span>
                        <hr>
                        <span CLASS="text">

                                <!--Top menu-->
                                <p>
                                <a href = "mon_mission.html">mission</a>  
                                <a href = "mon_events.html">events</a>  
                                <a href =
    ➥ "javascript:flashWin=window.open('flash.html', 'flashPopup',
    ➥ 'menubar=no, scrollbars=no, width=800, height=600,
    ➥ resizable=no');void 0;">flashub</a>  
                                contact  
                                <a
    ➥ href="javascript:polWin=window.open('mon_pol_con.html', 'polPopup',
    ➥ 'menubar=no, scrollbars=no, width=550, height=300, resizable=no');
    ➥ polWin.focus(); void 0;">polish help</a> </p>
                                </p>

                                <!--Content area-->
                                <br><br><br><br>

                                <!-- sub-menu-->
                                <p>
                                <a href = "mon_webdes.html">web design</a>  
                                <a href = "mon_photo.html">photography </a>  
                                <a href = "mon_generic.html">generic design </a>
     
                                <a href = "mon_casestud.html">case study </a>
     
                                <a href = "mon_past.html">past mondos</a>
                                </p>
                                <hr>
                        </span>

                        </td></tr>
                </table>
                <!--table main dimensions - end-->
        </td></tr>
    </table>
```

```
<!--table main center - end-->

</body>
</html>
```

5. You need to do the same to all the other non pop-up pages. It's a relatively easy process of copy and paste to do this, but it might be a little fiddly, depending on how simple your 'simple text editor' actually is! See the download for this chapter, where you will find the completed files to help out if you get stuck. They are:

- `index.html`
- `mon_mission.html`
- `mon_events.html`
- `mon_contact.html`
- `mon_webdes.html`
- `mon_photo.html`
- `mon_generic.html`
- `mon_casestud.html`
- `mon_past.html`

Copy these to your `mondoSkeleton` folder, allowing them to overwrite the old versions.

> *For those who want to compare the old and new files, rename the old versions first, but be sure to move/delete the old ones before you move on, so we all have the same set of files.*

Summary

As you can see, our case study is steaming along, as is our understanding of the core concepts of web design. In the next couple of chapters we'll introduce the last major topic we've still to cover – web graphics. You'll see how image-heavy websites are actually built, and get to flex your creative muscles even more.

Go have a cup of coffee, open up your favourite image editor and get ready...

Creating Web Graphics

What this chapter will do

Before we can start to think about graphics for an overall site, we need to understand the underlying processes used to create individual graphics, and how to turn general files intended for print-based use into the leaner, more optimized file formats required for use on the Web. In this packed chapter, we'll introduce:

- General color theory, what you need to know and why
- The main web graphics formats – GIFs, JPEGs, and PNGs
- Using Adobe Photoshop and Macromedia Fireworks to optimize your graphics

What you will have learned by the end of this chapter

By the end of this chapter you will understand how color works on the Web, including the issues behind the web-safe color debate. You will also have a firm knowledge of the GIF, JPEG and PNG file formats and how to ready them for website use.

Color

OK, you might be wondering how we're going to teach you about color in a black and white book. Well, we'll try, but for added illustration, head along to www.friendsofed.com/fwd/color.html where you can see the following diagrams in glorious full color!

Take a look at the first image. If you shone red, green and blue light beams at a darkened wall, you would see something like this:

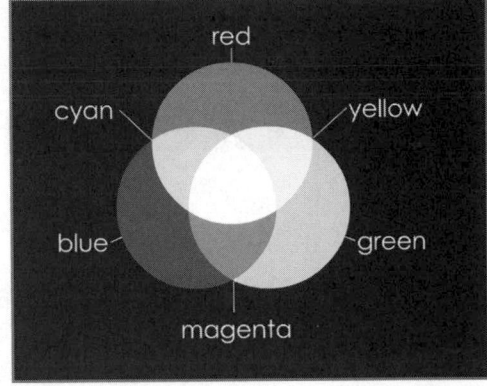

The areas of the three beams that don't overlap would retain their original color. The points where all three beams intersect would give you white, and the points where red-green, green-blue and blue-red intersect would give you the secondary colors yellow, magenta and cyan.

That's as far as you can go with torches, but if you could actually vary the **intensity** of each of the red, green and blue lights, then you could create any color imaginable. For example, if you wanted a gray, you would reduce the intensity of all three lights, and the central white areas would get dimmer, giving you your gray. If you wanted a yellow that was closer to red than green, you could increase the intensity of the red light and/or reduce the green light.

Modern monitors replicate this simple process many times across the face of the monitor screen with an array of red, green and blue dots. These dots don't actually overlap, but are so small that they give the same effect. Black is created by having all the dots turned off, and a colored screen pixel is created by a number of separate screen dots, each at a unique brightness to give the impression of a new color, but actually created by a combination of pure red, green and blue light.

For example, if we wanted to create a solid yellow, red and green dots would be used to give alternate red-green dots that the human eye is fooled into thinking is a solid yellow. Having all the red, green and blue dots full on creates white.

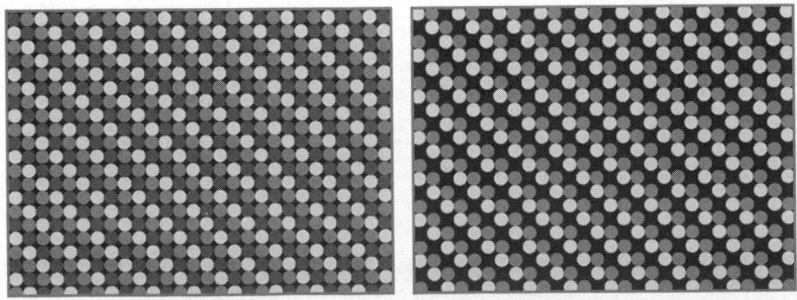

For each pixel on the screen, a computer has separate red, green and blue values that are required to give the final color. The bad news is that computers spend a lot of time writing color and pixel information to the screen, and the process has to be very fast to be efficient. This means that the color information is packed in a way that the computer understands, but which we have to think about to understand.

Hexadecimal

All digital systems use the **RGB** color system, named after the three color components: **R**ed-**G**reen-**B**lue. Unfortunately, a binary pattern to express the color of a typical pixel looks something like: *1000110110001010110001010*. There are easier ways to represent binary, and one of the most common is **hexadecimal**, which results in shorter numbers for us humans to work with. Expressed in hexadecimal, our binary number above becomes: *8D8D8A*.

So how do we create hexadecimal numbers that we can recognize as red-green-blue color mix definitions? Each of the three components - red, green and blue - can have a brightness level from 0 to 255. In hexadecimal, this is expressed as *00* to *FF*.

In case you want to convert from normal decimal to hexadecimal (or even from hexadecimal to decimal), we've included a little application authored in Flash with a full chart from 0 – 255 in the chapter download file. Double-click hexChart.html *to see this in your browser, or just run the* hexChart.swf *file to run it in the standalone Flash 6 Player.*

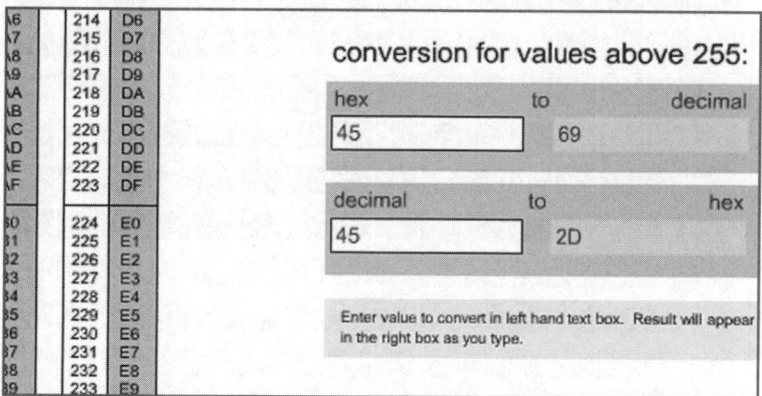

Supposing you wanted to mix a color that had a red value of *200*, a green value of *150* and a blue value of *0*. That gives us R, G, B values of *200, 150, 0*. In hex, these numbers are *C8, 96, 00*. The value that the computer would recognize as a meaningful color for the pixel is a single number, and to create this number, we simply put the hex R, G, and B values after one another in the form *RRGGBB*, so our color becomes *C89600*.

Finally, you have to let the browser know that the number you have come up with is in hexadecimal rather than normal decimal. There are two ways of doing this: if you're writing HTML, you add a hash to the front, so our color becomes *#C89600*; if you're writing in JavaScript, add an *0x*, so we get *0xC89600*.

As well as the hex values, both Internet Explorer and Netscape Navigator recognize a list of color names, such as *aliceblue*, *aqua*, *red* and *black*. Although many of these are more descriptive than the hex values, you are not recommended to use them, given that many of them are not part of HTML standards in use by a number of browsers. Some of the color names are a little, well, imaginative and are probably harder to visualize than the hexadecimal color values they replace anyway - *blanchedalmond* anyone?

Common RGB colors

Under the RGB system, white is the full value of the three R-G-B components, or 255-255-255, which gives us #FFFFFF. Black is the minimum values, giving us #000000. Pure red, green and blue are created by putting the active color to its full value, and the others to zero, giving us #FF0000, ##00FF00 and #0000FF respectively.

Grays can be created by making the red, green and blue values the same (which makes the final color a **neutral** - neither red, green or blue). There are 256 gray levels, shown below. You can get a good grayscale sequence by using the colors #000000 (black), #111111, #222222, #333333, #444444, #555555, #666666, #777777, #888888, #999999, #AAAAAA, #BBBBBB, #CCCCCC, #DDDDDD, #EEEEEE, #FFFFFF (white). These are the shades from diagonal top left to bottom right in the picture.

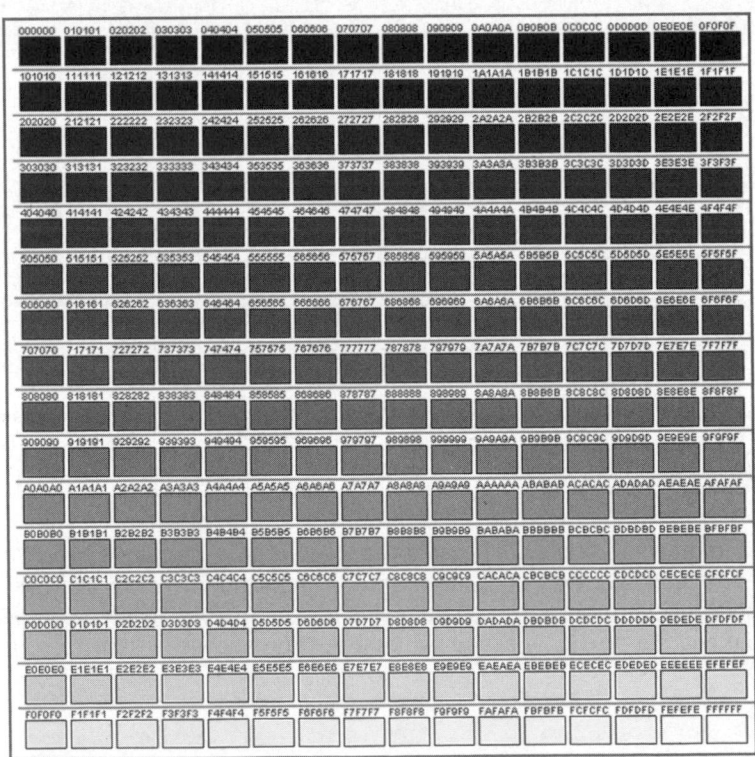

The secondary colors are also easily created: **yellow** is #FFFF00 (full value red + full value green), **magenta** is #00FFFF (full value green + full value blue), and **cyan** is #FF00FF (full value red + full value blue).

You can form other colors by starting with the primary and secondary colors as a base. For example, orange is simply a yellow with a higher proportion of red to green, such as #FF9900. A good way of creating pastel colors is to start with a grayscale and add or subtract small amounts to one or more of the RGB components to add a tint. For example, if we wanted a light blue of about the same intensity as the gray #E7E7E7, increasing the blue component to give us #E7E7F7 results in a subtle bluish gray.

Using color pickers to form the RGB value

Most graphics applications allow you to find out the hexadecimal value interactively. In Photoshop you can access the **Color Picker** by simply clicking on either the foreground or background color in the toolbox. The hex color value corresponding to your selected color will appear next to the value marked #, as shown:

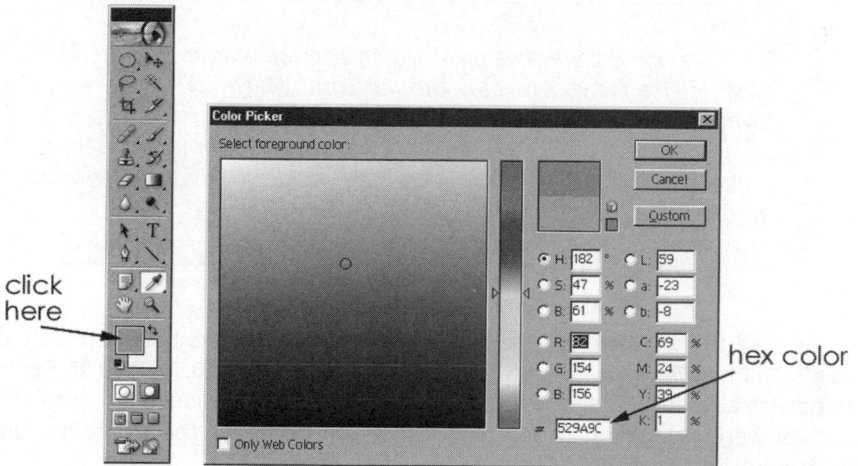

click here

hex color

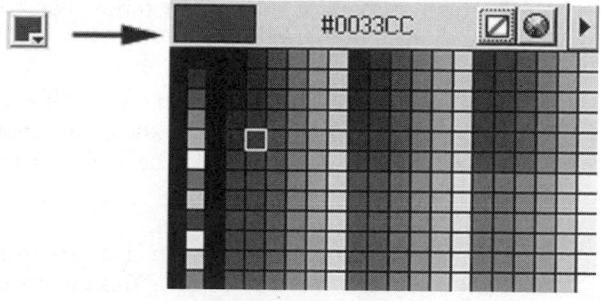

Macromedia MX applications use a common color system. Wherever you see a color that is presented as a block with a little down-arrow to the bottom left corner (you will usually find them on the toolbox and Properties panel, plus any panels that control color), you can select a new color by clicking on the block to reveal a Color Picker. The hex value will be shown for the selected color, and the means to enter a hex value directly is always available either next to the color block or on the Color Picker.

Web-safe palettes

As a multimedia designer, 'web-safe color' is one of the terms you will see bandied around quite often. Early computers were only able to show a limited number of colors due to video memory constraints - typically 256, 128, 64, 32, or even 16 colors. This raised a number of problems for web color usage, given that HTML can specify any color from #000000 to #FFFFFF, giving 1,677,216 possible colors.

The way round was to define a minimum number of colors that the designer could use for all web design work. This set of colors assumed that a computer that could display at least 256 colors, and 216 of these were used to form the **Web-Safe Palette**. The remaining 40 colors were reserved, and used by the operating system.

Web-safe colors are easy to identify: they consist of only the hex RGB component values FF, CC, 99, 66, 33 and 00. For example, #FF0033 and #66CCCC are both part of the web-safe palette. You can see the web-safe palette in the Macromedia Color pickers (it's the set of colors shown by default) and the Photoshop Color picker if you check the Only Web Colors checkbox at the bottom left of the window.

> For completeness, we have provided an electronic version of the web-safe palette for you to play around with, which you can see by downloading the files colorChart.swf and colorChart.html and double-clicking the HTML file to view the result in a browser or double-clicking the SWF to view the result in the standalone Flash 6 player.

Any design that used the web-safe palette was using only those colors that were actually available to the computer; so all browsers would show exactly the same colors. Restricting the colors in a site to the web-safe palette also ensured that the browser did not try to reproduce any graphic that contained more colors than were available (it would do this by approximating the colors it didn't have, which would quite often make a mess of the image).

So, using the web-safe palette is a good deal, right? Well, no, not any more. You will have noticed that the discussion above is in the past tense. Two things have happened since the days when web-safe colors were first thought up.

Firstly, the majority of people don't use 256-color screens any more. Most computers use bigger palettes, typically 16-bit color (also known as "thousands of colors" or "high color"). This doesn't need to restrict itself to web-safe color because it can display all the unique colors that the browser can specify.

Secondly, more recent hardware can also handle an advanced mode called 24-bit color (also known as "millions of colors" or "true color"). This color mode is the 'true computer palette' in that it includes all colors available – even more than the colors #000000 to #FFFFFF. This is also about the number of unique colors that the human eye can distinguish between, so we're not going to be able to see any more colors, even if our monitors get better.

Unfortunately, 24-bit color mode shows slightly different actual colors to the web-safe palette given the same hex values: there is no color consistency between 24-bit color and the web-safe palette.

> *Some machines can also handle 32-bit color, which is actually really only 24-bit color. The advantage of 32-bit over 24-bit is more to do with hardware optimization than 'more available colors'.*

The last issue to bear in mind is that different screen hardware actually shows different colors for a given hex value. Unless a computer screen is calibrated for absolute color (and no-one except print-based graphic designers seems to bother doing that these days), the colors you see on your screen will vary depending on:

- The operating system used. Macs and PCs show slightly different overall brightness (or **gamma**).

- The type of screen used. Flat-screen and conventional monitors use totally different technologies, and will therefore produce slightly different colors.

- The user's preferences. Unless a computer is calibrated, even two monitors of the same type will not be consistent because different people prefer different screen brightness, color and contrast settings.

Producing accurate absolute color for the Web is therefore pretty much impossible, but there are a few simple rules that tend to create good results:

- Use web-safe color values for web page background colors and text. As long as the user's computer can display the web-safe palette, any color you specify will be rendered accurately as a solid color. It might not show up as *exactly* the same color you specify if the user is using 24-bit graphics, but their eyes won't usually make the distinction, so don't worry.

- Use contrasting colors for your text and background. This ensures that your design is still legible even if the colors are a little different on some machines.

- Select web-safe colors for any large areas of color in graphics destined for the Web, so that everyone will see a solid (un-dithered) color irrespective of whether they are using 8, 16, or 24, bit color.

- Check your final pages in 256, 16-bit and 24-bit mode, making sure there are no really odd colors showing up in either Internet Explorer or Netscape Navigator. There are a few combinations that might show up wrong in the conversion from 16- to 24-bit (some grays may show up with a hint of red, blue or green, and this may be obvious if your site is otherwise color-neutral, but it's all pretty rare, and depends on you having good eyesight and a pro-level monitor!).

Don't worry about anything else. If your selected colors are a bit out, then that's life. The user's monitor brightness and color preferences will typically be the biggest change between the design you see on your computer and the one they end up seeing, anyway, and there's no way that you can gain control over that!

Color-blindness

A point worth noting is that up to a fifth of men are color-blind to varying degrees, so when choosing a background and text color for your web pages, it is always a good idea to make sure that your design is still legible when the user can see no color at all.

The easiest way to check this to take a screen-copy of your site (use Print Screen on the PC, or Apple-Shift-F3 on the Mac), and turn the picture into grayscale. To do this, select Image > Adjust > Desaturate in Photoshop, or select Filters > Adjust Color > Hue/Saturation in Fireworks and set the saturation slider to −100. If you can still read the text and make out the graphics, the site is OK for color-impaired users.

Now we've taken a stroll through color theory, it's time to put it into practice with some graphics for our websites...

Adding graphics to web pages

The Web started life as a way of linking up academic institutions, and you only have to look at the way HTML is structured to see what effect that has had. HTML has loads of text-specific tags (headings, block quotes...), but we meet some slightly different issues when we start adding graphics, specifically:

- Browsers can only display certain file formats
- Delivery on the Web is limited by the speed of the user's connection

It is now generally accepted that there are three standard options for image file formats: the GIF, JPEG and PNG file formats. Aside from the issue of which of these is best to use, the only remaining issue is image size. Although graphics are important in any web design, they also make up the majority of the file size that the user has to load up to see the page – text takes comparatively much less space.

> *These three web formats all compress images in some way, so you should use the TIFF format when saving your raw source image files from flatbed scanners or digital cameras, in order to save them with maximum image clarity.*

Working with Photoshop and Fireworks

The two most common applications used for preparing graphics for the Web are Adobe Photoshop and Macromedia Fireworks. Photoshop is a general image manipulation program traditionally used for print based and photographic work, but has evolved over the years to include web publishing. Fireworks is a more recent entrant to the market, and – as you'd expect in a Macromedia product – is more closely tied into web design.

Although they're two different programs, you use them identically to make images **web-ready** – the only differences are to do with the slightly different interfaces. With this in mind, you can use whichever is most convenient for the next exercise – if you don't have a copy of either, you can download fully functional 30-day trial versions from:

- www.macromedia.com/software/fireworks/download/ or
- www.adobe.com/products/photoshop/

> *Whenever we talk about Photoshop, we are also including its sister application, ImageReady. ImageReady is a separate application that comes bundled with Photoshop and specializes in the creation of web graphics. You won't really notice this, though – moving between the two is pretty seamless, as we'll see in a moment. The general idea is that you create your image in Photoshop, and then optimize it in ImageReady.*

Macromedia call their little floating interface windows **panels** whereas Adobe call theirs **palettes**. There's little difference between them except on PCs, where they can be **docked** in the Macromedia MX series of applications. To switch between a docked and undocked panel in MX, drag the window with the knurled area (three dots) to the bottom left of the title bar.

A point worth making is that to get best results from either program, you should use a good screen size (a good minimum is 1024x720) and the highest color depth your computer can handle (the best bet is true color, which may be listed on your machine as 24-bit, 32-bit or 'Millions of Colors').

File formats

As we've said above, there are three standard options for image file formats: GIF, JPEG and PNG. Let's take a look at them.

The Graphic Interchange Format (GIF)

The GIF format (pronounced to sound like 'giff' by almost everyone except the authors of the file format, who pronounce it to sound like 'jif') is the most common type of image on the Web. Pretty much any browser that supports images will allow GIFs, and the format allows some specialized features like the ability to include animation and transparency (both of which we will look at in **Chapter 9**).

The GIF dates from the days when computers could only display 256 colors at a time. This means that they don't make use of hardware advances that allow more colors to be shown, but neither do they take up the extra processing power needed to display the newer formats with more colors.

The GIF format is particularly good at compressing images with lots of solid blocks of color in them. For example, the Amazon logo shown in the next page uses very few different colors, and has a large area of solid horizontal color, which makes it an ideal candidate for the GIF format. Logos using text, simple graphics (like that arrow underneath Amazon), and whitespace are a good place to use GIFs.

Many websites use a faux metallic or shiny-plastic effect for their user interface - www.evolt.org is one example. The site top bar has a minimalist design, which uses black and a few dark grays. The site logo consists of three colored cubes, which contrast well with the black strip. This clever use of a small number of colors and large amounts of solid black in the design of the interface makes the GIF format a good choice for the graphics. When you're first thinking about the look of your site, it's worth thinking about ways in which the visual content can be simplified in ways such as this, while remaining effective and true to your vision.

Likewise, cartoons, line drawings, and sketches usually consist of areas of solid color and use a limited palette, both of which make the GIF format a good choice.

Many instructions specify that the GIF format should not be used for photographs, but it can be used successfully if the image has a reduced number of colors – black and white images, or images using a sepia, mono, or duotone effect, for example. Any complex or subtle gradations of color are best kept well away from the GIF.

In summary, you would use a GIF where:

- You want to make sure everyone will be able to view the image
- Your design requires you to use transparency (more on this in **Chapter 9**)
- You have graphics with large areas of solid color – such as background images, bitmap text, and charts, graphs or technical graphics
- You are sticking to the web-safe palette
- You want to create short animations: unlike software like Flash, the animated GIF requires no plug-ins or downloads to start working (see **Chapter 9**)

You shouldn't use a GIF where:

- You want some subtle gradations of color that step outside of the GIF's maximum of 256 colors (such as in a standard photograph)

Using GIFs

1. We will be using the `leaf.tif` image for this exercise, so open this up in either Photoshop or Fireworks with the usual File > Open command. You should end up with something like the images shown:

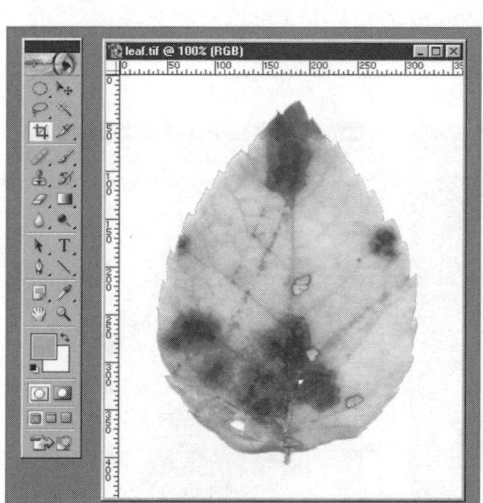
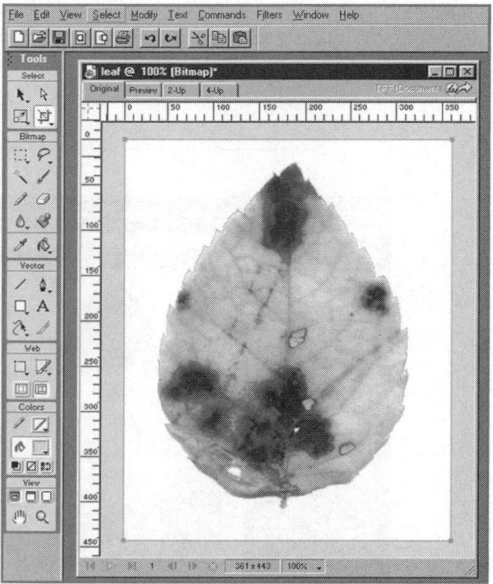

2. If you can't see rulers along the top and left edges as shown, select View > Rulers. The scale most useful to a web designer is pixels, and you can set this in Photoshop by CTRL/right-clicking on any ruler and selecting pixels in the pop-up menu that appears (Fireworks will automatically use pixels as a result of its greater emphasis on web work). The rulers give you an indication of the size of your work area, something that is easy to lose sight of when you zoom in and out.

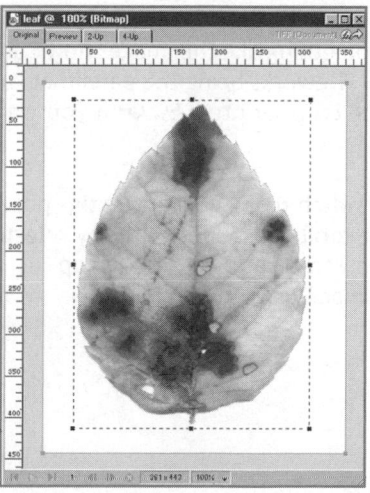

3. Before we start playing about with compression settings, one of the quickest (and often forgotten) ways to reduce file size is to simply make the image area smaller – we can add any whitespace we want later with HTML/CSS. By cropping the image, we not only reduce the file size, we also make it more relevant, keeping our content sharp and to the point. Our image has a big white border around it, so select the Crop tool from the toolbar (it's the  icon, and you can see it selected in the toolbar in the shots).

> *If you can't see the Toolbox, bring it up with* Window > Tools.

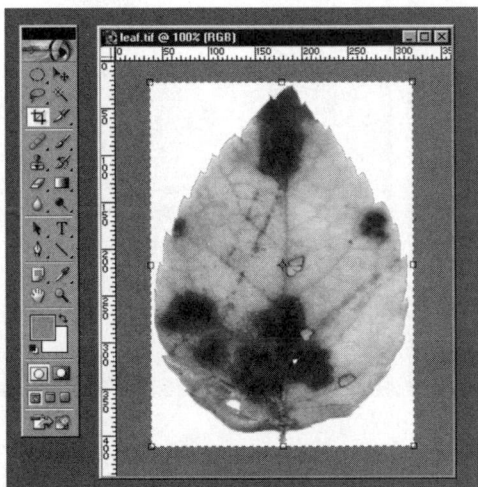
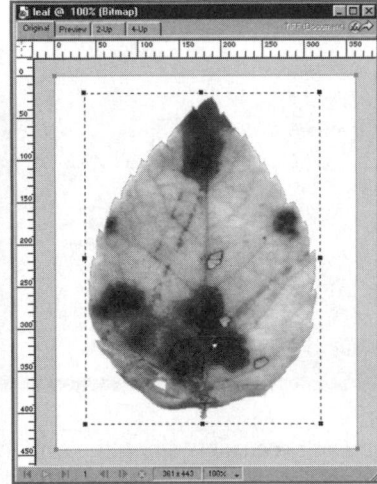

4. Click-drag anywhere on the leaf and drag out a small square. Using the little handles at the corners and edges of the shape, enclose the leaf within the square, leaving as little blank space as possible. If you need to get in close, use CTRL and the + or – keys to zoom in and out.

5. You should end up with something like the image shown above, with the gray area in Photoshop, or the dotted rectangle in Fireworks being the parts that will be cropped. Double-click anywhere on the leaf to perform the crop, or press ESCAPE if you want to have another go at defining the crop area.

6. Photoshop users need to switch to ImageReady at this point by selecting the little icon at the very bottom of the toolbar (as shown), or by selecting File > Jump to > Adobe ImageReady. (You can switch back to Photoshop at any time by clicking the bottommost icon in the ImageReady toolbar.)

7. Photoshop and Fireworks users, both select the 4-Up tab at the top of the image window. Use Window > Optimize to bring up the Optimize window if you can't see it. The 4-up window allows you to experiment with different file formats, and allows you to select the best web format to export our TIFF file.

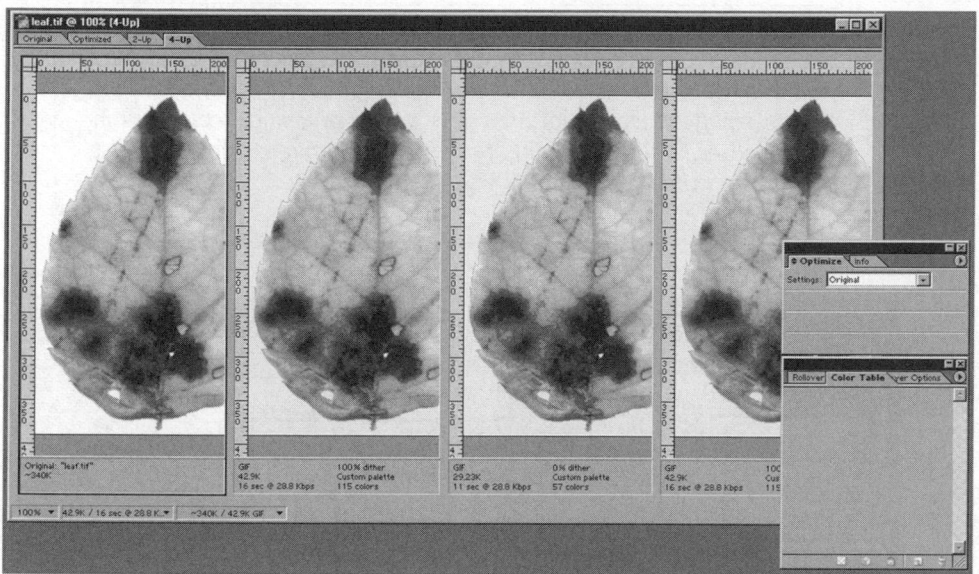

8. Photoshop users might also see some symbols and lines bordering the images, like the ones shown below, depending on the other palettes you have open. If you do, don't worry, we will explain their relevance when we look at image slicing in **Chapter 10**. For now, turn them off by hitting CTRL+H or selecting View > Extras. Your window may also show as a 2x2 window rather than the row of 4 shown, but this doesn't matter.

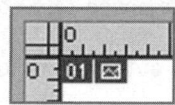

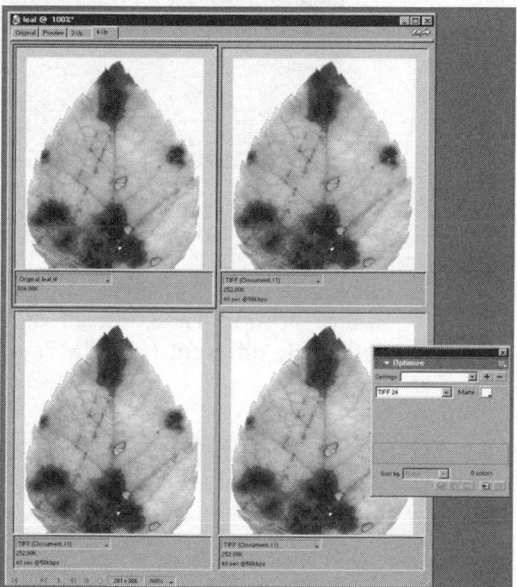

9. The first image will currently be selected, and it's best to keep this at the original setting, so that you've got something to compare the other three with. Select the second leaf, and change the file format to GIF in the Optimize panel. Change the other options as shown: 16 colors, no dither, web-safe colors.

> *16 colors is always a good setting to start with, given that it's usually the minimum setting. You may be able to go lower for images that are text only, or logos that are a few shades of a single color, but in most cases, you will want to raise the image quality whilst minimizing the increase in file size.*

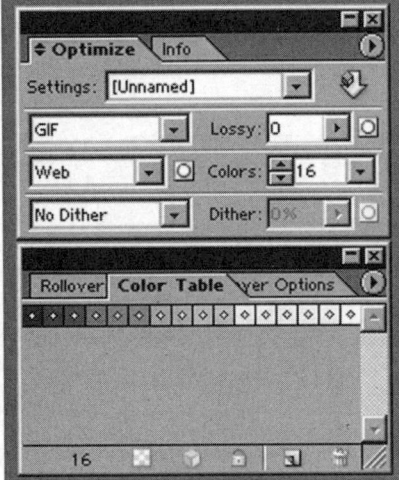 

The color table you'll see at the bottom of the panel (Photoshop users may have to click on the Color Table tab, to change from the Rollover one) shows the 16 colors used by the GIF. The little dot inside each color tells you that it's a web-safe color. Both applications will show you a file size of around 12KB instead of the initial 400-500KB, but you'll see that the image looks noticeably different from the smooth autumnal yellows of the original, with blotches of color showing.

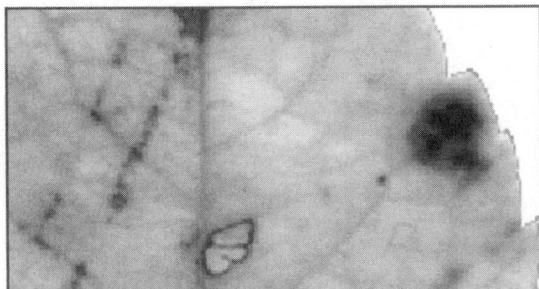 

10. There are two options to improve quality. The first is to add **dither**: if a monitor can't show a certain color, dithering will approximate the color by placing pixels in colors the monitor can display close together. This only really works when the main colors are close to each other, but we're in luck with our leaf, because we're playing around with shades of yellow. Choose Dither from the menu...

> You should never try to compress something that you have added dither to as a JPEG; always keep the source graphics and start from there if you want to use JPEG compression, because JPEG does not work well with dithered images.

11. You should see that adding dither gives you something close to the original image (at least, when seen without zooming in, which makes the dither pattern painfully obvious). It also doubles your file size because you're breaking up the solid colors that GIF likes so much.

 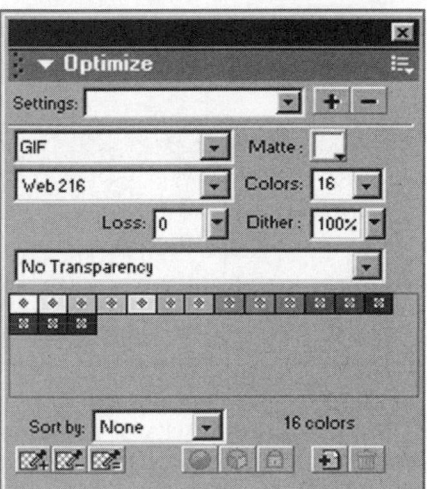

12. Your other option is to increase the number of colors. You can increase this to any value by typing something directly into the requester, but you should only increase it by powers of two (2, 4, 16, 32, 64, 128, or 256) - this is a much more efficient use of the format due to the way computer memory works. Remove the dither, and try increasing the number of colors.

> Fireworks users watch out: Fireworks has a sneaky habit of setting the dithering back to 100% every time you change color settings!

13. You're probably quite disappointed, because whilst keeping to the web/web 216 palette, you'll notice practically no difference in quality at all. The leaf can only use some of the colors in the web-safe palette, and increasing the number just gives us access to colors that the leaf can't use (like more shades of pink, for example). To fix this, select Adaptive instead of Web/Web216 and you will see a marked improvement, even at 16 colors. This time, you are allowing the application to chose the closest 16 colors to go for, irrespective of whether they are web-safe or not.

> *If we had created this image from scratch, we could have made sure to stick to web-safe colors wherever possible if we were concerned about this issue.*

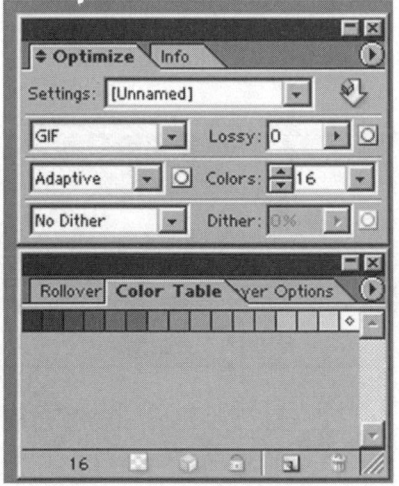 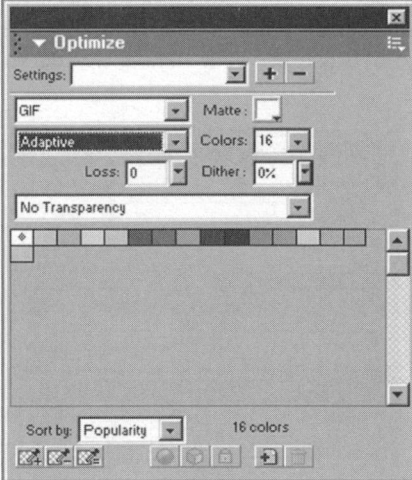

14. You can preview the results of the optimizations in any version of the leaf. Photoshop users, select the image by clicking on it, Ctrl/right-click and select Preview in followed by the name of the browser you want to use. Fireworks users, select File > Preview In Browser... followed by the browser you want to use. (Fireworks users can also hit F12 to go straight to the primary browser).

> *Leave your Fireworks or Photoshop window open for the moment, as we'll be coming back to this exercise shortly in the JPEG section.*

Safe colors with GIFs

Turning off web-safe color as we've just done gives a better image quality, but means that low-end computers will see odd colors (you can see from the colors in the display with a dot in them that only the white is web-safe). The best way around this is compromise. Forcing the main details in your image to be built of web-safe colors makes sure that the image will show the main details on all screens, and better machines will show the additional detail.

This is the core concept of **graceful degradation** at work again - everyone will see the minimum site that presents the basic content, but other users may see enhancements. To do this, you have to identify the major colors in the image, and then force them to become web-safe colors. The remaining colors will then be either remapped to the closest web-safe color for minimum systems (thus losing some detail) or shown as you see them on your machine.

To force a color to go to the nearest web-safe color, select the color, and then hit the icon at the bottom of the box – it's a three-colored cube in Photoshop, and a black and white cube in Fireworks (the cursor is pointing at them in both the screenshots). The selected color will then be forced to the nearest web color, and you can see this by the little icons that will appear over the colors.

When you do this, note that the overall coloring of the image may change. Whether this should worry you or not is down to the image: if the final leaf is more orange than the original, this probably won't matter, but a face that becomes bluer may cause problems!

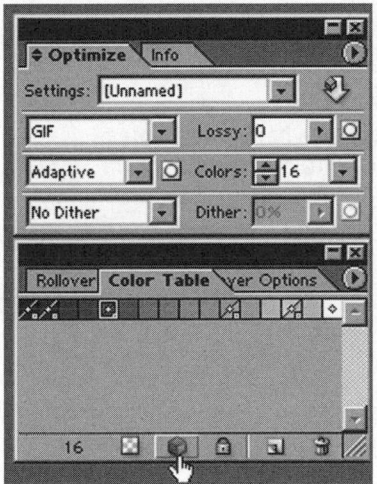 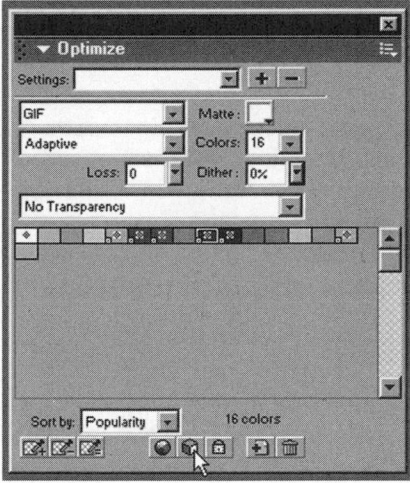

You can also consider making the GIF lossy, which means the image loses some information and detail. Although GIF is not usually a lossy format, you can tell the conversion process to lose data at the expense of detail. To make your GIF conversion lossy, enter a percentage value of 28% in the Lossy or Loss values boxes.

As with all things, you have to play about with all three settings (number of colors, level of dithering and allowable lossiness) to reach a compromise. The settings shown on the next page gave me an acceptable image quality and a file size of about 12KB.

I have given the image:

- A certain amount of lossiness, because the leaf has a lot of random textures in it in any case, and this tends to hide the effects of lossiness. Lossy GIFs will show up their shortcomings more if you have large areas of solid color.
- An adaptive color palette. The image uses lots of autumnal yellows, and there are very few of those in the fixed web-safe palette
- Diffusion noise because it's the best dither for this image; it compresses better than noise dither and isn't as apparent as patterned dither.

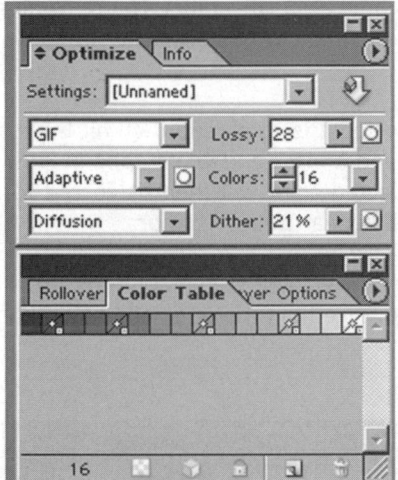
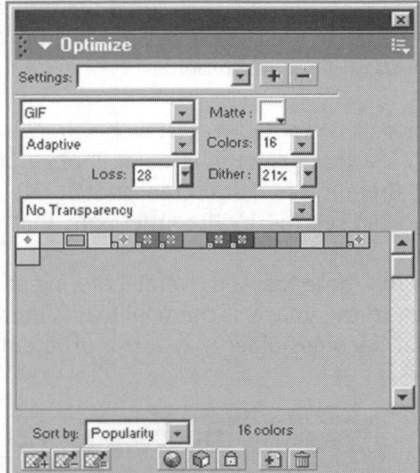

It's given us a chance to see a lot of the options, but we're being a bit unfair on the GIF, because the leaf isn't the best sort of image to convert to GIF. In most cases, you'll use GIF for simple two-to-ten color logos, using no dither and no lossiness, like this one:

Once you've sorted it to your satisfaction, you can export your GIF by making sure it's still selected in the 4-up view (click on it if it isn't) and selecting File > Save Optimized in Photoshop, or File > Export in Fireworks. Your file will be saved with a .gif extension. Some operating systems will hide the extension, so if you want to clearly delineate the difference between this and leaf.tif, save it as leaf_gif.

The Joint Photographic Experts Group Format (JPEG)

As its name suggests, the JPEG format was designed for use with photographs. The JPEG format works well with photographs and other real-world images, artwork based on real-life scenes, and images that contain complex color variations and textures. They don't work well with the sharp change of colors we saw in the logo in the last section.

 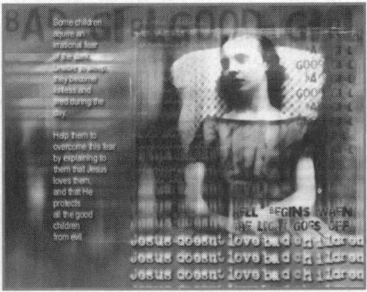 

The greatest advantages of the JPEG are its ability to display the full range of colors perceived by the human eye, and the fact that it allows you to set custom compression rates, allowing you to fine tune the trade-off between image quality and file size. The downside of JPEG is that the compression is lossy, meaning that once you optimize an image using the JPEG format, the final image contains less information than the original, and - unless you save the original - you lose this discarded information for good. This means that you should only use JPEG s to create the final web-ready images, and not any work in progress or original source files, which you should save as TIF or PSD files.

In summary, you would use a JPEG where:
- You want to make sure that everyone will be able to view an image that shows realistic full-color images
- You are using anti-aliased images (more on this when we look at compression later)

You wouldn't use a JPEG where:
- You have an image with heavily contrasting edges such as text or bright logos
- You need transparency or motion

Remember: you should never save your source or working files as JPEGs. Apart from issues with it being lossy, many designers have reported that it is a poor format when archiving data. If your archiving software uses its own compression routines before it burns your data onto backing storage, there is a fair probability that one or two of your JPEGs will corrupt.

Using JPEGs

1.   If you've got your Fireworks or Photoshop window still open from the GIF exercise, return to it now. If not, then follow steps 1-7 of that exercise again to open the leaf image, and crop it down to a better size.

2.   Assuming you've left the first leaf image as it should be, and the next has your GIF experimentations on it, select the next leaf image and this time select JPEG from the drop-down. Then select Low or JPEG - Smaller File from the Settings drop-down. Notice that neither application presents us with a color table or palette. This is because the JPEG format can always handle full 24-bit color.

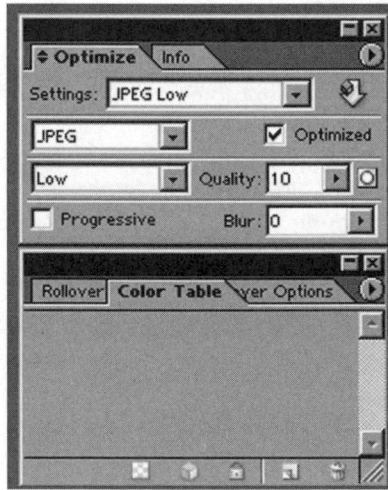 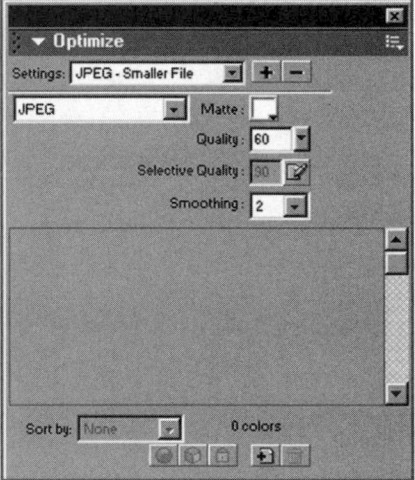

3.   Here, you have two settings to play with: **Quality** and **Smoothing/Blur**. The quality setting is a trade between file size and quality, with 100 being best quality, and 0 being worst. A quality setting of 50 is a good starting point; so try that for the moment.

4.   The Smoothing/Blur setting allows you to blur the image slightly before optimizing. JPEG prefers gradations of colors to sharp edges, so adding a blur helps stop the "noise" caused by JPEG trying to cope with large changes in contrast. It does however make the image more indistinct – which you go for depends on the image. Add a small amount of blurring to our leaf.

We can show this easily by looking at something that JPEG is particularly *bad* at; graphics that also contain text. Text has all the things that JPEG doesn't like:

- Big contrasts (black text, white background or other mutually contrasting colors) and no graduations of color
- Large areas of solid colors
- Content that doesn't like being blurred because it then becomes unreadable

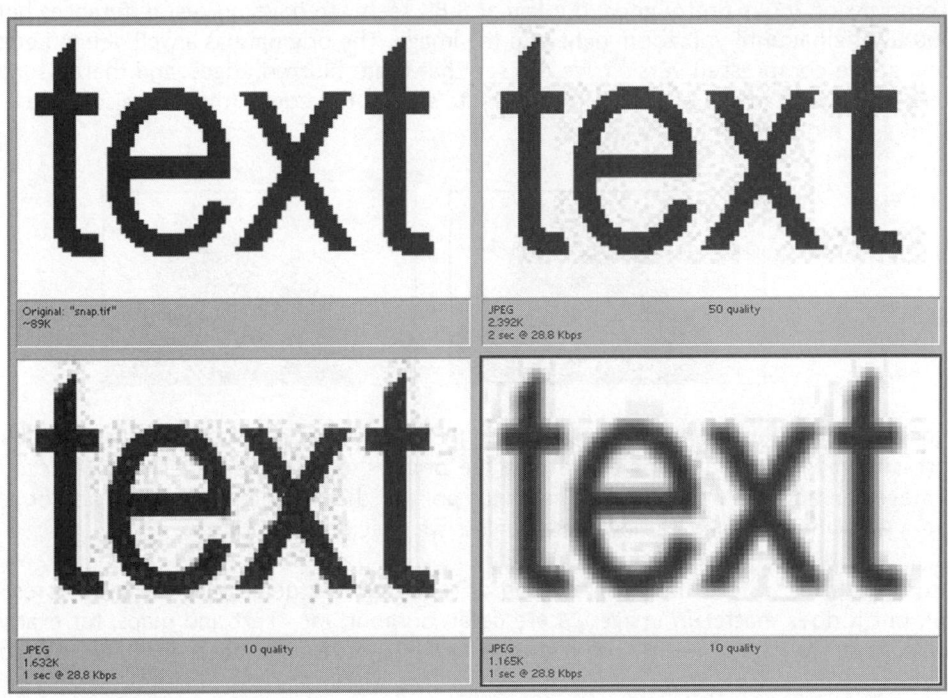

The top left image is the original, crisp text. The top right image is a JPEG at a quality setting of 50. It looks OK, but we're up to 2.39KB for just one simple word of text. For a big paragraph of the same text, we're looking at 100KB +. If we go right down to a quality of 10 (bottom left), we start to see noise (the random gray pixels) around the edges of the text. We can get rid of these if we kill the sharp edges and instead force a graduation via blurring (bottom right) but this causes another problem; our text is now blurred!

5. To save your compressed JPEG, select it and (as with your GIF) choose File > Save Optimized in Photoshop, or File > Export in Fireworks.

> *You should never recompress a JPEG. Start from a TIFF or 24-bit PNG, or you'll get inefficient compression. Equally, never recompress a GIF as a JPEG (or vice versa, except for high-quality JPEGs), for the same reason. This is another good reason why you shouldn't save your source files in JPEG or GIF format.*

The compression looks pretty good: the leaf at 6-8K seems to have no real differences between it and the 500KB original until you zoom right into the image. The original has a well defined edge, but when we look at the compressed version, we can see that it has blurred edges, and there's some odd pixels created, which we can see especially on the white side of the edges (they are also there on the darker side, but well hidden).

 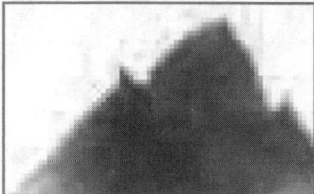

This shows up the pluses and minuses of using JPEGs. The plus point is that they work by making the compressed image appear to be as close to the original as possible by taking into account what the human eye can and can't see clearly. The minus point is that in doing this, it will add or remove pixels (unlike a GIF, which doesn't remove detail unless we specifically tell it to).

In natural pictures, where the brain is good at replacing lost detail that the eye misses, this doesn't matter, but it does matter in images where detail is important - text and maps, for example. In these circumstances, we have to either use high-quality JPEGs, or use the other formats we've looked at.

The images below contain some sample text. This image is full-quality:

- To stop the JPEG adding new pixels, we have to have a very high-quality image of around 70%:

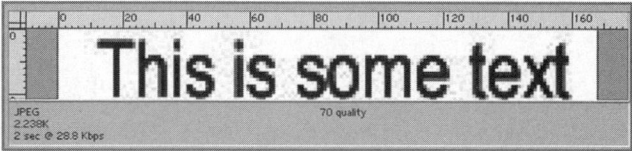

- As we saw earlier, if we go for low JPEG quality settings, we start to get extraneous pixels. These lose detail that may make the text difficult to read:

- The GIF format, on the other hand, compresses text much better, and doesn't change pixels around:

When you need to mix text and real-world graphics, it is *always* better to use JPEG for the image, and then add the text onto the web page separately with HTML. This uses the advantages of the JPEG format, and avoids its pitfalls.

The Portable Network Graphics Format (PNG-8 and PNG-24)

There are two types of PNG (pronounced 'ping' or just P-N-G), PNG-8, which can handle 256 colors and is much like a GIF, and the PNG-24, which produces a higher quality image.

The PNG-8 is a recent format that attempts to make up for the failings in the GIF format. The creators of the PNG-8 format state that it will usually give you a 5-20% improvement over the same GIF settings, although occasionally GIF does come out better (when it does, it is usually a sign that you would be better off using a JPEG!).

PNG-8 and PNG-24 are effectively different image formats, and many designers have been put off using PNG in the past, after finding that the format creates *bigger* files than the same GIF file. This is usually a result of compressing an image into a PNG-24, rather than reducing the number of colors to 256 (or less) and using a PNG-8. You should *never* use PNG not knowing which of the two you're actually compressing to, because the difference in file size can be up to an order of fifty different!

PNG also supports better transparency features than the GIF, and has some support for cross-platform consistency in that – unlike a GIF - it can allow for the differences in brightness or **gamma** between PC and Mac machines. The reduction in file size over a GIF must be weighed against the lower level of browser support in older browsers for PNG.

Browser support for PNG as a one-for-one GIF alternative is good for all current browsers, except that its more advanced features (such as better transparency) are not supported in the most prevalent browser – Internet Explorer for Windows. There is therefore currently no compelling reason to use PNG-8 over GIFs when catering for a general web audience. Although PNG-8 is significantly better than GIF overall, Explorer for Windows users can only really make use of the modestly better compression rate, which isn't a good enough reason for most web designers to change over.

PNG is a lossless format, compressing files without losing any data. Unfortunately, this means less efficient compression rates than the JPEG, which usually beats PNG compression rates for photographs.

In the past, some designers have noticed that their Windows-based browsers never showed PNG files. This was not due to lack of support, but a bug in Macromedia Fireworks 4, which fouled up the browser PNG support in some cases. If your machine has this problem, fix it by selecting Start > Run... *and entering* `regsvr32 thumbvw` *in the dialog that appears.*

So when would you use this rather accurate, but relatively bulky format? Well, if you are creating pages that contain detailed images (works of art, maps, technical/medical images) that you expect the user to want to print to a high quality, PNG-24 is an option. The PNG is the favored format of Fireworks MX: if you use Fireworks, then you'll usually store your work in progress and your source files as a PNG-24.

In summary, you would use a PNG where:
- You want a smaller image than a GIF and are not worried about people using older browsers
- You want a transparent full-color image
- You want an image that allows for the differences in gamma levels between a Mac and a PC

You wouldn't use a PNG where:
- You were worried about compatibility with old browsers
- You wanted to use the more advanced features of PNG for IE for Windows

Using PNGs

If you select your fourth leaf, and select PNG-8 from the Settings menu, you'll find much the same options as we saw with GIFs earlier. Select PNG-24, and you'll find much fewer options: it can display all the colors it needs anyway, so there's no need for Dither settings and so on.

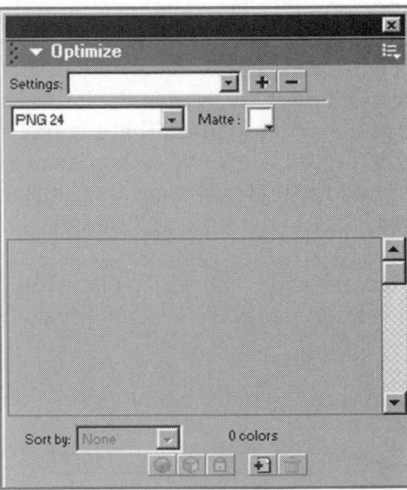

> *There is a PNG-32 mode available in Fireworks. You wouldn't use this format on the Web, because the human eye struggles to even perceive the difference between 24-bit color and 32-bit color. Only use this format if you expect folks to download your images from your site and use them in an image-editing program. When mixing pixels in Photoshop (and to a much lesser extent, Fireworks), the extra amount of color information makes for more accurate color processing during intermediate steps.*

Exporting to file size

Sometimes you're not really bothered about which format you use, just that you need to create an image of a given size. For example, a banner advert is usually constrained to being no more than 12KB. Both Photoshop and Fireworks offer you easy ways to achieve this. Fireworks users read on, Photoshop users skip to the next heading.

In Fireworks...

1. Select File > Export Preview… and then the file format you want to use in the Format drop-down menu.

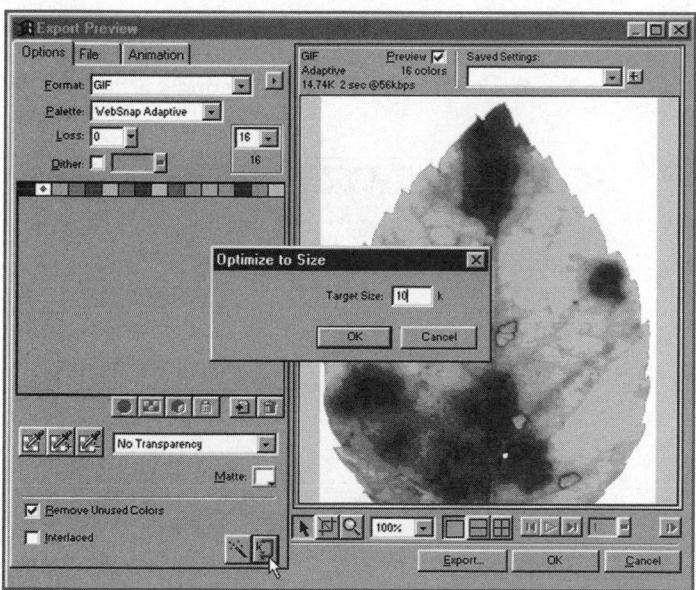

2. Hit the Optimize to size wizard icon (it's the one the cursor is over in the screenshot), and enter your target size in the Optimize to Size requester that appears.

3. Once you're happy with the result (and you can tweak it slightly in this window if you are not), hit the Export... button.

In Photoshop

1. Select Optimize to File Size in the menu for the Optimize panel (click on the little arrow to the top right to open it).

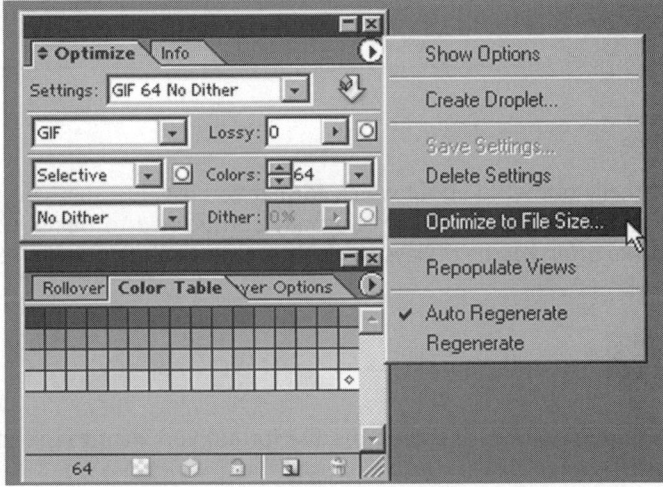

2. The Optimze To File Size window will appear, and this allows you to select a target file size, as well as allowing you to choose between the current format or to let Photoshop Auto select. This last option gives good results (or at least provides a good starting point), so don't be shy!

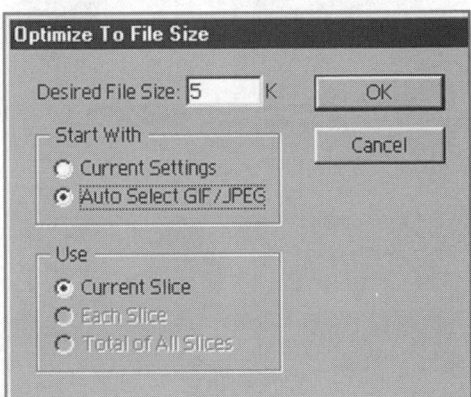

The Case Study: creating an 'Under Construction' page

So far in this chapter, we've looked at optimizing single images, but the Mondo site rarely uses single graphics in isolation. Instead, it uses a slightly more involved process where we use **slices**, which we'll be looking at in **Chapter 10.**

There are, however, a few pages that only use a single image. One page we don't have yet is a 'work in progress' or 'under construction' page to put up on the Web while we sort the rest of the site out.

If you do a search for 'under construction' in any of the search engines, you will see a multitude of sites with a 'work in progress' page. The trouble with many of them is that you don't know whether the page has been there for two days or two years – and people tend not to return unless you tell them when it will change.

Putting the launch date on the construction page is therefore recommended, as it tells the casual browser when to come back, and also implies to them that you *really* are building a site (assuming of course, that the said launch date isn't given as September 23rd 1997!).

There are lots of sites out there that use pre-built graphics for an 'under construction' page, but it's always a good idea to build a page in keeping with the final site design, because it implies that you know how to design, and suggests that the final site is going to be more than a bunch of shareware graphics.

Making the 'Under Construction' page

This is the Mondo logo that appears on many of the pages of the final site – you can find it in the download files as `mon_logo.tif`. We'll use this as the basis of our page. Currently, this file is 18-19KB, which isn't too bad, but I'm sure we can get it down to less than 2KB.

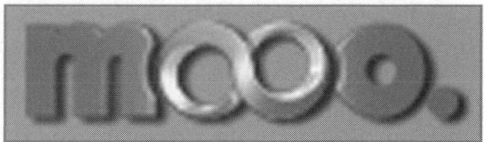

1. Open the file in Fireworks or Photoshop (go straight into ImageReady) and use the 4-Up tab to have a play around with different formats. Leave the original at the top left, and make sure to try both web-safe and non web-safe GIF settings. It's a fairly small image, so make sure you zoom in to see the full effects of your optimization.

> *You've probably already worked out that the GIF format will work out best here because we've got a reduced palette and a fairly big solid background area, and it's not a photographic or natural photograph of the kind JPEG loves.*

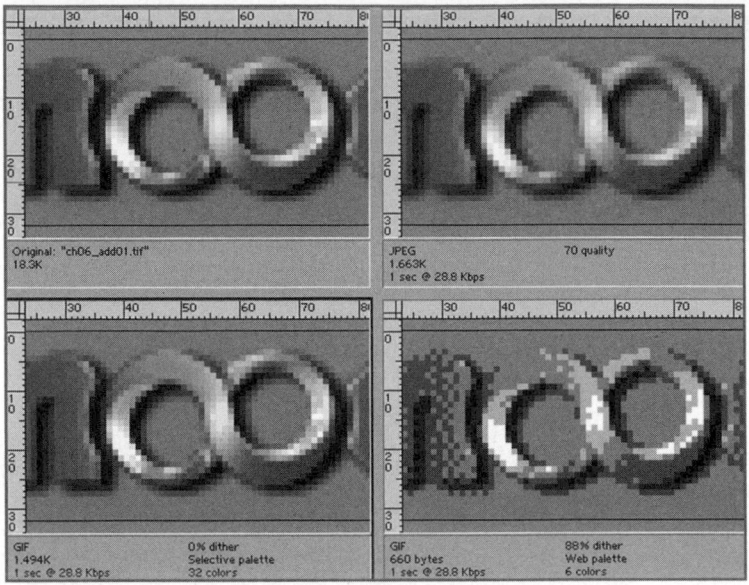

Compared to the original (top left)

- PNG-8 (not shown) did not do too well, being bigger than the same quality GIF image.
- JPEG (top right) came out badly, as expected.
- When forced to use the standard web palette, GIF (bottom right) resorted to dithering, giving a very poor-looking image.
- GIF using 32 colors of its own choosing (bottom left) gave the best likeness, and took the target 'less than 2KB' to do it.

2. The story isn't finished, because we need to be sure that the gray in the image is the same as the background of our web page (which will be #999999, as per the rest of the site so far). Photoshop users, go to the next step, Fireworks users go to step 4.

3. Select the Eyedropper ✒ tool and click on a background pixel. In the Color window (you may have to change from the Swatches tab to the Color tab), you should see the RGB values 99, 99, 99 appear (these values are all in hexadecimal). Click on several places on the background to make sure that the background is the same color throughout.

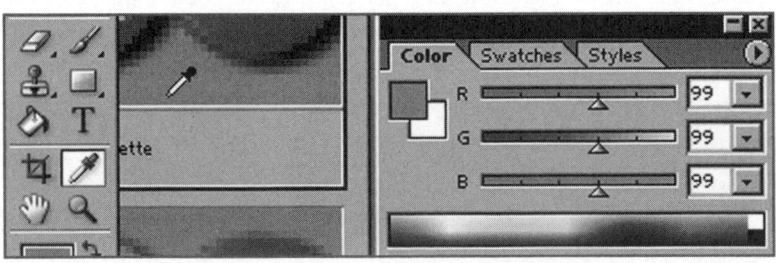

4. Fireworks users, click on the fill color in the toolbox (just under the Colors heading). The cursor will turn into an eyedropper. As you roll over the image, the color brick and hexadecimal value at the top left of the color picker pop-up will change to reflect the color currently under the eye dropper. Roll over several parts of the background and check that the color stays as #999999.

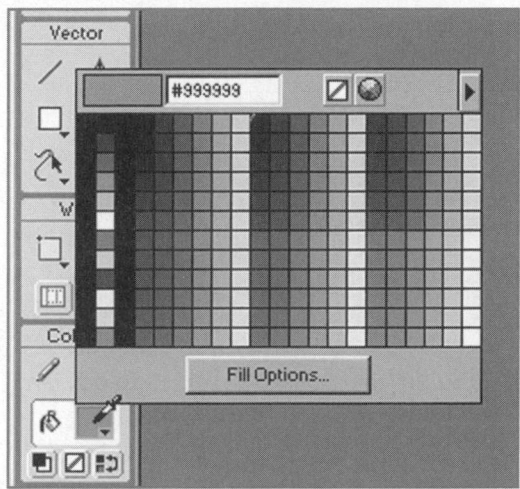

5. Finally, we need to save our file. With the GIF selected (click on the bottom right frame of the 4-up view) select File > Save Optimized in ImageReady, and File > Export in Fireworks, and save the file in your mondoSkeleton folder.

6. The first file that the browser will go to when a user goes to www.yoursite.com/ is www.yoursite.com/index.html, we need to name the 'under construction' page index.html. First though, rename the current index.html in the mondoSkeleton directory dev.html.

7. OK, we're ready for the HTML. We're going to use a variation on the two-table layout we saw in the last chapter – the new lines are in bold. Create the following, (or have a look at our version):

```
<html>
<head>
<title>welcome to mondo</title>
<link href="mon_style.css" rel="stylesheet" type="text/css">
</head>

<body>

<!—TABLE MAIN CENTER - START—>
<table BORDER="0" CELLPADDING="0" CELLSPACING="0" WIDTH="100%"
HEIGHT="100%" ALIGN="CENTER">
        <tr><td>
        <!—TABLE MAIN DIMENSIONS - START—>
        <table BORDER="0" CELLPADDING="0" CELLSPACING="0"
        ➡ALIGN="CENTER">
            <tr><td>
```

continues overleaf

```
                                    <img src="mon_logo.gif"><br>
                                    <span CLASS = "title">Mondo is
                                    ➡coming</span><br><br>
                                    <span CLASS = "text">Site launch 29th January
                                    ➡1967</span>

                            </td></tr>
                    </table>
                    <!—table main dimensions - end—>
            </td></tr>
    </table>
    <!—table main center - end—>

    </body>
    </html>
```

8. Save this as `index.html` in the `mondoSkeleton` folder, and test it. You should see the following:

It's everything an 'under construction' page should be: short and succinct, but giving a flavor of the style of the site to come, while including the all-important launch date.... and not a road sign in sight! Well, OK, I know - the launch date has expired a little. It's actually my date of birth, but you can change it to something achievable and in the future.

If you want to upload this page at this point, check out Appendix A: Getting your work online.

Further JavaScript

What this chapter will do

This chapter will take you through all of the building blocks that make up a top-notch JavaScript. We'll learn about:

- Syntax
- Expressions
- Value Types
- Variables
- Loops
- Functions

More importantly, given that these terms probably scare the living daylights out of you at the moment, we'll see them in action, and see how we can use them make our web pages **interactive**.

What you will have learned by the end of this chapter

By the end of the chapter, you'll have a good grasp of JavaScript, and what it can offer your web design. You'll be able to start writing your own scripts, and – equally importantly – you'll be able to understand what is going on in other scripts, so that you can customize them.

> *If things go wrong with any of your JavaScripts in this chapter, don't forget to go and take a look at the* **Appendix B – Debugging**, *which shows you how to get your browser to tell you where the problem in your script is located.*

If you go to the popular web design award sites such as the Webbys (www.webbyawards.com), you will see that most mainstream sites are more than just text and graphics. Take sites such as the award winning *360 Degrees* HTML site (www.360degrees.org) for example. As well as the usual text links, there is also an odd graphic at the top right of the page:

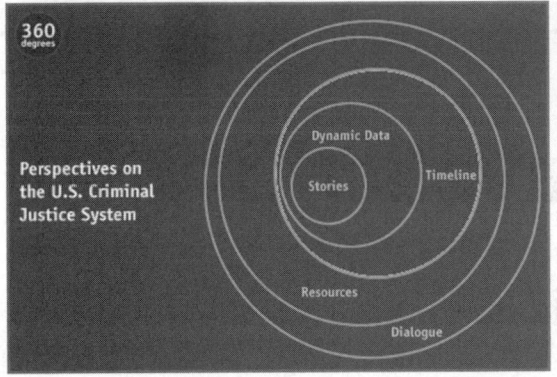 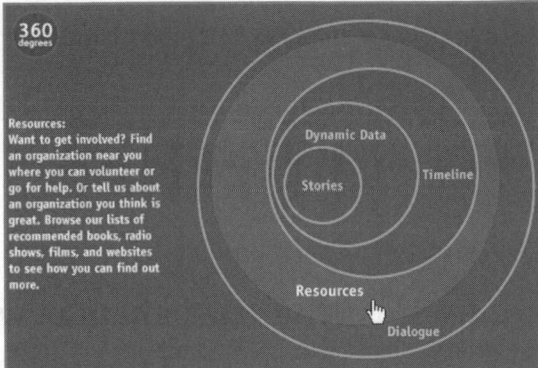

Roll the cursor over any of the circles and two things will happen. Firstly, a segment of the graphic will become highlighted, and secondly, a section of text describing the current option will appear to the left. Clicking on the highlighted area will navigate to the selected option.

This is nothing like the stuff we have created so far. The graphics *change*, and text can be made to appear and disappear in response to what we are doing. The word for all of this is **interactivity**; the site changes in response to user actions. To be able to do this, the site has to be more than just a collection of static text and graphics though; the page has to be programmed to do what it does.

> *It's not all about clever interfaces and pretty graphics; one of the main reasons that sites like 360 Degrees get awards is that they contain lots of relevant content.*

HTML and CSS are fine for site layout, but to do the sort of things we see above (and many of the things other Webby Award winners are able to do, such as interactive site searches, various interactive menu systems, and all sorts of other **non-static** page features) are at least in part to do with our other web design component, JavaScript.

JavaScript allows us to set up the page to respond to various **events** such as the cursor rolling over a graphic, or to allow the page to remember information that we have given to the page, so that it can act on that information. This includes being able to process our inputs, and make decisions based on the results. Taken together, these features can add interactivity to the page, but they can also do something deeper; it can allow the page to react in an apparently intelligent way.

We have already looked at the basics of JavaScript, but we actually bypassed a lot of the power of JavaScript so that we could introduce it early in the book. Now is when we'll really start to put it through its paces. To do this, we have to know some of the fundamental rules and techniques of programming in JavaScript. This chapter is therefore a little detour into the world of programming, before we get back onto the main road in the following chapters and start to apply what we learn here.

Syntax

Language has structure. When I speak to you, you will understand what I am saying if you know the rules of spoken English. There are two things you have to know for this to take place:

- You have to have to know enough of the English vocabulary to understand the meaning of my individual words.

- You have to understand the structure of my sentences to know what I am saying. This is called **syntax**, and it literally means 'to put in order' (from the root Greek *syn* – together, and *tassein* – to put in order).

For example, if I wanted to tell you...

```
I walked to the meeting.
```

...you know it is I that did the walking, not the meeting. You know this because of the relative relationship between *I walked* and *meeting*.

As well as having different words to express the same meaning, different human languages also have different syntax. For example, many Asian languages would express verbs, nouns and adjectives in a different order, so that if you applied the syntax of these languages, but converted the individual words into English, you would still see a different sentence:

```
To the meeting I walked.
```

Although different human languages use different words, it is actually the *syntax* changes that make languages truly different. Human languages are very diverse, allowing subtle changes in meaning, and it is the rules of syntax rather than vocabulary that allow this richness. It is also syntax that makes new languages hard to understand, because there are so many subtle rules in the *use* of words.

Computers also have languages, and the languages naturally have syntax. The cool thing about computers is that they don't need to be told subtle things, but need explicit instructions of the *do this, do this, do this, and then do this* variety. This means that the syntax of computer languages is simple - the creators want you to be able to pick it up in a matter of hours, rather than the fifteen years the English language requires.

This total simplicity wrong-foots many designers when they come to coding, because they see this simplicity as strange. Bear with it though, and remember that it looks different from any human languages you know because it is *much simpler*.

The other fundamental difference between a computer language and a human language is purpose. Human languages are used to communicate, but computer languages are used to instruct, and the syntax reflects this.

JavaScript syntax

The good news is that JavaScript has very few rules you need to know about before you can string its vocabulary into meaningful sections. The bad news is that although JavaScript has fewer rules, you do have to stick to them. In spoken English, the odd mispronunciation causes no real problem, but in computer languages it usually involves something much more serious. In our case, it means the JavaScript will do either nothing, only partially do what you want, or do the wrong thing.

The instruction

The most basic element of syntax is an **instruction**, and an instruction's syntax looks like this:

```
this is a line of JavaScript;
```

Why use semi-colons at the end? Well, computers are precise, and cannot handle anything that can have a potentially confusing dual meaning. Other potential 'end of line' signifiers are spaces and full stops, but these are already used for other things within the line (spaces are used to separate keywords from each other, and the full stop is used in the dot notation we've already seen in **Chapter 3**). A semi-colon is used because it is not used anywhere else.

A series of instructions would look like this (and we saw this sort of thing in **Chapter 3**):

```
do this;
then do this;
and then do this;
```

The JavaScript parser would read up to the first semi-colon and take what it had up to that point as an instruction. It would act on this, and when it had completed the task that this instruction defined, it would read the next bit of text until it met another semi-colon, and so on.

Because the semi-colon denotes the end of an instruction, you don't necessarily have to start each instruction on a new line. You can for example do this:

```
do this; then do this; and then do this;
```

The instruction block

The block is a sequence of related instructions. To define a block, you simply enclose it in curly brackets:

```
{
do this;
then do this;
and then do this;
}
```

Notice that neither of the curly brackets ends with a semi-colon. This is because they are not instructions themselves, but simply a way of structuring groups of instructions into blocks.

There are various other ways that you can format the line breaks and white spaces around a block, including:

```
{     do this;
then do this;
and then do this;   }
```

Or:

```
{ do this; then do this; and then do this; }
```

These are possible because the line returns are not the thing that the JavaScript parser is looking for when it looks for each instruction; it is simply looking for the semi-colon at the end of each instruction.

A block alone is not useful. What is important is the overall structure you put *around* the block, and this allows you to do things like conditionally execute the block (only run the block if certain conditions are present) or loop round the block (keep repeating the block for a defined number of times). There are a number of different types of block we can define:

```
if (condition exists) {
    do this;
    do this;
    do this;
}
```

The block that follows is called a **decision**. If the `condition exists` is found to be true, then the block is run through. If the `condition exists` is found to be false, then the block is skipped. By selecting which code we run, we can make our code do different things in different conditions.

```
for (as long as condition exists) {
    do this;
    do this;
    do this;
}
```

This block is an example of a **loop**. When it sees a loop block, JavaScript will keep going back up to the top of the block and re-running all the instructions as long as the `condition exists` remains true. This allows you to do things like this:

```
for (as long as I have sweets) {
eat a sweet;
}
brush my teeth;
```

We will loop though the block, getting fatter. As soon as we have no more sweets, we get out of the loop and carry on with the next instruction, which tells us to brush our teeth.

Loops are a fundamental part of programming. They allow us to tell the computer to carry out repetitive tasks without writing loads of code. A loop block could only contain six instructions, but if it loops 1000 times, the computer will actually run 6000 instructions.

Creating a new HTML document with JavaScript

You can create web pages from scratch using JavaScript, and we'll be doing this several times in this chapter. To create a web page from scratch, you first have to open a 'document stream' by using JavaScript to write something to a HTML page. Once this is done, you can write into the document, and then close the stream. If the document is written to after it has been closed, a new document is started, clearing the existing content.

`document.close()` closes a document stream, and `document.write()` adds text to a currently open document, or clears the existing document and starts a new one if the document is currently closed. `document.writeln()` is the same as `document.write()`, except that a `<br>` or line return is added to the end of every line automatically.

Our final listing uses these methods to create HTML documents on the fly. You don't have to type all this out: just use the `docwrite.html` document from the source files.

```
<html>

<head>
     <title>document example</title>
</head>

<body>
     <div align = "Center"><br>

             <h3>click on a link...</h3>

             <a href="javascript:
                     newWin = window.open('', 'popup', 'height=200,
                     ➥width=200');
                     newWin.document.write('
                             <html>
                                     <head>
                                             <title>.::window 1::.</title>
                                     </head>

                                     <body>
                                             <h3>This is the link 1 document</h3>
                                             <p>This window is generated by
                                             JavaScript.</p>
                                     </body>
                             </html>
                     ');
                     newWin.document.close();
                     newWin.document.bgColor = '#DD8000';
```

```
               newWin.document.fgColor = '#FFEEEE';
               newWin.focus();
               void 0;
          ">window 1</a><br><br>

          <a href="javascript:
               newWin = window.open('', 'popup', 'height=200,
               width=200');
               newWin.document.write('
                    <html>
                         <head>
                              <title>.::window 2::.</title>
                         </head>

                         <body>
                              <h3>This is the second document</h3>
                              <p>This window is generated by
                              JavaScript.</p>
                         </body>
                    </html>
               ');
               newWin.document.close();
               newWin.document.bgColor = '#AACC00';
               newWin.document.fgColor = '#EEFFEE';
               newWin.focus();
               void 0;
          ">window 2</a><br><br>


     </body>

     </html>
```

If you test this HTML in a browser, you will see that the HTML first generates some formatted text as shown:

click on a link...

window 1

window 2

Depending on which of the two links you click on, you will see one of the two focused pop-ups as shown:

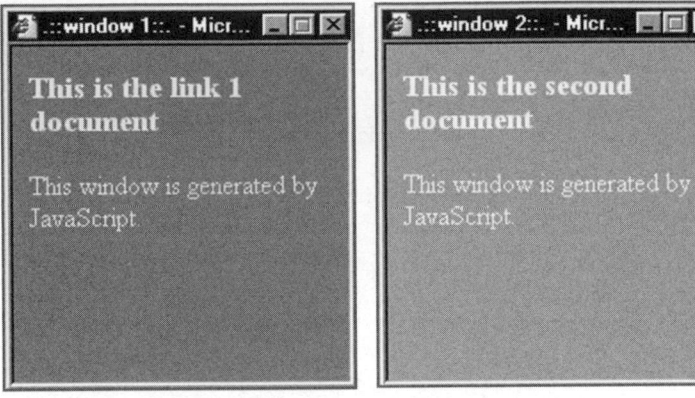

The original page is created by the boring old HTML formatted text:

```
<html>

<head>
     <title>document example</title>
</head>

<body>
     <div align = "Center"><br>

             <h3>click on a link...</h3>

             ">window 1</a><br><br>

             ">window 2</a><br><br>

</body>

</html>
```

The important part is the hrefs for the two <a> links. Both contain similar JavaScript that generates the HTML for the two pop-ups. The first line opens a new pop-up window 200 pixels square:

```
newWin = window.open('', 'popup', 'height=200, width=200');
```

Because we haven't defined any other attribute for the pop-up, they are assumed to be set to no, so no chrome appears at all, and the windows are not resizable. This new window is called popup and has a JavaScript instance name of newWin. Because both links open the same window, clicking either of the two links will open this window, but subsequent clicks will be written into the same window, so you only ever have one pop-up (which is a nice touch for most users who hate pop-up clutter).

Line 2 is split up over several lines. It starts with the dot notation `newWin.document.write`, which is asking the browser to write some text into the document object in `newWin`, the currently empty window we have just created in line 1. This text is actually the HTML that we want to put into the pop-up, and it defines a title and some formatted text:

```
newWin.document.write('
       <html>
              <head>
                     <title>.::window 1::.</title>
              </head>

              <body>
                     <h3>This is the link 1 document</h3>
                     <p>This window is generated by JavaScript.</p>
              </body>
       </html>
');
```

Finally, we close the document stream we have just opened. This means that any further writes to the window will erase the content we have just sent to it, effectively giving us a new page. This means that the second link will appear in the same window, overwriting the first window.

```
newWin.document.close();
```

Now that we have our HTML page in the pop-up, I have also changed the background and foreground colors of the page using the appropriate properties of the document object:

```
newWin.document.bgColor = '#DD8000';
newWin.document.fgColor = '#FFEEEE';
```

To make everything look a little more professional, I have then given the pop-up focus. This is so that the pop-up isn't immediately lost behind the bigger parent window. Because the parent window is bigger, the user can easily get back to the original window simply by clicking on it.

```
newWin.focus();
```

To end the `href = javascript:` attribute, I have added the obligatory...

```
void 0;
```

...at the end to avoid corruption. Now that we've seen how this works, we can get on to the meat of the chapter, and learn about Expressions, Value Types, Variables, Loops and Functions.

Expressions

An expression is a term for anything that contains numbers, algebra, and operators, including:

```
3+7

(4+6)/2

(1/2)*3
```

> *In scripting, we use * for multiplication to avoid confusion between multiplication 'x' and the letter 'x'.*

You probably know the answers to all of these, but let's write it in code and get the browser to tell us. You'll remember the basic form of HTML that allows us to enter JavaScript from **Chapter 3** (here's a clue):

```
<html>

<head>
        <script language = "JavaScript">
            ...
            ...
        </script>
</head>


<body>
</body>

</html>
```

Within the <head> ... </head> tags enter the code shown in bold:

```
        <head>
    <script language = "JavaScript">
        document.write(3+7, '<br>');
        document.write((4+6)/2, '<br>');
        document.write((1/2)*3, '<br>');
    </script>
        </head>
```

If you save this as expression.html and view it in a browser, you will see the following output:

```
10
5
1.5
```

How does this work? Well, we're using document.write to write things to the document being displayed by the browser. This method writes whatever is in the brackets to the browser document, having first evaluated any expression that it sees in the brackets. Let's look at one of our lines as a specific example:

```
document.write((1/2)*3, '<br>');
```

As implied here, you can write a list of things, each list item separated by a comma. The line above is exactly the same as:

```
document.write((1/2)*3);
document.write('<br>');
```

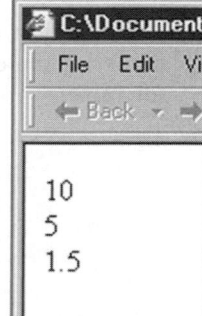

Whatever you send to the browser document is treated as HTML, so our three lines of `document.write`s will look like this:

> *Notice that our listing is simply a few instructions, each ending with a semi-colon, as per the standard syntax we talked about earlier.*

Value types

In JavaScript, there are three types of basic value. The first of these is **numerical** values, such as we've been using above. The next type is a **string** value, which is a series of values inside quote marks, `'sheep'`, for example. We've used these before, too.

> *As a refresher, recall that it's a good idea to use double quotes (" ") in HTML and single quotes (' ') in JavaScript, for the reasons mentioned in* **Chapter 3**.

Try amending your code above by enclosing the `3+7` in quotes, like so:

```
document.write('3+7', '<br>');
```

Why are we doing this? When we add quotes, we are creating a **string** value, where the browser will display the contents enclosed by quotes. Without any quotes around the value, the browser is free to evaluate the value, and change it by performing calculations or other actions on it.

So, the browser would take a look at `3+7`, and perform the calculation to give `10`, whereas '3+7' would result in the text `3+7` being displayed. The browser would look at text not contained in quotes and assume that it's a variable (more on these in a moment), so text that we want displayed is always contained in quotes.

You can add string values together:

```
<script language = "JavaScript">
      document.write('sheep' + 'dog');
```

```
        </script>
```

Would give you:

```
sheepdog
```

The final type of value is the **Boolean**. This is a logic state and can be either **true** or **false**. For example, on asking the question "am I wearing black today?" there can only be two answers: yes (or **true**), and no (or **false**).

> Booleans are named after the mathematician George Boole, who defined the theory that first included the logic values true and false.

For an expression to evaluate to a Boolean value (true or false), the expression can only be one thing: a **comparison**. There are several comparisons that can be made:

<	less than
<=	less than or equal
>	greater than
>=	greater than or equal
==	equals
!=	does not equal

Typical expressions using these would be:

```
5 < 4
5 > 4
2 >= 2
2 != '2'
```

Let's try them out. Change the code in the HTML document above to:

```
<script language = "JavaScript">
        document.write(5 < 4, '<br>');
        document.write(5 > 4, '<br>');
        document.write(2 >= 2, '<br>');
        document.write(2 != '2', '<br>');
</script>
```

This will give you:

```
false
true
true
false
```

...because...

- (5 is less than 4) is false
- (5 is greater than 4) is true
- (2 is greater or equal to 2) is true

The last one is a bit more difficult – we're asking whether 2 does **not** equal '2'. If it wasn't the same, then we'd get a true value. But because they are equal, we get a false value... watch out for the 'is that not so?' expressions; they can be real mind twisters!

You're probably thinking, "what use are all these value comparisons and expressions? – I could do all this much faster with a calculator", and you would be absolutely correct. The code we have written is useless at the moment. It only ever gives one set of fixed results every time you run it, and our time would be better spent just working it out ourselves: the answer is fixed and known when we come to write the script, so we could have just put 9 instead of 7+2.

The real usefulness of computation with code is when you write code that can solve a *general* problem. We don't want to keep being told what 7+2 is, but we might be interested in code that can add *any* two numbers. We know 5 is greater than 4, but we would rather a web page used Boolean logic to make itself smart enough to check if the number of CDs we have bought at the online record store is enough for us to get free postage and packaging yet.

What we really want to be able to do is form expressions that give us results that we cannot know at the time of writing the script. For this to be possible we need to move away from fixed values, and get acquainted with something a bit more flexible...

Variables

As humans, we are defined by what we know. I have written a few books, and remember how I did it, so my accrued memory of writing has left me with certain skills that make me an author.

More importantly, what we know affects the future. I know I can go to the local shop and buy some milk for my breakfast after finishing this section because I can remember how much money I have in my pocket (I had a look this morning at 7.30am, and as I write, it's now 8.45 and I'm starving!).

At a simple level, this is called *memory,* but at a more specific level, we have individual bits of information that tell us something about ourselves and stuff around us, such as how many brothers and sisters we have (for me, 2 and 0 respectively) or the results of the Boolean comparison 'is the money in my pocket > the cost of a carton of milk?' which is just about `true`.

Just as I needed to remember how much money I had, a computer needs to store values and results all the time so it knows what to do in the immediate future. The way this is done is by using a **variable**. A variable has two parts to it.

The first is its **name**. This allows us to differentiate between our variables. A variable name cannot consist of spaces, anything that might make JavaScript think the name is an expression, or anything that may make JavaScript think the name is actually an instruction or part of the syntax of the language.

So:

- `Shams milk money` is out, as no spaces are allowed: the JavaScript interpreter will see this as three different variables, but will raise an error because it doesn't look like a proper expression.

- `shams_milk_money` is OK, because we're using underscores in place of spaces.

- `ShamsMilkMoney` is OK.

- `shams-money` is wrong – it looks like we're trying to take `money` away from `Sham`, rather than naming anything

- `5cents` is out, because the leading `5` will make the JavaScript interpreter expect a number, and the cents part will throw it, leading to an error.

- `Cents5` is OK - the first letter in the name means JavaScript will expect a name, which is exactly what it's getting.

- `{money}` isn't good at all, as the curly brackets will spook JavaScript into thinking you have done something odd with an instruction block, because the curly brackets are reserved for defining code blocks.

Most web programmers tend to use variable names like the third one, where the variable is a short bit of text (with no spaces in it) that describes what the variable is, and where the second and subsequent words start with a capital letter to allow it to be readable. So you can have variable names like `myAnswer`, `todaysDate`, and so on.

The second part of a variable is its **value**. This can change in the same way the value of gas remaining in your car or money in your pocket varies (hence the "variable" name, as I'm sure you've worked out).

You can set a value by treating variables in several ways. The easiest is by equating variables to literal values like we were using in the last section. Create a new HTML file called `variable.html` as follows:

```
<html>

<head>
     <script language = "JavaScript">

             // set the variables...
             myAnswer = 'blancmange';
             gasRemaining = 34.654;
             browserIsNetscape = true;

             //output values...
             document.write(myAnswer,'<br>',gasRemaining,'<br>'
             ➡ ,browserIsNetscape);
     </script>
</head>
```

```
<body>
</body>

</html>
```

This will give you the following output if you test it:

```
blancmange
34.654
true
```

The first part of the script sets variable myAnswer to the string 'blancmange', the variable gasRemaining to the number 34.654, and the variable browserIsNetscape to the Boolean true. The second part (the document.write) displays the three variable values back to the browser.

Note that when we write the variables to the screen, we write the variable myAnswer to the browser, we see the **value** (blancmange) and not its *name*, myAnswer. It's important to see why we haven't output our values by referring to blancmange, 34.654 and true. This is what we have done every time so far, and this is because we were simply sending dumb string literals to the browser every time. This time we are not using quotes, and are instead sending dynamic variable values.

Except of course, we haven't made our variables very dynamic yet; they still always show the same old boring values. Let's change that to prove that we can make the browser work out stuff we can't work out easily...

Storing user input in variables

We can get our code to equate our variables to values from the user. Although they are still literals, *we don't know what they are when we write the code,* which is a first for us. We do this via the prompt() instruction, which does just what it suggests: it prompts the user for a value via a pop-up requester with a prompt message and a text input box.

prompt() takes the form:

```
variable = prompt(message, defaultValue);
```

Here, *variable* is the name of the variable you want to set, *message* is the text you want to prompt the user with, and *defaultValue* is the default value in the text box.

If you used the following:

```
userInput = prompt('prompt message', 'enter something here');
```

Like this:

```
<html>

<head>

<script language = "JavaScript">

// get user inputs...
    userInput1 = prompt('enter a value', '');
    userInput2 = prompt('enter an animal name', 'aardvark');

    //output values as an unordered HTML list...
    document.write('<br><br>You entered: <ul>','<li>', userInput1,
    ➡          '</li><li>', userInput2, '</li></ul>');

</script>

</head>

<body></body>

</html>
```

This script will prompt you for two values, which will be stored in the variables userInput1 and userInput2:

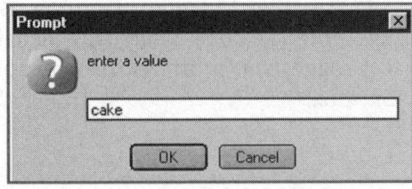

Once the script has got our values, the document.write() sends the values of our two variables to the browser, formatting them into an unordered list (via the <ul> and <li> tags):

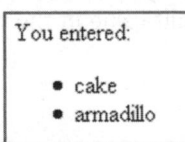

Notice that the browser doesn't make any checks on what you enter, so you could easily enter the number 6 as your animal, and nobody would be any the wiser. So now, although the page is using variables instead of fixed literals (allowing us to create different pages that depend on what the user does), it is not actually doing anything useful; we are simply echoing what the user tells us and adding nothing new. It would be better if we took the user inputs and did something useful to them before writing our outputs to the browser document.

> *Variables are the way you can get the web page to create new information rather than the fixed HTML we have used elsewhere. As soon as you start writing variables to the screen instead of fixed string literals, your script can adapt what is actually seen by the user on what has gone on before, or make it conditional.*

Loops

Loops are useful because they make the computer do all the work. They allow your code to do a lot of work by using a simple script that applies the same code many times, a process called **iteration**.

The `for()` loop has the following general form:

```
for(initialisation; conditional; update){
    // do this block as long as the
    // conditional expression is true...
}
```

The `for` loop uses a variable to control how many times it loops, and this is called the **loop variable**. The starting value of this loop is set with the *initialization* value, and it is updated at the end of every loop by running the *update* algorithm. Finally, the *conditional* expression is tested at the start of every loop. A plainer way of putting that would be that we give it a starting value, an instruction on when to run, and an instruction of what to add to the value each time the loop runs.

Try entering the following into the `<head>` section of a blank HTML document, for example:

```
<script language = "JavaScript">
        for(count=1; count<=12; count=count+1){
                document.write(count,'<br>');
        }
</script>
```

This will make the browser count to 12 – we set it to start at 1, and stop when at 12.

You don't have to count upwards or in 1s; you can just as easily count backwards or in other steps:

```
<script language = "JavaScript">
        for(count=12; count>=1; count=count-1){
                document.write(count,'<br>');
        }
</script>
```

...will output 12, 11, 10, 9, 8, 7, 6, 5, 4, 3, 2, 1.

```
<script language = "JavaScript">
        for(count=0; count<=10; count=count+2.5){
```

continues overleaf

```
                              document.write(count,'<br>');
                    }
          </script>
```

...will output 0, 2.5, 5, 7.5 ,10.

A good shortcut to remember when using the `for()` loop is that:

`count = count+1`

...can also be written:

`count++`

(It's the same for count = `count-1`, which is the same as `count--`).

This is like this purely because coders add one to a variable so often that someone created a quicker way of writing it. It doesn't result in noticeably faster code, so if you prefer the longhand way because it's more obvious to you, you can just go with that.

I passed Math at college but hate even checking my change after buying a soda. I need a calculator if I ever need to get serious with numbers. Let's get the browser involved in sorting out my weakness: supposing I wanted to enter a number and make it work out the times table of that number from 1 to 1000.

What we need to do is prompt for the number called (say) `userInput`, and keep multiplying it by 1, 2, 3, 4... and so on, each time displaying the result until the result is more than 1000. The following should achieve this:

```
<html>

<head>
      <script language = "JavaScript">

              // Set up variables...
              userInput = prompt('enter a number greater than zero', '1');
              userInput = Number(userInput);
              timesTable = 0;

              document.write('<h3>', userInput, ' times table</h3>')
              for(count=1; count<=12; count++){
                      timesTable = userInput*count;
                      document.write(count,' x ', userInput, ' = ',
                      ➥timesTable,'<br>');
              }

      </script>
</head>
```

```
<body>
</body>

</html>
```

Our script sets up a user input variable `userInput` and two other variables, `timesTable` (which it sets to 0) and `count` (which it sets to 1). We have a slight problem with entering numbers, in that JavaScript will assume that anything entered is a string if it has a choice. We can fix this by forcing a string to be read as a number by using `Number()`, which will try to read anything in the brackets as a number, so we can make sure that whatever the user enters is treated as a number with `userInput   = Number(userInput);`.

Once the user enters a value for `userInput`, the script displays some text in the browser, and runs these two lines:

```
timesTable = userInput*count
count = count+1
```

The result of the calculation is then displayed in the browser. Say the user enters a 6, then this will be calculated the first time:

```
timesTable = 6*1
```

The line in bold in the code listing above is what actually tells the loop to run what follows after the first time – that is, after the initialization value is 1. We tell the loop to run when this value is less than or equal to 12.

How does it remember how many times we've run through? Well, the final value is the update value, and we simply add 1 each time the loop runs. This value is also used to determine what we multiply the originally input number by, so on the first time through the loop, the number gets multiplied by one, on the next it gets multiplied by two, and so on. This stops after the twelfth loop (when the user input number has been multiplied twelve times), as `count` no longer equals a value of 12 or less, and so the loop stops.

Functions

If we just stick to basic instructions and blocks, we come across a pretty insurmountable problem in our syntax; our language can only solve *linear problems*, where the problem is solved by performing a fixed number of steps in a fixed order. Real-life isn't like that, though.

Say I was writing a script to make myself coffee, then I'd have to add a line to add some decaffeinated coffee powder:

```
add 1 teaspoon of decaffCoffee;
```

In real life, I want to go for something a little stronger after certain conditions:

```
if (I went out last night and woke up with a bad head){
    add 2 teaspoons of coffee;
}else{
    add 1 teaspoon of decaffCoffee;
}
```

The first version always gives me the same healthy start to the day, and is a linear solution. The second code *conditionally* makes either standard decaffeinated or a strongly caffeinated cup of coffee, depending on whether I'm drinking coffee for pleasure or medication. This makes the code non-linear; the number of steps and their order is no longer fixed, but conditional (in this case, on the state I'm in).

So now you're thinking "Eh?" Well, I don't blame you. You see, we're used to reading sequentially – starting at the beginning and working to the end, often in a fairly narrative fashion. We don't only go and read paragraph four after two hours have passed, and then return to read it every two hours.

Computer languages are not just a means for us to communicate to the computer; they are a *real-time definition of what the computer needs to do*. When we write a video game, we don't tell it the rules of the game before it starts playing. Instead, we feed instructions at the same rate as which we want things to happen. It's a bit like a little drill sergeant who sits on your shoulder barking monosyllabic instructions in your ear as you try to navigate an assault course blindfolded:

Go LEFT NOW. STOP! WAIT! Turn right 45 degrees… MOVE! Go! Go! GO!

In our case, this would probably give us all nervous breakdowns before the end of the course. Unsurprisingly, it even causes problems for computers. Firstly, the computer reads the code in the same way as we read, starting from the top and ending at the bottom, such as **code listing A**. Here, we run 4 code blocks in sequence:

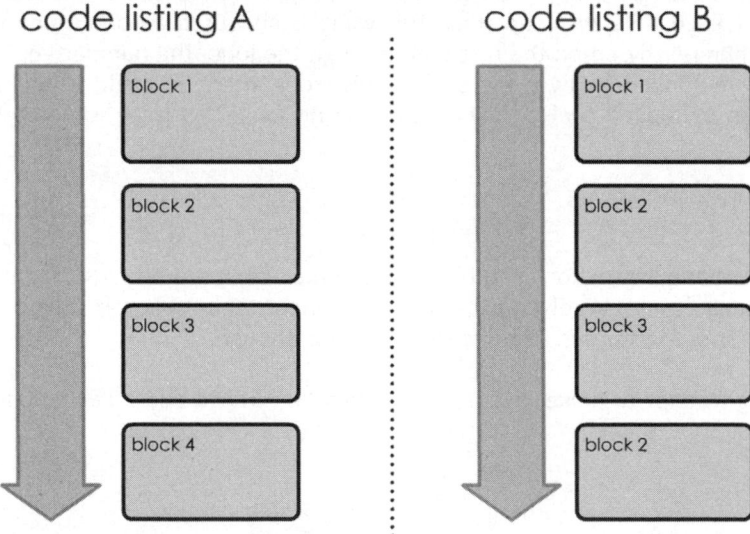

What if block 4 is actually the same as 2; in that case we'll actually want to write something like **code listing B**? The computer will read our blocks one after another sequentially down the listing, and we currently have no way of telling it "repeat code block 2 as block 4". So instead, we have the rather undesirable alternative of writing code block 2 again.

There must be a cunning plan that stops this repetition, right? Here's how it works. You define a block and give it a name. Say I called block 2 `fred`. Then, every time I say `fred`, the computer says "A-ha! He doesn't want me to execute the instruction `fred`, but the code block called `fred`".

code listing C

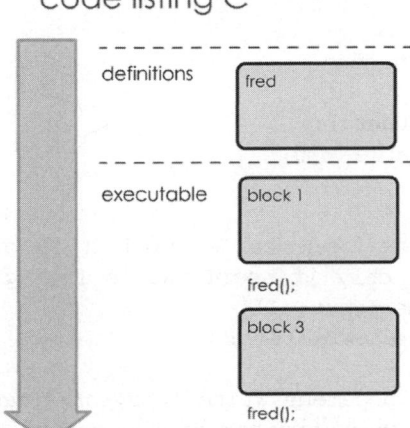

That's cool because our code now gets much shorter, because we're not repeating ourselves. If we look at our listing from the last section, we can rearrange it using **functions** so that our code blocks are now ordered in a more sensible way.

A function at its simplest level is a named block that is defined early on in the listing, and then called later in the main code. In other words, a function will do a specific task that we assign it, whenever we call it. This is extremely useful, as we'll be seeing in our **Case Study** section in a moment.

Here, we have two functions, `promptUser()` and `showTables()`, which are code sections to prompt the user to give us the variable `userInput` and display the times table respectively. If we look at the function `promptUser()` and the place where it is called, the instruction `promptUser();` we can see that nothing much has really changed; we have just moved things around a bit.

```html
<html>

<head>
    <script language = "JavaScript">

        // Functions

        function promptUser(){
            userInput = prompt('enter a number greater than zero',
            ➡'1');
            userInput = Number(userInput);
        }
```

continues overleaf

```
                    function showTable(){
                            while (timesTable<=1000){
                                    timesTable = userInput*count;
                                    document.write(count,' x ', userInput, ' = ',
                                    ➥ timesTable, '<br>');
                                    count = count+1;
                            }
                    }

                    // Main code

                    promptUser();
                    timesTable = 0;
                    count = 1;

                    // Write times table until it is over 1000
                    // but only if userInput is 1 or greater...
                    if (userInput>=1){
                            showTable();
                    }else{
                            document.write('<br><br>Please hit REFRESH and enter 1
                            ➥ or greater at the prompt.<br>Thanks!');
                    }

            </script>
      </head>


      <body>
      </body>


      </html>
```

The cool thing about functions is that we can easily reuse them. Stay with this function and change the first bit of our code to:

```
            <script language = "JavaScript">

                    // Functions

                    function promptUser(){
                            userInput = prompt('enter a number greater than zero',
                            ➥ '1');
                            userInput = Number(userInput);
                            return (userInput);
                    }
```

Now delete all the code after the `// Main code` comment, and add these three lines:

```
        // Main code

        userInput1 = promptUser();
        userInput2 = promptUser();
        document.write(userInput1*userInput2);


    </script>
```

This will multiply the first value you enter by the second value that you enter, and display the result. What's really important is that we're using the same function twice. Instead of using something like:

```
    userInput = prompt('enter a number greater than zero', '1');
    userInput1 = Number(userInput);
    userInput = prompt('enter a number greater than zero', '1');
    userInput2 = Number(userInput);
```

We set up our function, but don't run it. Then we equate it to `userInput1` and `userInput2`. When the browser sees `userInput1 = promptUser();`, it runs the function we've set up, which prompts the user for an input, turns it into a number, and then gets to this line:

```
    return (userInput);
```

When you use `return(something)`, the function ends, going back to where it was called, but it returns the value of `(something)` before it does so. So here, the function returns the user input number to `userInput1`, and finishes, allowing `userInput2` to run the whole process over again to gain another number from the user. Finally, the last line writes the result of the multiplication of the two numbers to the browser.

Now, the use of a function like this here has only really saved us writing the `prompt('enter a number greater than zero', '1')` line twice, but imagine how much it could save us if we were designing a site where we regularly needed to allow users to multiply two input numbers. We'll see just how useful a function can be in the practical world of web design when we use one to create all of our JavaScript pop-up windows in the **Case Study** section in a moment.

We've now learned the building blocks that make up JavaScript scripts:

- **Values** can be numerical, strings, or Booleans. They can be literal (unchanging), or they can be **Variables**.
- **Variables** store the value of a piece of (often changing) information for us.
- **Loops** are a way of running the same piece of code over and over, until a particular value is met.
- **Functions** are a way of setting a block of instructions for a particular task aside, so that we can run that set of instructions whenever we want to.

We'll now take a quick look at how we can separate out our longer scripts into a separate file to prevent confusion, before putting what we've learned in this chapter into practical use in our Case Study site.

> *Now that you understand the constituent parts of JavaScript, you're free to go and have a look at the many places on the Web that have banks of free JavaScripts for people to download and use. Try sites like:*
> http://www.hotscripts.com/JavaScript
> http://hotwired.lycos.com/webmonkey/programming/javascript/
> http://javascript.internet.com/

How to use external JavaScript files

As you've seen already, you can easily include JavaScript files inside your HTML document inside `<script language = JavaScript>` ... `</script>` tags. If you remember back to when we used some images, our HTML document didn't contain the images; it used the `<img>` tag to provide a *reference* to where the image could be found. We can do the same thing with a script created as a separate text file, by using tags like these:

```
<script language = "JavaScript" src= "myscript.js" >
</script>
```

Rather like the `<img>` tag, the `<script>` tag has been given a `src` (source) attribute, and this tells the browser where to find the actual script, which is simply a text file with a `.js` extension. So what are the advantages of this? Well, there are a few:

- You keep all your different code types separate. The HTML file contains only HTML, and the JS file contains only JavaScript. If you use a dedicated web design application, and open a file with a JS extension, it will immediately recognize what it's dealing with.

- You can use the same JS file in a number of HTML pages, and this makes the overall download for several pages smaller (the JS file is only loaded in for the first .html page that uses it).

- It allows you to build up a library of common JS files. If you have written a general bit of JavaScript then you only need to write it once, and simply refer to it from any later HTML page you decide to use it with. That's cool, because you only have to develop and debug your JS file once. This idea of writing code that you can use again and again is a core concept in good scripting

In general, it's not worth using separate JS files until your scripts start to get big.

You can also include JavaScript by defining it as the `href` hyperlink reference of an `<a>` (hyperlink anchor) tag. This is a quick and easy way to run a short script: if you start the `href` with `javascript:` the browser will treat the rest of the tag as JavaScript (separated by semi-colons as necessary). Including this line inside the `<body>` of an HTML document:

```
This <a href="javascript:window.alert('boo!'); document.write
    ➡ ('scary huh?');">link</a> will do something!

</body>

</html>
```

...will create the text *This link will do something!* in a new window, with the word 'link' as a link.

Notice that the `href` attribute definition uses two sorts of quotes. The JavaScript code section is included in "..." quotes, whereas the text `'boo!'` and `'scary huh?'` are in single '...' quotes.

The reason for this is that when the browser sees an `href` definition, it expects to see it equated to something in "..." quotes. If we enclosed the `"boo!"` in double quotes as well, the browser would take the `"` at the start of it as the **end** of the `href` attribute *value*, giving us...

```
href="javascript:window.alert("
```

...instead of the correct:

```
href="javascript:window.alert('boo!'); document.write('scary
   ➥ huh?'); "
```

Because of this, it's a good idea to get into the habit of using single quotes with all JavaScript (and in fact, with all web based computer languages that allow it) and double quotes only within HTML tags.

The Case Study

Looking at the HTML for our case study, there's some JavaScript that uses the `<a>` (hyperlink anchor) tag in just the way that we've discussed above. This means that the JavaScript is mixed in with the HTML, which is a bad thing because we really want to keep our HTML separate from both our CSS and JavaScript.

Worse still, it's always the same JavaScript: the code to open a pop-up. Instead of having this same code all over the place clogging up our HTML, we're going to use the knowledge that the last two sections have given us to tidy things up. First of all, we're going to make it into a function, and then we're going to place our function in an external JS file.

First off, let's identify our JavaScript. Here's a typical example:

```
<a href = "mon_events.html">events</a>  
<a href="javascript:flashWin=window.open('flash.html', 'flashPopup',
➥ 'menubar=no, scrollbars=no, width=800, height=600,
➥ resizable=no');void 0;">flashub</a>  
<a href = "mon_contact.html">contact</a>  
<a href="javascript:polWin=window.open('mon_pol_casestud.html',
➥ 'polPopup', 'menubar=no, scrollbars=no, width=550,
➥ height=300, resizable=no'); polWin.focus(); void 0;">
➥ polish help</a> </p>
```

Since this scripting is almost always the same, we can use a JavaScript function to simplify our code.

Designing our function

We will call the function `openPop()` because that is what it does; open pop-ups. The function should be able to open our three pop-ups. You can see these if you look at `dev.html`; they are the Polish language translation pop-up, the Flash version pop-up, and the news pop-up:

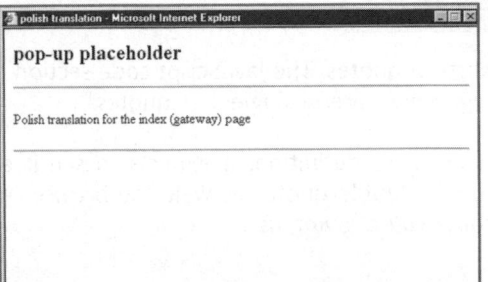
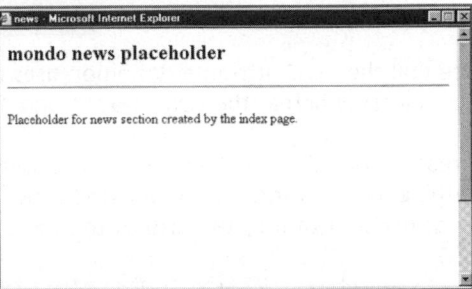

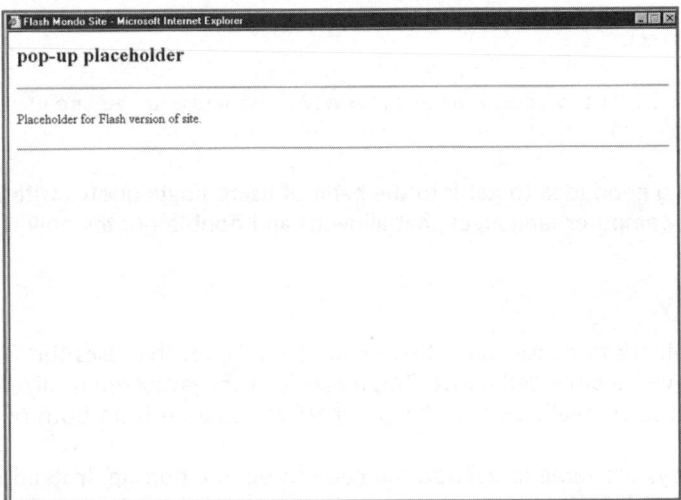

The windows open in a variety of sizes, sometimes have scrollbars, and sometimes (but not always) have focus. The windows also have different HTML (`flashPopup` and `polPopup` in the code above) and JavaScript names (`FlashWin` and `polWin` for the same windows in the code).

In addition, we'll have to specify different source URLs for the content we actually want to go into the pop-up windows, because there are several HTML documents we want to put in them. Let's look closely at these features, because we will create a more general and efficient function if we only keep the differences we actually need.

If you need to refresh your knowledge of pop-up conventions and terminology like **focus** *(appears on top), or HTML and JavaScript names, check back to* **Chapter 3**.

We have to be able to open the windows at different sizes, so we need to be able to change the height and length. The same goes for the scrollbars; sometimes we need them, and sometimes we don't, and there's not much we can do about this.

Changing the HTML/JavaScript window names is an odd issue. We need the HTML name to be different between windows, because that is the name that the `<a>` tag looks at. We also need to be able to differentiate between the JavaScript names, because that is the name the JavaScript window object needs to know about when we use methods such as `window.focus()`.

What is not obvious is that the HTML and JavaScript window names can be the same for each window. We can make both the HTML and JavaScript names of the Flash pop-up `flashPopup`. If we do that, we have less to worry about.

The decision to give a window focus depends on what the window does. When a new window is opened for the first time, it always gets focus, so we don't have to bother giving it focus then. When the window is already open, but we load new content into it (as we do all the time with the Polish translation pop-up), the window will not get focus because it's already there, even though we use `window.open()`.

The upshot of that is that we could simply give all windows focus every time we load anything in them. Sometimes we don't actually need to, but it makes our code simpler if we do, because we then don't have to think about it.

Okay, so now we know that the function will be called `openPop()` so we will start with:

```
function openPop(){
}
```

We also know that we have to be able to change the following **arguments**:

- The width and height of the window we want to open. We will address these with the variables `w` and `h` that we will pass to the function as arguments.
- The URL of the content to go into the window, so let's give that a variable `src`. This will be a string value such as `'flash.html'`.
- The name of the window, which will be both the HTML and JavaScript name; let's call that `name`. Again, this will be a string value, such as `'flashPopup'`.
- Whether or not we want to have scrollbars. We could make this a Boolean value, given that it can be either true or false, but the `window.open()` method accepts the more intuitive 'yes' or 'no', and since we have been using these instead, we will go for a string called `scrollbars` which can either be **'yes'** or **'no'**.

So we now have:

```
function openPop(src, name, scrollbar, w, h ){
}
```

Somewhere along the line we need a JavaScript `window.open()` method to actually open the window (or to put new content in an already open window), and for that we need to have:

```
JavaScriptWindowName = window.open(sourceURL, htmlName, windowFeatures);
```

That's four bits of information we need to specify :

- JavaScriptWindowName
- SourceURL
- htmlName
- windowFeatures

The `JavaScriptWindowName` and `htmlName` will be the same thing, the `name` argument that we gave our initial function:

```
function openPop(src, name, scrollbar, w, h ){
}
```

Similarly, the `sourceURL` is the `src` argument. That leaves `WindowFeatures`, and this will be a string containing a comma separated list of the features we do/do not want the window to have. Looking at the HTML we saw earlier, this can be stuff like:

```
'menubar=no, scrollbars=no, width=550, height=300, resizable=no'
```

The 'no' in 'scrollbars = no' is our `scrollbars` argument, and the width and height values are our `w` and `h` arguments.

```
function openPop(src, name, scrollbar, w, h ){
}
```

The other features are always 'no'. The window open requires this list as a single string, but that's not a problem because we can create a string of our own, which we will call `features`. This list **concatenates** (joins together) the values we need to create one big list. You can see that we use the scrollbar and w and h variables passed as arguments in the first line, and set the rest to literal values.

```
function openPop(src, name, scrollbar, w, h ){
    features='menubar=no, resizable=no, scrollbars=' + scrollbar +
            ➥ ',width=' + w + ',height=' + h;
    name=window.open(src, name, features);
}
```

This means that when we use this function, the literal values are always set, but we can change the others by passing different arguments to the function – so we can create windows of different sizes, but they'll never be resizable. This is where our earlier careful planning comes in useful!

The final line then finally takes all the values we've set up (i.e. the src and name variables that we supply as arguments in the first line, and the list of features that we set up in the second line), and opens the window with window.open().

That's almost it. All we have to do now is give the window focus and finish with a void 0 to make sure we don't write to the HTML document that this function is part of:

```
function openPop(src, name, scrollbar, w, h ){
        features='menubar=no,resizable=no, scrollbars=' + scrollbar +
        ➡ ',width=' + w + ',height=' + h;
        name=window.open(src, name, features);
        name.focus();
        void 0;
}
```

Adding the function

Okay, that's our function developed, but where should we put it? Well, we will start by trying it out on one of our pages. Try opening dev.html from the last chapter, and add/change the following:

- Add the function in a new <script> section in the document <head>
- Change the three <a> tags that open a window so that they now call the function openPop:

```
<html>
<head>
<title>table test</title>
<link href="mon_style.css" rel="stylesheet" type="text/css">
<script language="JavaScript">

function openPop(src, name, scrollbar, w, h ){
        features='menubar=no,resizable=no, scrollbars=' + scrollbar +
        ➡ ',width=' + w + ',height=' + h;
        name=window.open(src, name, features);
        name.focus();
        void 0;
}

</script>
</head><body>


<span CLASS = "title"> gateway placeholder</span>
        <hr>
        <span CLASS = "text">
        <p> <a href="javascript:openPop('mon_pol_sta.html', 'polPopup',
        ➡ 'no', 550, 300);">polish help</a> </p>
        <p> <a href = "mon_mission.html">HTML version</a> </p>
        <p>
        <a href="javascript:openPop('flash.html', 'flashPopup', 'no', 800,
        ➡ 600);">flash version</a>
```

continues overleaf

```
      <a href = "http://www.macromedia.com/shockwave/download
➥ /download.cgi?P1_Prod_Version=ShockwaveFlash">
➥ Flash plug-in</a>
        </p>
        <p> <a href="javascript:openPop('mon_news.html', 'newsPopup',
➥ 'yes', 550, 300);">news</a> </p>
        <hr>
      </span>
```

So what have we gained by doing this?

- We have separated our JavaScript from the HTML, putting the code where it belongs - in the <head>. This makes our solution more structured, and therefore easier to change should we need to alter it in the future.
- We have lessened the amount of repetition in the JavaScript, and centralized our code, so it becomes easier to debug and modify.

If you test dev.html, you will see that nothing much appears to have changed; the pop-ups open as before. The only way you will know that the function is being used is if you roll over one of the pop-up opening links and look at the browser status area. This will show the contents of the <a> tag that will be executed when you press the link, and you can see it now shows the function call.

Adding the function to other pages

That's cool, but the function could be called from other pages as well if we let it. We *could* simply put the function in the head of every page that could do with using it, but there is a better way. Remember the mon_style.css file, which contains a site-wide style definition that allows us to link one file to many HTML files? Well, we can do the same with our JavaScript.

1. Copy the function as it is at the moment by highlighting it, and using Edit > Copy, or CTRL+C.

2. Change the <script> tags in dev.html like this:

    ```
    <link href="mon_style.css" rel="stylesheet" type="text/css">
    <script language="JavaScript" src="mondo_script.js"></script>
    </head>
    ```

3. Create a new file within the site folder called mondo_script.js.

4. Into this new file, paste the function that you copied in step **1** (or type it all out again as follows):

    ```
    function openPop(src, name, scrollbar, w, h ){
         features='menubar=no,resizable=no, scrollbars=' + scrollbar +
               ➥ ',width=' + w + ',height=' + h;
         name=window.open(src, name, features);
         name.focus();
         void 0;
    }
    ```

5. If you test `dev.html`, you will find that it works as before, but this time is using the function in `mondo_script.js`.

6. To alter all the other pages to do the same thing, you need to change all the HTML documents from previous chapters (except those that open in a pop-up) in the same way. These include the following files:

    - `mon_mission.html`: the mission page.
    - `mon_events.html`: the events page.
    - `mon_contact.html`: the contact page.
    - `mon_webdes.html`: the web design page.
    - `mon_photo.html`: the photography page.
    - `mon_generic.html`: the generic design page.
    - `mon_casestud.html`: the case study page.
    - `mon_past.html`: the past mondo sites page.

> *The completed files (and the modified* `dev.html` *and new* `mon_script.js` *files) are included in the download for this chapter.*

The skeleton site

The skeleton site is now complete. We have all the major pages set up and our navigation defined. The most important files are now in place. We may later add or subtract the odd link or page, but we have the basic site working. We still of course need to add some content, but because we have defined most of the other details, we are less likely to have to keep changing the content because we have forgotten something.

Events and User Interaction

What this chapter will do

This chapter continues the examination of JavaScript we started in **Chapter 3** and continued in **Chapter 7**, and introduces the final pieces to the puzzle. In this chapter, we'll introduce:

- The concept of **events**
- How JavaScript can be combined with CSS to provide Dynamic HTML
- Using JavaScript and **forms** to create more complex user interaction
- **Checking** that our user has enable JavaScript before proceeding into our site

What you'll have learned by the end of this chapter

By the end of this chapter, you will have learned the core JavaScript you need for a start in web design. You will have covered browser control basic JavaScript syntax, and the common programming blocks, and also setting up events. Lastly we'll have touched on more advanced topics like using JavaScript with CSS to set styles interactively.

Introducing events

Last chapter, we looked at the JavaScript that allowed us to write the basic code blocks that make up most scripts. By combining some of these blocks, particularly **functions**, we can create the basis of interactivity: **events** and **event handlers**. Supposing we had a large block of code that contained a number of other smaller blocks as shown:

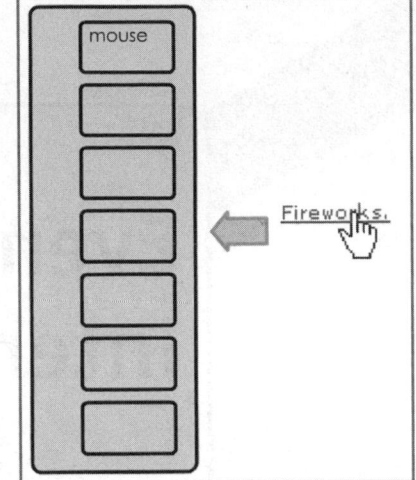

If the large block was a loop, then we would have the seven smaller blocks of code constantly running one after another. If this was a website interface, then one of the blocks might be looking for user interaction from the mouse.

Great, except what if the user manages to press and release a link during the part of the loop that mouse was not looking for interactions? Well, because nothing in our code would be looking for any mouse interactions, our loop would miss it! The user could have to click for several minutes on the Fireworks link before the mouse code was actually running at the same time as the user was clicking, thus causing nothing to actually happen except by happy coincidence!

The code blocks that need to run as soon as something beyond the control of the code happens – like a user's mouse click – are called **event handlers** and the 'something' is called an **event**. As soon as an event happens, the computer looks to see if there is a corresponding event handler. If there is, then whatever else is happening with the code is temporarily halted while the event handler is run. Once the event handler is run, the previous code is allowed to carry on as if nothing happened.

That's pretty useful, but we can take it further. When you open a web page and interact with it, everything you do generates events. When you open a page, an event triggers when the page is fully loaded. When you move the mouse, there's a corresponding event. There's a separate event for when you roll over, roll out of, click, and release a button. There are events generated when you click inside a form text field, and another when you click anywhere else and stop entering text into it.

Event handlers waiting for their respective events to fire, and cause code to run is a whole lot more efficient than the loop-and-pray affair we saw earlier. Such code is called **event driven**, and it's what you need to use if you want to create code that interfaces to the real world and/or real users. Not only is this sort of code what drives most web pages, it's the sort of code that typically runs for all interactive applications - everything from word processors to computer games.

So how do you set this up? Well, you simply declare some blocks (as we did earlier in the last chapter) and associate them with events. When the events occur, the required function block will execute. In the diagram, we have created three function blocks: button1Handler, button2Handler and docLoaded. We then have to associate them (or attach them) to the specific events we want to cause each function to run. As soon as the listing has got to the end of the definitions section, no more instructions are executed. The browser just sits there, waiting for an event to fire.

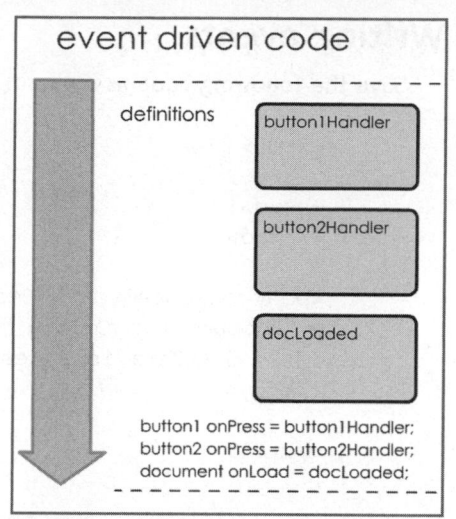

The way we have set it up, button1's *someone pressed me* event will cause the button1Handler to execute. In the same way, as soon as the web page is loaded up, the function docLoaded will execute. Although the button events are generated by user input, some events – such as the *is the current web page loaded* event – are not; they're caused by the browser. This makes your code very flexible – not only can you respond to user input, but you can also respond to browser events.

This means that your code appears to work much quicker than it would any other way, because it responds to the initial event immediately. It also means that your code can appear to be responding to events in an intelligent way. Suppose you pressed button1, setting off button1Handler, and then immediately afterwards pressed button2. What would happen? Well, the button2 pressed event would temporarily stop the button1 event handler, and run button2Handler. When button2Handler finished, button1Handler would resume.

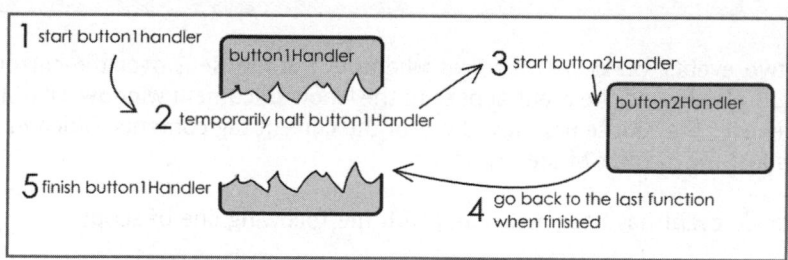

Writing events

Save the following code as `event01.html` and view it in a browser:

```
<html>

<head>
</head>

<body onMouseOver = "document.bgColor='#FFFFFF';" onMouseOut =
➡ "document.bgColor='#DDDDDD';">
    <h2>This is a test page</h2>
</body>

</html>
```

> Note that we don't need the `<script>` tag to tell the browser this is a script. That's because the argument after the `onMouseOver` is expected to be a script.

You will see that if you move out of the browser frame area, it turns gray. Open another browser window, and the browser that your mouse is over turns white, and the other one turns gray. If you are over neither browser, both of them will turn gray.

> Note, on some versions of Netscape on the Mac, you might have to click to see the proper effects!

We are using two events. `onMouseOver` fires whenever the mouse is over the current tag – in our case, the current tag is `<body>`, so the event applies to the whole document window. Likewise, the `onMouseOut` event fires whenever the mouse has moved out of the current tag contents, which in our case means that the mouse has just moved out of the window.

The `onMouseOver` event has been associated with the following line of script:

```
document.bgColor='#FFFFFF';
```

This turns the background color property `bgColor` to white. The `onMouseOut` event has been associated with the following line:

```
"document.bgColor='#DDDDDD';
```

This turns the background a light gray. Each color change is caused by a single event. When you are in a browser, causing it to turn white, the onMouseOver is not being constantly generated. It only runs once when you enter the browser. If your browser windows overlap so that you immediately leave one window and enter the other, the above rule still applies. The left browser goes gray because its onMouseOut occurs, whereas the onMouseOver of the rightmost browser causes it to turn white.

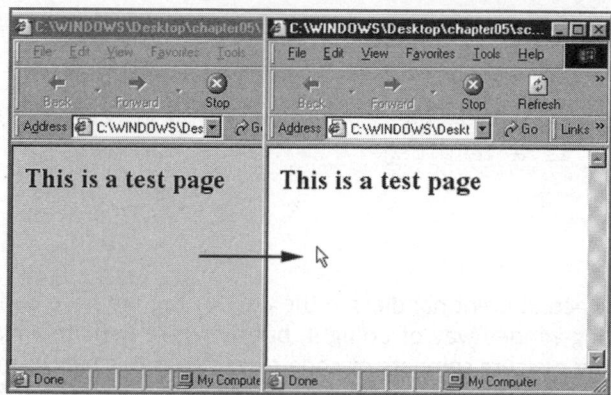

The user would see this as one more complicated event; 'I have moved from the left browser to the right browser, and the two browsers must have communicated this fact between each other'. This shows how multiple simple events can be used to look like some more complicated interaction is occurring.

Although this looks good, you'd normally be more interested in which browser window has **focus**. A browser has focus when its title bar isn't grayed out, meaning it's the currently active browser window. To make our color change consistent with that, change the <body> tag to:

```
<body onFocus = "document.bgColor='#FFFFFF';" onBlur = "document.bgColor
    ='#DDDDDD';">
```

When you test this, you'll have to have another application not fully maximized, so that you can see the color change when you activate another window. Rather than simply have the mouse over its window, an in focus window also has to be clicked. It looks less good, but the concept of focus is important. The in-focus browser contains the in-focus web page, and this is the page that can take inputs from a user's keyboard, amongst other things.

The code we are writing is a little like the code we wrote in **Chapter 3**, where we ended up with tags with long code blocks in them. That's a quick and dirty way of writing scripts, but now we know about functions, we can tidy up our code by keeping code and HTML separate:

```
<html>

<head>
    <script language = "JavaScript">

        function makeActivePage(){
            document.bgColor='#FFFFFF';
        }
```

continues overleaf

239

```
              function makeUnActivePage(){
                    document.bgColor='#DDDDDD';
              }

      </script>

   </head>

   <body onMouseOver = "makeActivePage();" onMouseOut = "makeUnActivePage();">
         <h2>This is a test page</h2>
   </body>

   </html>
```

Instead of including the actual event handlers in the <body> tag, we have defined them as functions. This may seem like more long-winded way of doing it, but there are definite advantages to always using this format. Instead of having obscure snippets of code clogging up our tags in the <body> as previously, we have now put meaningful function names in. This allows us to see what is happening more easily, and prevents massive ten line tags with whole blocks of JavaScript in them.

We're also sticking to defining all our code in the <head> and then defining the events-event handler associations as the page is being rendered (the <body> section). This keeps all our JavaScript in one place and all our HTML in another, which makes for neater, easier to debug, web pages. The only interface between the two is function calls from the HTML to the <head> scripts. This makes it easier to write separate .js files for our domain, building up a single script file suitable for all our pages.

JavaScript and CSS

You can also use JavaScript to change our CSS definition. The following script changes the style definition for the <body> and <h2> tags – try testing it in a browser, and you'll see the change of color when we move our mouse out of the browser that we've seen previously, but you'll also see that the text enclosed by h2 tags changes.

We first have to define which particular tags we want to change with the ID attribute. We have named the <body> tag doc (because style changes to this tag will affect the whole visible document) and the <h2> tag is called title. This allows JavaScript to act on our individual tags by using these IDs, which is a very powerful feature - it allows us to change the HTML after the page has been created.

```
   <html>

   <head>
      <script language = "JavaScript">

              function makeActivePage(){
                    doc.style.backgroundColor = '#FFFFFF';
                    title.style.color = '#000000';
              }
```

```
            function makeUnActivePage(){
                    doc.style.backgroundColor='#DDDDDD';
                    title.style.color = '#B7B7B7';
            }

        </script>

    </head>

    <body ID = "doc" onMouseOver = "makeActivePage();" onMouseOut =
    ➡  "makeUnActivePage();">
            <h2 ID = "title">This is a test page</h2>
    </body>

</html>
```

This way of HTML, CSS, and JavaScript working together goes by the name of **DHTML**, or Dynamic HTML. It isn't a new language, just a way of using the best features of all three of our web design components together to create dynamic pages. To change a tag's style in JavaScript, we use:

```
ID.style.property = 'value';
```

- The ID is the ID of the individual tag (note that we're effectively making inline changes: we're changing the style of a specific <h2> tag in the code above, and not all <h2> tags).
- The property is the CSS property you want to change. (Check back to **Chapter 4** for more information on these.)

There is a problem with CSS and JavaScript, in that CSS properties such as background-color will look like an expression (in this example, it looks like the variable color should be subtracted from the variable background). To avoid this confusion, we ignore the dash, but make the first letter of the second word a capital: hence backgroundColor.

Notice that our scripts are now running more than once. The scripts in **Chapter 7** only ran once, because they were run as the <head> part of the document was being parsed. The <head> is only run once when the page is opened or re-opened. Running such scripts thus overwrites whatever else was originally on the page. Events called from the <body> run every time they are seen and do not require a page reload.

Now, not only does the background color change on these events, but so does the color of the title text. You can also change between your own custom styles dynamically, by changing between CSS classes directly:

```
<html>

<head>
<style>

.redText    {color:'#FF0000';}
.grnText    {color:'#00FF00';}
.normalText {color:'#0000FF';}
```

continues overleaf

```
        </style>
        </head>

        <body>
            <h2 ID = "title">This is a test page</h2>
            <a href ="#" onMouseOver = "this.className='redText';" onMouseOut =
    ➥ "this.className='normalText';"> Make me red</a>
            <a href ="#" onMouseOver = "this.className='grnText';" onMouseOut =
    ➥ "this.className='normalText';"> Make me green</a>
        </body>

        </html>
```

The CSS Style Sheet simply sets up three classes. These allow us to change the color property of any tag between red, green, and blue. The HTML will create two links (neither of which will actually go anywhere because I have given them the dummy location '#', although you could put in a URL if you wished).

The two links have onMouseOver and onMouseOut events defined, so stuff will happen if you move the mouse over or out of the links. Let's have a look at the first link. We have an onMouseOver of:

```
this.className='redText';
```

this is a very useful bit of code to know about; it refers to the current tag you are defining an event for, and stops you having to define an ID, because JavaScript knows you are talking about the current (or *this*) <a> tag. The className is the name of the CSS class you want to define, and we have the three names (redText, grnText and normalText) to choose from.

When you roll over the 'make me red' link, this line forces a style change to the current link, making it red. When you roll out of it, this forces it back to blue. Ever wondered how the text turns red when you enter an incorrect number in an online order form, or how a text entry box is highlighted when you click on it? Well, now you know.

Introducing forms

Using JavaScript for simple effects isn't all you can do: you can also use it to process information that users enter. We do this with **forms**. There's only so much you can do with point and click; as soon as real communication involving real information passing hands needs to be done, you have to get involved with text, and that means inputting the stuff. Form building is also conveniently one of the main uses of event code.

To show what can be achieved, we're going to build something that's useful: a calculator. So now you're thinking 'uh … that's not a form!'. In web design, anything that requires dynamic text (where you don't want to use the nice but eventually annoying alert and prompt boxes) is a form. Creating forms always follows the same process:

- Plan what the form will do (what we want).
- Plan what you need it to look like (what our form needs to look like).
- Note all the inputs and outputs you want (what our form needs to do).
- Identify all the events you want to set up, and what you need to happen for each one.

What we want

We want a calculator – something that allows us to add, subtract, divide, and multiply numbers. We won't go for one of those clever scientific ones that allow us to do trig or have memories and so on, although there's nothing stopping you carrying on after this chapter (HINT - you might have to read up on the JavaScript Math object).

What our form needs to look like

What do we need to have in our form? We want a display to show the numbers as we put them in, and we also need the display to spit out the answer. We also want the number keys 0 to 9, and the "+", " /", "*" and "-" keys. Oh, and an "=" key. We can do away with the cancel/reset/clear key, because we have the browser refresh, which will give us a blank new version of the page, with a reset calculator.

In essence, our form needs to look like this:

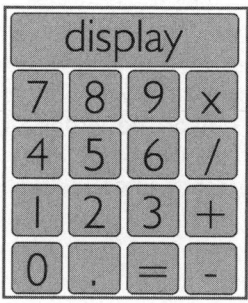

Our calculator looks much simpler than many of the online forms you see on the web, but it's actually more complex when you consider the fundamental issue of efficient, event-driven interfaces. In an online form, the fact that the user can enter data out of order isn't a problem, because there's a big Submit button at the end, and the form doesn't actually do anything until someone hits that button. A calculator is a much truer real-time problem because it has no submit button (the "=" key is not a submit button in disguise because stuff also has to happen when you press any other key; the display has to update on every key for one thing).

What our form needs to do

So what do we want our form to do?

- When we click on any of the digits or the decimal point, we want them to appear in the display, and build up our number. So, if we entered "7", ".", and "5", we should end up with "7.5" in the display.

- As soon as we hit any of the operators (* / + -), we need to remember the number displayed so far (let's call it `firstNumber`) and clear the display. We should also note which operator was pressed, so let's call the operator `sumType`.

- As soon as we hit equals, we should do our sum: `firstNumber` (* or / or + or -) `secondNumber`, and we should put the answer (say `result`) into the display.

Notice that I've defined each key in isolation, because we cannot expect that one key will be pressed before any other. Life would be so easy here if we could always expect the user to press:

```
'number' 'operator' 'number' ' = '
```

...but there's nothing stopping the user pressing:

```
'- 5 - =.7.7.7'
```

We can assume a certain amount of intelligence from the user, so we can reasonably send out garbage if the user is feeding us garbage, but we have to tell the user it is garbage, and our calculator must never become as confused as the user. It must certainly not crash on any input for example. One of the easiest ways to do this in event driven code is to assume as little as possible, and if your inputs don't meet up with the expected sequences, tell the user it's garbage.

This is also where you need to think about your audience. If your site needs the user to reach into their pocket and enter a credit card number, then obviously, your site needs to bend over backwards to make that happen. Like a perfect shop assistant, your interface must always smile and gently correct the customer even if said customer got out of the wrong side of the bed and into a strange planet this morning. If you don't mind too much about people who got out of the wrong side of bed, then there's nothing stopping you creating an interesting interface that requires some thought from the user.

Setting up the form

We need to be able to walk before we can run, so we will be adding in the basic functionality of our calculator first, so that we can look at the basic event driven framework. We will look at two of the most common form elements: the **text field** and the **button**.

> If you get stuck, the code up to the end of this section is saved as `calculator01.html`.

1. Start with a basic HTML document, and add the following: (I've added a pair of `<script></script>` tags because I know I'll be adding some JavaScript later).

   ```
   <html>

   <head>

   <script language = "JavaScript">

   </script>

   </head>

   <body>
   </body>

   </html>
   ```

2. The first thing to add is a `<form></form>` tag. As you can potentially have several forms on one page, you have to give each form a name, and you do this with a name attribute. Add the following inside the `<body>` section, (the `<br>` tags simply place our form two lines down from the top of the page):

   ```
   <body>

   <br><br>

   <form name="calculator">
   </form>

   </body>
   ```

3. To add a form input element, we use the `<input>` tag, and the most common attributes we have to specify include the **type** of input element, the **name** of the element (so that JavaScript can refer to it), and a **value** (this is the text you see displayed). For our text field, add the following within the `<form></form>` tags:

   ```
   <form name="calculator">
           <input type="text" name = "lcd" value= "0" size = "16">
           <br>
   </form>
   ```

4. Test the page so far. We've created a text box (`type="text"`) named `lcd` (as in calculator LCD screen), and set the initial value to 0. You can change this by clicking in the text box itself when you run the page in a browser.

> *Notice that this zero is a string not a number, a fact that we will be using later.*

5. Looking at our form layout, we have the display. We now need a row of 4 buttons, the first one being a 7 key. Add the following, still within the `<form></form>` tags:

```
<form name="calculator">
        <input type="text" name = "lcd" value= "0" size = "16">
        <br>
        <input type="button" value = "   7   ">
</form>
```

6. Test this in a browser, and you should see something like the screenshot. If you press the button, um ... nothing happens. Well, we knew that would happen, right? Given there's nothing to tell the browser what to do when the button is pressed, it's no surprise.

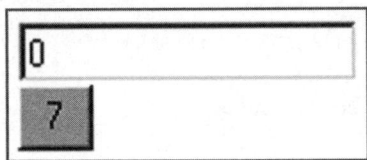

7. Anyway, we might as well do the rest of the line of buttons while we're here, so add:

```
<form name="calculator">
        <input type="text" name = "lcd" value= "0" size = "16">
        <br>
        <input type="button" value = "   7   ">
        <input type="button" value = "   8   ">
        <input type="button" value = "   9   ">
        <input type="button" value = "   x   ">
        <br>
</form>
```

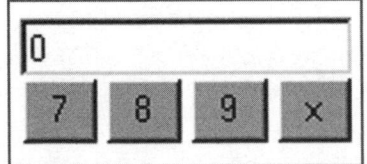

Note that the value attribute of the button is simply the text that appears on the button, and has no other significance, so we can use the more people friendly x for the multiply button rather than the more geeky *.

8. We can now add the rest of our buttons:

```
<form name="calculator">
        <input type="text" name = "lcd" value= "0" size = "16">
        <br>
        <input type="button" value = "   7   ">
        <input type="button" value = "   8   ">
        <input type="button" value = "   9   ">
        <input type="button" value = "   x   ">
        <br>
        <input type="button" value = "   4   ">
        <input type="button" value = "   5   ">
        <input type="button" value = "   6   ">
        <input type="button" value = "    /   ">
        <br>
        <input type="button" value = "   1   ">
        <input type="button" value = "   2   ">
        <input type="button" value = "   3   ">
        <input type="button" value = "   +   ">
        <br>
        <input type="button" value = "   0   ">
        <input type="button" value = "    .   ">
        <input type="button" value = "   =   ">
        <input type="button" value = "    -   ">
        <br>
</form>
```

Note that you need a **double** space either side of the character inside the speech marks, except in the case of the "/"," "." and "–" symbols, which need three spaces before them.

9. Save your file as `calculator01.html`, and test it. (If you'd rather not, have a look at `calculator01.html` from the downloads).

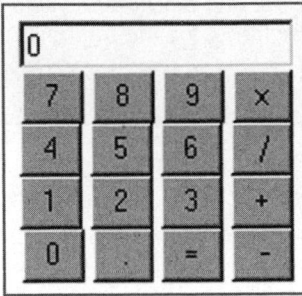

Adding the input events

So far we have a form, but it just sits there. What we need is some way to make our buttons enter values into our text field. To do that, we need to know how to make the browser place values in a text field. As with most interaction, it involves JavaScript, and JavaScript invariably uses the DOM when it is being used to change something that can be seen on a browser.

We know the text field is within the current document, that it is in a form called `calculator`, and the text field is called `lcd`, so it makes sense to identify the field like this:

```
document.calculator.lcd
```

To change the value of the text field, we used the value attribute in the `<input>` tag that defined it, and we can do the same thing here:

```
document.calculator.lcd.value = "test";
```

1. Let's try it. Enter the following into the `<script></script>` tag in the `<head>` part of our document:

```
<head>

<script language="JavaScript">
    document.calculator.lcd.value = "test";
</script>

</head>
```

2. This doesn't work. Why? The `<head>` part of the document is run *before* the `<body>`, which means that the text field doesn't actually exist when our script is run. Instead, we have to try the line after the form is defined (because we know that the text field actually exists by then). Cut the line of script we just added into the `<head>` and paste it into the `<body>` like this:

```
<input type="button" value = " = ">
```

```
                    <input type="button" value = "   -  ">
                    <br>
          </form>

<script language ="JavaScript">
          document.calculator.lcd.value = 'test';
</script>

</body>

</html>
```

3. Test the page in a browser, and you should see the word `test` appear in the text field. Delete the code you've just added (so you end up with the same listing we started this section with - `calculator01.html`).

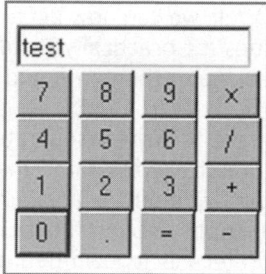

4. Let's try making a 7 appear in the text field when we hit the seven, an 8 when we click the eight, and so on. For the first two keys, add an `onClick` attribute to the first two button tags:

```
          <input type="text" name = "lcd" value= "0" size = "16">
          <br>
          <input type="button" value = " 7 " onClick ="numeralSeven();">
          <input type="button" value = " 8 " onClick ="numeralEight();">
```

5. This defines the `onClick` handlers for our two buttons as the functions `numeralSeven()` and `numeralEight()`. Now we need to add these functions:

> *We are adding these functions in the* <head>. *Despite the fracas that resulted when we tried this earlier, we can do this because when the functions are run (by a user pressing the button), the buttons will exist.*

```
<head>

<script language="JavaScript">

function numeralSeven(){
     document.calculator.lcd.value = '7';
}

function numeralEight(){
     document.calculator.lcd.value = '8';
}

</script>

</head>
```

6. View the page in the browser. Well, we can now get a 7 or 8 in the text field by clicking the buttons, but the code has so many issues it's practically certifiable. For example, when we click the seven followed by the eight, we get a 7 and then an 8 and not the 78 we might be hoping for.

    This might suggest that we'll have to write a separate function for each button, which is a shame because all the functions do practically the same thing. We can get around this by using a single function with an **argument**. An argument is a value that you can pass to a function. It works in much the same way as JavaScript's inbuilt functions. When you write `alert('hello');` for example, the JavaScript interpreter has its own defined function that prints whatever you enter in the brackets in an alert pop-up window. You can even have more than one argument, for example:

    `prompt('enter a value', 'enter something here');`

    ...would give us something like the screenshot. The point is that with `alert()`, you wouldn't dream of having a different JavaScript function for every different message you could possible want - `alertWelcomeToMySite()`, `alertAprilFool()`, and so on. In the same way, we can write **one** function to handle all the number buttons.

7. Let's see this in action. First, change our form buttons to give them all the same `onClick` handler, a new function called `numeral` (which we'll write next):

    ```
    <form name="calculator">
         <input type="text" name = "lcd" value= "0" size = "16">
         <br>
    ```

```
<input type="button" value = " 7 " onClick ="numeral(7);">
<input type="button" value = " 8 " onClick ="numeral(8);">
<input type="button" value = " 9 " onClick ="numeral(9);">
<input type="button" value = " x ">
<br>
<input type="button" value = " 4 " onClick ="numeral(4);">
<input type="button" value = " 5 " onClick ="numeral(5);">
<input type="button" value = " 6 " onClick ="numeral(6);">
<input type="button" value = "  / ">
<br>
<input type="button" value = " 1 " onClick ="numeral(1);">
<input type="button" value = " 2 " onClick ="numeral(2);">
<input type="button" value = " 3 " onClick ="numeral(3);">
<input type="button" value = " + ">
<br>
<input type="button" value = " 0 " onClick ="numeral(0);">
<input type="button" value = "  . " onClick ="numeral('.');">
<input type="button" value = " = ">
<input type="button" value = "  - ">
<br>
</form>
```

8. Next, the function. Replace the two functions we added earlier with the following in the head `<script>`:

```
<head>

<script language="JavaScript">

function numeral(buttonValue){
    document.calculator.lcd.value = document.calculator.lcd.value +
    ➡buttonValue;
}

</script>

</head>
```

Our argument is the variable `buttonValue`. Whenever a `numeral` *(something)* is clicked, the function is run with a *buttonValue = something;* at the start of the function block. This means that if we do `numeral(7)`, the block will effectively become:

```
buttonValue = 7;
document.calculator.lcd.value=document.calculator.lcd.value+buttonValue;
```

This is good because it makes our text field whatever it already is (`document.calculator.lcd.value`) plus `buttonValue`, which is 7 if we press the seven button.

9. Try the calculator now, and you will see that you can enter a number.

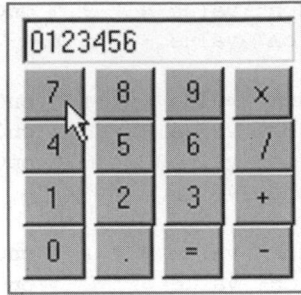

We are performing string concatenation here, rather than adding the numbers. In this case, it's actually what we want to happen, but if it wasn't, we would have to use Number() to force the strings to become numeric.

Removing the leading zero

There's always a 'but' and here it's that it would be good if we could get rid of that leading zero, unless that is what the first digit of the entered number actually is. How do we do that? Well, we need to:

- Make the display show the button pressed if we are on the first digit in the number.
- Make the display show whatever it is already plus the button just pressed if it isn't.

We can do this with Booleans and if. Change our scripts like this:

```
<script language="JavaScript">

function numeral(buttonValue){
    if (startNumber){
        startNumber = false
        document.calculator.lcd.value = buttonValue;
    }else{
        document.calculator.lcd.value =
document.calculator.lcd.value+buttonValue;
    }
}

// Initialize...
startNumber = true;

</script>
```

The important thing to remember when looking at this is that when the head <script> section is first processed, functions are defined, but do not run. So the only thing that runs during this time is the instruction that sets startNumber to true.

That means that after the first button is pressed at the start of a new number, `startNumber` is `true`, and the display will become the button pressed, and not `0+` the button pressed. We then set the `startNumber` to false, so that on subsequent presses, the `else` part of the code runs, and this takes into account what is already in the display. If you try it now, you will see that the leading zero disappears when it is not required.

Operators

We still haven't looked at the operators, though. Not only do we need to store the operator pressed when the +, -, x or / keys are pressed, we need to set `startNumber` to `true` again, because the next number button pressed will be the start of the second number. We also need to store the value of the first number entered, which is currently in the display, or it'll be overwritten and lost when the second number is entered. Let's set that all up:

> The `calculator02.html` *file contains these changes if you get stuck.*

1. In the form, make the following changes to define a new `onClick` handler for the operator buttons:

```
<form NAME="calculator">
    <input type="text" name = "lcd" value= "0" size = "16">
    <br>
    <input type="button" value = " 7 " onClick ="numeral(7);">
    <input type="button" value = " 8 " onClick ="numeral(8);">
    <input type="button" value = " 9 " onClick ="numeral(9);">
    <input type="button" value = " * " onClick ="operand('*');">
    <br>
    <input type="button" value = " 4 " onClick ="numeral(4);">
    <input type="button" value = " 5 " onClick ="numeral(5);">
    <input type="button" value = " 6 " onClick ="numeral(6);">
    <input type="button" value = "  / " onClick ="operand('/');">
    <br>
    <input type="button" value = " 1 " onClick ="numeral(1);">
    <input type="button" value = " 2 " onClick ="numeral(2);">
    <input type="button" value = " 3 " onClick ="numeral(3);">
    <input type="button" value = " + " onClick ="operand('+');">
    <br>
    <input type="button" value = " 0 " onClick ="numeral(0);">
    <input type="button" value = "  . " onClick ="numeral('.');">
    <input type="button" value = " = ">
    <input type="button" value = "  - " onClick ="operand('-');">
    <br>
</form>
```

2.   This calls up a new function `operand()`. So we now need to define this in the `<script>` section. Add the following function after the definition for `numeral()`:

```
}else{
            document.calculator.lcd.value =
    ➥ document.calculator.lcd.value+buttonValue;
        }
}

function operand(operator){
    firstNumber = document.calculator.lcd.value;
    sumType = operator;
    startNumber = true;
}

// Initialize...
```

We store the value of the first number in the `firstNumber` variable and the type of sum in the variable `sumType`. Assuming that the calculation you wanted to do was 56 + 44, so far:

`firstNumber` would be 56
`sumType` would be +

3.   It's always good practice to initialize all your variables to a starting value, so we might as well set `firstNumber` and `sumType` to something at the start of the page. Add the two bold lines to the code:

```
// Initialize...
startNumber = true;
firstNumber = 0;
sumType = '';
```

4.   Save your file as `calculator02.html`.

We now have our entire interface set up, and all the buttons do something. Well, all of them except the most important one: the equals key. If you try the calculator, it all works fine until you hit that magic key.

Adding the final calculation

> *This section starts with* calculator02.html, *and the final file is* calculator.html.

1. It doesn't take too much to realize that we need to add a third and final event to the equals key, so lets do that first:

```
<input type="button" value = "   .   " onClick ="numeral('.');">
<input type="button" value = " = " onClick ="doCalc();">
<input type="button" value = "   -   " onClick ="operand('-');">
```

2. We now need to add this function in the `<script>` section. Add the following code just after the definition for `operand()`, but before the instructions that start with the initialize comment: we already have our first number as a string, and the first line of this block turns it to a number. The second number we need to grab is currently in the display, so we get that as well in the second line, again turning it into a number.

```
function operand(operator){
      firstNumber = document.calculator.lcd.value;
      sumType = operator;
      startNumber = true;
}

function doCalc(){
      firstNumber = Number(firstNumber);
      secondNumber = Number(document.calculator.lcd.value);
}
```

We now need to decide what sort of sum we need to do. To do this, we simply look at sumType and if...
- it is * we need to multiply `firstNumber` and `secondNumber`
- it is / we need to divide `firstNumber` and `secondNumber`
- it is + we need to add `firstNumber` and `secondNumber`
- it is - we need to subtract `firstNumber` and `secondNumber`

3. The easiest way is to add a series of if decisions like this:

```
function doCalc(){
      firstNumber = Number(firstNumber);
      secondNumber = Number(document.calculator.lcd.value);
      if (sumType == '*'){
            result = firstNumber*secondNumber;
      }
```

```
if (sumType =='/'){
        result = firstNumber/secondNumber;
}
if (sumType =='+'){
        result = firstNumber+secondNumber;
}
if (sumType =='-'){
        result = firstNumber-secondNumber;
}
}
```

4. This gives us our answer, which I have equated to a new variable `result`. We need to put this value into our display. Thinking ahead, we also need to get ready for the next sum, and to do that we need to set up the calculator to expect the first digit in a new number. The two lines in bold do this:

```
function doCalc(){
        firstNumber = Number(firstNumber);
        secondNumber = Number(document.calculator.lcd.value);
        if (sumType == '*'){
                result = firstNumber*secondNumber;
        }
        if (sumType =='/'){
                result = firstNumber/secondNumber;
        }
        if (sumType =='+'){
                result = firstNumber+secondNumber;
        }
        if (sumType =='-'){
                result = firstNumber-secondNumber;
        }
        if (Number(result) != result){
                result = 'Error'
        }
        document.calculator.lcd.value = result;
        startNumber = true;
}
```

5. Finally, we had better initialize the two new variables we've created:

```
// Initialize...
startNumber = true;
firstNumber = 0;
sumType = '';
secondNumber = 0;
result = 0;
```

Error trapping

As a finishing touch, there are still a few ways a user could get an incorrect result. In particular, if the conversion from a string to a number doesn't work, you get a result of NaN (Not a Number). This is correct, but is a message really aimed at the programmer, and not the final user. We should really put up a more user-friendly message. Add this near the end of doCalc() to display error instead:

```
if (sumType =='-'){
        result = firstNumber-secondNumber;
}
if (Number(result) != result){
        result = 'Error'
}
document.calculator.lcd.value = result;
startNumber = true;
}
```

Making it better

You can now test the final results, or see it in calculator.html. I based this code on an old calculator I have in my drawer: one of those really old ones with red LED displays and requires more batteries than a Flashlight. It doesn't allow you to do things like 1+2+3+4= and you have to press the equals button after each sum: 1+2=, +3=, +4=. Our HTML page does exactly the same thing, so one thing you could do is change it so it can do the chained sums shown, rather than requiring the user to press the equals button every time. You could also add a cancel button - at the moment, you have to simply start a new sum, which suits me, but you might prefer a cancel key.

This is actually the simplest calculator code I could come up with (most JavaScript calculators cheat by using the rather clever JavaScript eval(), which evaluates its argument, so eval('40+(30*2)') would return 100. This script is about the most complicated level you'll need to write at for standard websites that don't need to talk to remote files or servers, so it's a good one to sit down and pore over.

The Case Study – Catering for Mondo's JavaScript

Now it's all well and good having JavaScript in your site, but given that it's possible to disable JavaScript, and some businesses even insist on disableing it on employees' work machines, how do you account for what happens when your fancy new JavaScripted site comes up against a browser that simply doesn't want to know?

In general with HTML, when a browser doesn't understand the newer tags that your site is using, it will *ignore them and go onto the next thing in the HTML*. It's that graceful degradation thing again, and it's one of the best things about HTML.

That's fine, except when we're actually dealing with a JavaScript <script> tag or CSS <style> tag, where the next thing the browser will see is your code or CSS definition. Because it sees plain text after these tags, the browser will simply plough through it, displaying it on screen, leaving you with horror stories like the one on the next page:

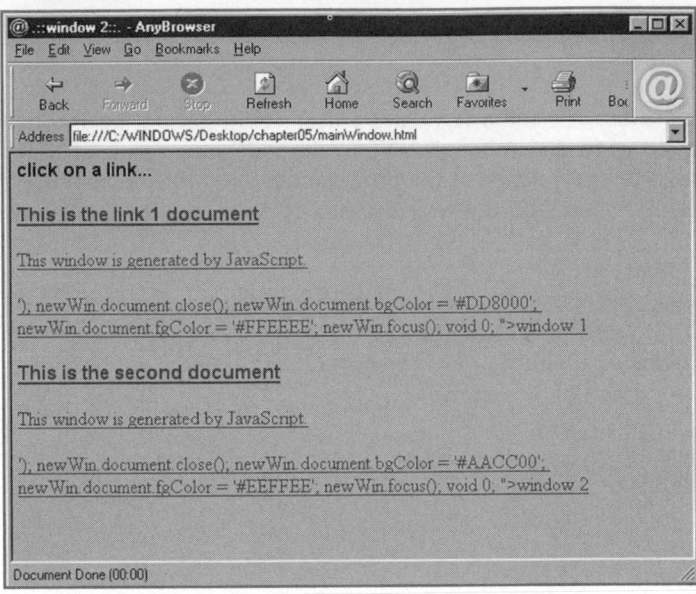

The general rule for graceful degradation here is to *hide the JavaScript or CSS definitions* by either:

- Leaving the space between the opening and closing tags empty
- Making the browser ignore the text between the script or style tags by commenting them.

In the Mondo site, we use the first way. Because our `<script>` and Style Sheet `<link>` tags are actually empty (they simply define a linked object *within* the tags rather than have the definitions *between* or *after* them), a browser that ignores the `<script>` or `<link>` tag misses the definition totally and simply carries on, rendering the next thing it can:

```
<link href="mon_style.css" rel="stylesheet" type="text/css">
<script language="JavaScript" src="mondo_script.js"></script>
```

> *You see the browser will ignore any* **tags** *it doesn't understand but not ignore any* **text** *between them. Our links above are all* **attributes** *within but not between the tags, so we're OK.*

When you are not using linked JavaScript code or CSS Style Sheets, the way to go is to comment out the listing:

```
<script>

<!--
JavaScript code goes here;
```

```
//—>

</script>

<Style>
<!—
Style definitions go here
—>
</style>
```

In this listing, any browser that ignores the `<script>...</script>` or `<style>...</style>` tags will instead see a HTML `<!— comment —>` and will ignore that as well.

What this will usually do is cause the browser to render the rest of the page, after ignoring the parts that it cannot handle.

If the user's browser understands JavaScript, as most do these days, the user might still have disabled it, or their company might have a policy of disabling it for security reasons. In this case, we can again do two things.

Testing for user preferences

1. Firstly, we can use the `<noscript>...</noscript>` tag, which will cause the browser to render whatever is seen between it, assuming that the browser understood the `<script>` tag, but is set to ignore scripting by the user.

2. You can see this in Netscape Navigator if you first disable scripting (check **Appendix A** if you're not sure how to do this) and then try this script with the same browser:

```
<html>
<head>
<script>
document.write('this browser will run JavaScript');
</script>

<noscript>
<br><br>
<hr>
<h2> This site requires you to enable JavaScript</h2>
<p>Please enable JavaScript for your browser and retry.</p>
<p>To do this in Netscape 6;<br>
Select <b>Edit > Preferences...</b><br>
Select the <b>Advanced</b> category.<br>
On the right hand side of the window, check <b>Enable JavaScript for
Navigator</b><br>
Select <b>Ok</b> and Hit the browser<b>Refresh</b> icon to try again.<br>
<hr>
</p>
```

continues overleaf

```
</noscript>

</head>

<body>

</body>
</html>
```

3.   You will first see the following page:

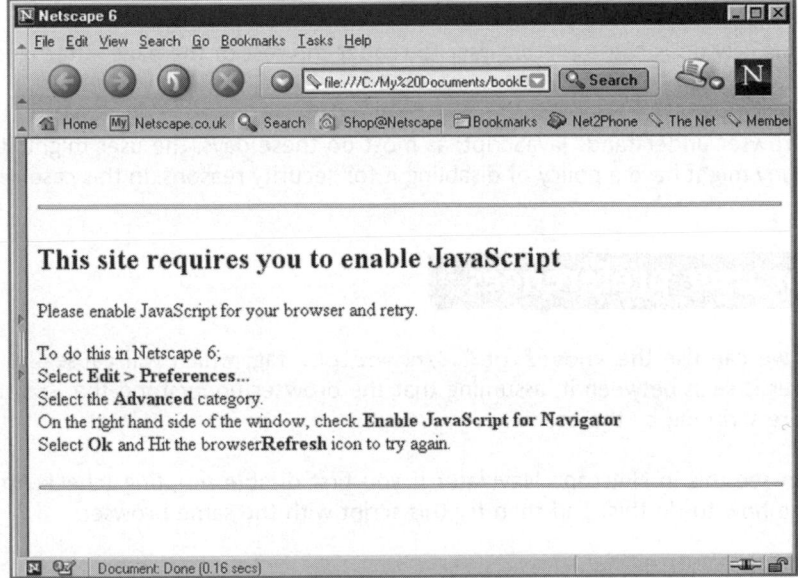

4.   If you follow the instructions, as soon as you hit the Refresh icon (third from left icon), the page will be reloaded, but this time with JavaScript enabled. We know this, because the .document.write() actually works this time:

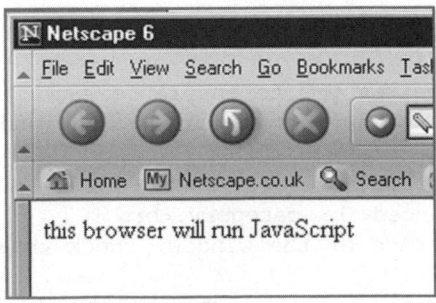

5. Alternatively, we can simply jump to a page that doesn't actually need JavaScript. This HTML will look for the file www.mysite.com/index.html after 5 seconds if the current browser doesn't support JavaScript, and if it does, will simply stay at the current page:

```
<html>
<head>
<script>
document.write('this browser will run JavaScript');
</script>
<noscript>
<h2>You don't seem to have JavaScript enabled</h2>
Redirecting you to a script free version of the site...
<meta http-equiv="refresh" content="5; http://www.mySite/index.html">
</noscript>

</head>

<body>

</body>
</html>
```

The problem is, we can't use JavaScript within the `<noscript>` to set up the delayed action (we wouldn't be here if we could do that!). The `<meta>` tag allows us to do this another way, and is set up to do a 'client-pull' which is essentially the same as you entering a new URL in the browser and hitting return; it requests (or 'pulls') a new document from the server.

This method is better when you don't want the user to know what the problem is (such as when the user is browsing from a company computer that routinely has JavaScript disabled to prevent virus infection, so the user hasn't really got a choice), or you don't want to ask them to undo something they obviously feel strongly about enough to set up in the first place (such as a user who has disabled JavaScript intentionally because it stops pop-ups).

> We will be looking at `<noframes>`, a similar tag to `<noscript>` when we tackle **frames** in **Chapter 11**. The great thing about the Web is that as well as having all these great different technologies working together, you've got the means to allow for their absence too.

Applying this to the Mondo site

The final Mondo site will not work properly unless JavaScript is enabled. We therefore need to check for this in the file dev.html in folder mondoContent. Add the following code in the `<head>` part of this document's HTML:

```
<html>
<head>
<title>gateway</title>
<link href="mon_style.css" rel="stylesheet" type="text/css">
<script language="JavaScript" src="mondo_script.js"></script>
<noscript>
<p align="center">
This site requires a JavaScript enabled browser.  
Please enable Scripting and refresh your browser.
</p>
</noscript>
</head>
<body>
```

This will cause a warning message if the site is viewed with JavaScript disabled. Easy!

Summary

We've now covered JavaScript to the level you need to begin creating reasonably complex web scripts. Well done! Now, we need to approach another key topic in a bit more detail.

We introduced the basics of designing and deploying graphics on the Web in **Chapter 6**, and in the next two chapters we'll take that further, looking at using event-driven code to create interactive graphics like **rollovers** and using software like Fireworks or Photoshop to **slice** our graphic designs into working web pages.

Stand by for some really amazing results...

Special Image Features

What this chapter will do

We learned the details of **image formats** back in **Chapter 6**, but we have not yet really touched on how they're used in practice. In this chapter we will learn how to use the special features that some image formats possess, including:

- Transparency
- Progressive loading
- Animation

What you'll have learned by the end of this chapter

By the end of this chapter, you will have learned about some of the special options that the image formats we looked at earlier allow you. These might be simple options, but they're absolutely key in creating effective graphical web experiences.

You'll also be able to design and animate your own image sequences, and then optimize and export them ready to spice up your web pages.

Earlier in the book, we had a look at optimizing graphics. What we can do with graphics doesn't stop there, though. You can also use special features of your graphic format, including **transparency**, **animation**, and **progressive loading**.

After the last two chapters, I'm sure you'll be glad to hear that, from a technical standpoint, doing this isn't very hard. With these features, and the further image information that we'll learn about in the next chapter, we are moving from knowing the tools to being able to use design in a really creative sense. The real magic of designing a page is seamlessly mixing text and graphics so that the finished page has a mood and ambience, where the user no longer feels that they're interacting with just another web page.

> *We are now starting to add content to our skeleton site, so it might be a good idea to move on from the* mondoSkeleton *folder. Copy the* mondoSkeleton *folder and its contents, renaming the new folder* mondoContent.

Transparency

Currently, index.html is our 'under construction' page. It's cool in a minimalist kind of way, but perhaps we could add a little more to it. The Mondo logo is made up of the letters m and o with an ∞ sign between them, implying infinite possibilities. I like the use of the infinity symbol, and thought it might be cool to make that more prominent. The ∞ symbol in the logo appears again in the first page of the final site, bottom right:

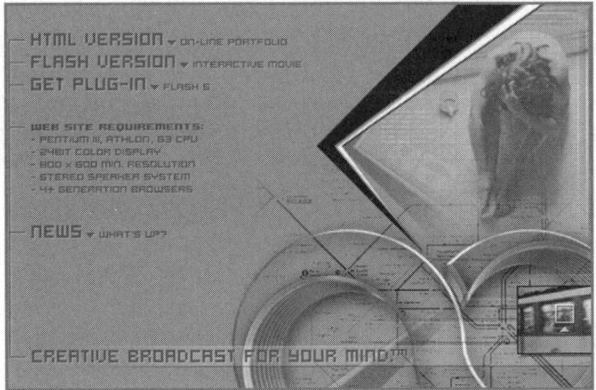

This time, the symbol appears to be made of glass, and it sits on top of a route map, with a grainy shot of someone on a train over it. To me, it signifies an infinite journey, which I'm guessing is what Mondo is all about to Tom; a self-imposed but fragile creative journey that may never end...

It also has the Mondo strapline across it: creative broadcast for your mind™. Put together, all that says a lot to me about not only the Mondo site, but Mondo as a concept itself, so if anything needs to go on the 'under construction' page, this would do it for me. We'll start with the image shown, which is a version of the infinity symbol, journey symbolism and the strapline separated from the other graphics.

You can find this file as `creative.tif` in the source files. The first thing we need to do is turn this into a low-bandwidth version. The TIF file is around 250 KB, but I think we can get this down to below 15 KB if we export it as a GIF.

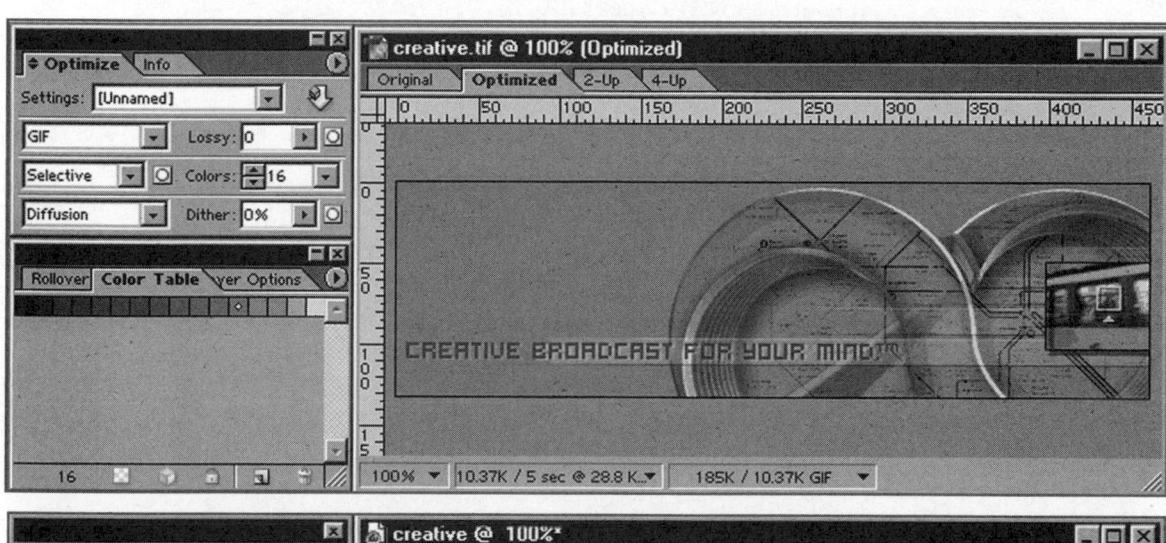

I'll leave you to do this using the lessons we learned in **Chapter 6**. Whether you use Fireworks or ImageReady, make sure you set the lossy/loss and Dither settings to zero so that the background remains a solid color and blends into the rest of our 'under construction' page. When you're finished, save the optimized image as mon_strapline.gif in the mondoContent folder.

The image is cropped so that it is designed to sit at the bottom right corner of a box, so we will have to place it in the same place in the browser window. Edit the code in index.html like this:

```
<html>
<head>
<title>Under Construction</title>
<link href="mon_style.css" rel="stylesheet" type="text/css">
</head>

<body>

<!--table main center - start-->
<table BORDER="0" CELLPADDING="0" CELLSPACING="0" WIDTH="100%"
    ➥ HEIGHT="100%" ALIGN="CENTER">
        <tr><td HEIGHT="100%">
        <!--table main dimensions - start-->
        <table BORDER="0" CELLPADDING="0" CELLSPACING="0"
        ➥ALIGN="CENTER" valign = "bottom">
            <tr><td>

                    <span CLASS = "title">Mondo is coming</span><br>
                    <img src="mon_logo.gif"><br>
                    <span CLASS = "text">Site launch 29th January
                    ➥ 1967</span>

            </td></tr>
        </table>
        <!--table main dimensions - end-->
</table>
<!--table main center - end-->

<img src="mon_strapline.gif" align="RIGHT" >

</body>
</html>
```

This will give you the following page:

Well, actually, you will see the same page as before with just the Mondo logo, centered in the middle of the page, but if you notice that the scrollbar is actually active, and scroll down, you will see the strapline. I actually prefer not having everything visible from the start; the ability to have little hidden extras that the user has to find is always fun.

Adding a background graphic

Another graphic element that Tom has tended to enjoy using is geometric grids as backgrounds. Have a look at the file `back.gif`: a simple 'r' shaped pair of lines. If this is repeated as a 'tile', you end up with a grid:

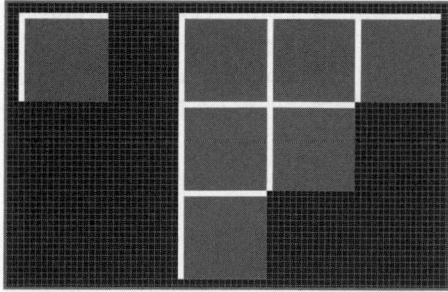

If you're interested in how to create this, see the note in the **Chapter 9** *source files folder.*

You can add a background like this by using the BACKGROUND attribute. Place the back.gif file into the MondoContent folder and change the <body> tag in index.html to:

```
<body BACKGROUND="back.gif">
```

This tells the browser to make back.gif the background image for the entire page (the whole page in within the <body> tag). The image is not actually big enough to cover the background, so what happens is that the image is repeated (or **tiled**) as many times as is necessary to fill the browser. That's a cool effect, given that it breaks the solid background, and makes our page look like it has larger graphic content than it actually has. On the downside, this kills the illusion that the page is one big image, as the Mondo logo and infinity images now show up their backgrounds against our new background.

The way round this is to make the mon_strapline.gif background pixels render as **transparent**. There are two routes here: Fireworks or ImageReady.

Giving images transparent backgrounds in ImageReady

1. Load mon_strapline.gif, and select the Optimized tab in the image window.

2. ImageReady tends to get confused if you load images into it that are already optimized (it may make the optimized version a 256-color GIF), so reselect 16 as the number of colors in the Optimize window to remind it otherwise. Do this even if the Colors setting already shows a value of 16.

    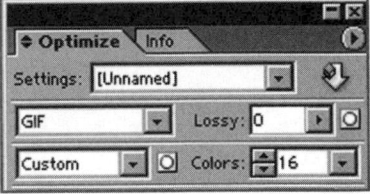

3. Select a background pixel with the color picker and the background color in the color table should now become selected.

    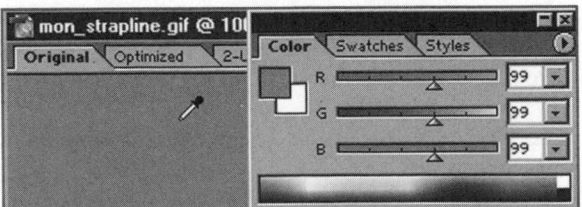

4. At the bottom of the color table, hit the icon to the far left that looks like a checkerboard. If you're not already viewing the image in 2-Up or 4-Up view, switch to the Optimized tab at the top of the screen, and you'll find that the background color has disappeared in the image, to be replaced by a checkerboard pattern (which is how most applications represent transparent pixels).

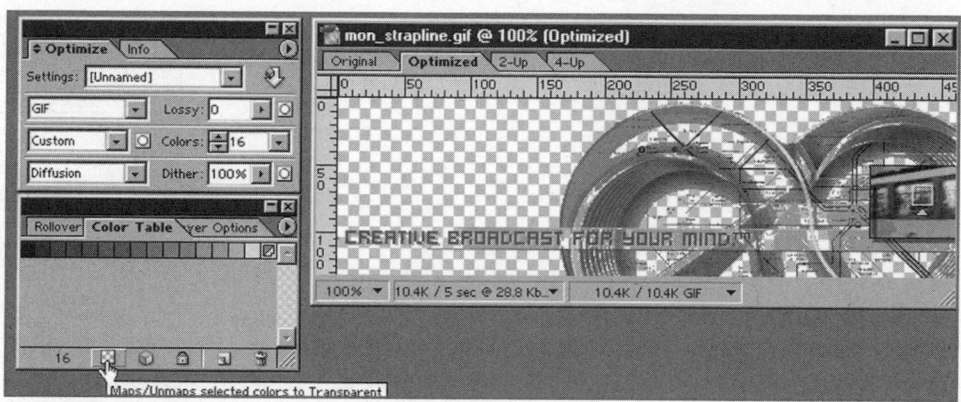

5. Save the optimized image as `mon_strapline_trans.gif` in the `MondoContent` folder with File > Save Optimized as....

6. Load up `index.html` and change the `<img>` tag at the bottom so that it points to our transparent version of the image:

```
<img src="mon_strapline_trans.gif" align="RIGHT" >
```

7. Test the page, and you should see that the background does what we would expect.

Giving images transparent backgrounds in Fireworks

1. Load the image, and select the Preview tab in the image window.

2. In the Optimize window, hit the Select transparent color icon, third from the bottom left. (If you can't see the Optimize window, bring it up with Window > Optimize.)

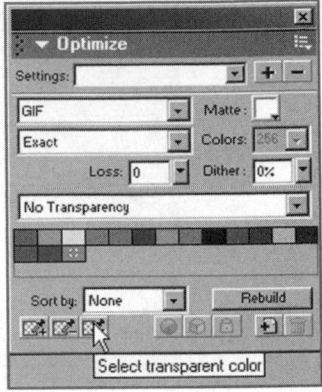

3. Click on the image background with the cursor, which should by now have turned into the color picker. Change from the Original to the Preview tab if you're not viewing the picture in 2-Up or 4-Up, and the background color will disappear, replaced by the checkerboard pattern that represents transparent pixels.

4. Save the optimized image as `mon_strapline_trans.gif` in the `mondoContent` folder with File > Export.

5. Load up `index.html` and change the `<img>` tag at the bottom so that it points to our transparent version of the image:

```
<img src="mon_strapline_trans.gif" align="RIGHT" >
```

6. Test the page, and you should see that the background does what we would expect:

Progressive images

One of my earliest Photoshop works was the rather dark 'Desire'. These images are fairly difficult to compress: they are quite busy and contain a number of conflicting requirements. Not only are they 'photo-like' and therefore better suited to JPEG compression, but they include integral text that is not incidental and therefore difficult to separate from the pieces. This text will be negatively affected by low JPEG compression rates, and this means that we may have to go for larger files to maintain the overall quality.

An alternative approach is to use **progressive** rather than standard images. A progressive image format starts showing things on screen before the full image is loaded into the browser, so there is always something for the user to see whilst they wait for the page to load up. JPEG is the only popular format that supports this feature, so this is a particularly good solution for my 'Desire' images.

> *The term for showing useful content before it is all loaded in is* **streaming**. *By allowing the user to see the beginning of a file before the end of it is actually ready, you hide the true loading time. Streaming is used in a number of web technologies – most notably video/sound formats – but is only really suitable for content that the viewer watches in a linear fashion. An interactive presentation where the viewer selected a section that hadn't loaded yet wouldn't be much use to anyone!*

Making an image progressive

1. Open the files `desire1.jpg` and `desire2.jpg` in either ImageReady or Fireworks. I have already optimized them from the original 24 MB Photoshop files, so you don't need to make any further changes to them (unless you really want to!).

2.   In **ImageReady**, select JPEG, specify High quality and check the Progressive checkbox in the lower left corner of the Optimize options (as shown in the screenshot):

3.   In **Fireworks,** select File > Export Preview, set the Quality to 60, and check the Progressive box under the Options tab in the window that appears:

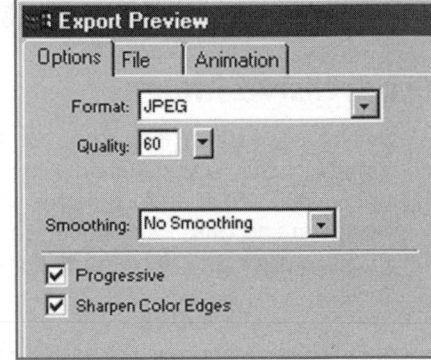

4.   You won't be able to see the image streaming in action unless you upload it to your server, so if you want to do that, then save your files in a new folder called prog_test, create the following HTML document in the same folder, and upload all three documents:

```
<html>
<head>
<title> Desire by Sham B</title>
<style>
IMG {margin: 10px 0px 0px 20px;}
</style>
</head>

<body>
<img SRC="desire1.jpg">
<img SRC="desire2.jpg">
</body>

</html>
```

These are simply adding margins around the images, so they don't touch right up to each other; kind of like picture frames. Prior to CSS, you would have done it via a table, but CSS is neater and easier.

Normally, large images are shown in a separate window to ensure that users can carry on doing other stuff whilst the image loads. When doing this, it is sometimes a good idea to make the link to the full-sized image a **thumbnail:** a smaller (typically 100x100) version of the final image.

If the image has lots of detail, you lose some of it when you reduce the size, so a top tip is to add a Gaussian Blur first, which creates some averaging so that the pixels you discard when you reduce still have an effect on the pixels in the final thumbnail.

You might also want to make a note that another way is simply to add a small section of detail at full size instead of the thumbnail. For the images in this example, you might, for example just use an image of one of the eyes as the thumbnail. Its something that art galleries traditionally do; eg 'Detail of *Man with Cake*, Leonardo de Bhangal, circa 1645 (pm)'. Doing that with images can sometimes produce more interesting thumbnail-type pictures that make the user more curious.

Animated GIFs

Almost everyone knows and hates animated GIFs even if they don't realize it, as they're the technology behind the much-hated animated banner adverts. Although now somewhat superseded by the more efficient and interactive Macromedia Flash, animated GIFs have one big advantage, and that is that all browsers can handle them without requiring a plug-in.

An animated GIF is simply a series of static GIF images that are played in sequence to give the impression of motion. Obviously then, a ten-frame animated GIF may be up to ten times bigger than the static version. Used sparingly, animated GIFs can occasionally serve a purpose.

Converting external animations to GIFs

Supposing you have created a sequence of images externally, and now want to use them to create a web animation, such as the rotating logo below:

Notice that we have chosen our logo design carefully; few solid colors, and a simple design. Obviously, less colors and lots of solid areas are good for high GIF compression ratios, but the fact that our logo is simple also means that it can be small and still discernable. As always, cropping and simplifying the image *even before* you start thinking about compression technology is the way to create *really* small files for the Web.

Importing animation in ImageReady

1. From the download file, place all of the files from `futuremedia00.tif` to `futuremedia18.tif` in a folder called `animation`.

2. Select File > Import > Folder as frames and pick the `animation` folder in the file browser window that appears.

> *Be sure not to open the folder, just select it, because ImageReady finds the images by looking inside the folder. If you open the folder, then it gets lost. Really pedantic I know, but that's what it does!*

3.   You should end up with an animation window that consists of all the frames of your animation, as shown below. To test this animation, hit the Play button.

> *You can also test the animation in a browser by selecting* File > Preview in > [Browser].

4.   The option to loop Once or Forever is also available to the left of the Play and other animation buttons and this will affect how the final animation is run in the browser, but not here in ImageReady.

5.   To export the animated GIF, we treat it just like a normal GIF. Our exported version, `animatedLogo.gif`, uses eight colors.

> *An important point to note when creating this type of animation is that adding dithering can sometimes spoil the animation by creating either 'shimmering' (where the dither pattern pulsates) or odd effects where the dither pattern seems to stay still as the animated effect moves.*

Importing animation in Fireworks

1. From the download file, place all of the files from `futuremedia00.tif` to `futuremedia18.tif` in a folder called `animation`.

2. Go to File > Open, select all the files in your sequence, and check the Open as animation option. (If you select the first file and then SHIFT-click the last one, you will automatically block-select all the files in between.)

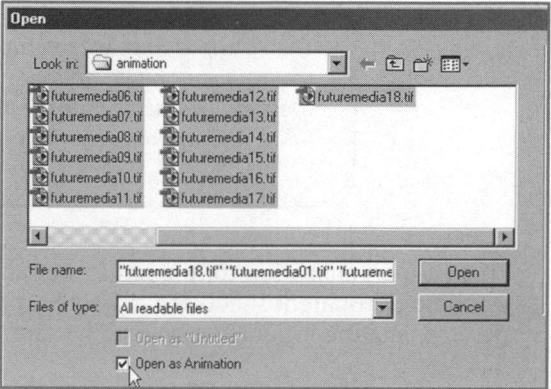

3. In the Optimize panel, select Animated GIF as the file format. The animation frames will appear in the Frames and History window, and the animation controls are below the main image window.

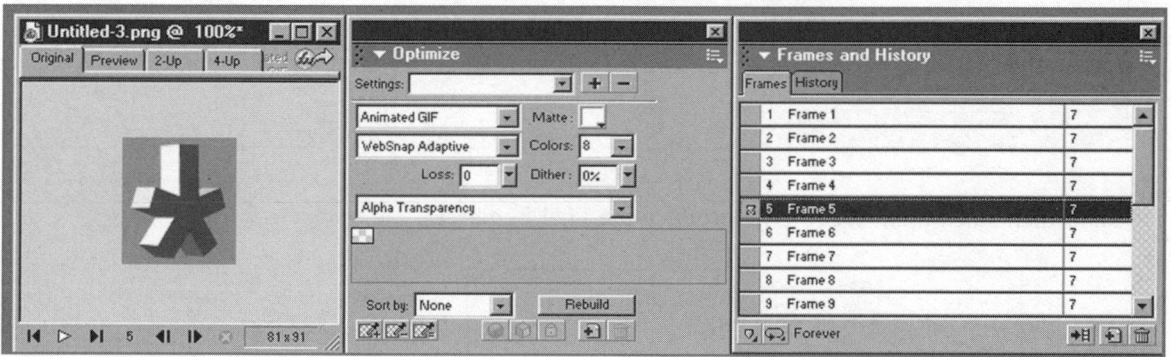

So what can you do with your animation? Well, you can treat it just like any other GIF, except that of course it will animate. You can actually use an animated GIF wherever you can use a normal GIF. You can even use one as your background, though this almost always looks horrible: try this to see why (you'll need the `animatedLogo.gif` file you've just created to be in the same directory as this HTML file)...

```
<html>
<head>
<head>

<body background="animatedLogo.gif">
<p> It won't be long before the novelty wears off!</p>
</body>

</html>
```

Creating your own animation from scratch

The rotating logo frames in the main exercise were actually created externally to both ImageReady and Fireworks, but we'll now have a brief look at how you would create animation from these applications from scratch.

> *The rotating logo was actually created in a 3D application. When creating specialised animations, it is always better to use a program specifically designed for the purpose, given that animation in general takes a long time to produce!*

True cartoon animation (of the sort Disney and Warner Bros do) is based on acetate sheets called **cel**. It's on these transparent sheets the characters, props and backgrounds are painted. Supposing we wanted to do an animation including a boy and his kite. Our individual animation components might look like this...

We separate the boy, the kite, and the background into separate sheets of cel.

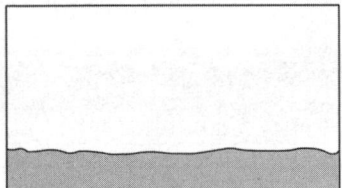  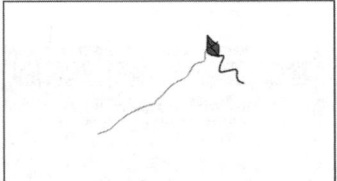

...and then stack them together to produce the final frame...

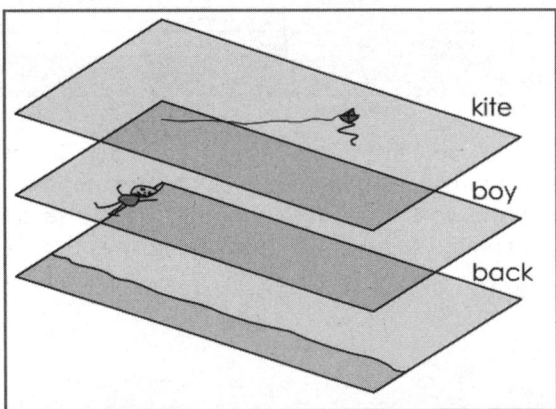 

What are the advantages of this separating? Well, animation is a frame by frame and laborious process at the best of times, and what this process does is make sure we can *isolate* the frames into animating and non-animating sections.

For example, the background stays still; the boy may walk into view with his kite, but then stand relatively still. Meanwhile, the kite is bobbing around all the time. Instead of having to redraw the background for every frame, because it is separate, we can get away with making it a static image. The boy moves, but not in every frame, so we can separate the animation of him from the kite. Finally, the kite has to be animated in every frame to give the impression of being blown about.

Another advantage of the cel-based approach is that you can simplify some parts of the animation simply by moving the acetates around, rather than having to paint lots of separate frames. For example, the kite swaying and bobbing may be recreated simply by moving its cell slightly relative to the others. In short, using cel prevents you having to draw the whole animation every frame.

The cells are simply a real world implementation of *layers*, so it comes as no surprise that layers play a strong part in the creation of animation digitally. Knowing that this is what our layers are emulating will make the walkthroughs below make much more sense. We will, as usual, look at ImageReady first, then Fireworks...

> *If you haven't used* **layers** *before, you might want to read* **Appendix D: Layers** *before continuing*

Original animation in ImageReady

The finished source file for this exercise is available as `animated_gif.psd` if you get stuck or want to look ahead to what we are aiming for.

Animation occurs via the Animation and (surprise, surprise...) the Layers windows.

In this example, we will create a simple animation including text and a couple of circles. We will then optimise the animation for GIF export and produce the final animated GIF.

1. Create a new file with File > New, making it 200 pixels wide by 100 high. Make the contents of first layer white.

2. Using the Type tool T , add the text 'circles...' in the center of the image, giving you a new text layer of the same name.

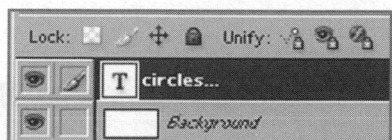

3. Create a new layer called red circle. In it, draw a red circle via the following steps:

4. Using the Create New Layer icon ▣ at the bottom of the Layers palette, create a new layer and name it red circle. Select this new layer and use the Marquee tool to draw out a circular selection anywhere on the image.

> *The Marquee tool will most likely be set to draw a rectangular selection (it's the first icon on the toolbox), but if you click-hold on it, you will see the correct icon* ◯.

5.   Next, click on the Foreground Color brick in the toolbox and select a red (it's a good idea to select a web-safe red by checking Only Web Colors in the color picker window that will appear, for maximum compatibility). Using the Paint Bucket tool 🪣, click inside the circular selection. Voila! One red circle.

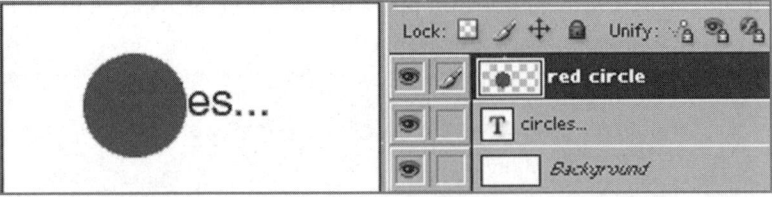

6.   Repeat the process, this time creating a green circle in its own layer green circle. Finally, drag the text layer circles … so that it is the topmost layer. As shown below, this will put the text in front:

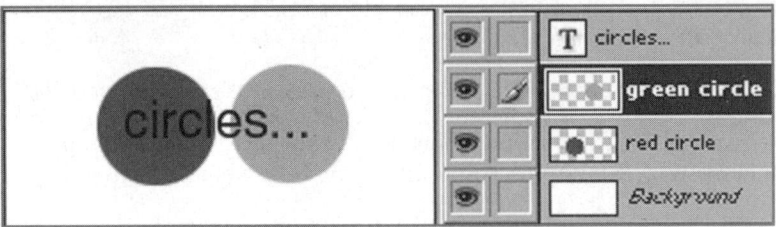

OK, what we now need to do is create something called **keyframes**, and a **tween** animation between them. We will look at what these are, and where they come from in terms of hand-drawn animation when we look at Flash in the final chapter of this book, but for now, we will simply carry out the steps (you can look ahead to **Chapter 12** if you are feeling curious).

Think of this window as a reel of film. The little thumbnail images will form a film reel-like sequence containing your animation.

8. Copy the current frame by clicking the Duplicate current frame icon at the bottom of the palette:

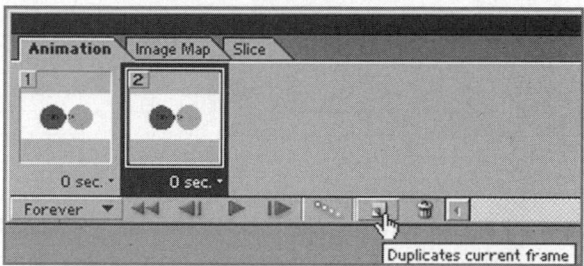

These are our two **keyframes**. They define the start and end point of our animation. What we will do is create an animation where the two circles shoot across the image, from left to right (red) and right to left (green), crossing in the middle.

9. Select the first frame in the animation window, and on the actual image, select the red circle and green circle layers, and using the Move tool ▸⊕, move each circle so that the red one is almost off screen, bottom left corner, and the green one is the same at the top right, then, select frame 2 and swap the positions of the two circles.

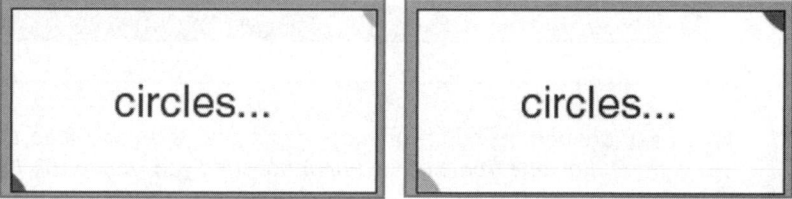

10. Now, here's the clever part. In the Animation palette, select frame 1 and SHIFT-SELECT frame 2, so both are highlighted. Then, hit the Tween animation frames icon ⚬⚬⚬ (it's at the bottom of the animation palette).

11. In the pop-up that appears, make sure Tween With is set to Selection, This will create an animation transition between the two selected frames. In Frames to Add enter 10, and make sure all the other options are as shown (they should be the default settings when the dialog appears).

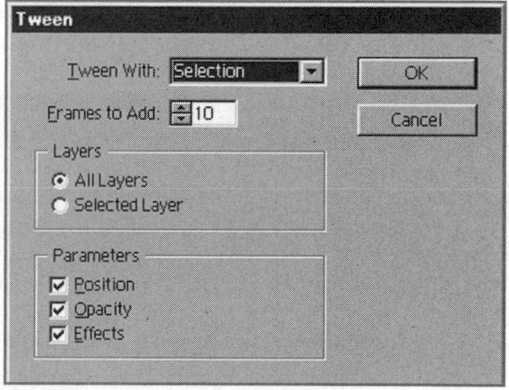

You should now see your animation, and pressing the Play button on the Animation palette will run the sequence.

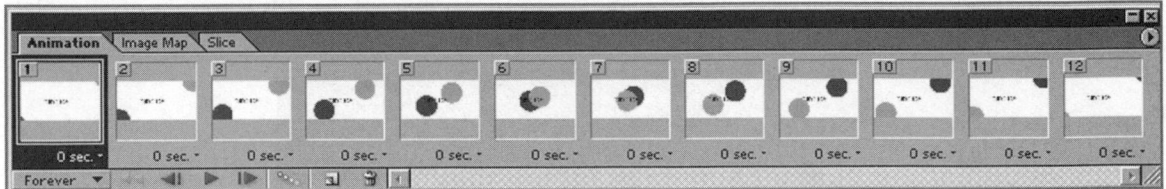

12. To optimize this, simply go to the Optimized, 2-Up or 4-Up tab in the main image window, and optimize as you would with a static image, but make sure you select GIF as the file type. You can preview the animation with File > Preview in > [browser] and export the final GIF with File > Save Optimized as (again, all just the same as you would with a non-animating image).

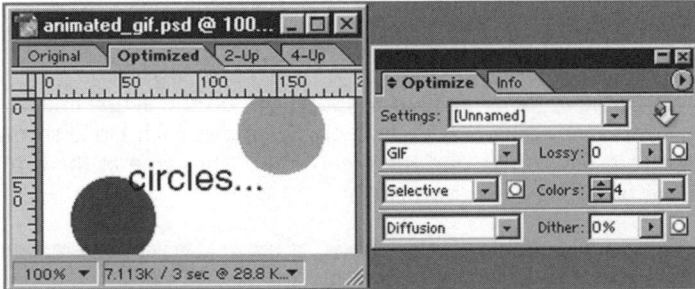

When you are optimizing an animation, it's always a good idea to check more than one frame of the animation, and you can do this by selecting frames in the Animation *palette and checking that they all look OK in the main window.*

As well as adding motion as we have here, you can also add other effects by selectively showing/hiding layers. For example, if you select every other frame in turn in the Animation palette, and then hide the text layer for those frames, you will end up with flashing text!

Original animation in Fireworks

The finished source file for this exercise is available as `animated_gif_fw.png` if you get stuck or want to look ahead at what we will be creating.

Animation occurs via the Frames and History panel and (surprise, surprise...) the Layers panel.

In this example, we will create a simple animation including text and a couple of circles. We will then optimize the animation for GIF export and produce the final animated GIF.

1. Create a new file with File > New, making it 200 pixels wide by 100 high, and at a resolution of 72 pixels per inch. Next, fill the first layer with white.

2. Using the Text tool **A**, add the text 'circles...' in the center of the image, giving you a new text layer.

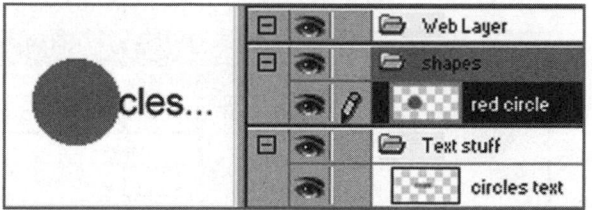

3. Rename the new text object (it is currently called Text in the Layers palette) to circles text. Rename Layer 1 to Text stuff.

4. Using the New/Duplicate Layer icon ![icon] at the bottom of the Layers panel, create a new layer and rename it shapes.

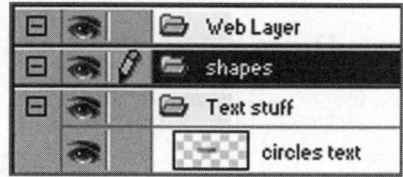

5. Select shapes and use the Marquee tool to draw out a circular selection anywhere on the image. The Marquee tool will most likely be set to draw a rectangular selection (it's the first icon on the Bitmap section of the Tools panel), but if you click-hold on it, you will see the correct icon ![icon].

6. Next, click on the Foreground Color brick in Tools and select a red.

7. Using the Paint Bucket tool ![icon] , click inside the circular selection. Voila! One red circle. Rename the new bitmap created to 'red circle'.

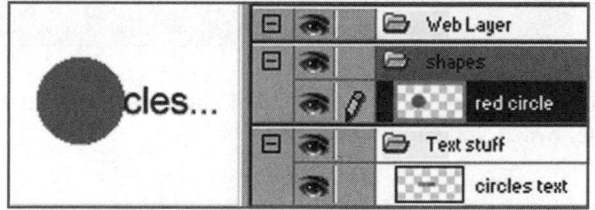

We want to repeat the process, adding another circle, but Fireworks will assume anything else we draw is part of the Bitmap object red circle. That would be OK for a static image, but we will be looking towards making the two circles move independently, and that means they have to be separate objects.

8. To start a new object, with the layer shapes still selected, go to Edit > Insert > Empty Bitmap. This lets Fireworks know we want to start a new bitmap graphic. Draw out a new circular marquee selection as before, but this time color it green.

9. Rename the new bitmap green circle. Finally, move the Text stuff layer to the top of the stack (you won't be able to put it above the Web Layer, which is always at the top).

10. Finally, lock the Text stuff layer (by clicking in the column pointed at by the cursor in the image below). We won't be animating the text, so it's a good idea to do this to get it out of the way for now.

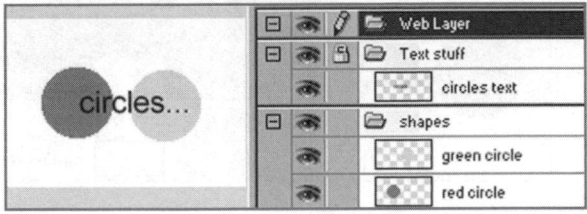

What we will do next is animate the two circles whizzing around the image. Fireworks displays animations as a combination of *paths* and *frames*.

11. Select each circle in turn, and bring up the Animate dialog by either right-clicking on the circle and selecting Animation > Animate Selection or the same thing from the Modify menu. In either case, you'll see this:

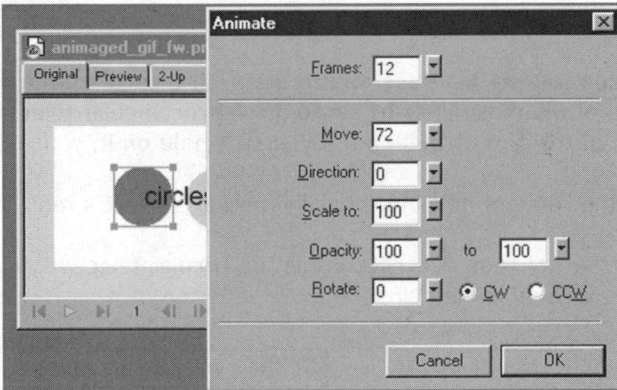

12. Leave all the values at the default (we'll change them interactively in a moment in any case), except the Frames value, which you should change to 12.

> *You will get a warning message asking if you want to automatically add more frames. Click* OK *in response.*

You will see a line of dots starting from the center point of the circle (and in green) to a red one. This path maps out the journey the circle will take on its animation. You will also see 11 new frames appear in the Frames and History panel, and you can check what any frame will look like by clicking on a particular frame and looking at the main image.

13. Drag the green and red dots so they take the circle from the bottom left corner to the top right-hand corner as shown below, checking that the circle is just visible at frame 1 and 12;

> *You may have to temporarily move the green circle out of the way as you do this.*

14. Select Frames within the Frames and History panel to see the circle move along the path. Note that the green circle currently exists on frame 1 only, as does the text.

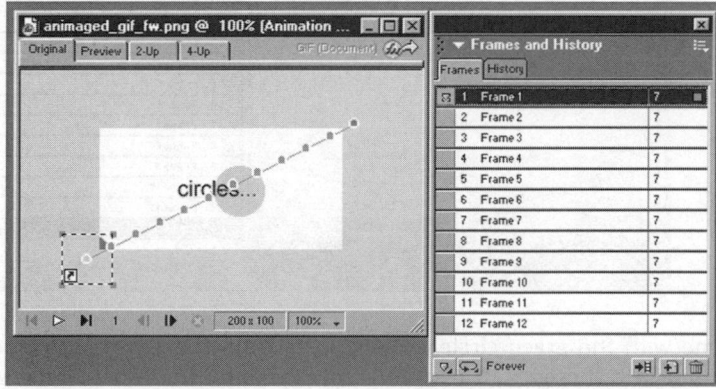

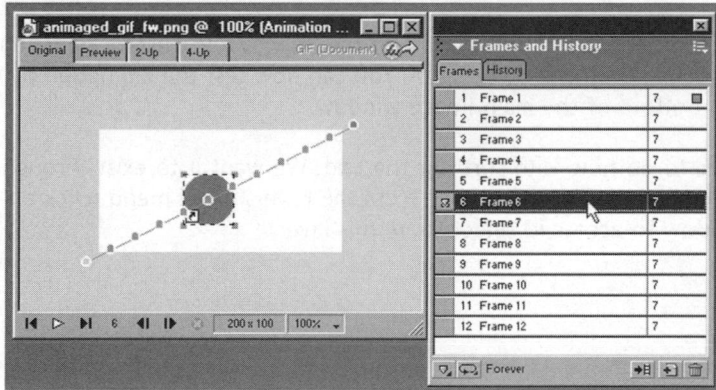

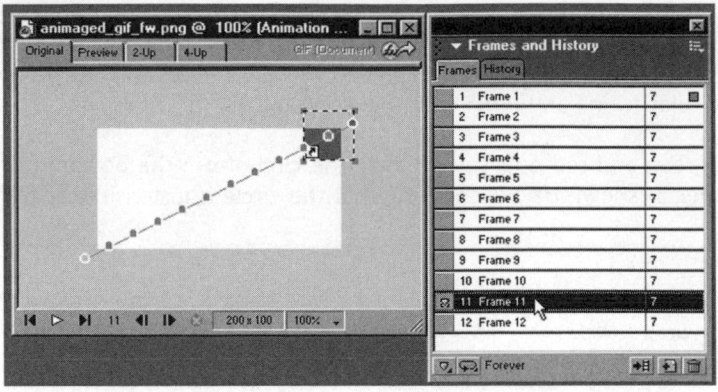

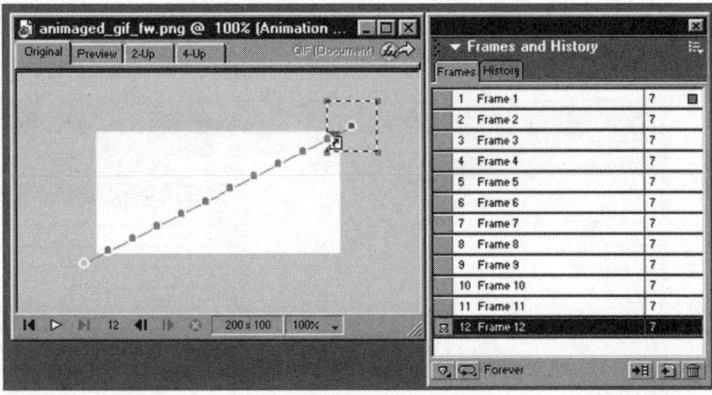

15. Do the same with the green circle, making it go from the top right to the bottom left (you will have to find it first though ... it currently only exists on frame 1 so select that frame before you proceed).

16. Click the icon ⟲ at the bottom left of the Frames and History panel and make sure Forever is checked (it should be this by default). You can now test the animation by clicking the Play icon ▷ at the bottom of the main image window.

17. All we have to do now is to sort out the text. We want it to exist throughout the animation, and to do that unlock the layer and then from the Layers panel menu (click on the ▤ at the top right of the window to access it) select Share this layer.

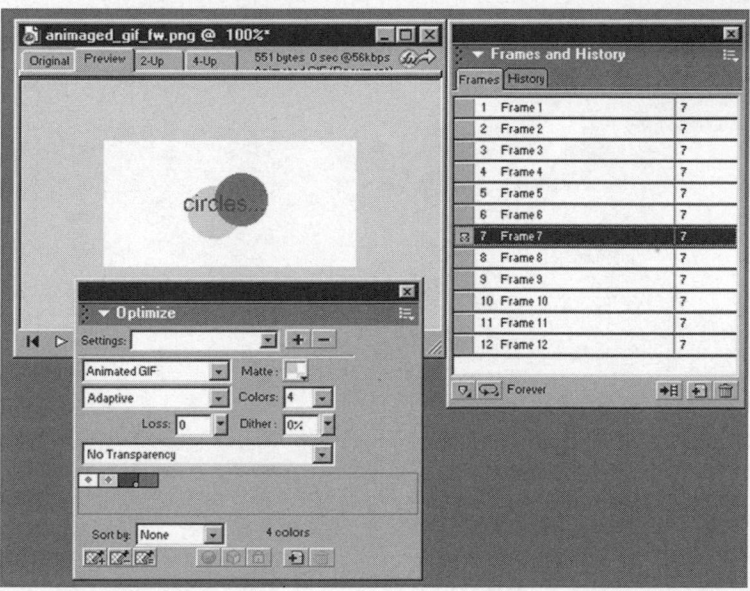

18. To optimise this, simply go to the Preview, 2-Up or 4-Up tab in the main image window, and optimise as you would with a static image, but make sure you select Animated GIF in the file type. You can preview the animation with File > Preview in browser > [browser] and export the final GIF with File > Export (again, all just the same as you would with a non-animating image).

> *When you are optimising an animation, it is always a good idea to check more than one frame of the animation and have the* Frames and History *panel open whist you optimize to do this (as shown above).*

Summary

We've now gone substantially further than our last foray into web graphics, delving into the animations features of ImageReady and Fireworks. You're now competent enough to start creating your own animations and transparent graphics, even maybe a dreaded banner ad or two! At least you now know how they make them.

The next chapter continues and concludes our study of graphics, with slicing and rollovers, the very basis of website interactivity...

Slicing Images

What this chapter will do

We've learned about the different image formats and how to optimize images in
Chapter 6, and we've learned about the special features unique to some formats
in **Chapter 9**. Now it's time to move on and add our graphics into the wider mix
of our overall web page. In this chapter, we'll look at:

- **Slicing** large graphics
- Turning slices into **buttons**

What you'll have learned by the end of this chapter

In this chapter, we'll start by taking you through the slicing of one of the Mondo
pages. This will then allow us to create the buttons for the menu on the page. The
process of creating the buttons is fairly different in ImageReady and Fireworks, but
don't worry – we'll cover each program in turn. By the end of the chapter, you'll
be able to slice your images, and turn individual slices into buttons.

Slicing

We know that we should optimize our graphics, but all we have really done is optimize single images. A typical website consists of several image areas, all of which may require different image types. We haven't yet seen how to separate a design into different files, rather than use one big image, and then put it back together as a final web page.

The process of separating our content into image areas is called **slicing**, and produces a number of different **image slices**. These slices are then arranged in a table to give the user the impression of one big image.

Slices have several benefits:

- You can specify different levels of image quality for each slice (just select each slice and optimize it in the same way that we did for individual images in **Chapter 6**).
- You can turn individual slices into buttons.
- You can replace areas of images with plain HTML background.
- Placeholder slices can later be used to house objects such as Macromedia Flash movies (more on Flash in **Chapter 12**).
- It can make re-designing the site (or customizing it for different people) easier, as you can just replace specific key slices.

Here, we're going to use slices primarily for the second reason – to let us create a menu bar. The great bonus here is that ImageReady and Fireworks can take a lot of the pain out of this process for us.

Source files

The source files that you use to create your website are called **assets**. You will occasionally have to build them all entirely from scratch, but you will often be starting with some material. You might have some images that you've made in the past, or some photos. In the commercial world, clients will often supply logos and other graphics for you to include.

The first step is to bring these assets into a program like Photoshop. In the commercial world, the Photoshop files with the graphics on them are often printed and signed by the client before any further work continues, as making changes after this stage can be particularly arduous. A simple logo change could mean the tables holding the slices have to be completely redesigned on every page where the logo appears, for example.

There is a lot of job satisfaction in web design, but the downside is always the number of seemingly small changes that cause major reworks, so getting things right at this stage is important, if only for your sanity! We're going to be using the original Mondo storyboard files that Tom put together. These were created in Photoshop, but you can open them in Fireworks if you haven't got Photoshop.

Starting the slicing

1. To start, you need to install the font that Mondo uses – `hoog055.ttf` – and you can find this in the source files. If you don't (or can't) install the font, then you might meet with a few warning windows when you first open the files – select No in each window, and everything should be fine.

2. Unzip the files for this chapter to a new folder called `mondo assets`. Open up `mon_t_upper.psd` – we start with the PSD file, whether you're in Photoshop or Fireworks.

> *For the work in progress and final files, you'll need to open the correct version – the Fireworks files are in PNG format, and the Photoshop files in PSD format. These are different because we're going to use both programs to write some HTML/JavaScript later, and they tend to create slightly different files.*

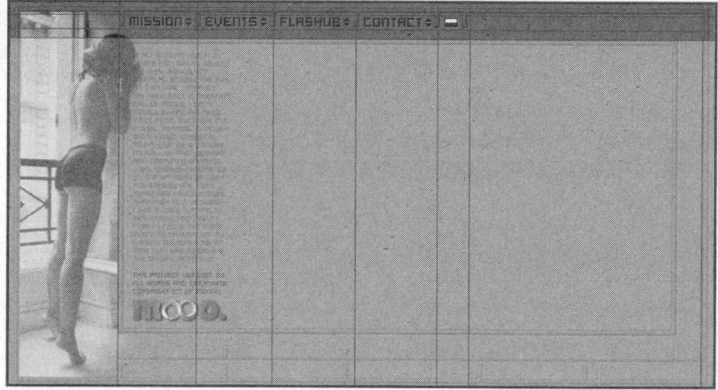

3. So, what are those blue lines all about? These are the lines (or **guides**) along which we need to slice the graphics. The graphics will then be placed in a table so that they display perfectly as one to the user.

4. Select the Slice tool from the toolbox. In Fireworks, it's simply a matter of clicking on the ⬚ icon. Photoshop users need to go to ImageReady here, and ImageReady has a Slice *and* a Slice Select tool in the same place in the toolbox: to make sure you get the right one, press-hold the icon ⬚ and select Slice Tool from the pop-up menu that appears.

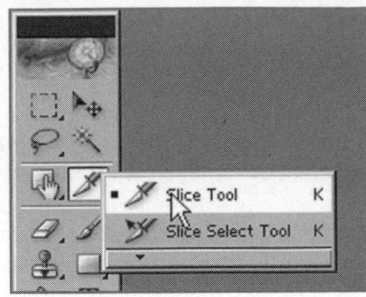

5. Starting from the top left-hand corner, use the Slice tool to select each area within the image area to be separated. Do this by click-dragging from the top left-hand corner of each segment marked out by the ruler lines, to the bottom right. Zooming into the image so that you get the slices right on the ruler lines really helps.

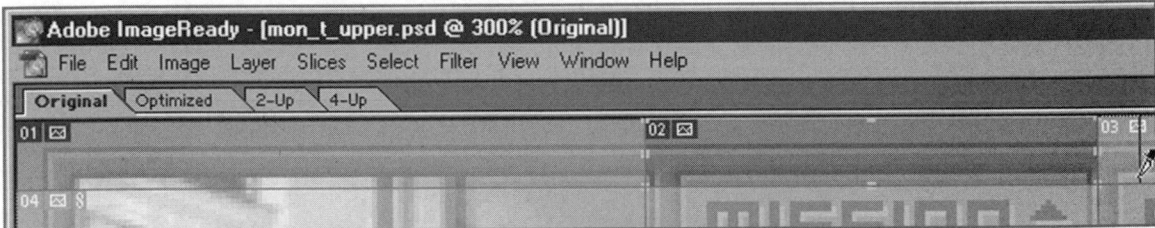

> This isn't that easy, so a couple of tips. First, make sure that View > Snap to Guides *(ImageReady)/* View > Guides > Snap to Guides *(Fireworks) is switched on, and the application will help you by snapping to the nearest ruler line when you get close to it. Second, remember the undo key (*CTRL+Z): it's a life-saver in this process.*

6. As you add each slice, ImageReady will number them and Fireworks will simply add a semi-transparent colored rectangle.

7. If ImageReady makes it difficult to see the faded out areas after you make the first slice, select the Slice Select tool (by clicking and holding on the Slice tool and selecting it from the menu that pops up), and hit the Show auto-slices button that appears at the top of the screen.

8. In Fireworks, you'll notice the slices appearing in the Web Layer in the Layers panel as you create them.

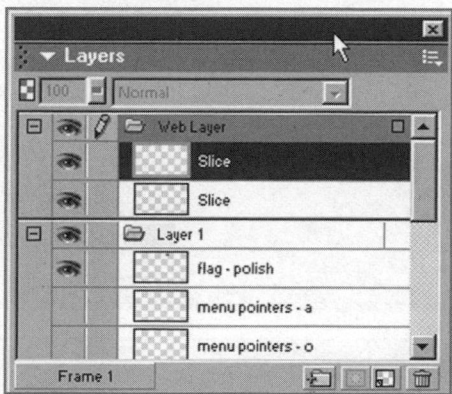

> *To temporarily hide the slice lines in ImageReady, select* View > Extras, *or simply hit* CTRL+H *to toggle them. In Fireworks, use* View > Guides, *or* View > Slice guides, *or* View > Slice overlay, *or simply click the eye icon on the* Layers *panel* Web Layer.

9. Carry on slicing until you have a slice for all the parts of the image we need to cover – that's twenty-four slices in all (three rows of eight).

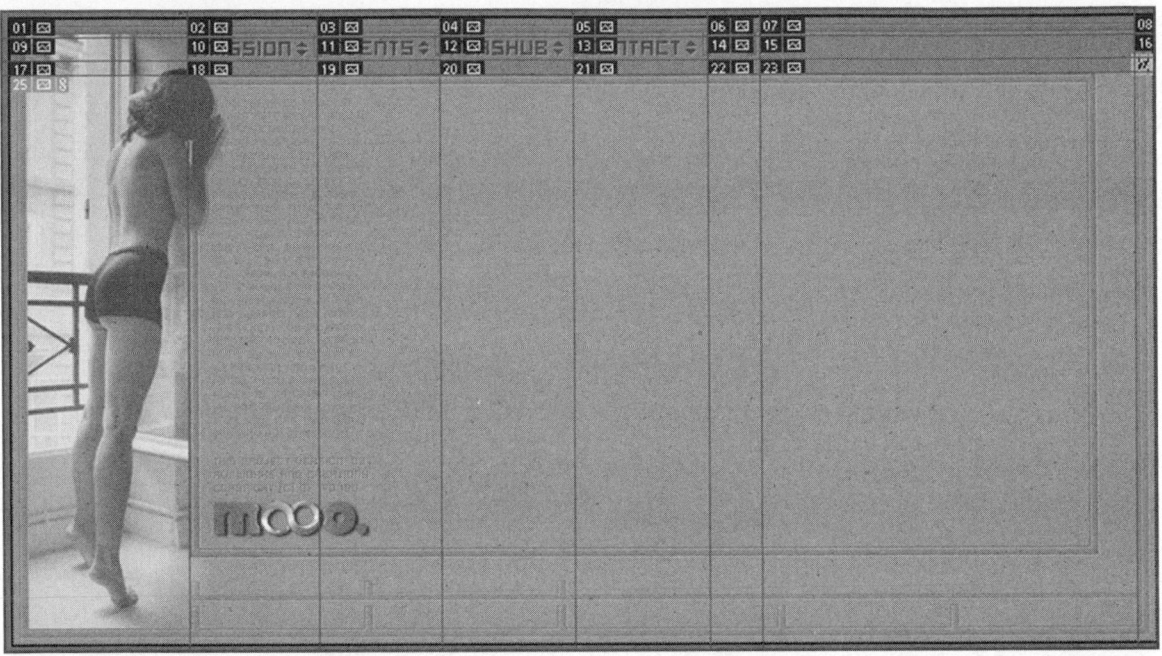

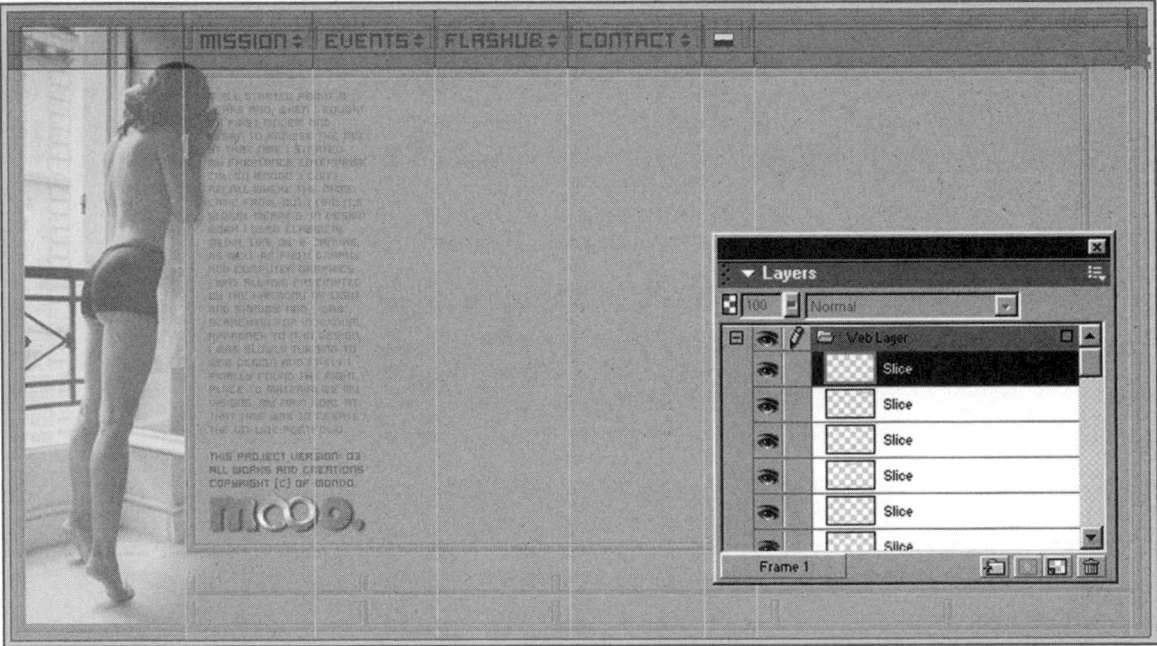

10. To check that you have not inadvertently created more slices than you need, ImageReady users should have consecutively numbered slices, and Fireworks users should see the selected slice move along by one as you select each slice object in the Layers panel (be careful not to move slices when selecting them – wait until the single cursor pointer displays).

11. We don't actually need the part of the image that we haven't specified as slices. Select the Crop tool, highlight the area you've turned into slices, and double-click to get rid of the rest of the image. Make sure that you crop at the exact ruler lines (using zoom is recommended!): we don't want any extra slices around the edges!

12. Save your files in a new folder called `mondo slice files` - ImageReady will save to PSD, whereas Fireworks prefers to save as PNG, both of which is fine. That's it - congratulations, you've just created your first slices.

Working with our slices

Each slice that we've just made is now effectively a single graphic, so any settings that we want to apply can be applied to them individually.

1. We're going to give all our slices the same compression, so we need to select all the slices. ImageReady users, select the Slice Select tool, and click-drag a box that encloses all of the slices. Fireworks users need to shift-select all the slice objects in the Layers panel or shift-select each slice directly with the Pointer tool.

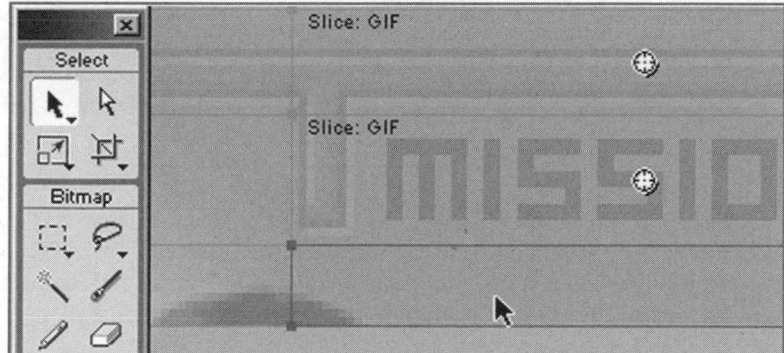

2. Once you've selected all the slices, turn them into 32-color GIFs, using an adaptive color palette. Make sure that there's no Dither specified – dithering across slices can create "seams" between the slices. We're dealing with solid colors here anyway, so noise won't look great.

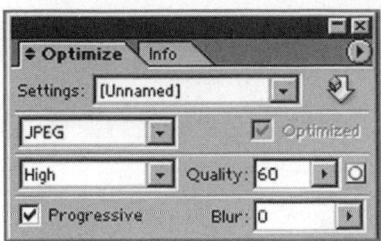 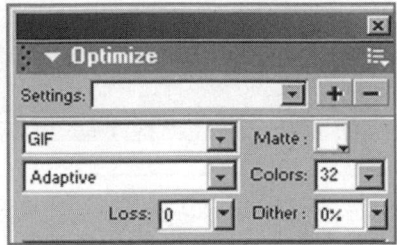

3. We're now going to give our slices some attributes. ImageReady users, make sure you can see the Slice Tab (Window > Slice), Fireworks users make sure they can see the Properties panel (Window > Properties).

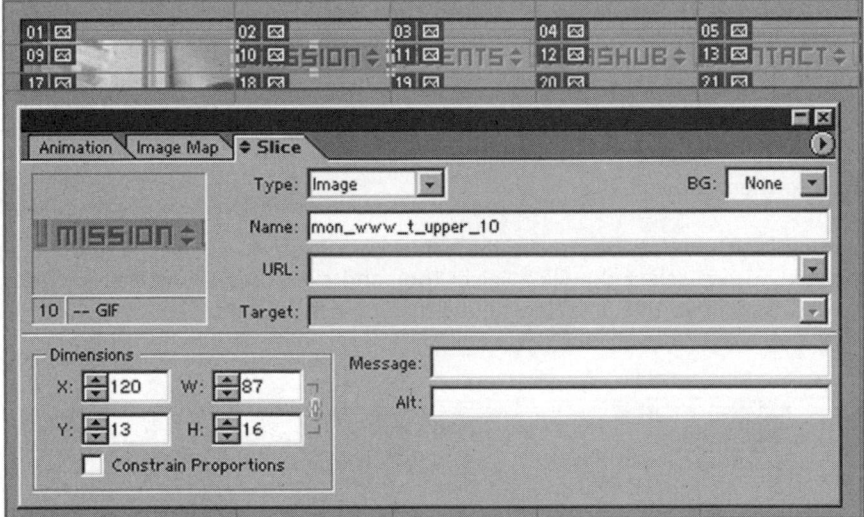

*Each slice has already been given a name based on the name of the source file. ImageReady and Fireworks will give slightly different names; **so make sure you stick to one or other application** for the rest of the exercise if you have both.*

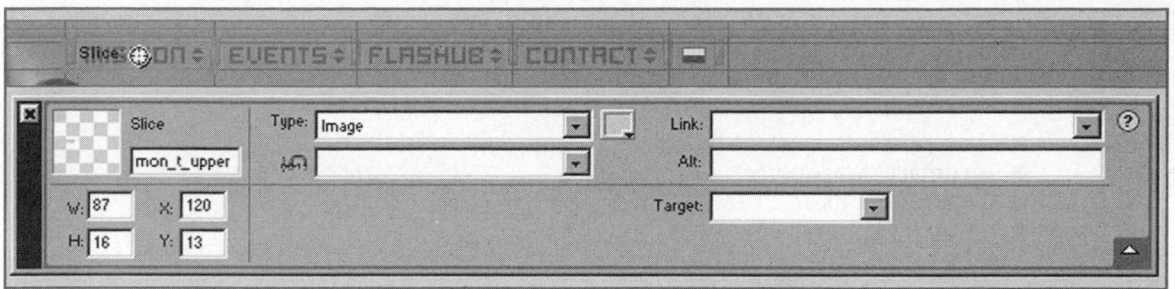

4. You can now deselect the entire group of slices by clicking outside them. The Link/URL option allows us to specify a link for a graphic – effectively making a button. Add the following links to these slices by clicking on the text to select the slice, and entering the value into the panels we've just opened:

- events slice: mon_events.html
- contact slice: mon_contact.html

5. We can also add the JavaScript to open a pop-up as part of the link/URL. We're going to make use of that handy openPop() function we included in mondo_script.js in **Chapter 7**, so add the following Link/URLs:

- flashub slice: javascript:openPop('flash.html', 'flashPopup', 'no', 800,
  ➥ 600);
- Polish flag slice: javascript:openPop('mon_pol_mis.html',
  ➥ 'polPopup', 'no', 550, 300);

The application already knows this is a string, so there's no need for speech marks here.

6.   We discussed Alt text in **Chapter 2**: it will display in browsers configured not to show images, be used by screen readers for the visually impaired, and finally display when users hover their mouse over the graphic. Add the following Alt: values:

- events slice: events
- contact slice: contact
- flash slice: flash
- Polish flag slice: tekst Polski

7.   ImageReady users will see a Message option. This allows you to make text appear in the browser status area when the user's mouse passes over the image. All browsers will show this, but some will show it, and then immediately overwrite it with the URL or 'document done' text. If you are using ImageReady, add the following message texts:

- events slice: What's up in mondo land
- flashub slice: Open Flash site in a pop-up
- contact slice: contact mondo
- Polish flag slice: Polish language translation

8.   Some of our slices are simply a section of background color. Given that it will be faster to download, we might as well have an empty cell in the final table instead of loading this in. Select one of the pure gray cells, and choose No Image (in ImageReady) or HTML (in Fireworks) to create a blank table cell.

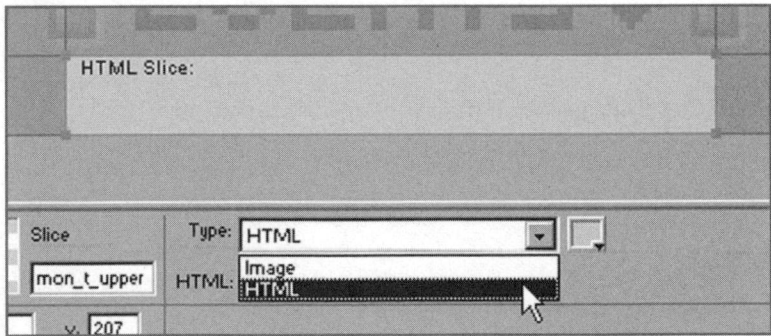

9. You also need to specify no background color for the cell, so that the background color of the page will show through. To do this, select NONE for BG in Imagready. In Fireworks, you'll need to select the No Color option from the color brick next to the Type drop-down in the Properties panel (as shown by the white with a red line through it).

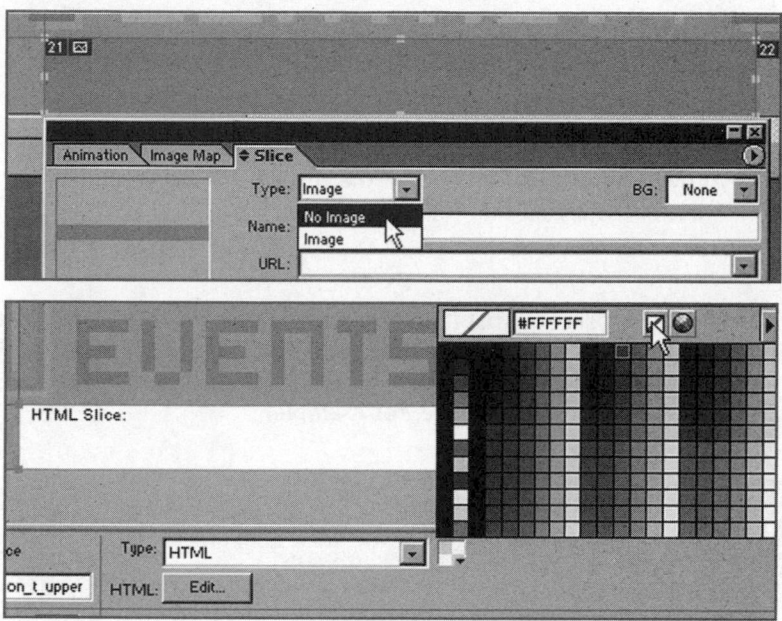

10. You can do this for the other empty cells too if you want, but the graphics that we're talking about here are small enough that it's less of an issue than other pages.

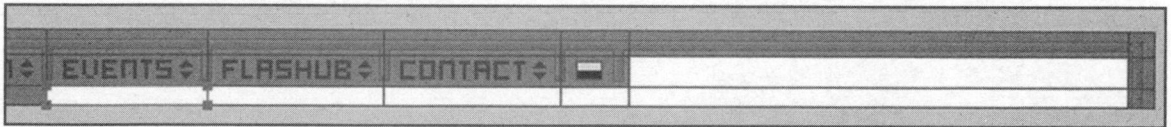

Another slice?

As you might have worked out by now, that tricky bit of slicing that we've just done is only a small part of the overall slicing work for the Mondo site. This is unfortunately one of the side effects of taking apart an absolute top-level creative site for our case study, rather than a quickly knocked-together example. Not that many sites are going to be as complex – in terms of content or artistic direction – as Mondo, so you can rest assured that the twenty-four slices you've just lovingly created are probably as complex as you're going to need to get.

The way that we've shown you offers you the maximum amount of control, but ImageReady users may want to investigate the Slices > Create Slices from Guides *option to automate things in future: just create guides by click-dragging them out from the rulers, and ImageReady will slice along them for you.*

All the original files are supplied in the downloads area, for those of you who want a little more practise or even those of you who want to go and do all the rest of the slicing. Otherwise, keep reading for the explanation of the rest of the slicing that follows...

The Mondo slices

The other point behind using slices is that it means that you can separate the content that doesn't change from the content that does. You can then use **frames** (as we'll see in the next chapter), to create a more efficient site where we don't have to keep loading the content that never changes (take a look at the `mon_www_t_something` files in the final site, for example).

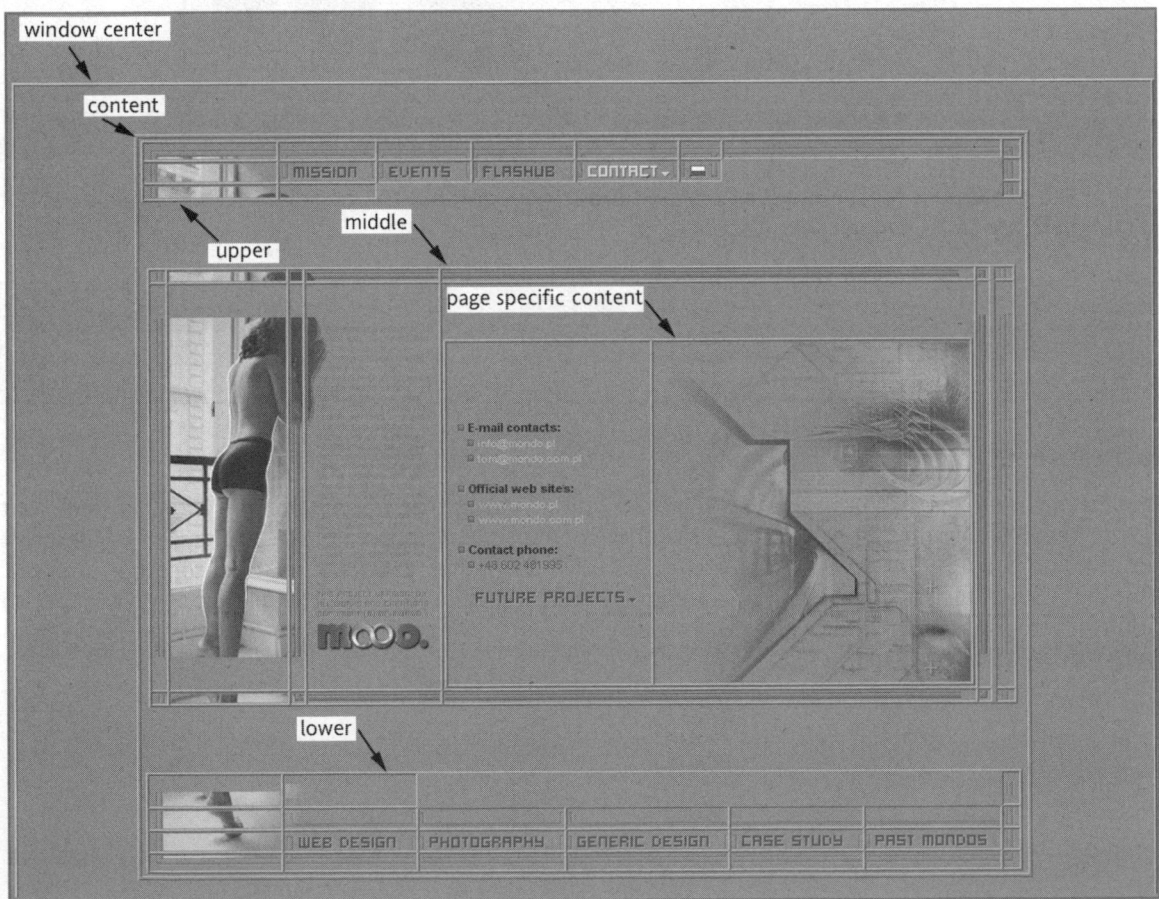

The diagram above can be simplified into the one below:

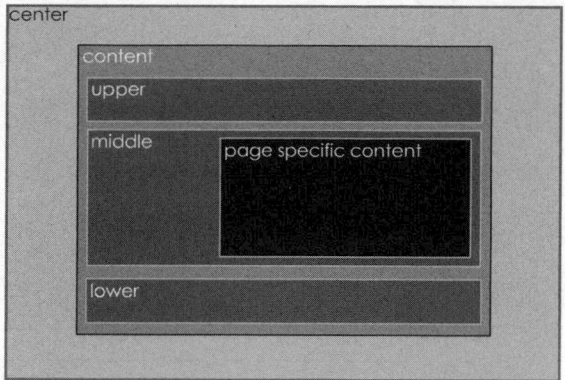

The file that we've just completed – `mon_www_t_upper.psd` in the Mondo files – specifies the slices we need to create to populate the upper table:

The file `mon_www_t_middle.psd` specifies the slices we need to populate the middle table:

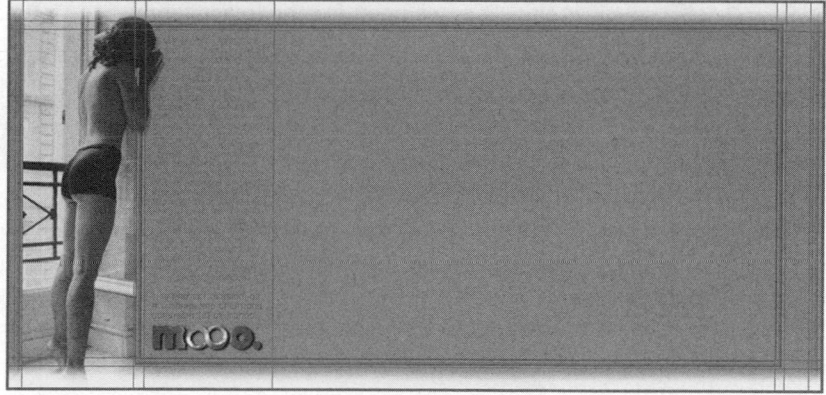

Notice that the page specific content area is blank in `mon_www_t_middle`. We will be filling that with the content seen in the files `mon_www_start`, `mon_www_mission`, `mon_www_events`, `mon_www_webdes` and `mon_www_contact`. The first three of these are shown on the next page:

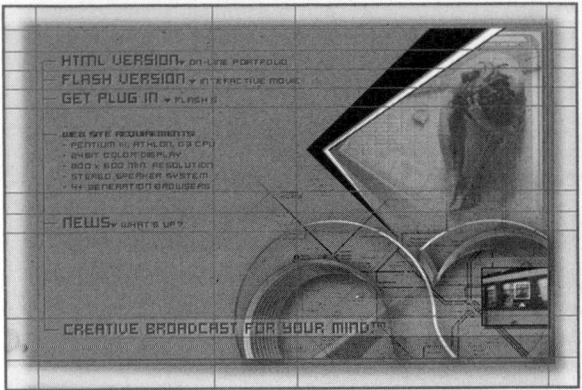

Finally, `mon_www_t_lower` specifies the slices we need for the lower table:

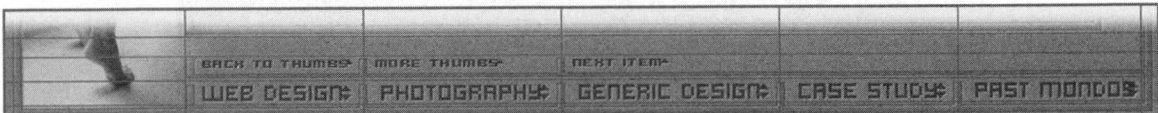

Creating rollovers

Normally, the mission graphic is as below, left. In the final site, we want the text to become highlighted if the mouse is rolled over it (below, middle). If the graphic is not an active link, meaning that you're already at that page, then we want the text to be highlighted for as long as you're on that page (below, right).

normal state

over state

active state

We're going to spend the rest of the chapter talking about how to do this. As before, this process is a little different for ImageReady and Fireworks users, so Fireworks users need to go to page 315.

Again, we stress that files between ImageReady and Fireworks are not compatible in these exercises: so choose one, and stick with it!

Adding rollovers in ImageReady

To build the menu for the mission page, we need the events, flashub, and contact slices to be buttons, and the mission slice to remain highlighted (as shown).

We'll start by giving the different images separate layers, so that we can alter one button at a time, rather than all of them at once. We'll then set up the graphics that change, and add the rollovers to make that happen.

Preparing our layers

1. Open up `mon_t_upper_sliceStart` from the source files, and open ImageReady.

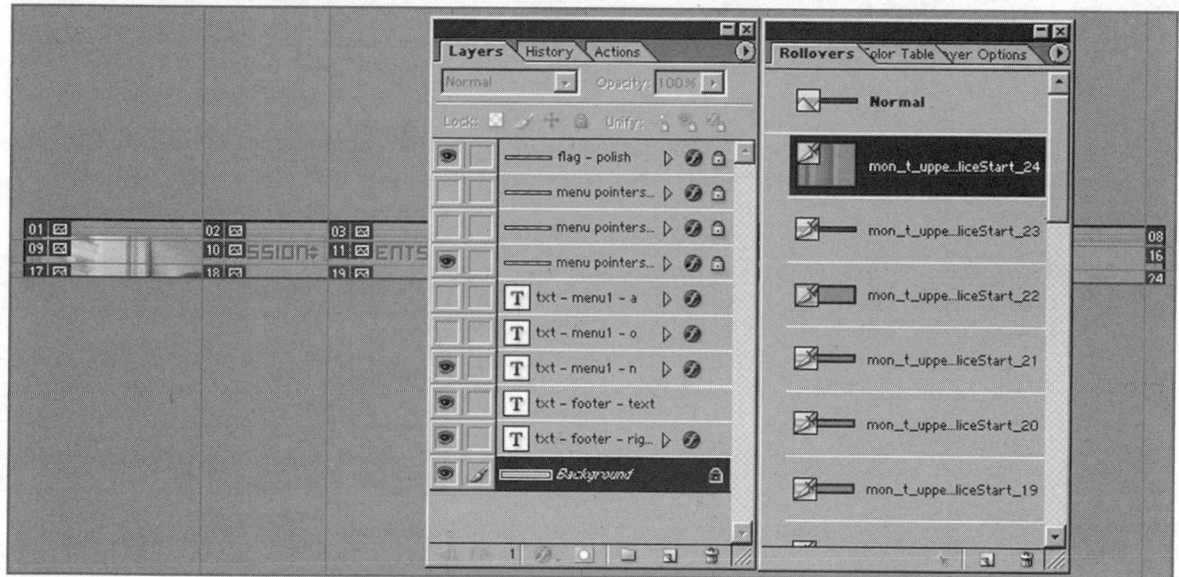

2. Make sure the two tabs you can see in the screenshot - the Layers and Rollovers tabs – are open (you can open them both from the Windows menu if you can't see them).

3. Make all the layers in the list invisible, by clicking on the eye symbols to the left of them. Now, make the Background layer at the bottom of the list visible by clicking on the eye symbol next to it.

4. Click on the eye icon in the Layers palette for the first three text layers (txt - menu1 - a, - o and - n), and you will see that the mission text in our graphic will change between the three states we want.

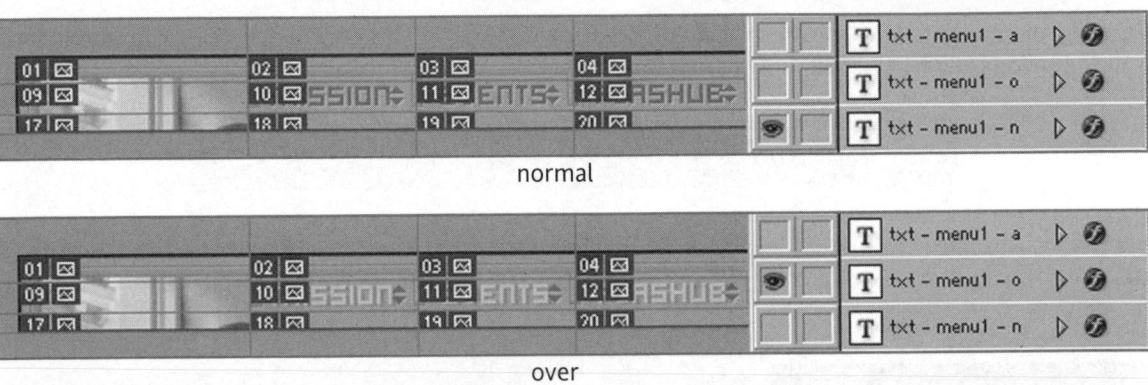

normal

over

active

The problem is that any layer changes affect all of the buttons at the same time. We need to create a set of layers for each button, so that changes only affect one button at a time.

5. Select the top text layer (txt1 - menu1 - a), and create a new layer set by clicking the folder-like Create a new set icon at the bottom of the layer window (as shown). This creates a new folder for us to keep stuff specific to this layer in.

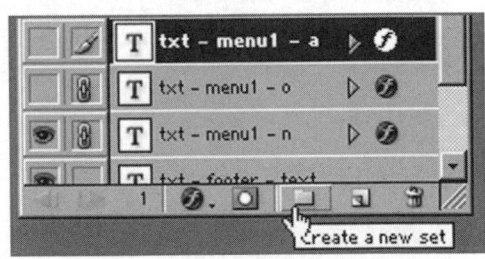

6. Double-click the new folder's name, and rename it button text.

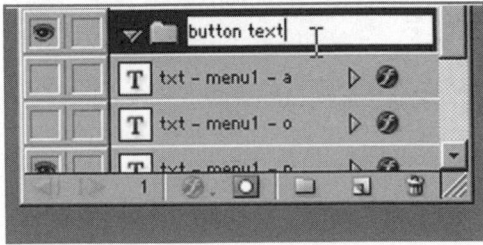

7. We now need to fill this set with our three text layers. Click-drag each of the three text layers (txt – menu1 – n) and drop them into the button text set.

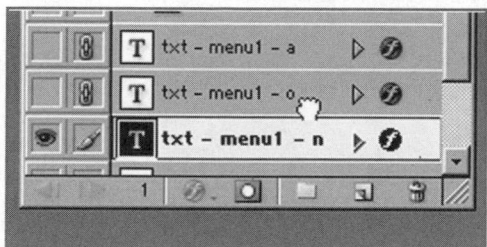 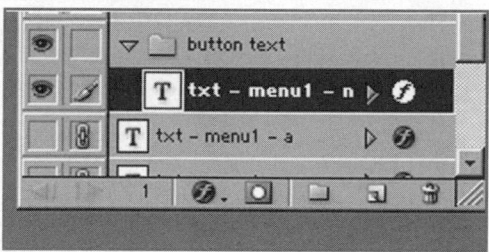

8. If the three folders are not in the order shown, simply re-order them by click-dragging them to the correct positions within the folder (you can tell where the layer will end up if you release at any time by the little line that appears as you drag up and down the layer stack).

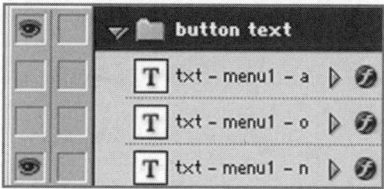

9. We now need to change the text from true text to bitmap text (a process sometimes called **rasterization**), which will mean that we can't change the text easily, but can now edit it using the normal pixel-based tools. To do this, select each layer in the button text set in turn, and select Layer > Rasterize > Type. As you do this to each layer, the T icon will disappear, signifying that the layer is no longer editable text.

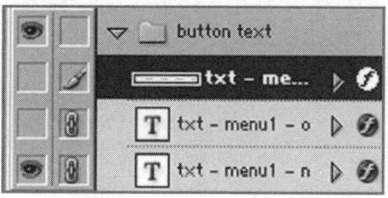

10. When you have done all three, we are ready to start copying the layer sets. Click the folder so that the set is selected, and select Layer > Duplicate Layer set. Do this four times.

11. Rename the four new sets to mission button, events button, flashub button and contact button.

12. Now, remove the `copy` bit that Image ready adds to the end of each layer within the folders. Your layers should look like the screenshot when you're done:

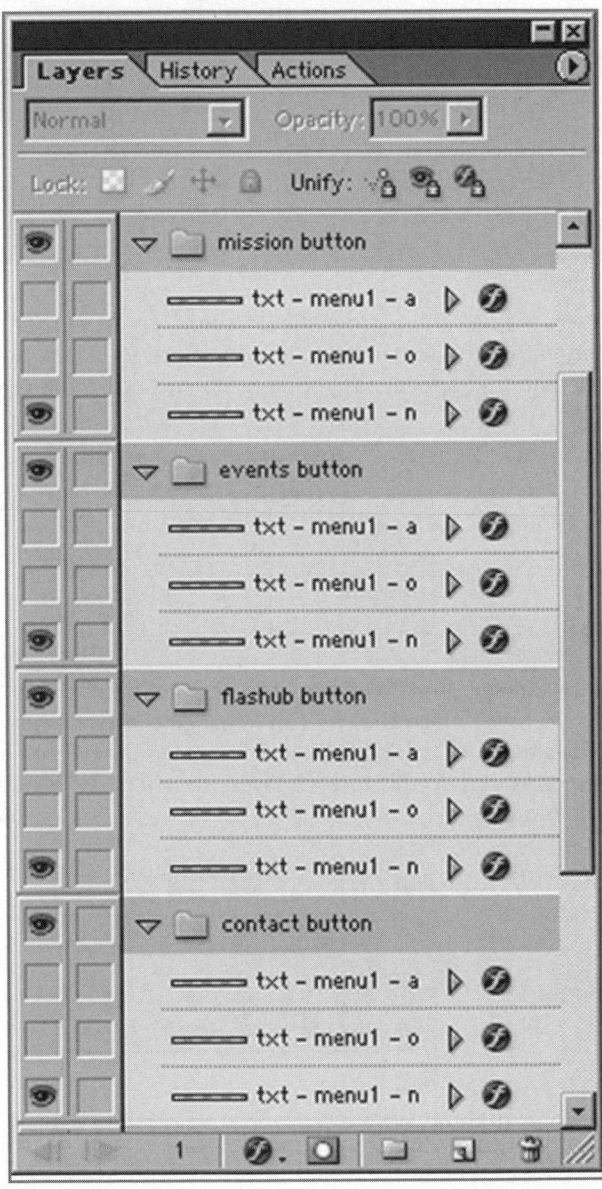

The file so far is saved as `mon_t_upper_slicestep2.psd` *if you have got stuck or need to compare notes.*

Setting up the graphics

1. Hide all the layers except the `mission button` set and the `background` layer by clicking the eye icons. Make sure the `background` layer is locked, as we only want to change the `mission button` set. Close the other sets by clicking on the little down arrows.

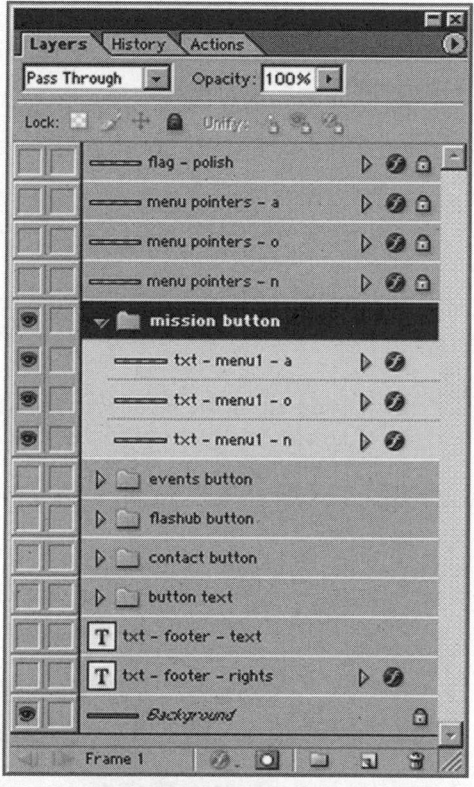

2. We now need to delete all text in the `mission button` set *except* the text for the mission button. To do this, select the first icon in the toolbox: the Marquee tool ⬚ . This may not be set to a rectangle shape – if it isn't, click and hold on the icon, and select the rectangular icon from the pop-up that appears.

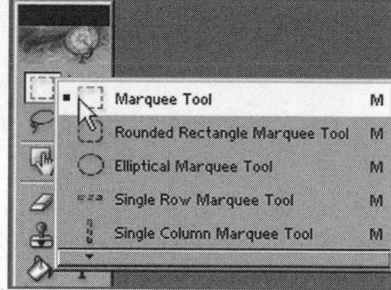

3. Now, drag out a marquee that covers the events, flashub and contact text, but doesn't cover mission.

Don't forget that View > Extras (or the shortcut CTRL+H) gets rid of all those slice lines, so that you can see what you are doing...

4. Select each layer in the mission button set in turn, and hit the DELETE key. You should now only be able to see the mission text:

5. Hide all of the mission button set (you can do this quickly by just clicking the eye icon for the mission button folder, which hides the contents of the whole set).

6. Follow steps 1 to 5 for the other three sets: flashub, events, contact. To speed things up, try creating multiple marquees to delete the unwanted text either side of the events and flashub buttons by holding the SHIFT key down to drag out additional Marquee sections after creating the initial marquee (a little + will appear below the cursor to tell you that you're adding an additional marquee selection).

The observant will now have realized why we had to rasterize the text; if we deleted the mission text in the screenshot when it was still text, the rest of the text would just have moved along to fill in the missing spaces. By turning the text into a bitmap, we stop this happening.

7. When you have done all four folders, delete the `button text` set that we started off with by selecting the folder and hitting the trashcan icon at the bottom (delete Set and Contents if prompted).

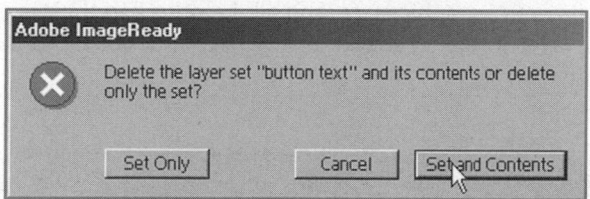

8. Delete the layers `txt - footer - text` and `txt - footer - rights` in the same way (they were tied up in the areas of the image we deleted when we cropped the full sized page after slicing earlier). You should end up with the layer structure shown in the screenshot.

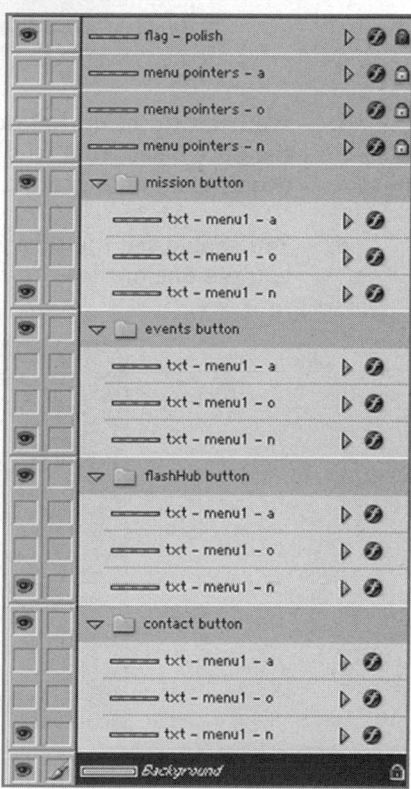

The file so far is saved as `mon_t_upper_sliceStep3.psd` *if you have got stuck, or need to compare notes.*

Adding the rollovers

To add the rollovers, we need to use the rollovers tab in conjunction with our layers.

1. Start with the layer visibilities (the 'eye' icons) set up as shown in the screenshot on the last page (that is, with the button sets all expanded and visible, the last layer in each set visible, and the Background and flag – polish layers visible).

2. As this is the mission page, we're already at the page, and we want the mission button set permanently to its active graphic state, and all the others to their normal states. To do this, change the a (active) layer in the mission button set to visible, and make the n (normal) layer in the same set hidden.

3. We need to set up rollovers for the other three buttons. We'll do the events button first. Select the Slice Select tool, and the slice overlay will appear. Select the events slice by clicking on the events text in the graphic.

4. You should see the slice is now selected in the Rollover tab. Scroll down the Rollovers tab, until you see one of the entries is highlighted.

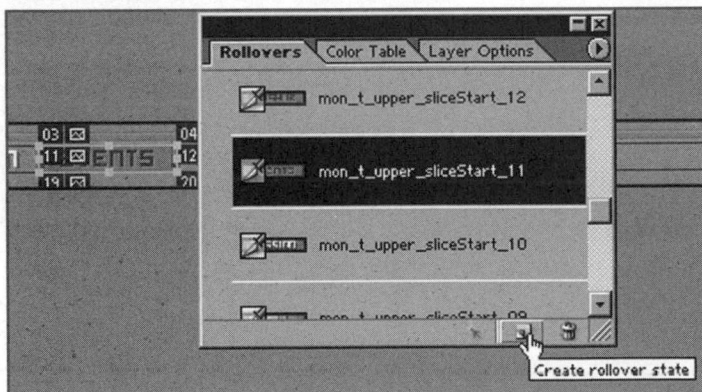

5. Hit the Create rollover state button at the bottom of the window:

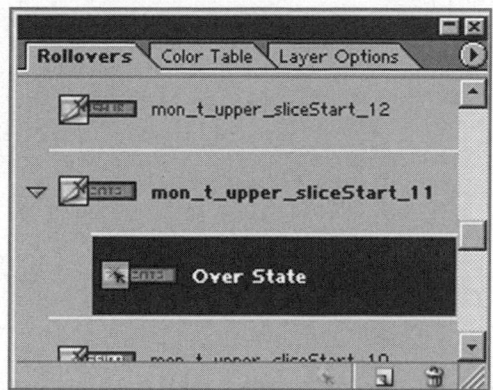

6. With the new Over state still selected in the Rollovers palette, change the layer set events button so that the n layer is now hidden and the o layer is visible.

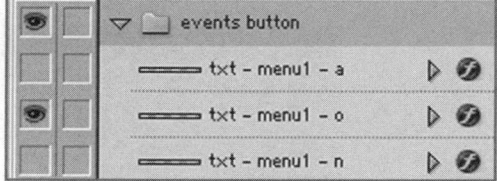

7. That's it! We've done it, and you can now test this. Save the file, hit Ctrl+H to hide the slice overlay, and select Image > Preview Document. If you now roll over the events button, it will animate. You will also see the Rollovers palette reflect the changes in the image slices.

To recap, what we've done is created two slices for the buttons. These will act as a two-frame animation that is triggered by user interaction with the button; when the user rolls over it, the slice images are swapped to show the button change, and the slices are swapped back when the mouse rolls away.

If it doesn't work, take a look at our working file:
`mon_t_upper_sliceStep4.psd`.

8.   We now need to do the same for the other two buttons. Get out of preview by unchecking Image > Preview, as you can't edit in this mode. Select the `flashub` and `contact` slices in turn, and add a rollover state in the Rollovers tab.

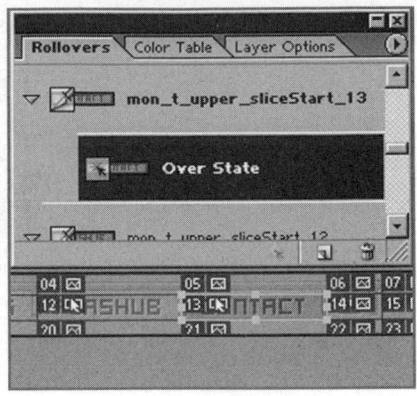

9.   For each of the two new Over states, select the Over state, and change the layer set so that the o (over) state is associated with the rollover.

You can actually add other mouse states corresponding to the available mouse events – you can even add multi-frame animated GIF animations, but we'll stick with this for the moment...

10.   If you now preview the animation again, you should see that the menu works for all the animations.

11. You can test the menu in a browser now, without leaving ImageReady with File > Preview in > browser from list... If anything goes wrong, the file with all of this information entered is saved as `mon_t_upper_sliceStep6.psd`.

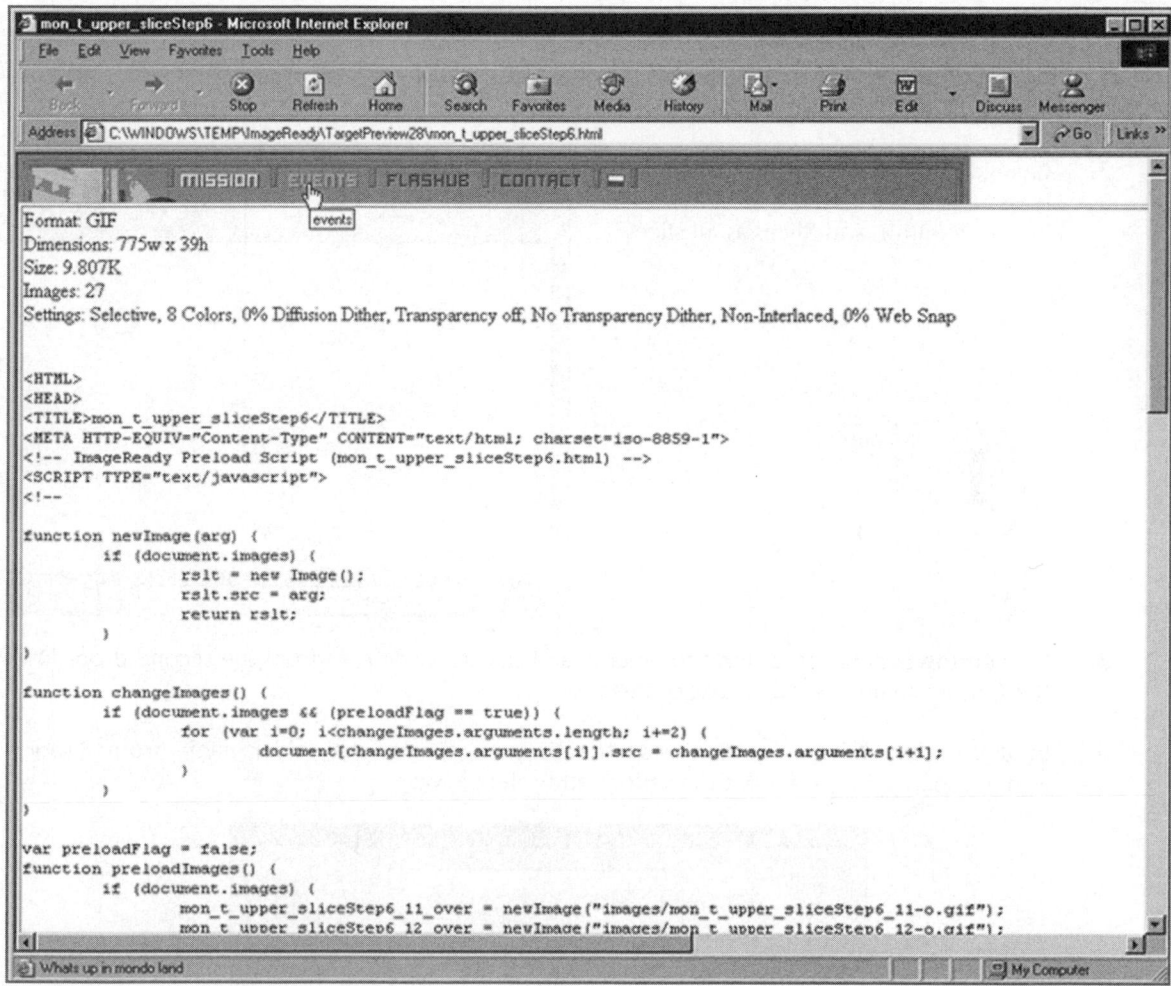

If you click the links that would normally open a pop-up, you either won't see anything happen, or will get an odd 'object not found' error. That's because we're using our popup() function without telling ImageReady what it is (the error is saying 'I can't find this function, sorry'). If you click any of the other buttons or links, the page won't be found, as ImageReady doesn't know where they are yet. What's important is that the menu works in terms of the mouse-over animations.

As you'll have noticed, telling ImageReady that a slice has a rollover state isn't the simplest process, but it's almost always the same – you need to:

1. Select the slice on the image
2. Give it a rollover state in the Rollovers tab
3. Set up the layers for the rollover state by changing the layer visibilities

Saving the file

We can also get a full listing of the HTML that creates our menu, and ImageReady has written all the JavaScript and the HTML to create it!

1. We should really export all this and stick it in our skeleton site, so select File > Save optimized as (This will save your slices *and* the JavaScript/HTML to drive it).

2. Change the filename to mon_t_upper, leave the Save as type as HTML and Images (*.html), and Slices as all slices.

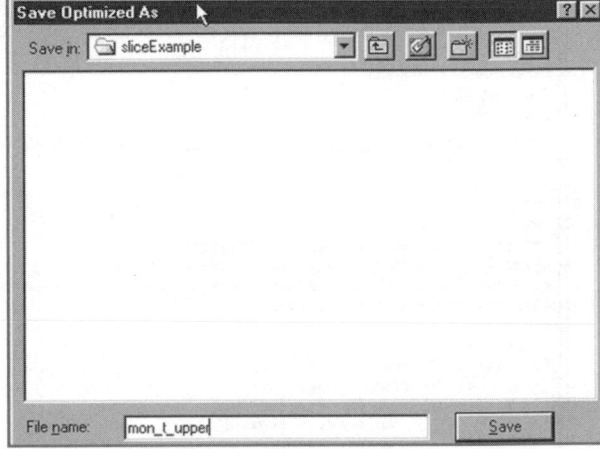

3. Change the Settings drop-down to other... and select Saving Files from the second drop-down on the Output settings window that comes up.

4. In the Optimized files section near the bottom, change the folder name from images to mon_t_upper_images. OK this window, and select Save.

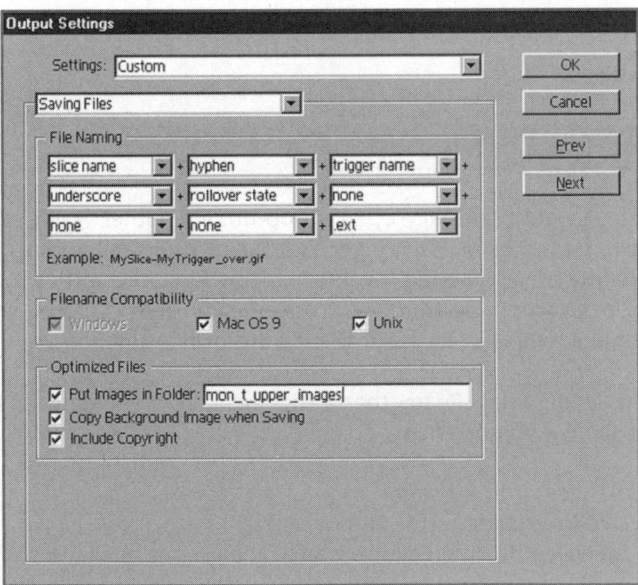

This will create a folder called `mon_t_upper_images` with all our slices in it, plus an HTML file, `mon_t_upper.html`, that uses them (this will be in the same place as the directory, and not inside the directory with the files). Have a look inside the folder and you will see the same number of GIFs as we had slices (24), plus the three _over states.

If you copy both the folder and HTML file into the `mondoContent` folder, it will almost work. What we need to do is add our JavaScript `mondo_script.js` file. Open `mon_t_upper.html` in your editor, and add the following line immediately after the `<head>`:

```
<script language="JavaScript" src="mondo_script.js"></script>
```

> You can have more than one separate `<script></script>` in the head.

This allows our HTML to now find the missing function. Save and try again. Voila! We've now sliced our images to make them ready for the Web, and all we have left to do now is put this and the other tables into the pages. Stay tuned for the next chapter...

Adding rollovers in Fireworks

To build the menu for the mission page, we need the events, flashub, and contact slices to be buttons, and the mission slice to remain as an inactive graphic stuck on the 'active' appearance.

To create any animated features in Fireworks, we first have to set up our layers for animation. To do this we have to add **frames**, and alter the appearance of the graphics between them. We want two frames for each button: the first frame will hold the normal button appearance, and the second frame will hold the image that'll appear when the user runs their mouse over the button.

> The concept of frames is unique to Fireworks. ImageReady (and HTML web design in general) uses a more standard method that concentrates on the slices themselves, as you'll see if you glance through the previous section. Using Frames can be quicker though, so it's no disadvantage – just a little different.

We'll start by looking at the effect we want to create, and then we'll organize our layers, set up the text for the rollovers, and finally add the rollovers. This will take the rest of the chapter, so make sure you're sitting comfortably...

Test run

1. Either continue with your file from the last exercise, or open `mon_t_upper_sliceStart_fw.png` from the download file. Make sure the three panels you can see in the screenshot – the Behaviors, Frames and History and Layers panels – are open (these can all be opened from the Window menu if you can't see them).

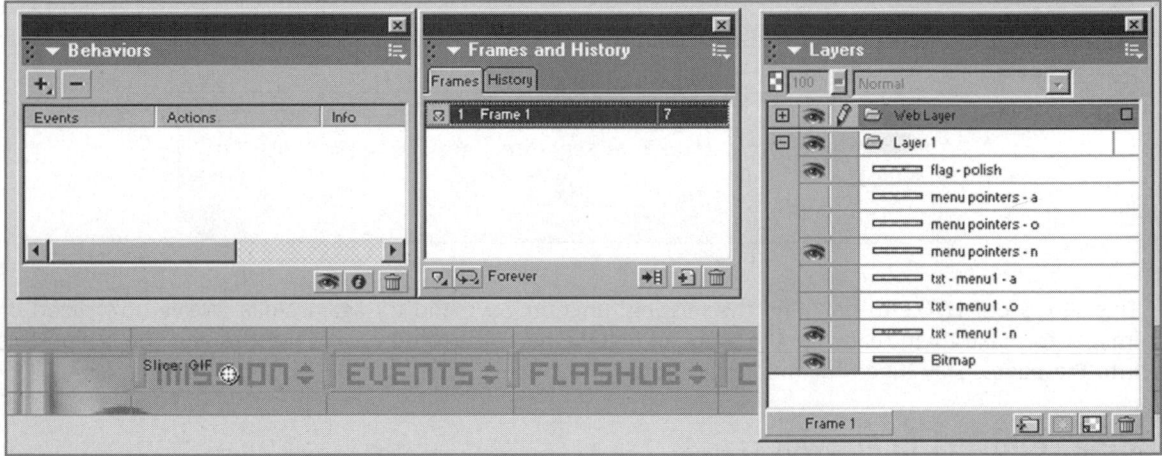

2. We're going to make the change manually to check that our rollover actually works, before implementing it fully. Start by hiding the `web layer` in the Layers panel (by clicking the eye icon) so that we can see what's going on.

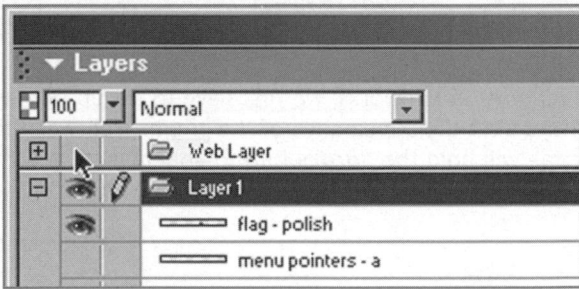

3. When a button is not being interacted with, it will be in its **normal** state, which you can see by clicking the eye icons so that only `txt - menu1 - n` is visible.

4. When the button is rolled over by the user, it will be in the its **over** state, which you can see by making only txt - menu1 - o visible.

5. When we see the mission button on the mission page, we don't need it to work, but we want it to look **active** to let the user know that they are on the mission page. You can see this final state by making only txt - menu1 - a visible.

Shared and normal layers

The problem is that we need some of our layers to be there all the time (i.e. both frames) and some to be there only for one of the frames to create the animation. To do this, we have two types of layers; **shared** layers and **normal** layers. A shared layer is there all the time (*shared* between all the frames), whereas a normal layer is able to appear/disappear with the use of **behaviors**.

> **Behavior** *is Macromedia terminology for 'a piece of code attached to something that makes it act (or behave) in a certain way'. There are a number of these pieces of code supplied as standard with Fireworks, ready for us to use, and among these is a rollover behavior, with the code to create a rollover animation.*

The first step is to split our graphics into shared layers and normal layers - at the moment, we have all our graphic objects on layer 1. The main problem then is working out what changes and what doesn't change between the frames. It *looks* like the three text layers txt - menu1 - a, - o and - n change, but only the **over** state needs to be in frame 2 because as soon as it appears, it will cover any other text in the same position.

If you need to convince yourself, have a look at the final Mondo site and how the menu works. The active text is always there, the normal text is much the same; it only appears as long as the user doesn't interact with it. Only the **over** text changes when the user passes a mouse across it.

Organizing our layers

We'll be working in the Layers panel a bit here, so you might want to make this a bit bigger before you start.

1. Hit the duplicate/create layer button at the bottom of the window twice. This will create two new layers, `layer 2` and `layer3`.

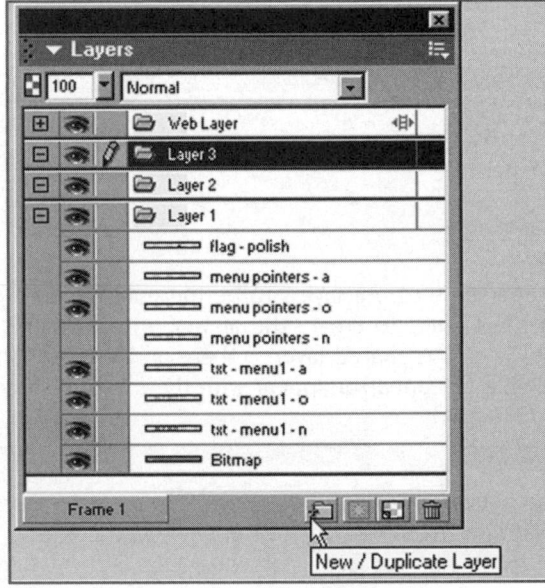

2. Double-click the `layer1`, 2 and 3 text to rename the layers `shared`, `over` and `pointers`.

3. Make `shared` a shared folder by checking the Share Across Frames checkbox when you change the name.

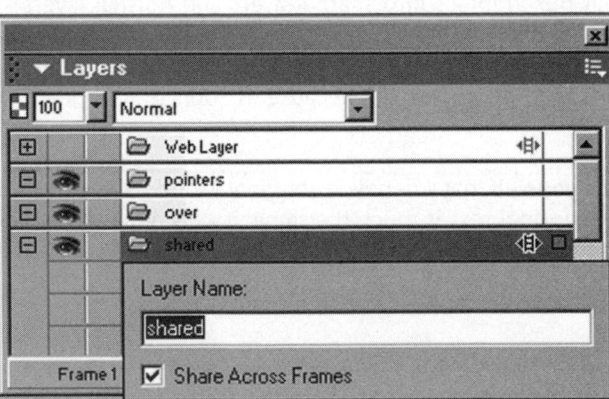

4. We now need to split our objects between the layers. Click-and-hold the three `pointer` objects currently in `shared` and drop them each in turn into the `pointers` layer.

5. We won't look at the pointers here, so make the `pointer` layer invisible by clicking on the eye icon next to it.

6. Click-drag the `txt - menu1 - o` layer into the `over` layer. Your Layers stack should now be ordered like the screenshot.

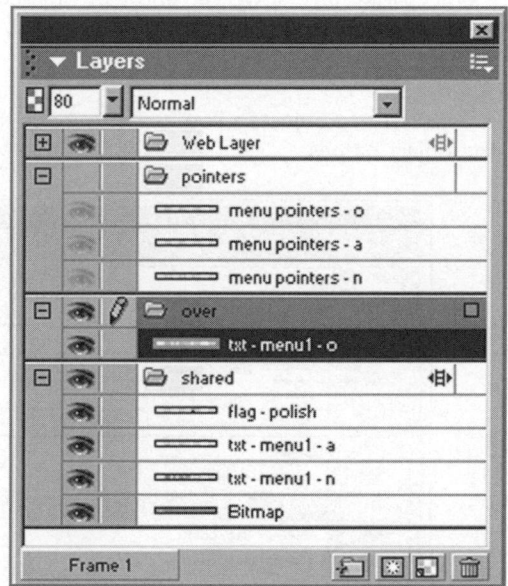

> *Take a look at our version,* `mon_t_upper_sliceStep2_fw.png` *if you get stuck.*

The text

What we need to do is create several *normal* and *active* static text combinations, so that we can use this single file to create all the menus we need for the site. For example, the combinations below are what we would need for the mission and events pages:

First, we need to change some of the shared text from true text (text that you can still edit) to bitmap text (where you can't edit the text, but can edit the appearance with the pixel-based tools).

1.　To do this, select the txt - menu1 - a object on the shared layer in the Layers panel, and choose Modify > Flatten Selection. Flatten Selection is Fireworks speak for 'I have converted your text to the simplest object I can - a bitmap'.

2.　We need to separate the active mission, events, flashub and contact text so that each is on a separate layer. Once on separate layers, we can show or hide each of the four words. Select txt - menu1 - a and press CTRL+C to copy the text, then CONTROL+V three times to paste three copies (making four txt - menu1 - a layers in all).

3.　Rename the four txt - menu1 - a objects mission-a, events-a, flashub-a and contact-a by double-clicking on the object names.

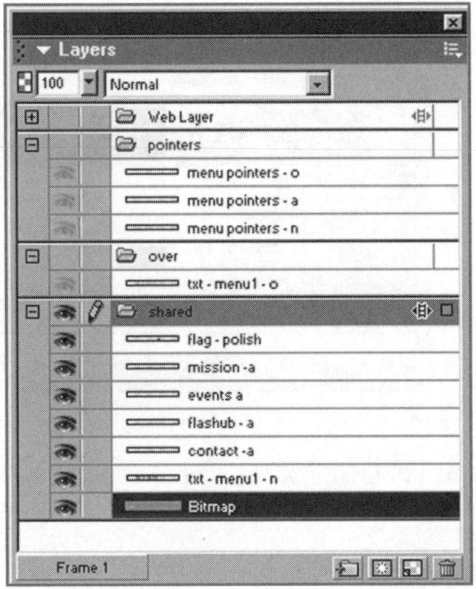

4.　We want only the mission text on mission-a, the events text on events-a, and so on. To do this, select the Marquee tool. This may not be currently set as a rectangle – if it looks like on oval, click-hold the icon, and select the rectangular icon from the pop-up that appears.

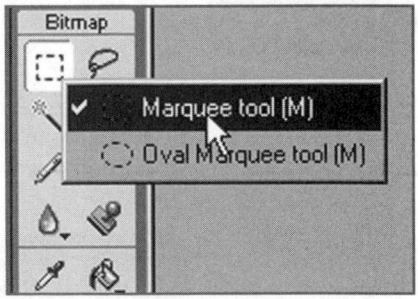

5.　Make everything hidden except the mission-a object and the background Bitmap object by clicking the eye icons.

6. Select the `mission-a` object in the Layers panel, and click-drag a marquee out to select all of the text except the word `mission`.

7. Hit the DELETE key to erase them, leaving only the word `mission` as the `mission-a` object.

8. Now, hide the layer, and make the `events-a` layer visible. Delete the text, leaving just `events` behind.

9. Hide the layer, and do the same for `flashub-a` and `contact-a`, keeping the title text (`flashub`, and `contact`), and deleting the rest.

> *You now know why we had to change the text into a bitmap: if we hadn't, then when we deleted the* mission *text, the rest of the text would have moved over to the left to fill in the missing spaces!*

10. Now make the `txt - menu1 - n` object visible, and try making the `-a` objects visible:

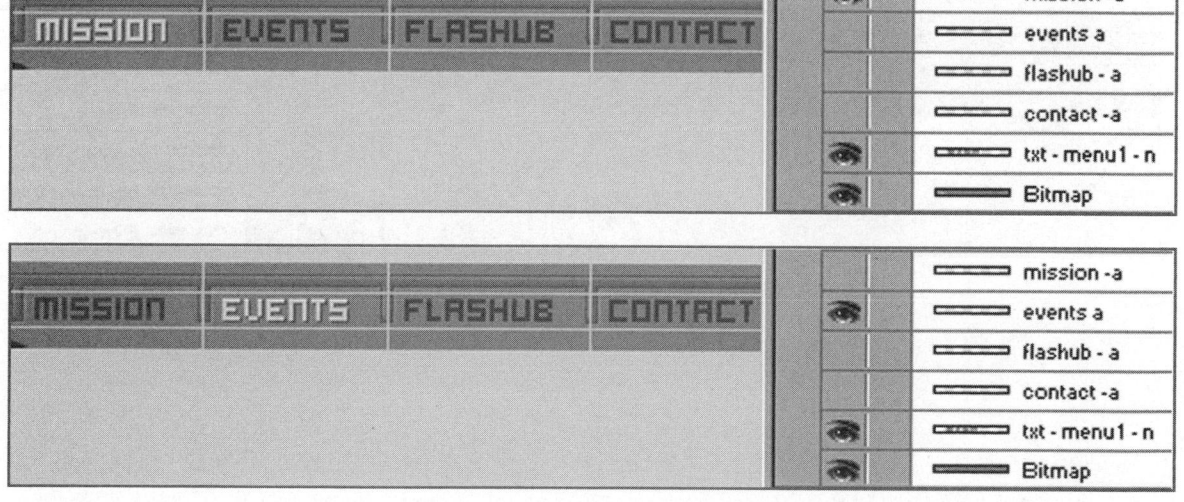

You can see our work in progress file for this point by looking at
`mon_t_upper_sliceStep3_fw.png`.

Adding the rollovers

Make the `text – menu1 – n` and `mission-a` layers visible. Leave the background image at the bottom of the list visible, but hide the rest. We should now see the `mission` text highlighted – just as we want it to appear for our `mission` page:

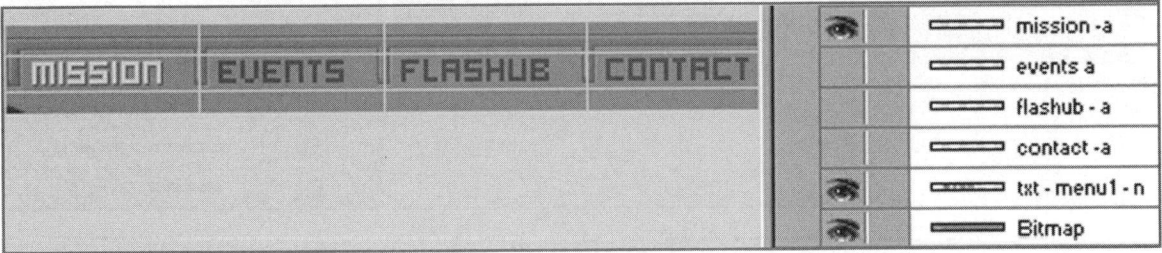

1. The first step in adding the rollover animations is putting in our second frame. In the Frames and History panel, hit the New / Duplicate Frame icon (as shown) to create a second frame.

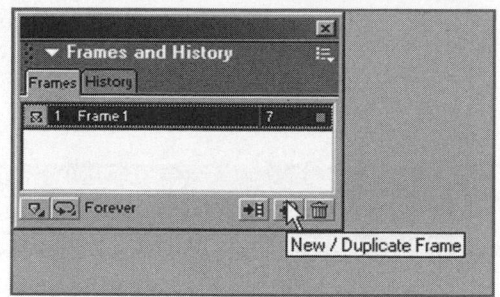

2. Behaviors are a cool way of adding script to slices; simply attach your behavior to a slice and forget it. Select the Pointer tool (first tool in the toolbox).

3. Make the Web Layer visible in the Layers panel, and select the events slice by clicking directly on the image. Click the + button at the top-left of the behaviors panel and select Simple Rollover.

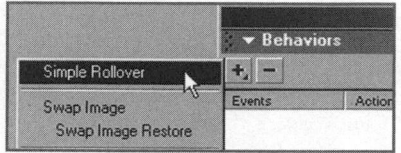

4. Do the same for the flashub and contact slices.

5. We can now test the animation. Make sure that Frame 1 is selected in the Frames and History panel, and check that your layer visibilities are the same as shown below. Select File > Preview in browser > ... You will see that the animation is 'back to front'; a rolled over button goes darker instead of lighter.

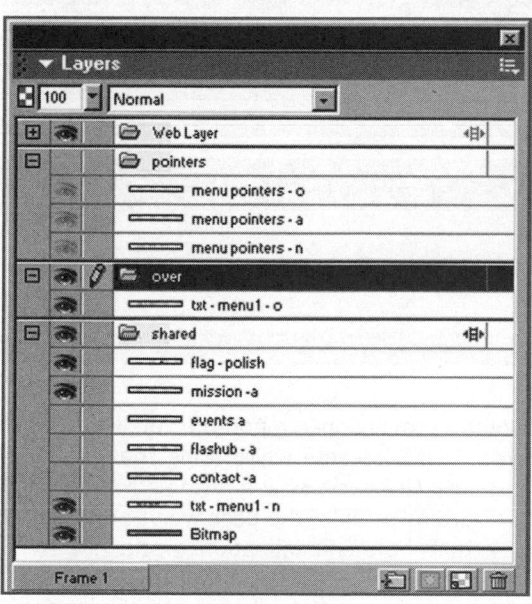

6.   This is because each slice we defined to be a rollover button will move to frame 2 when we rollover it. The *over* text that we want to display exists on frame 1, though, as that's where we created the *over* layer. To fix this, simply drag frame 1 in the Frames and History panel below frame 2 to reverse the animation.

You can actually see the animation states in step time if you select a frame in the Frames and History panel and look at the image itself. You can also see what the layers are doing if you look at the Layer panel.

> The file to this point is saved as mon_t_upper_sliceStep4_fw .png *if you need to take a look at our version.*

Saving the file

Test the menu in a browser now, with File > Preview in > browser...

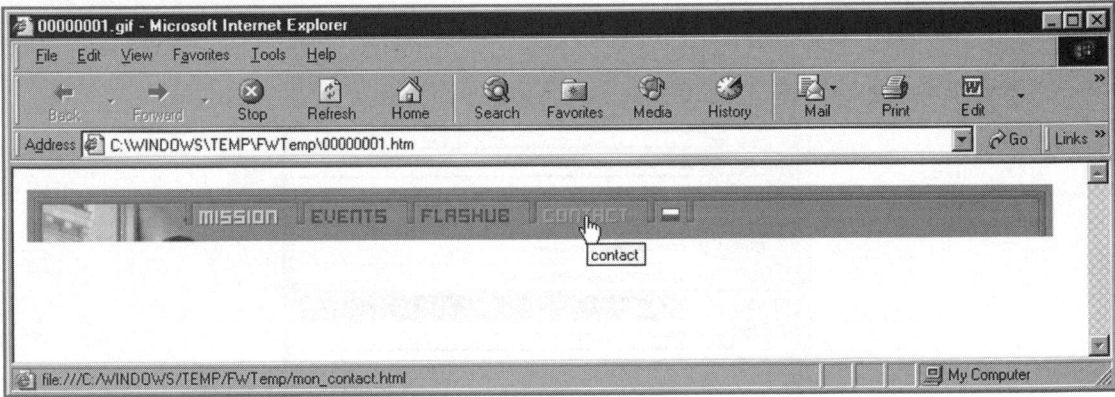

If you click the links that would normally open a pop-up, you'll either not see anything happen, or get an odd 'object not found' error. That's because we're using the openPop() function we wrote earlier in mondo_script.js without telling Fireworks what it is (the error is saying 'I can't find this function, sorry'). If you click any of the other buttons or links, the page won't be found, as Fireworks doesn't know where they are. The important bit is that the menu animations work.

What's even better is that Fireworks has written all of the JavaScript and HTML to create the menu for us. It's time to export this into our skeleton site, so that we can check that the pop-ups and links work.

1.   Select File > Export - this will save your slices and the JavaScript/HTML to run them.

2. Change the filename to mon_t_upper, and check the Put images in Subfolder option. Use the file explorer window to create a new folder called mon_t_upper_images to put them in.

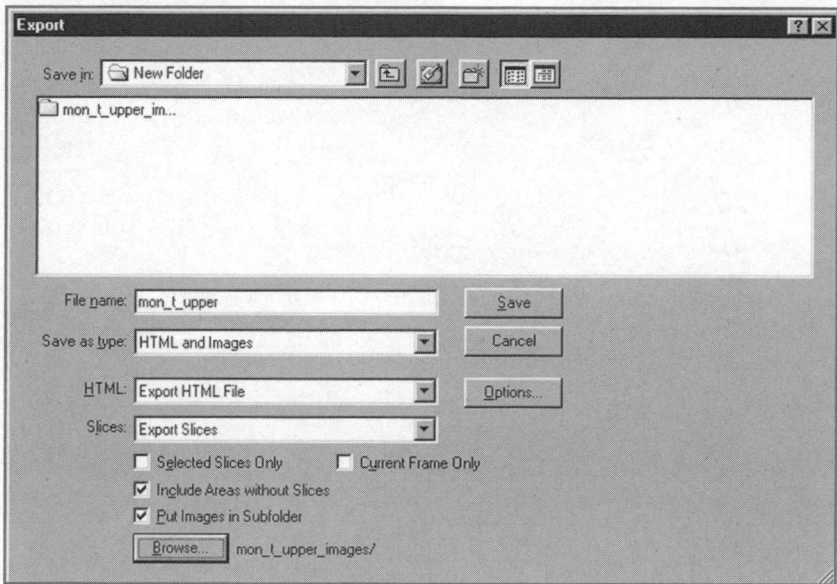

3. Select Save, and Fireworks will create a folder called mon_t_upper_images with all our slices in it, plus an HTML file, mon_t_upper.html, that uses them. Have a look inside the images folder and you will see the same 24 GIFs for our 24 slices, plus the three _f2 ('frame 2' or rollover) states.

4. Copy both the folder and HTML file into the mondoContent folder.

5. Finally, we need to add our custom JavaScript file mondo_script.js into the mix. Open mon_t_upper.html in your text editor and add the following line immediately after the <head>:

```
<script language="JavaScript" src="mondo_script.js"></script>
```

> *You can have more than one separate* <script></script> *in the head.*

6. This allows our HTML to find the missing function, so save and try again. Well done!

We've now sliced our images to make them ready for the Web, and all we have left to do now is put this and the other tables into the pages. Stay tuned for the next chapter....

Frames

What this chapter will do

In this chapter, we will introduce you gently to pages that are created from more than one HTML document via the magic of **frames**. You'll see how to create rows and columns of framed documents, update individual frames and design unique layouts not possible with other technologies.

What you'll have learned by the end of this chapter

By the end of this chapter, you will have learned all the basic skills needed to design a standard HTML website:

- HTML – formatting and tables
- CSS
- JavaScript
- Creating web graphics, animations and rollovers
- Frames, framesets, and inline frames

We will also have put the finishing touches to our Mondo case study and uploaded it to our webspace online, just in time for a quick sprinkling of multimedia in the next and final chapter.

In this chapter we will look at one final basic skill that you need to know about before finishing up on the Mondo site – **frames**...

Introducing Frames

A real window is usually built up of several different panes of glass held together in a frame. There are several reasons why we do this:

- Glass is fragile and prone to breaking. By splitting a large glassed area into separate smaller window areas, we prevent the whole window breaking if our weekly game of indoor baseball goes awry, and we only have to replace the affected pane before my wife gets back, rather than the whole window frame.

- Also, we want to split up the window so that we can do different things with each pane. For example, we might want one half of the window to be hinged so that we can open it.

Looking closer at our window, we see that it is made up of two main parts, the *frame* and the separate *panes*:

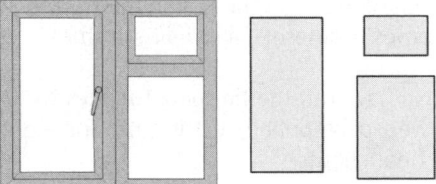

It comes as no surprise that we can do exactly the same with the virtual window that is the browser. Instead of glass panes, we have *frames* that can hold separate HTML documents, and instead of a wooden 'master' frame, we have an overall document, or **frameset**, that holds our separate frames together.

The frameset describes how many frames there are, how big they are, and where they sit. The individual frames then tell the browser where to find the source documents they contain.

Why use frames?

Using frames to divide your web page has one key advantage. Using a frameset allows us to treat each frame as a separate entity, and we can configure each to a specific purpose. For example, we can decide whether a particular frame should have its own scrollbar, or whether it should contain HTML or a Flash movie. We can also use JavaScript to write text messages (or anything else for that matter) into one frame whilst preventing it overwriting the other frames.

It is this last point which differentiates frames from tables. Although both can be used for layout and for separating content, only with frames do you get truly individual and independent sections. Think for example of a site with navigation down the side; you click each link and the navigation bar doesn't change, only the content in the right hand section does. This is a classic use of frames – one you're bound to have seen in action.

A frame-based approach does have disadvantages though. You cannot easily bookmark a particular frame, only the frameset. It's also more difficult to print an entire page, and search engines have been known not to sniff out the content in the individual frames.

The final issue against frames used to be that you would typically have to create two sites if you wanted to use frames; one for frames-ready browsers, and one for non-supporting browsers. This was a major headache in the early days, but support for frames is high nowadays (refer back to the chart in **Chapter 1** for the evidence):

- Frames are included in the HTML 4.01 specification; so all current browsers support them.
- They were introduced in Internet Explorer 3 and Netscape 2 (although neither of these browsers supported HTML 4.01), which means they have been around for years.

Although we don't actually need to use frames in the Mondo site (we need to center the Mondo site, something much easier with tables), we'll have a quick look at how to set up a simple example.

> We will be using a special type of frame though, the **inline frame** later in the final site.

You can think of a frame as being very similar to a pop-up (although they look different). Both a frame and a pop-up share the following features in common:

- They open new browser HTML pages, each of which creates a new set of JavaScript DOM objects (including document, history, etc)
- Each new document downloads separately to the main document
- Once a new document is open, you can communicate between all currently open documents by using JavaScript.

Unlike pop-ups, the frames are simply sections of the original browser window, and although they are different HTML documents, they share the same Window object. The picture below shows this. On the left, we see a pop-up based navigation. The original document causes three pop-ups to be created, each of which will contain content via its own HTML document.

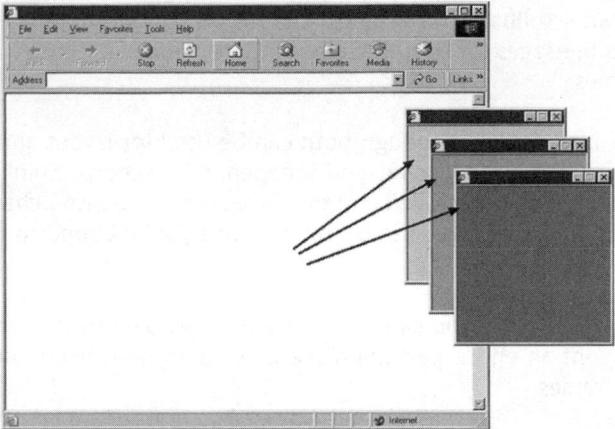 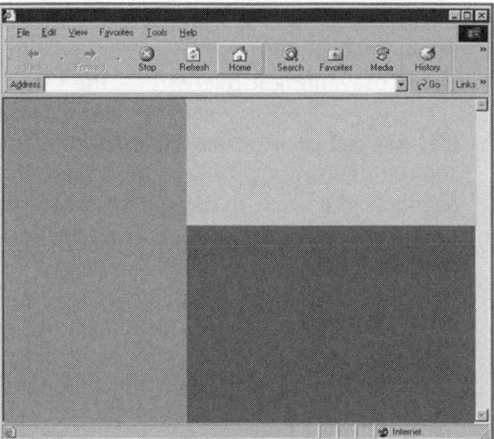

The browser on the right also opens up three new documents, but creates them as frames. There are several advantages to doing this, the biggest one being that users are now more than a little tired of multiple pop-ups. Because frames don't look as untidy (and in many cases, it is possible to hide them well, so the user doesn't even notice them), folks don't seem to mind them as much!

The frame-based solution also has advantages over a regular page. Because the three frames that the right-hand browser now contains are actually *separate* HTML documents, you can change only the parts that you really need to, rather than having to refresh the whole page every time the user goes to a new page – just like the navigation bar analogy earlier.

OK, enough talk, let's start playing....

Frame tags

Now that we have got past the hurdle of learning tables earlier in the book, frames are actually quite easy, because they are essentially the same thing; a cell-like definition.

> *Perhaps like tables, frames can get very complicated very quickly, so when hand-coding, you are strongly advised to stick to a small number of frames per frameset. This is not a real problem, because in most sites you only need a few frames anyway.*

Building the frames and the frameset

1. Create a new folder called `frameTest` and inside it create a new document called `one.html`.

2. Add the following basic HTML to your new document:

```
<html>
<head>
</head>

<body BGCOLOR="#999999">
<p ALIGN="center"><br><br><br>This is one..</p>
</body>
</html>
```

3. Enter the following HTML in a new file called `two.html` (or just make the changes to `one.html` and save it as `two.html`:

```
<html>
<head>
</head>

<body BGCOLOR="#BBBBBB">
<p ALIGN="center"><br><br><br>This is two..</p>
</body>
</html>
```

> *Note, we're going to create the **frameset** in a moment – these documents do not contain any new tags – they are just the placeholder files our frameset will bring into our master document. For this reason, we're changing the background color of each, so we can easily distinguish them.*

4. In the same way create `three.html` and `four.html`, with **BGCOLOR="#DDDDDD"** and **"#FFFFFF"**, and with text *This is three..* and *This is four..* respectively. You should end up with four HTML files as shown over the page:

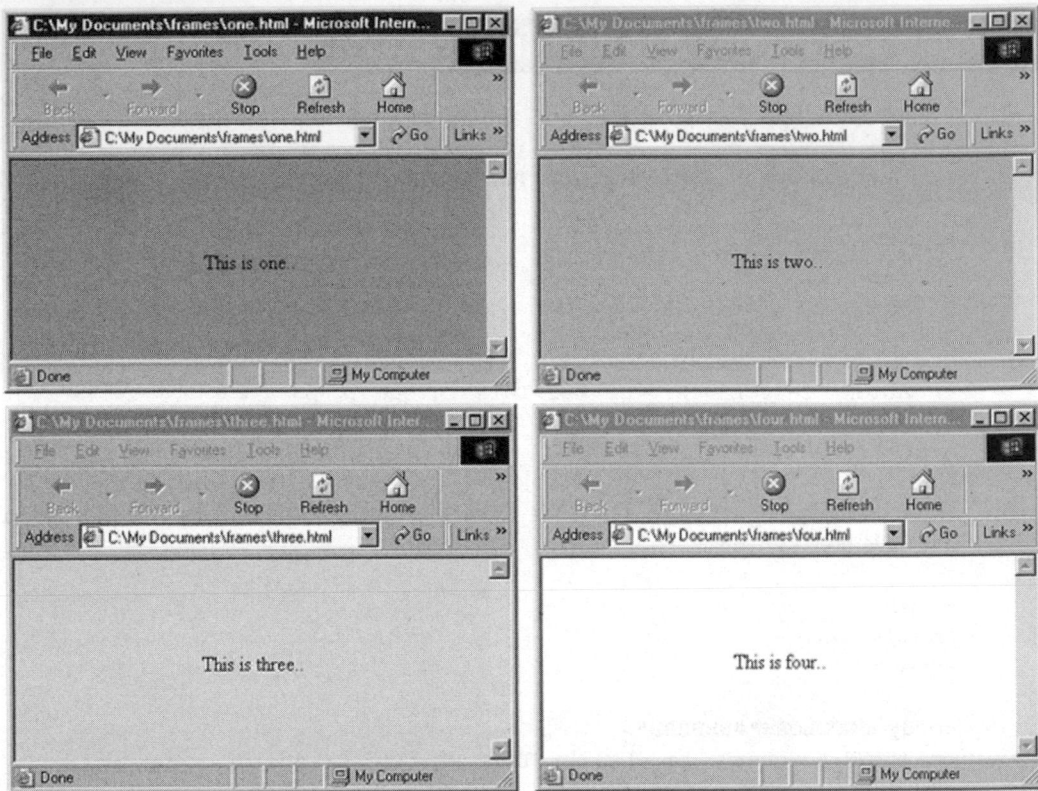

Now it's time to pull all these files together.

5.   Add a new file in the same directory called `index.html`. This will be our frameset, the *master document* that places all the other frame documents in their appropriate places. In the new file add the following HTML:

> *You can actually call these files anything you want normally; the file names you choose are not important (as long as the links to them are consistent of course!)*

```html
<html>
<head>
<title>frameset document</title>
</head>

<frameset cols="*,*">
 <frame src="one.html" name="frame1">
 <frame src="two.html" name="frame2">
</frameset>
```

```
<body>
</body>
</html>
```

The `<frameset>...</frameset>` tag is where our frameset definition is kept. It is neither in the `<head>` nor `<body>` because it is a new *structural tag* in its own right. A frameset is not a *formatting-related* tag, but instead defines something about the structure of the overall web page definition.

6. Before we delve deeper into the attributes and the other new tag, `<frame>`, let's have a look at the output:

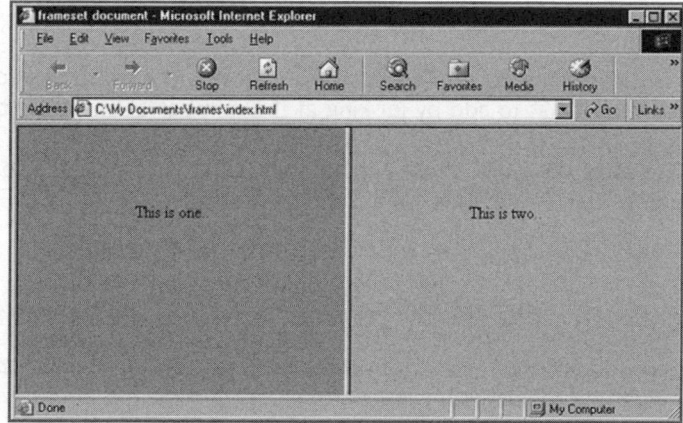

Our first two documents, `one.html` and `two.html` have now become embedded within the frameset document `index.html`. Resizing the browser window will cause the two frames to also resize.

7. If you resize the main window small enough to hide the text, notice that the two frames both inherit a scrollbar and these can be used independently of each other:

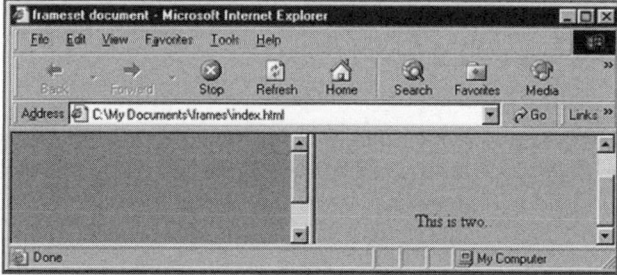

8. Finally, if you place the mouse at the dividing line between browsers, you can drag it to resize the two frames as you wish:

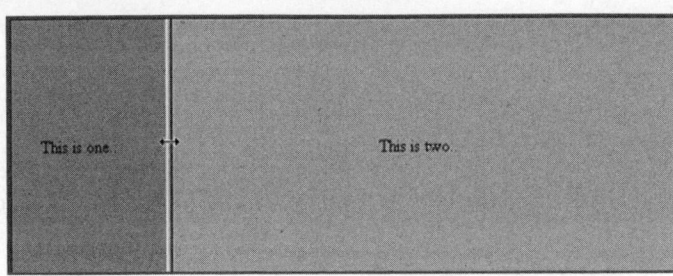

So how is this all set up? Well... let's look at each line of code in turn. The first line in our frameset definition is:

```
<frameset cols="*,*">
```

The COLS attribute is a comma *separated string literal* that lists the width of each column. The frameset knows how many columns it has to add by looking at the number of entries in this list.

Both our list items are asterisks, which means 'make them fill up the available space'. We can change this setting by making one of our frames take up a definite size;

```
<frameset cols="200,*">
```

> *Setting both frames to pixel values won't give you your exact values, because if the browser window is bigger than the total pixels you've set, it will adjust your setting to fill up the space. At least one of them should be set to auto-size via the *.*

OK, let's have a look at the next tag, `<frame>`. This tag specifies the documents we need to load into the frameset, and there *must* be one for every entry in the COLS list.

```
<frameset cols="200,*">
  <frame src="one.html" name="frame1">
  <frame src="two.html" name="frame2">
</frameset>
```

The SRC attribute tells the browser which file it needs to pull in, and the NAME attribute gives each newly defined frame a name. This name is required for the same reason as pop-ups have to be named; so that we can reference the individual frames later on and change their content.

> *After the closing* </frameset> *you can also add in* <noframes>…</noframes>
> *set of tags. These are identical in operation to* <noscript> *that we met* **Chapter 8***; they define what to do if the current browser has frame support turned off. They are pretty obsolete nowadays, partly because the latest browsers no longer have an option to disable frames (unlike with JavaScript), so I've chosen to ignore them in this example.*

Let's look now at an example with three frames:

```
<frameset cols="200, 300, *">
 <frame src="one.html" name="frame1" noresize>
 <frame src="two.html" name="frame2">
 <frame src="three.html" name = frame3">
</frameset>
```

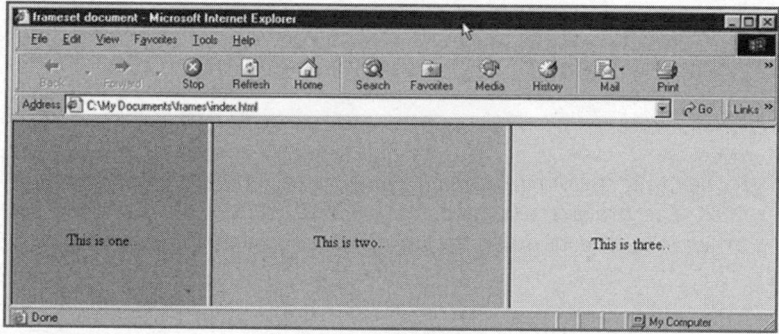

Notice that to add a new column we have had to add a new size to the COLS list (in this case a 300) and we have to define a new <frame src> attribute to tell the browser where to get the additional document from. We also have to give the new frame a unique name, in this case frame3.

We also introduce a new attribute this time, NORESIZE. This tells the browser not to allow resizing of the frame we specify (frame1).

OK, that's columns. How about rows?

Adding rows

1. Creating rows in your frameset couldn't be easier. Just take your first line...

```
<frameset cols="200, 300, *">
```

...and change it to...

```
<frameset rows="200, 300, *">
```

...and the columns become rows.

2. Of course, we can also specify rows and columns at the same time. Take a look at this frameset:

```
<frameset rows = "*, *" cols="*, *" >
 <frame src="one.html" name="frame1" noresize>
 <frame src="two.html" name="frame2">
 <frame src="three.html" name = "frame3">
 <frame src="four.html" name = "frame4">
</frameset>
```

> Notice that the order in which the `<frame>` tags are listed is important here. The browser will read from left to right, top to bottom on the browser as it reads down the list of `<frame>` definitions.

Here, we specify a 2x2 grid of frames. The list defines all four frames to be auto-sized, but the first one is set to no resizing, which means that none of them can be resized (because they all share a corner in common that must always stay in the browser center to prevent the first frame from changing):

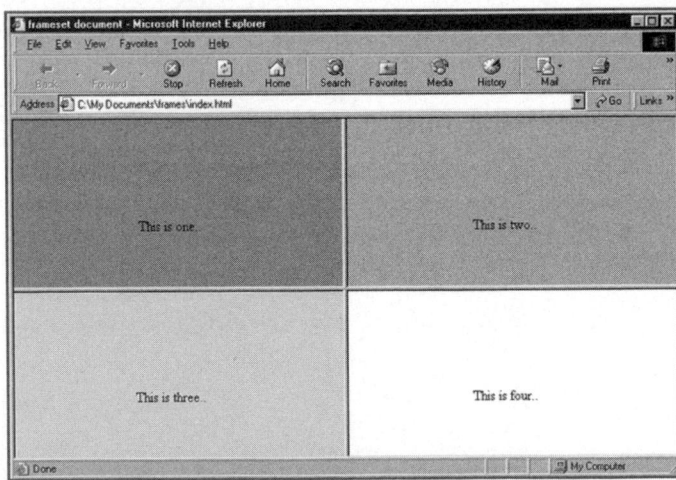

3. You can use combinations or rows and columns together to create all sorts of regular framesets (where regular means every row has the same number of frames):

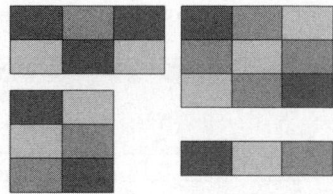

> Remember, the more complex your framesets are, the trickier it is to keep track of them. Make sure you always draft your plans on paper and keep a good visual record of how your framesets are looking, for future reference.

4. To create more complex layouts, you have to use **nested frames**:

```
<html>
<head>
<title>frameset document</title>
</head>

<frameset cols="100, *" >
     <frameset rows = "*, *">
             <frame src="one.html" name="frame1" noresize>
             <frame src="two.html" name="frame2">
  </frameset>
  <frame src="three.html" name = "frame3">
</frameset>

<body>
</body>
</html>
```

Here, we have two columns, but have split the first column into two rows. As always, a picture shows this better:

We start by defining two columns but the first column is a nested set of two rows:

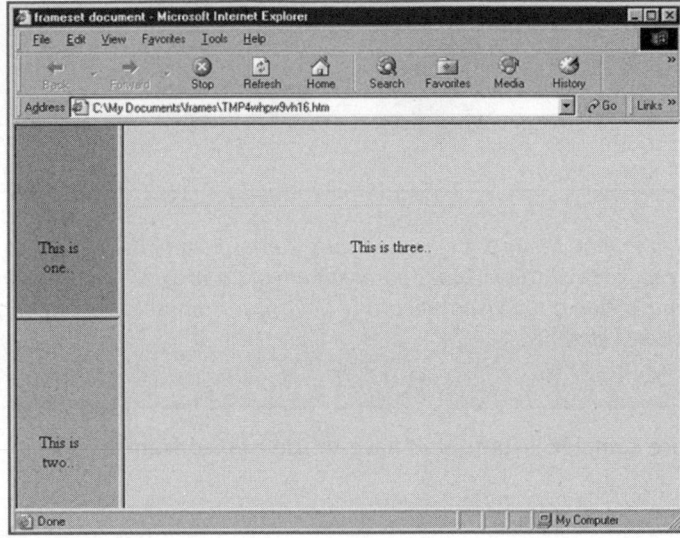

Because 1 and 2 are nested, the top to bottom, left to right ordering is broken.

So to recap:

- The **frameset** is a content free HTML document that contains a frameset definition within its `<frameset>...</frameset>` definition.
- The frameset splits up the current browser window object into a number of rectangles, called **frames**.
- The frameset contains a number of `<frame>` tags, each of which links to a separate HTML document that will be loaded into one of the frames. When loaded, this document will work just like a normal HTML file would in a full-sized window.

OK, that shows us how to lay out our basic frameset, but how do we actually implement navigation using them?

Time for a worked example!

Sham's artwork

Supposing we wanted to present a simple site showing an online portfolio of a renowned artist. Well, we haven't got the budget, given that we've already spent it getting Tom on the book, so a *renounced* artist will have to do instead; me.

1. The first thing we need to do is plan our layout:

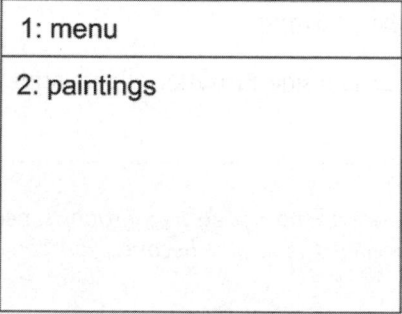

We will have a two frame layout, with the top one being a menu, and the lower one being an area to show images showing detail work from a number of paintings. We'll give them frame names of `menu` and `paintings`.

2. I have already created the menu document via a scan of some artwork and some slicing with ImageReady. Here's what I ended up with after the slices were placed into a table:

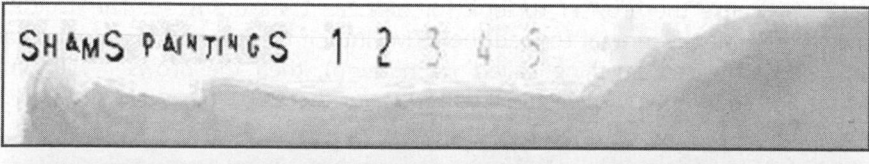

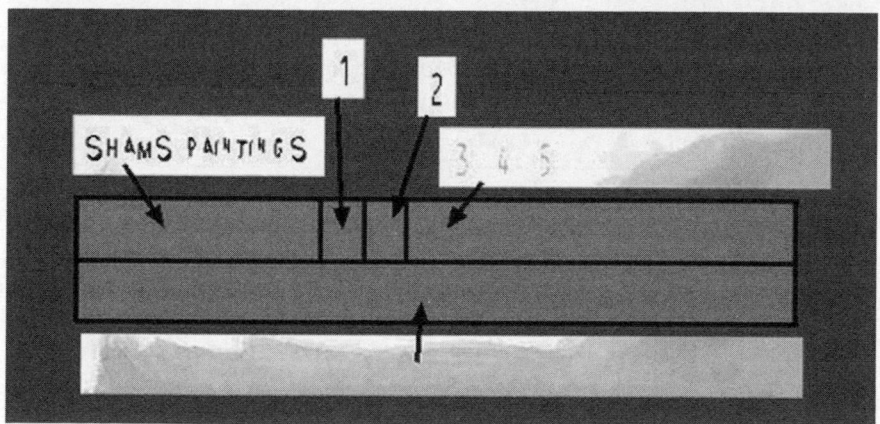

The numbers are inside `<a>` tags, making them links. Well... two of them are anyway. Painting may be therapeutic for me, but I think it may not be so for my audience, so I've only included two.

3.   To see all this in action, first create a new folder called `framesArt`.

4.   Into it, copy the files `index.html`, `topBar.html`, `zero.html`, `one.html` and `two.html` from the book's source files.

5.   Now create a new folder `topbar_images` within `framesArt`, and inside it, put the files `topbar_01.jpg` to `topbar_05.jpg`.

Now add one last folder `paintings` inside `framesArt`, and inside this put the files `zero.jpg`, `one.jpg` and `two.jpg`.

> *Notice that there are no* `mouseOver` *graphics, because I didn't think the design needed them. Just because you can doesn't mean you have to!*

6.   If you now view the HTML file, you will see the menu. Clicking on the buttons will cause either of the two `<a>` links corresponding to the number '1' and '2' slice to run, and they look like this respectively;

```
<a href="one.html" target="paintings">
<a href="two.html" target="paintings">
```

The '1' will cause the browser to look for `one.html` via the `href`. The TARGET attribute is the name of the object you want to load the HTML into. If there is nothing around called by this name (there currently isn't anything called `paintings`), then the browser will simply open a new browser and load `one.html` inside it. Likewise for the '2' button.

> *This is exactly the same sort of deal as the pop-ups in the placeholder site. If a named pop-up is already open, then content is loaded into it. If it doesn't exist yet, then it is created.*

7.   Now open `index.html`. This is our frameset. It defines two frames called `menu` and `paintings`.

```
<html>
<head>
</head>

<frameset rows="83,*" cols="*" framespacing="0" frameborder="0" border="0">
  <frame SRC="topbar.html" NAME="menu" SCROLLING="no" NORESIZE>
  <frame SRC="zero.html" NAME="paintings" SCROLLING="auto" NORESIZE>
```

```
    </frameset>

    <body>
    </body>
    </html>
```

There are also a few new attributes spread around this HTML, so let's have a look at those:

<frameset>

There are frame spacing and border attributes here, all set to zero. They collectively set the spacing between frames to zero and/or make sure the spacers between frames are not drawn. Different browsers have slightly different ways to make the frame spaces and the gray bit of chrome that is drawn between them disappear, and these three attributes make sure almost all browsers do it.

The `<frameset>` tag also sets the first row to 83 pixels high (the height of the menu) and the frame `paintings` is set to `auto` to make it fill the remaining space in the browser.

<frame>

The `SCROLLING` attribute tells the browser whether it needs to add scrollbars to the current frame. `menu` is set to `no` because it is set to exactly the right size already. `paintings` is set to `auto`; it will add scrollbars whenever it needs them.

The two frames `menu` and `paintings` are also loaded with the documents `menu.html` and `zero.html` respectively at start-up, to give you the following:

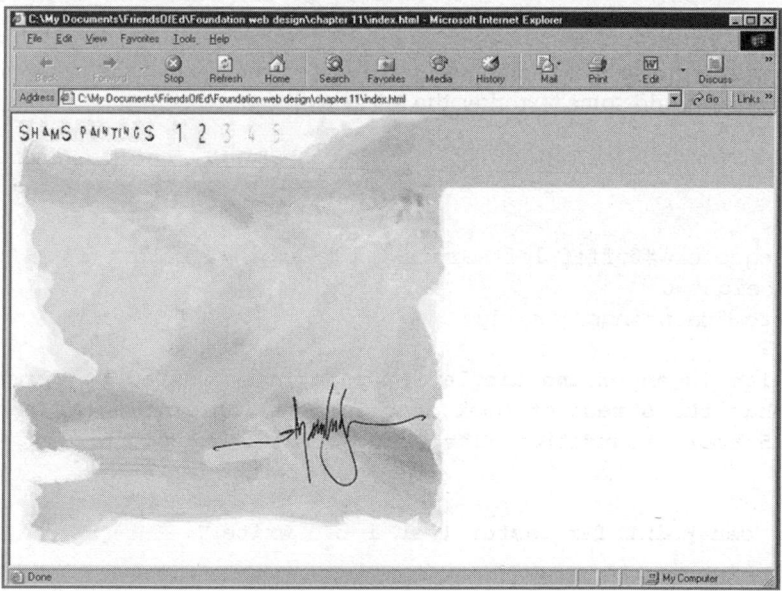

8. If you now click on one of the two numbers, the associated `<a>` links will again load up the documents `one.html` and `two.html`, but this time the frame object `paintings` exists, so the HTML is loaded into that.

Notice also how the scrollbars work; the lower frame has its own auto-scrollbars that only appear when required, whereas the top menu doesn't allow itself to get fouled up by overzealous scrollbars that would look pretty ugly and tend to hide the image anyway:

9. I designed the site so that I could add some text to the right of the image in zero.html. Open zero.html and add some text after the image as shown:

```
<html>
<head>
</head>
<body bgcolor=#ffffff leftmargin=0 topmargin=0 marginwidth=0
marginheight=0>
<img src="paintings/zero.jpg">
<br><p>
This site is an online display of paintings created by myself
to combat the stress of book deadlines during writing of the
Flash 5 books Foundation Flash and Foundation ActionScript.
</p>
<p>
NB - i can paint far faster than i can write...
</p>
</body>
</html>
```

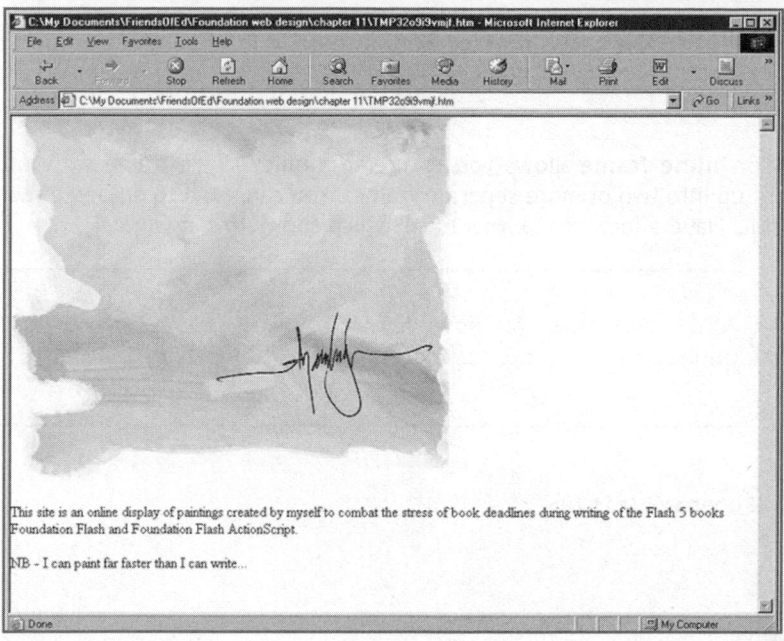

Hmmm. Not what I had in mind. The text seems to have missed the spot somewhat! Rather than go for tables to help us out, we can instead use the very useful ALIGN attribute. This not only allows you to align the image left or right, it also makes text align itself to the opposite edge of the image.

10. Add the following to the `<img>` tag:

```
<img src="paintings/zero.jpg" ALIGN="left">
```

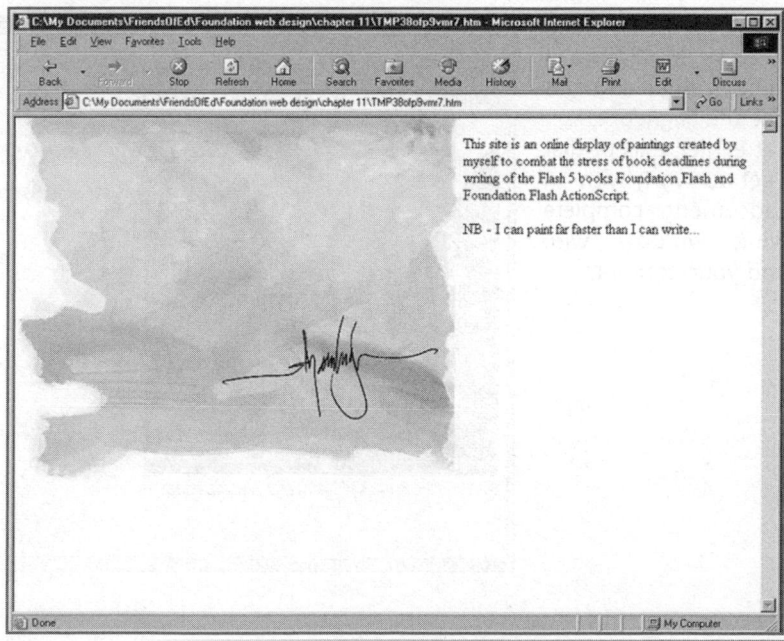

As you can see, the text now knows that we want it to go in the free space around the image. Cool!

Inline frames

The `<iframe>` or **inline frame** allows you to create a quick single frame without having to split your whole document up into two or more separate frames. You can use it to embed a second document inside the current HTML. Have a look at `iframe.html` which shows this at work:

> NB - *You need to have* `iframe.html`, `phoenix.jpg` *and* `phoenix.html` *in the same directory for this to work.*

```
<html>
<head>
<title>Phoenix</title>
</head>

<body>
<hr>
 <iframe src="phoenix.html" align="left" width="440" height="440"
➥scrolling="auto" frameborder="0" border="0"></iframe>
        Phoenix started out as a pencil and watercolor drawing,
        which was then imported into Photoshop for digital manipulation.
        <br><br>
        Art and Words by Sham B, 1998
</body>
</html>
```

The `<iframe>` tag loads a second HTML file, `phoenix.html` into a left aligned inline frame, and this will work just like the aligned `<img>` tag we looked at earlier, except that this time you get to work with an entire HTML document, complete with a viewing window with scrollbars around your content.

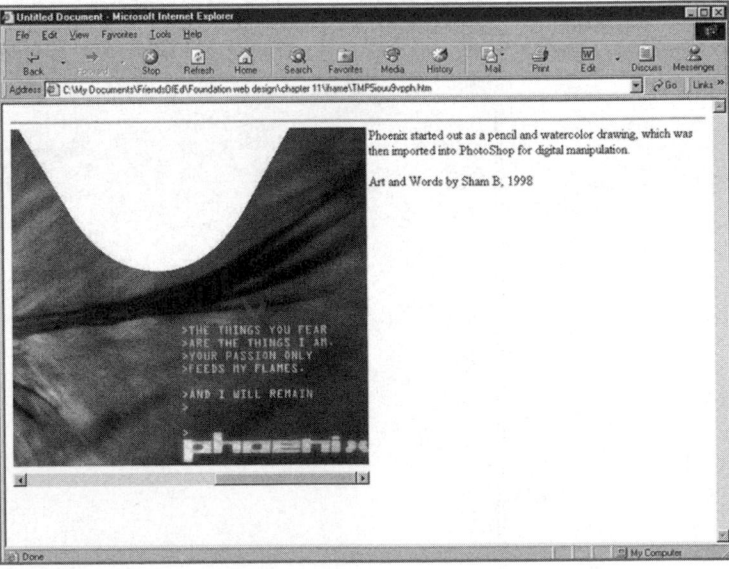

The Case Study – Frames and finishing touches

We now have all the bits we need to put together the Mondo site. This is another 'find a quiet few hours to do this' exercise, because we will need to place all our sliced tables into the appropriate placeholders, and do a fair bit of close-editing as we copy-paste our sliced sections to create the final pages.

The process will be slightly different, depending on whether you used Fireworks or ImageReady. As usual, we will do a typical example in the book, but the source files folder for this chapter contains instructions for the whole site.

Let's go through the game plan first....

We have our separate slice tables for every page in the site, each of which has the right URLs etc set up from **Chapter 10**. What we have to do is place each one into the right placeholder page.

As an example, we will look at the mission page again, and show how to put the first slice table into the placeholder page.

The files so far

In your mondoContent folder, you will now have the following (assuming you have followed the readme file in the download for **Chapter 10**, or used the files we have provided).

You will have four directories in the mondoContent directory:

- mon_t_upper_images
- mon_t_middle_images
- mon_t_lower_images
- mon_t_page_images

Each one holds the slices for our four page areas:

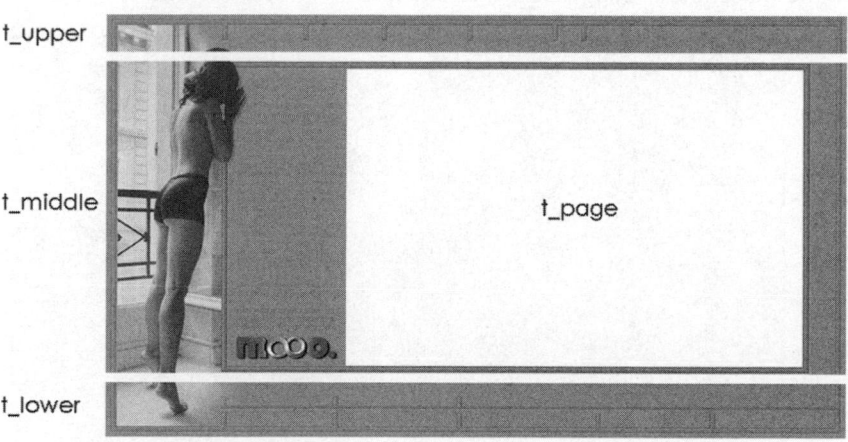

We have so far created the following HTML files for the mission page. Each of these contains the slice table for the general page sections illustrated above:

- mission_t_upper.html
- mon_t_middle.html
- mon_t_lower.html
- mission_t_page.html

As explained in the readme files for **Chapter 10** (in the download for that chapter), the 'mon_' files are general (the same for every page) but anything that starts with one of the page names (such as 'mission_' or 'events_') is for that specific page.

The top menu is unique because it has the mission text highlighted, and the '_page' is always different, given that it is the page specific content area.

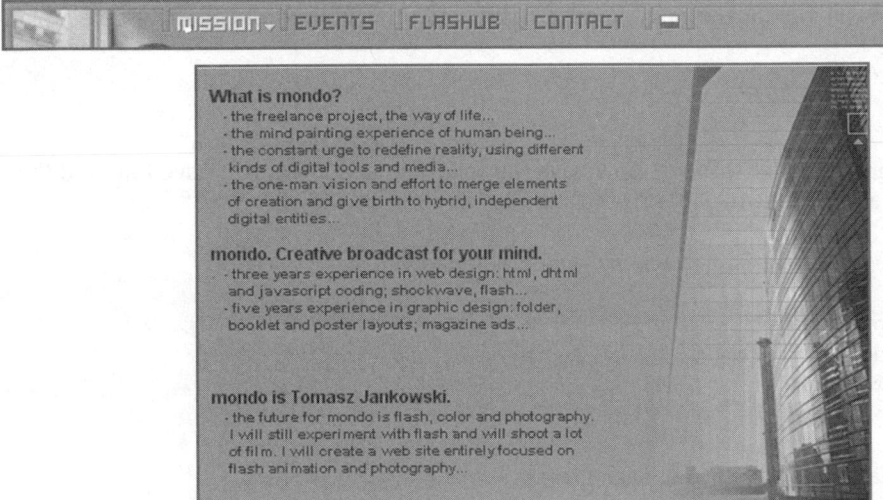

We also have the placeholder page mon_mission.html in mondoContent:

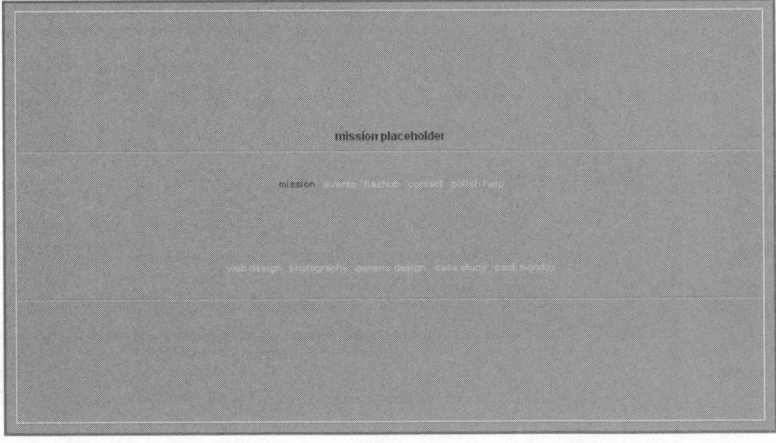

So to finish our site, we have to paste the currently separate files `mission_t_upper.html`, `mon_t_middle.html`, `mon_t_lower.html` and `mission_t_page.html` into `mon_mission.html`. That will give us the final page we need.

Easy, huh? Well, the problem is that we can't just paste them straight into each other. What we have to do is:

- Make sure we paste each slice table into the correct position in the table already in `mon_mission.html`.
- Make sure we also copy the right bits of JavaScript (the stuff that either ImageReady or Fireworks created for us in **Chapter 10**) so that it still works when we move the slice tables across.

Before we can do all this, we need to have a look at a couple of details, and they are different from both ImageReady and Fireworks, so choose your weapon and skip the inappropriate section...

ImageReady

If you look at the `<script>` part of the HTML `mission_t_upper.html`, you'll see something like this:

```
<SCRIPT TYPE="text/javascript">
<!--

function newImage(arg) {
    if (document.images) {
        rslt = new Image();
        rslt.src = arg;
        return rslt;
    }
}

function changeImages() {
    if (document.images && (preloadFlag == true)) {
        for (var i=0; i<changeImages.arguments.length; i+=2) {
            document[changeImages.arguments[i]].src =
changeImages.arguments[i+1];
        }
    }
}

var preloadFlag = false;
function preloadImages() {
    if (document.images) {
        mission_t_upper_11_over =
newImage("mon_t_upper_images/mission_t_upper_11-over.gif");
        mission_t_upper_12_over =
newImage("mon_t_upper_images/mission_t_upper_12-over.gif");
        mission_t_upper_13_over =
newImage("mon_t_upper_images/mission_t_upper_13-over.gif");
        preloadFlag = true;
```

continues overleaf

347

```
            }
        }

        // -->
    </SCRIPT>
```

All this code is concerned with **preloading** the rollovers. Normally, when you load a new page in a browser, content comes across to your browser when you need to see it. When you are creating interactive animation though, you don't want this to happen. What would happen if you did? Well...

1. The page content would load in.
2. You would then rollover a button to start doing stuff.
3. The browser would not have the graphic associated with the rollover animation (because it is not defined as part of the page *until you do something*), so the browser would have to request it.
4. This process would take some time, so the first time you press a button, the rollover animation will take up to a few seconds to change.

This looks really slipshod, so the solution is to *preload* all the graphics that will be needed during user interaction later. That way, the animations respond immediately.

So... for every slice table, we also need to make sure we also copy over the list of rollover slices to preload, and that is defined in the function preloadImages(). It is called in the <body> tag as the **onLoad** event, which means it will run as soon as the page is loaded.

As well as copying over the slice table, we also have to copy over this function (and the call to it in <body>) into mon_mission.html.

> We will also have to append the preload list from other slice table documents we put into the mon_mission *page, so that we really do preload everything we need.*

Because the images to preload are different for every page, the *preloadImages()* function will be different per page. To make life easier though, we can copy the functions that are the same for every page (the first two) into our script file *mon_script.js*. You need to copy the new stuff shown in bold below (make sure you get all the braces!):

```
function openPop(src, name, scrollbar, w, h ){
    features='menubar=no,resizable=no, scrollbars=' + scrollbar +
',width=' + w + ',height=' + h;
    name=window.open(src, name, features);
    name.focus();
    void 0;
}


function newImage(arg) {
```

```
        if (document.images) {
                rslt = new Image();
                rslt.src = arg;
                return rslt;
        }
}

function changeImages() {
        if (document.images && (preloadFlag == true)) {
                for (var i=0; i<changeImages.arguments.length; i+=2) {
                        document[changeImages.arguments[i]].src =
changeImages.arguments[i+1];
                }
        }
}
```

OK, skip the next part, because we're going to say the same thing for the Fireworks people...

Fireworks

If you look at the `<script>` part of the page `mission_t_upper.html`, you will see something like this:

```
<script language="JavaScript">
<!--
function MM_findObj(n, d) { //v4.01
 var p,i,x; if(!d) d=document;
if((p=n.indexOf("?"))>0&&parent.frames.length) {
   d=parent.frames[n.substring(p+1)].document; n=n.substring(0,p);}
 if(!(x=d[n])&&d.all) x=d.all[n]; for (i=0;!x&&i<d.forms.length;i++)
x=d.forms[i][n];
 for(i=0;!x&&d.layers&&i<d.layers.length;i++)
x=MM_findObj(n,d.layers[i].document);
 if(!x && d.getElementById) x=d.getElementById(n); return x;
}
function MM_swapImage() { //v3.0
 var i,j=0,x,a=MM_swapImage.arguments; document.MM_sr=new Array;
for(i=0;i<(a.length-2);i+=3)
   if ((x=MM_findObj(a[i]))!=null){document.MM_sr[j++]=x; if(!x.oSrc)
x.oSrc=x.src; x.src=a[i+2];}
}
function MM_swapImgRestore() { //v3.0
 var i,x,a=document.MM_sr; for(i=0;a&&i<a.length&&(x=a[i])&&x.oSrc;i++)
x.src=x.oSrc;
}

function MM_preloadImages() { //v3.0
 var d=document; if(d.images){ if(!d.MM_p) d.MM_p=new Array();
   var i,j=d.MM_p.length,a=MM_preloadImages.arguments; for(i=0; i<a.length;
i++)
```

continues overleaf

```
            if (a[i].indexOf("#")!=0){ d.MM_p[j]=new Image; d.MM_p[j++].src=a[i];}}
    }

    //-->
    </script>
```

Don't worry if it looks a bit dense; Macromedia are simply trying to keep it as short as possible, but to do that, they have also made it look pretty unintelligible!

All this code is concerned with **preloading** the rollovers. Normally, when you load a new page in a browser, content comes across to your browser when you need to see it. When you are creating interactive animation though, you don't want this to happen. What would happen if you did? Well...

1.   The page content would load in.
2.   You would then rollover a button to start doing stuff.
3.   The browser would not have the graphic associated with the rollover animation (because it is not defined as part of the page *until you do something*), so the browser would have to request it.
4.   This process would take some time, so the first time you press a button, the rollover animation will take up to a few seconds to change.

This looks really slipshod, so the solution is to *preload* all the graphics that will be needed during user interaction later. That way, the animations respond immediately.

So... for every slice table we also need to make sure we also copy over the list of rollover states to preload, and that is defined in the <body> tag a bit lower down:

```
<body bgcolor="#ffffff"
onLoad="MM_preloadImages('mon_t_upper_images/mission_t_upper_r2_c3_f2.gif','
mon_t_upper_images/mission_t_upper_r2_c5_f2.gif','mon_t_upper_images/mission
_t_upper_r2_c6_f2.gif');">
```

The **onLoad** event fires off as soon as the page is fully loaded, and this causes a call to the function MM_preloadImages(). This function will preload every image in the argument list.

To make life easier though, we can copy the functions into our script file mon_script.js, so that they become available throughout the site. You should end up with a mon_script.js as shown below (the text in bold is the copied stuff):

```
function openPop(src, name, scrollbar, w, h ){
    features='menubar=no,resizable=no, scrollbars=' + scrollbar +
',width=' + w + ',height=' + h;
    name=window.open(src, name, features);
    name.focus();
    void 0;
}

function MM_findObj(n, d) { //v4.01
 var p,i,x; if(!d) d=document;
if((p=n.indexOf("?"))>0&&parent.frames.length) {
```

```
         d=parent.frames[n.substring(p+1)].document; n=n.substring(0,p);}
      if(!(x=d[n])&&d.all) x=d.all[n]; for (i=0;!x&&i<d.forms.length;i++)
   x=d.forms[i][n];
      for(i=0;!x&&d.layers&&i<d.layers.length;i++)
   x=MM_findObj(n,d.layers[i].document);
      if(!x && d.getElementById) x=d.getElementById(n); return x;
   }
   function MM_swapImage() { //v3.0
      var i,j=0,x,a=MM_swapImage.arguments; document.MM_sr=new Array;
   for(i=0;i<(a.length-2);i+=3)
      if ((x=MM_findObj(a[i]))!=null){document.MM_sr[j++]=x; if(!x.oSrc)
   x.oSrc=x.src; x.src=a[i+2];}
   }
   function MM_swapImgRestore() { //v3.0
      var i,x,a=document.MM_sr; for(i=0;a&&i<a.length&&(x=a[i])&&x.oSrc;i++)
   x.src=x.oSrc;
   }

   function MM_preloadImages() { //v3.0
      var d=document; if(d.images){ if(!d.MM_p) d.MM_p=new Array();
      var i,j=d.MM_p.length,a=MM_preloadImages.arguments; for(i=0; i<a.length;
   i++)
      if (a[i].indexOf("#")!=0){ d.MM_p[j]=new Image; d.MM_p[j++].src=a[i];}}
   }
```

Adding the mission_t_upper menu to mon_mission

Yet again, the process is different depending on the application you are using … ImageReady first, then Fireworks:

ImageReady

1. Open both `mon_mission.html` and `mission_t_upper.html`. We will be copying parts of the latter into the former, so you might want to open them up side by side.

2. The first thing we need to do is sort out the preloading. Copy the function (and the line that sets `preloadFlag=false`) into a new set of `<script>…</script>` tags within `mondo_content.html`. When you are done, the script tags in `mondo_content.html` will look like this:

```
<script language="JavaScript" src="mondo_script.js"></script>

<script>
var preloadFlag = false;
function preloadImages() {
       if (document.images) {
               mission_t_upper_11_over =
newImage("mon_t_upper_images/mission_t_upper_11-over.gif");
```

continues overleaf

351

```
              mission_t_upper_12_over =
newImage("mon_t_upper_images/mission_t_upper_12-over.gif");
              mission_t_upper_13_over =
newImage("mon_t_upper_images/mission_t_upper_13-over.gif");
              preloadFlag = true;
      }
}
</script>
```

Note that we are loading up our JS file (which contains our common functions) via the existing `<script>…</script>` tags, and the new set define the functions that are *specific to this page*.

> As we add further slice tables to build up our page with the final graphics, we will need to add further entries in this function, so that it lists all the rollover preloading we need to do; for some pages it will get quite large!

3. Also change the `<body>` tag in `mon_mission.html` to add the `onLoad`, thus wiring `preloadImages()` up to the event that will make it run:

    ```
    <body ONLOAD="preloadImages();">
    ```

    Next, we must copy the slice table itself over.

4. In `mon_mission.html`, we need to delete the placeholder text, so delete the lines *between* the `<!--Top menu-->` and `<!--Content area-->` comments (the text marked in bold below):

    ```
    <!--Top menu-->

    <p>
    mission  
    <a href = "mon_events.html">events</a>  
    <a href="javascript:openPop('flash.html', 'flashPopup', 'no', 800,
    600);">flashub</a>  
    <a href = "mon_contact.html">contact</a>  
    <a href="javascript:openPop('mon_pol_mis.html', 'polPopup', 'no', 550,
    300);">polish help</a>
    </p>

    <!--Content area-->
    ```

5. Also delete the title text and rule that appears directly above the `<!--Top menu-->` comment. It looks like this:

    ```
            <span CLASS="title">mission placeholder</span>
            <hr>
    ```

```
<span CLASS="text">
```

6. ...and delete the ending `</span>` near the bottom of the file (there's only one, so there's no chance of getting the wrong one).

7. Finally, we need to insert the slice table. In `mission_t_upper.html`, you will see two comments at the start and end of the table that will look something like this:

```
<!-- ImageReady Slices (filename.psd) -->
...
...
...
<!-- End ImageReady Slices -->
```

8. Copy the comments and the rather large table between them and paste it right after the `<!--Top menu-->` comment in `mon_mission.html`.

9. When you are done, you can now view the result by viewing `mon_mission.html` in a browser:

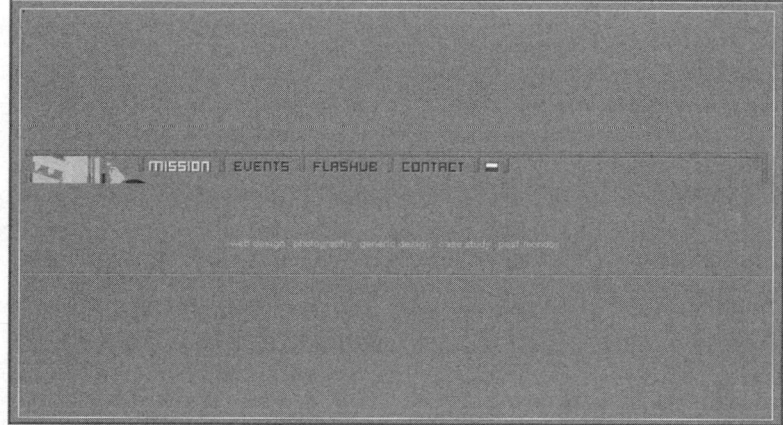

10. To completely replace the page, we also have to replace the rest of the placeholder text with the other slice tables in `mission_t_middle.html`, `mon_t_middle.html` and `mission_t_page.html`.

> *The reason the top menu bar is not at the top is because there is currently nothing in the table pushing it up into place. When you have added mission_t_middle and mission_t_lower, it will move neatly into place.*

11. If you click on the menu items, they should still do the same things as the finished page.

12. The rest of the exercise is simply repeating the process, adding the other slice tables until we have the finished page. As you can see, this is a fairly repetitive task (and you can appreciate why the rest of the exercise is in the readme file!), but offset slightly by the fact that you see the final site appearing slowly but fully working as you go. If any step doesn't work, you can simply stop and correct the current page section before moving on.

Although doing the site the way we have may have seemed a little slow at times, because we have effectively built two sites (a placeholder site and the final site), you may be seeing why we have to do that with most commercial sites; they have so many damn links and fiddly little slices everywhere, that if you tried to put it all together straight away or (worse still) built it up with no real plan, you would be spending about 80% of your time simply reworking to 'add that little bit you forgot earlier'!

Also, we have put you in the deep end a little by starting you off with a simple looking site, but which has some fairly complex, tightly fitting text and graphics. Don't worry too much if the HTML of the finished pages looks massive, giving you panic attacks, because that's a consequence of HTML being a simple formatting language – you usually need lots of it to do anything cool.

OK, let's give the Fireworks people the drill ... skip the next section and go to **Upload and play**.

Fireworks

1. Open both mon_mission.html and mission_t_upper.html. We will be copying parts of the latter into the former, so you might want to open them up side by side.

2. The first thing we need to do is sort out the preloading. Copy the onLoad event from mission_t_upper.html's <body> tag and add it to the <body> in mon_mission.html. You should end up with a <body> tag in mon_mission.html that looks like this:

```
<body
onLoad="MM_preloadImages('mon_t_upper_images/mission_t_upper_r2_c3_f2.gif','
mon_t_upper_images/mission_t_upper_r2_c5_f2.gif','mon_t_upper_images/mission
_t_upper_r2_c6_f2.gif');">
```

> As we add further slice tables to build up our page with the final graphics, we will need to add further entries in this function, so that it lists all the rollover preloading we need to do; for some pages it will get quite large! Remember that you can split the tag over several lines if it makes it more readable:

```
<body onLoad="MM_preloadImages(
'mon_t_upper_images/mission_t_upper_r2_c3_f2.gif',
'mon_t_upper_images/mission_t_upper_r2_c5_f2.gif',
'mon_t_upper_images/mission_t_upper_r2_c6_f2.gif'
);">
```

Next, we need to copy the slice table itself over.

3. In `mon_mission.html`, we need to delete the placeholder text, so delete the lines between the `<!--Top menu-->` and `<!--Content area-->` comments (the text marked in bold below):

```
<!--Top menu-->

<p>
mission  
<a href = "mon_events.html">events</a>  
<a href="javascript:openPop('flash.html', 'flashPopup', 'no', 800,
600);">flashhub</a>  
<a href = "mon_contact.html">contact</a>  
<a href="javascript:openPop('mon_pol_mis.html', 'polPopup', 'no', 550,
300);">polish help</a>
</p>

<!--Content area-->
```

4. Also delete the title text and rule that appears directly above the `<!--Top menu-->` comment. It looks like this:

```
<span CLASS="title">mission placeholder</span>
<hr>
<span CLASS="text">
```

5. ...and delete the ending `</span>` near the bottom of the file (there's only one, so there's no chance of getting the wrong one).

6. Finally, we need to insert the slice table. In `mission_t_upper.html`, copy everything between the `<table>`...`</table>` tags (including the tags themselves).

7. Then, paste it right after the `<!--Top menu-->` comment in `mon_mission.html`.

8. When you're done, you can now view the result by viewing `mon_mission.html` in a browser:

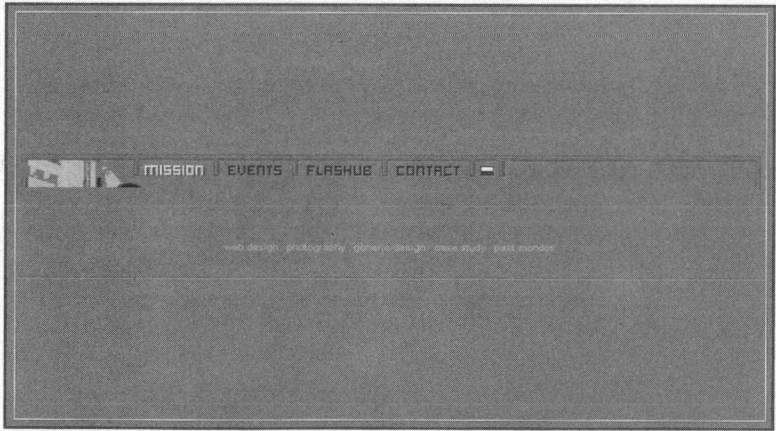

9. To completely replace the page, we also have to replace the rest of the placeholder text with the other slice tables in `mission_t_middle.html`, `mon_t_middle.html` and `mission_t_page.html`.

> *The reason the top menu bar is not at the top is because there is currently nothing in the table pushing it up into place. When you have added* `mission_t_middle` *and* `mission_t_lower`, *it will move neatly into place.*

If you click on the menu items, they should still do the same things as the finished page.

10. The rest of the exercise is simply repeating the process, adding the other slice tables until we have the finished page. As you can see, this is a fairly repetitive task (and you can appreciate why the rest of the exercise is on the `readme` file!), but offset slightly by the fact that you see the final site appearing slowly but fully working as you go. If any step doesn't work, you can simply stop and correct the current page section before moving on.

Although doing the site the way we have may have seemed a little slow at times, because we have effectively built two sites (a placeholder site and the final site), you may be seeing why we have to do that with most commercial sites; they have so many links and fiddly little slices everywhere, that if you tried to put it all together straight away or (worse still) built it up with no real plan, you would be spending about 80% of your time simply reworking to 'add that little bit you forgot earlier'!

Also, we have put you in the deep end a little by starting you off with a simple looking site, but which has some fairly complex, tightly fitting text and graphics. Don't worry too much if the HTML of the finished pages looks massive, giving you panic attacks, because that's a consequence of HTML being a simple formatting language you usually need lots of it to do anything cool.

Upload and play

Once we have all repeated the process above for all the pages in the site, then deleted all the individual construction files containing the individual slice tables (as discussed in the `readme` file), we are ready to upload our site to the Web and point our friends to what we've learned.

You might already be familiar with putting work online and copying your files to the Web – perhaps through some free webspace provided by your ISP. In any event, most providers supply you with full instructions on how to transfer your files onto your own website.

Appendix A – Getting Your Work Online will cover all the main issues you need to be aware of when getting yourself a web presence – from finding a domain to understanding all the jargon. You can leaf through that to fill in the gaps in your knowledge or indeed go right ahead and upload the Mondo site, if you already know how.

Our case study is now finished but in the next chapter, we'll take a look at Flash, a powerful tool for creating animation and highly visual web interfaces, and the last feather in your web design cap.

Introducing Flash

What this chapter will do

In this chapter, we will introduce you to the world of Macromedia Flash, an animation tool that can work equally well in creating entire sites and as part of a HTML based site. We'll take a look at:

- The Flash interface and environment
- Using **tweens** to create animation
- Using Flash to create buttons instead of JavaScript

More importantly, we'll take you through a couple of examples to show how you can use Flash alongside the knowledge that you've gained from the rest of this book. We'll show you:

- How to create a Flash pop-up
- How to add a simple Flash navigation bar to the site we looked at in the last chapter

What you'll have learned by the end of this chapter

What's most important is that, by the end of this chapter, you'll have a feel for what Flash can offer you, and why it's so potentially useful. Flash is rapidly becoming more and more important in the field of web design, so this is your chance to take a look and see what all the fuss is about.

This chapter can of course only be an introduction – Flash is a large subject area that can cover a whole range of tasks. If you want to take it further, we'd recommend starting by taking a look at *Foundation Flash MX* from friends of ED.

Your browser is designed to show web pages based on the premise that web pages are essentially electronic versions of book pages. The real differences between web and book pages are that web pages use hyperlinks, (allowing you to pick your own route through the information) and can also use *dynamic* data (a share price web page can be continually updated, for example).

These are both significant advantages over printed material, but what about a full multimedia presentation, including sound, video, and animation, all reacting to user input? A few folks thought this was a cool idea, and went to work. To add new functionality to the browser, they used a series of 'extras' called **plug-ins**. For example, if you wanted to add a video stream into your web page, you would make sure the user had a plug-in that could recognise the video, and take over from the browser to display it.

This works via two HTML tags: `<object>` and `<embed>`. These point to a specialized file, in the same way that the `<img>` tag points to a graphic, they also point to the plug-in that can display the file. If the user has the plug-in already installed, then the multimedia is parsed by the plug-in, and the user thinks the browser is doing it all seamlessly. If the user doesn't have the plug-in, the browser requests that it be downloaded from the web and installed.

This way of adding multimedia into a web page was dynamite, because it changed HTML from a simple text formatting language to something that allowed web designers to specify areas on a page and say 'put a streaming video there, and, oh, how about we make that section there a portal to a real-time reactive 3D simulation'.

The big problem was that the whole process was not seamless in practice, as there were a lot of different plug-ins involved, each of which were big, and took a long time to download. Not only this, but the content that the plug-ins allowed access to, was bandwidth-heavy, and users ended up with hour long downloads just to see a postage stamp-sized video.

All this made using plug-ins quite risky and difficult, until Macromedia Flash came along with a plug-in that was small to download, supplied a variety of content that was usable by folks on a 56k modem, and allowed for user interaction as well as enhanced graphics. The Flash plug-in is now a worldwide standard; Macromedia estimate that over 98% of all browsers have it installed. It can deal with a variety of different elements, including:

- low-bandwidth animation
- sound in the compressed MP3 format
- video compressed with the Flash codec (provided by industry giant Sorenson)
- talking to standard HTML content by issuing JavaScript commands to the browser

The Flash plug-in allows designers to program some sophisticated behaviors into web projects by way of Flash's internal scripting language **ActionScript**. The beauty of ActionScript is that it has exactly the same syntax as JavaScript, so it shouldn't look that strange to you.

Nothing is perfect, of course, and Flash's ability to create stunning visual experiences led to a rash of bloated site intros a while back, that created some negative press. There are also significantly greater inherent problems in making animated content accessible than there are in making traditional static HTML accessible. These points both underline that Flash is not the answer to everything, but it can be a very useful part of your overall web design, as we're about to see...

If you haven't got access to a copy of Macromedia Flash, you can download a fully functional trial version from www.macromedia.com/software/flash. You can also download the latest version of the plug-in. As you'll see from the screenshots, we're assuming that you're using Flash MX in this chapter, but what we're doing is also possible in previous versions...

The interface

Open Flash, and if the application has been used previously, select Window > Panel Sets > Default Layouts. Select Windows > Toolbars and check all three of the options that appear (Main, Status and Controller). You should now see a screen something like the screenshot.

You may see a request to connect to the Web at this point. This is Flash trying to update the Answers *panel. You don't need to connect, so hit* Cancel. *You can prevent this happening again by selecting* Window > Answers, *so that the panel doesn't try to display.*

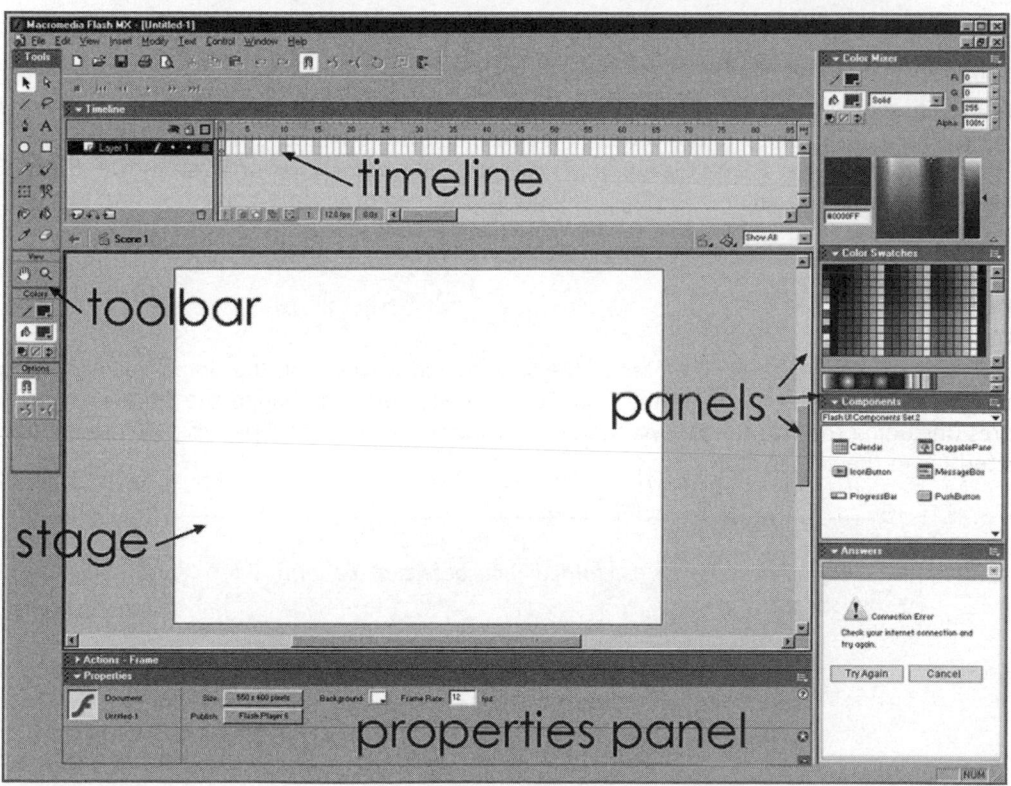

If you're using a PC, you will find that the panels are dockable – that is to say, that if you click-drag them with the little knurled area onto the right-hand side, the panel will dock onto the stack. To drag a panel so that it doesn't dock, use the upper dragbar. If you're using a Mac, the panels won't dock.

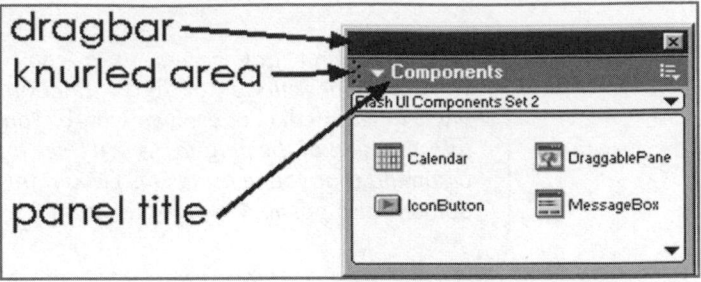

On either platform, clicking on the panel title or the little down arrow in front of it will cause the window to toggle to its collapsed appearance.

Two special panels are the **Properties** and **Actions** panels. The Properties panel is very similar to the Properties panel in Fireworks (or the Tool Options bar in Photoshop). It is **context sensitive**, which is to say that it will change to reflect the current tool or selection you are working with. It is always worth having open. Make sure that you've got the Properties panel fully open by hitting the little down arrow at the bottom right corner of this panel.

The Actions panel is where you add ActionScript. In our screenshot, it's collapsed (you can see the title bar just above the Properties panel), but clicking on the Actions title will open it. We'll look at ActionScript and the Actions panel later.

The timeline

As Macromedia Fireworks fans will already know, Macromedia tends to like film-based analogies. With Flash, animations are created with a series of **frames**, and the timeline is the physical representation of many frames in sequence. Each little square represents one frame in your Flash movie. Every time you click on a frame in the timeline, the stage will jump to the point in time corresponding to that frame in the animation, rather like looking at a movie reel frame by frame.

The stage

The stage is the white area in the center of the screen, and is where all the drama takes place: anything that happens here will be visible in the final Flash movie. You can change the stage's appearance and attributes (including the **frame rate**) via Modify > Document or in the Properties panel when nothing else is selected (as in the screenshot).

> *A good frame rate is somewhere between 12 and 24 frames per second.*

Creating tween animations

There are two ways of creating Flash animation: using **tweens**, and using ActionScript.

Tween based animation

In tweened animations, the timeline will move along frame by frame and the corresponding animation will play out on the stage. The terms tween and keyframe are borrowed from traditional animation. When animators create cartoons, they have a principal artist who creates the main (or *key*) frames for each sequence. Once these are defined by the principal, other animators will create the in-between frames, and the frames they produce are known as tweens.

In the simple animation below, where a circle becomes a square, the 'fully circle' and 'fully square' frames are the **keyframes**, and the intermediate ones are the tweens. In Flash, we only need to create the keyframes, and Flash generates the tween frames for us.

There are two types of tween: shape tweens, and motion tween. This is a shape tween, so we'll take a look at these first.

Shape tweens

A shape tween is an animation of the basic shape data of a primitive Flash graphic. A primitive shape is an unstructured collection of lines and fills. Everything you place on a timeline is a primitive unless you make it into one of Flash's more structured graphic elements (called **symbols**), which we'll look at in a moment.

1. To help us draw stuff, make sure View > Grid > Show Grid, and View > Grid > Snap to Grid are checked. This will make our drawings snap to the nearest grid line.

2. Look at your timeline: it should look like the one pictured. The single frame with a hollow circle is an **empty keyframe**. The orange rectangle and vertical line (currently highlighting the '1') is the **playhead**, which is Flash's way of telling us where we are at the moment: whatever frame is highlighted by the playhead will be shown on the stage. At the moment, there is only one frame, so it can't move anywhere.

3. In the Toolbar, select the Oval tool 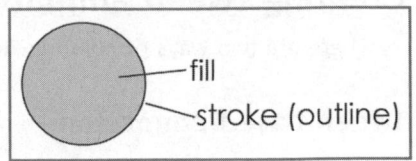. By default, Flash creates basic shapes in two parts, a **fill** and a **stroke**.

4. Shape tweens work best if they only have to deal with one of these. To prevent the Oval tool drawing the stroke, look down the toolbar to the Color section. Here, you will see separate color bricks for the fill and stroke colors. Click on the stroke color to select it, opening the color picker, and hit the 'no color' icon ▨ - the square with a red diagonal line through it.

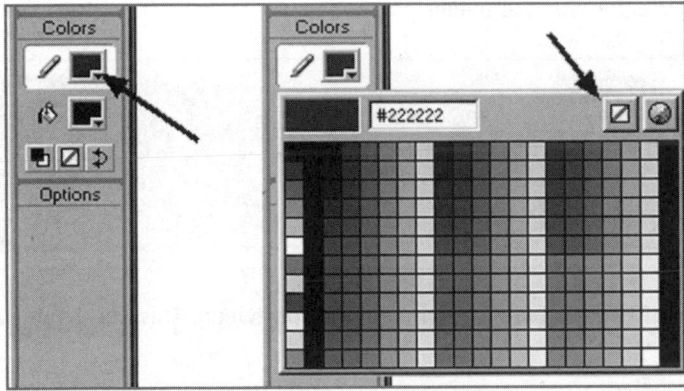

5. If you want to change the color of the fill (represented by the Paint Bucket symbol, below the Stroke color that we've just changed), use the same method to select a new color.

6. Using the grid as a guide, draw out a circle by click-holding at a grid intersection and dragging out a shape as shown. As well as seeing the finished circle on the stage, the keyframe in the timeline will now change to a solid circle, signifying a keyframe with content in it.

Try holding down the SHIFT key to constrain your oval to a circle.

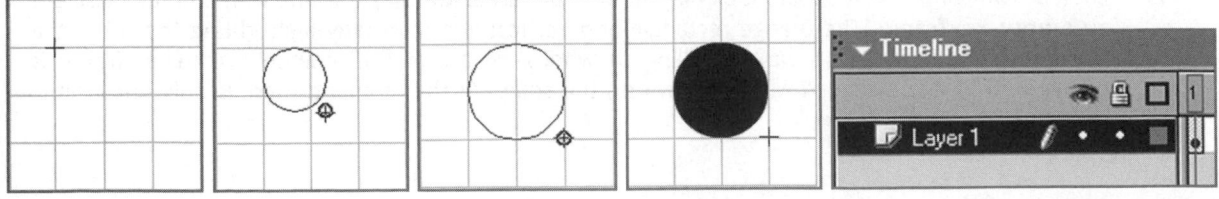

7. We now have the starting keyframe. We need an end keyframe as well, so select frame 10 on the timeline by clicking on it. Choose Insert > Keyframe, and a keyframe will be added at frame 10, and new frames will be added to frames 2-9.

 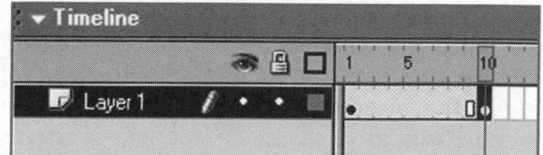

8. Select the Rectangle tool from the Tools panel, and make sure that the Stroke is still turned off.

9. Check that frame 10 is still selected, and draw a rectangle.

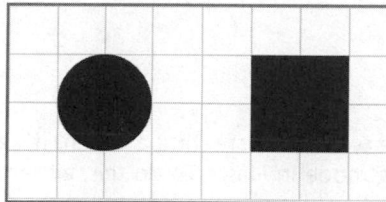 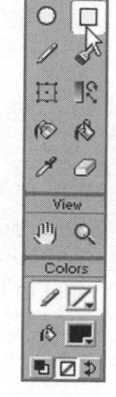

10. Select the Arrow tool, select the circle in frame 10, and delete it.

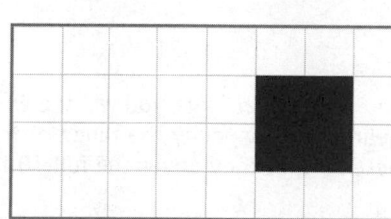

Let's recap what we've done. We have a circle in a keyframe on frame 1, we have a square in a keyframe on frame 10, and we have some frames in between. You can see what is currently in the in between frames by clicking on them or dragging the playhead along: they all contain the circle. We need to change these in-between frames to an animated transition.

11. We do this by defining frame 1 as a tween, so select frame 1. In the Properties panel, select the tween drop-down, and change it from none to shape. The intermediate frames in the timeline will now turn green to signify the tween.

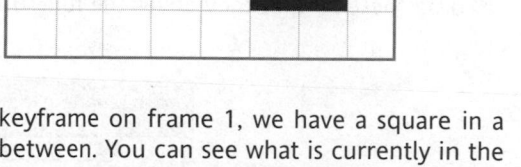

12. The timeline should look like the one above, with a solid arrow line inside the green area. If the line is dotted, as below, then you have done something wrong: either the keyframe at frame 1 or 10 is empty.

Onion skinning

When animators create tween frames by hand, they first use tracing paper to define the outlines of the in-between frames. This helps because they can see the outlines of *all* the frames in the animation, and helps to create a smooth transition. This process is usually called **onion skinning** because many layers of tracing paper are involved, and creating the animated effect involves quickly taking away the top piece of paper and working down the layers; rather like skinning an onion.

In the diagram below, we see a tween of a circle moving diagonally upwards as it shape tweens into a square. We can tell how good the animation will be by inspecting the closeness and smoothness of the intermediate outlines.

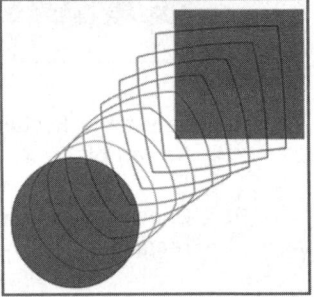

Because we will be creating a tween, it's a good idea to switch to the onion skinning mode in Flash. To do this, either click the Onion Skin or the Onion Skin Outlines icon at the bottom of the timeline (as shown).

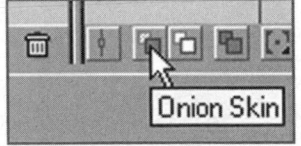

Once you click either icon, you will see what looks like { } brackets appear over the frame numbers above the timeline. These specify the range of frames that will show up as part of the onion skinning. Click and drag these so that they cover the full 10 frames of our tween.

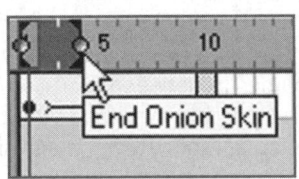
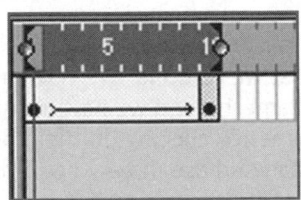

Now, you can select either keyframe, and use the Arrow tool to move the square or circle around and see how this will change the animation.

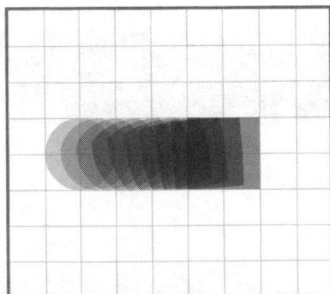
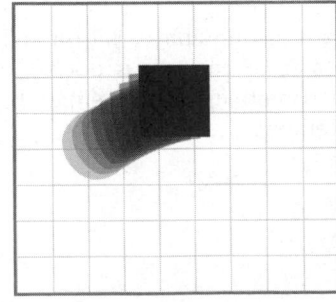
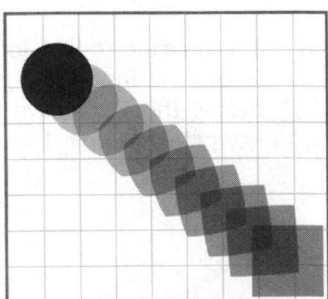

Testing the movie

Now that we've fine-tuned our animation, it's time to save it with (File > Save As), and see how our animation will look when we play it in the Flash player. Do this by selecting Control > Test Scene (or CTRL+ALT+ENTER). You can also test it by using the controller buttons at the top of the screen 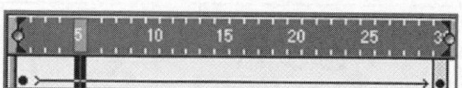 (Window > Toolbars > Controller).

You can see how it would look in a browser by hitting File > Publish Preview > HTML (CTRL+F12). This will create a SWF (the exported Flash movie) and an HTML file in the same place as you've saved the Flash file (which will be in FLA format). If you take a look, you'll see that the SWF is smaller than the FLA, and this is why Flash generates them: a SWF is a version of the FLA with all the non-essential details stripped out so that it's as small as possible for use on the web. We will look at how to use the files generated in this way later in the chapter, when we look at integrating Flash with HTML/JavaScript.

The animation will get less smooth as you make the start and end points (the square and the circle) of the animation further apart on the stage. You can fix this by inserting additional frames - select a frame part way between the two keyframes (such as frame 5), and use Insert > Frame (or F5) several times to add more frames to the tween. More frames means that the amount of movement between each frame decreases: test again to see this in action.

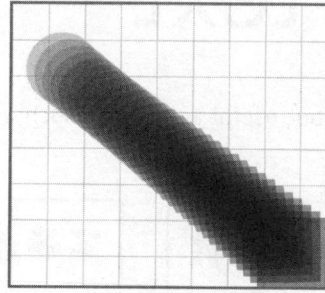

Text tweens

Shape tweens can be used with any primitive shape you draw on the stage. (You know a shape is a primitive if it looks like the screenshot on the left – if it has a blue bounding box around it like the screenshot on the right, then it's not a primitive.)

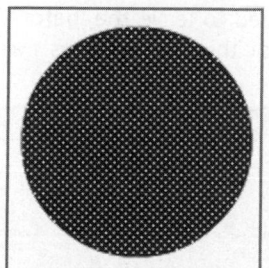
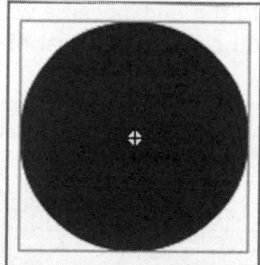

About the only thing you can create that is not immediately a primitive is text with the Text tool. To turn text into primitives, you can use Modify > Break Apart. You need to do this twice: once to break text apart into individual letters, and then again to break it into primitives.

normal text

text broken apart into letters

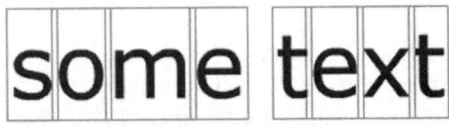

text completely broken apart

some text

Text is cool, because you can quickly create simple but useful animations such as the one shown using shape tweening.

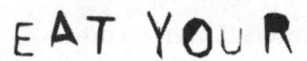

Here's the timeline that creates something like this. Notice that the tween doesn't start immediately, and neither does it carry on to the end, because we need to leave the 'before' and 'after' text up for a while so people can read it. You can see the final file for this animation as `tween1.fla` if you want a closer look.

Layers

OK, that's one animation, but what about adding a background or other tweens at the same time? Just like Photoshop, Flash uses layers (see **Appendix D**). Have a look at tween2.fla for an example of a more finished version of our animation, complete with layers, and all sorts of other tricks...

The timeline looks like the screenshot. It might look different, but it is still the same basic effect, with some extra trimmings.

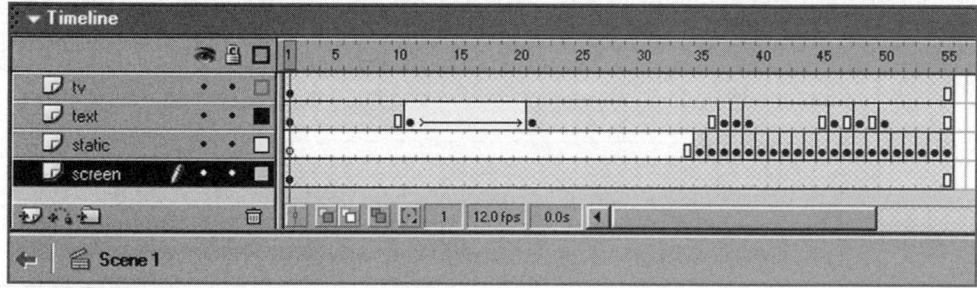

You create new layers by hitting the Insert layer icon 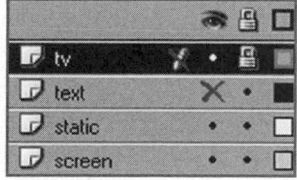 at the bottom left of the timeline. The Delete Layer icon to the right 🗑 does just what it says. You can rename a layer simply by double-clicking on its title.

Finding your way around a layered system depends upon being able to **lock** or **hide** a layer, and this is done with the icons to the right of the layer titles. Clicking on a layer in the eye 👁 column will hide a layer, and bring up a cross ✖ (as shown on the *text* layer below). Click on the red X to make the layer visible again. The **lock** icon 🔒 locks a layer, so that you can make sure that you don't make changes to it (in the screenshot, the tv layer is locked).

The final icon, Show Layer As Outline will make a layer appear as outlines. This is more useful than it may sound, because it allows you to see through a layer without fully hiding it. The positioning of the test card color stripes was achieved by making the tv layer into an outline while the positioning was carried out.

 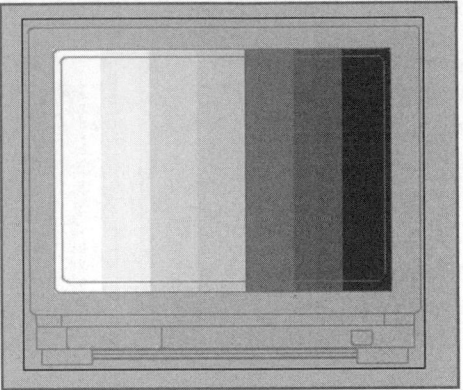

A final point to notice is how I created the TV static. Flash is a vector-based system that works best when dealing with artwork created inside it, but it can also handle imported bitmap images (albeit slowly, so keep them small). Sometimes vectors are unsuitable for representing a graphic, and the static is one such case. Instead, I imported a JPEG (with File > Import) and put this behind the TV window. This was then jiggled around a bit to appear as static.

> *Vectors are mathematical instructions about lines, shapes, and color fills, and are a different way of storing image details from the bitmaps we've used previously, which are made up of pixels laid side by side in a big grid.*

Motion tweens

Several pages ago, we said there were two types of tween, so it's about time we got around to taking a look at the second type: the **Motion** tween.

1. Create a new Flash movie with File > New.

2. Draw a circle like last time. Once you've done this, select it and go to Insert > Convert to Symbol.

3. You should see the window pictured (you might also see a bigger window – just hit the Basic button if so, you don't need the other options). Enter `ball` as a Name: and select Graphic for the Behavior:

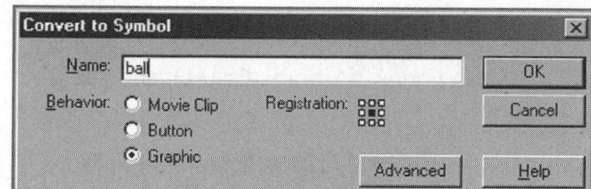

4. The circle is now a **Symbol**, rather than a primitive, and you can tell this from the bounding box around the shape.

5. Select frame 30 and chose Insert > Keyframe (or F6) to create a keyframe.

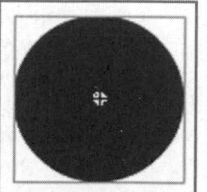

6. In frame 30, move the circle away from its starting position, so that we can create some motion.

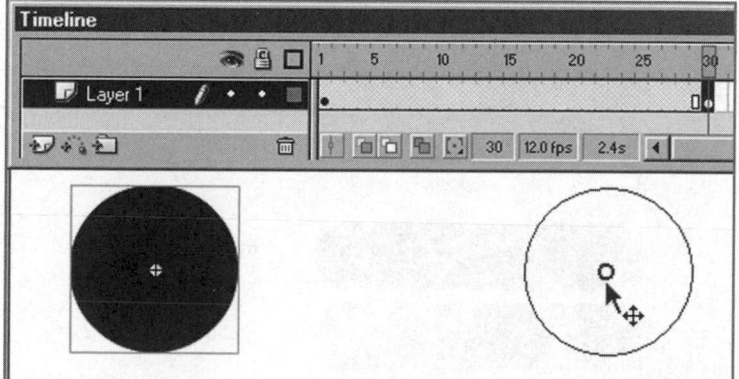

7. Select frame 1, select the Tween drop-down in the Properties panel, and change it from none to motion. The intermediate frames in the timeline will now turn blue to signify the tween.

8. Test as before, and the circle will move happily between the two points that you've given it.

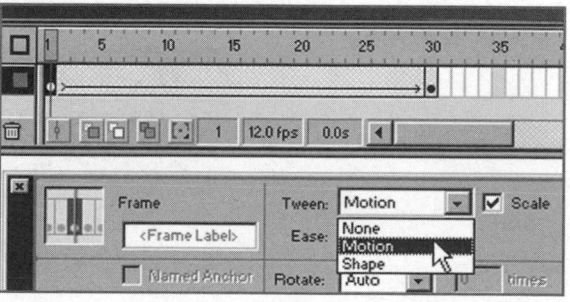

The Library

Now you're thinking 'so what? I could have done that with shape tweens'. True, but we are not changing the primitive data with a motion tween, we are changing the *position* property of the *ball* object. The great thing is that ball has a property for every other visual attribute – color, size, width, transparency, and so on. Additionally, now that we've created a ball object, we can reuse it. Go to Window > Library (CTRL+L), and you'll see something like the screenshot.

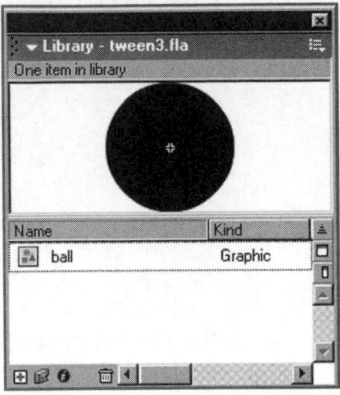

The ball graphic is a symbol, so it's remembered by Flash, and kept in the Library. If you want to use ball again, you can simply drag and drop it from the library as many times as you want (so you can have a whole screen full of moving circles if you want). This is great, because no matter how many times you use ball, Flash will only download one version of it, reducing the download time for the Flash movie no end.

The version in the Library is the original, and, using Flash terminology, the copies are **instances**. Once placed on the stage, you can vary the properties of each instance as you like. You can see an example of this in tween3.fla. Here, I've copied a number of ball instances from our Library, one per layer. All the instances do something other than just change position during the animation.

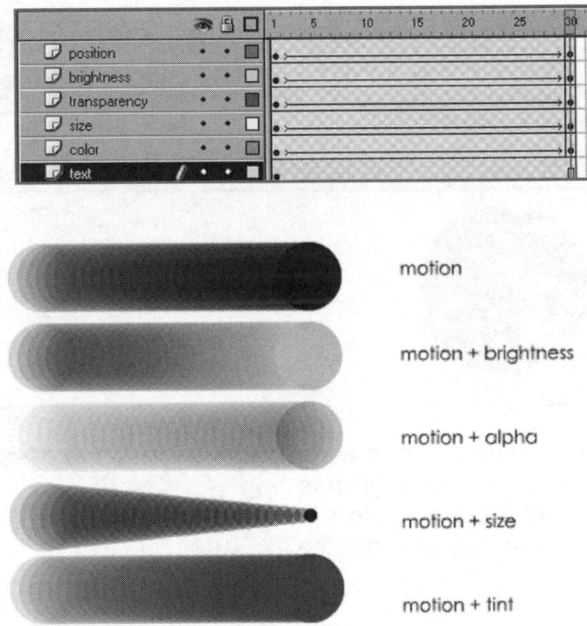

motion

motion + brightness

motion + alpha

motion + size

motion + tint

Now you see it...

How do we access these properties? The more complex properties - changing the lines and fills of the circle to create a different shape, for example - can only be accessed by ActionScript. Others can be accessed easily. Let's make our ball disappear, for example.

1. Select the ball in frame 30.

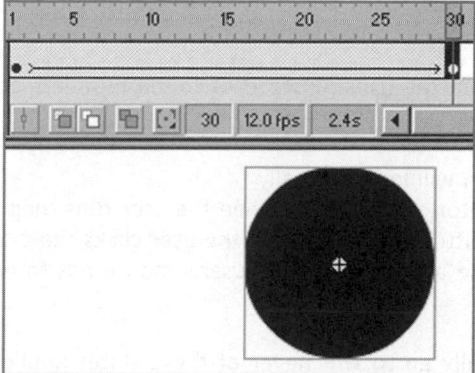

2. In the Properties panel, select the Color drop-down and choose Alpha. A new value will appear next to the drop-down, and will currently be 100% (totally opaque). Change it to a lower value (such as 20%).

3. Test the movie - the motion tween will change the alpha property from 100% on the first frame to 20% on frame 30, giving you a smooth transition.

Although shape and motion tweens may seem a little odd at first, have a think about what you can now do. With some layers to add depth, you've got everything you need to create a simple logo animation.

Buttons and movie clips

When we turned our circle into a graphic symbol, there were two other options: the **button** and the **movie clip**. We'll take a quick look at these before going on to use them in an exercise.

If you chose Button instead of Graphic when you turned your circle into a symbol, you'd see a timeline that looks like this:

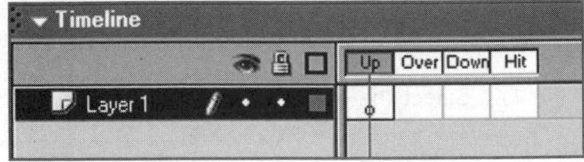

This is slightly different from the usual: instead of frame numbers above the timeline, you can see the button states:

- **Up** - how the button will look normally
- **Over** - what the button will look like when the user runs their mouse over the button
- **Down** – what the button will look like if the user clicks the button
- **Hit** – this defines the area in which the user's mouse has to enter to set off the Over and Down states

The button will automatically go to whichever of these states applies – none of that tricky slicing and rollovers business that we had to go through to create buttons in ImageReady and Fireworks in **Chapter 10**.

You add content to any of these states by inserting a keyframe into it in the normal way, but you don't need to add content to each frame. Just like a normal timeline, if the frame doesn't have any content, Flash will just assume that it's the same as the previous frame, so you don't need to add content to all of the states. Most buttons have at least Up and Hit states – something to tell the user that the button is there, and something to define the area in which the user's mouse has to be for the button to function. If you don't want to create your own, Macromedia have prepared some for you to use, and you can see these in Window > Common Libraries > Buttons.

A common trick in Flash is to have a button, but only define a Hit *state, which creates an invisible button – the user can't see it, but you can make things happen as soon as their mouse passes over it.*

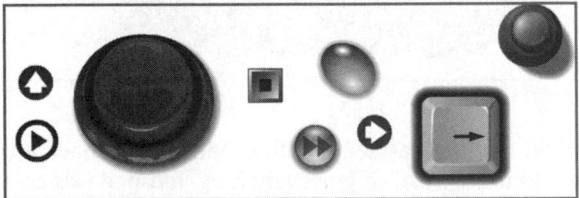

Here's something I created for some Flash-related work a while ago. Each key has a down state (plus a keyboard click sound). Just imagine how long we'd have been in ImageReady or Fireworks if we had to slice and define the rollovers for this: the more complicated your interactive or animated work becomes, the more time that Flash can save you.

One of the reasons that Flash took off is the small size of the plug-in, but the other is more subtle; it is much easier to work with than most other systems for creating web motion graphics. One of the reasons for this is the movie clip. All it consists of is a graphic object that has its own built-in timeline.

Have a look at `logo.fla`. If you test it you will see the Flash version of our GIF animation. Not only does the logo spin, it changes size and color. How do we do this? We do it by using both the main timeline and the movie clip's timeline.

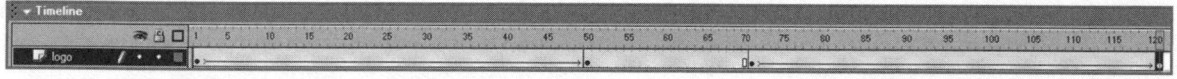

The main timeline has a couple of tweens on it. These cause the color and size changes. Double-click on the logo on the stage, and you will be taken inside the movie clip. You will see the area just under the timeline change to reflect the fact that you are now inside the movie clip (it's always important to keep an eye on this to make sure that you are where you think you are!).

This is rather like a file path in a file explorer - Scene 1 is the main timeline, and 3D futuremedia logo is the name of the movie clip. You can go back to the original (or *parent*) timeline by clicking on the 'scene 1' link, or the left pointing arrow.

Once inside the movie clip, the timeline will change to something like this:

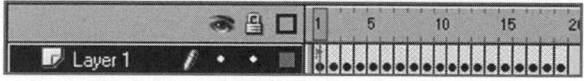

> *Sometimes the animation you want to create is too complicated or changes between frames in a non-uniform way. When that happens, you have to take over from Flash and do all the frames, rather than just the key frames, as here.*

What we have is a rotating logo animation that is itself animated. This process is useful when you want to animate something that has animated parts itself. For example, if you wanted to animate a figure walking, you would create an animation of a figure walking on the spot inside a movie clip. You would then place the movie clip on the stage, and use some sort of animation or tween to make it walk around the screen: the figure would be moving, but so would the figure's legs.

We won't really be using movie clips in this book – that's a book in itself, and we've only got time to scratch the surface of what can be achieved – but it's the way to create some really cool stuff.

A Flash pop-up

A lot of people hate Flash pop-ups, mainly because they usually carry advertising of one sort or another. They can be useful, however, so let's take a look at how to create one. Most pop-ups are pretty simple because they're usually loaded up in addition to the main site and have to be fairly small as a result.

1. Create the following HTML, saving it as `flashPopup.html`. You should recognize this – it's simply our pop-up window function being used to open a new pop-up containing `popup.html`.

```html
<html>
<head>
<title>pop-up launcher</title>
<script language="JavaScript">
function openPop(src, name, scrollbar, w, h ){
        features='menubar=no,resizable=no, scrollbars=' + scrollbar +
            ➥ ',width=' + w + ',height=' + h;
        name=window.open(src, name, features);
        name.focus();
        void 0;
}
</script>
</head>

<body>
<br><br>
click for <a href="javascript:openPop('popup.html', 'flashPopup',
        ➥ 'no', 310, 270);"> pop-up</a>
</body>
</html>
```

2. If the user decides to click on our pop-up, it should close itself and take them to the client's site. Create a new HTML page to represent this, calling it `client.html`.

    ```
    <html>
    <head>
    </head>

    <body>
    <br><br>
    who says web advertising doesn't work?
    </body>

    </html>
    ```

3. Open `tween2.fla` in Flash - we'll use this for our pop-up content. What we have to do though, is change it so that whenever the user clicks on it, the pop-up will close itself, and redirect the user to the client's site.

4. To do this we need an *invisible* button. Select the topmost layer tv and hit the Create new layer icon. A new layer should appear at the top.

    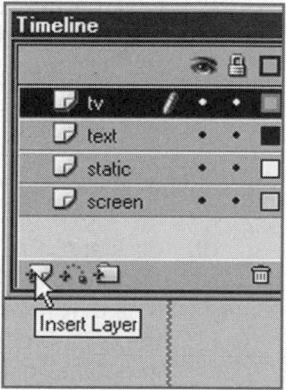

5. Rename the new layer `link` by double-clicking on the name. Lock all other layers, and your timeline should look like this:

    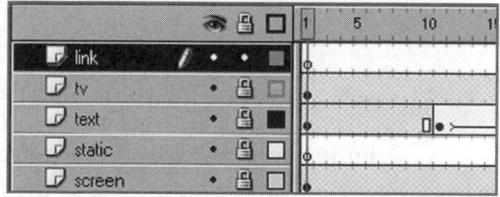

6. We need to create our button. Bring up the Library (Window > Library) and click on the + at the bottom to create a new symbol. Call it `linkButton`, and make sure you specify Button in the Behavior: section.

    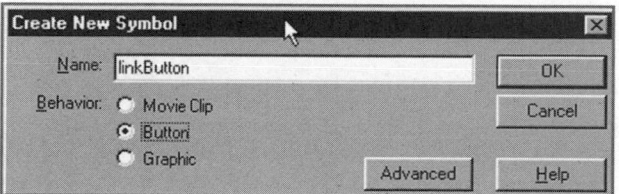

7. We don't actually need to see the button, so we only need to set a Hit state. Select the frame under Hit and use Insert > Keyframe to create a keyframe.

8. With the Hit state still selected, draw a rectangle – the color doesn't matter, as the button won't be seen (it will appear as a cyan shape on the Flash stage to let you know where it is, but won't show up in the final Flash file). The size doesn't matter, either, as we'll change that in a moment.

9. Click on the Scene 1 link at the bottom of the timeline to go back to the main timeline. On the main timeline, make sure the Link layer is still selected, and drag an instance of linkButton from the Library and onto the stage.

10. Click and drag your button so that the top left corner of the button is at the top left-hand corner of the stage. If this means you can't see your button anymore, make sure that the color block on the tv layer is selected to make it show up in outlines only (as shown).

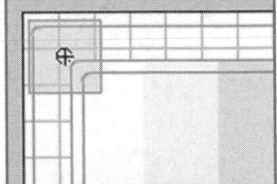

11. Select the Free Transform tool icon from the toolbar 🔲. The button should become bounded by a box with handles around it – if it doesn't, click on the button. Using the handles, enlarge the button so that it covers the entire stage.

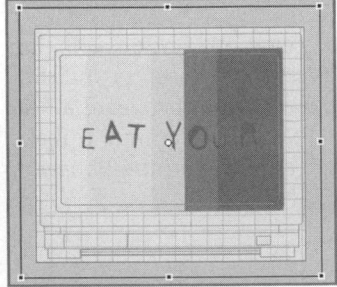

12. We need to give the button an **instance name**, so that the ActionScript we add in a moment can refer to the button. Make sure that the button is selected on the stage, and enter `link` into the Properties panel just under the drop-down menu reading Button, to replace the gray `<instance name>` text.

13. We now need to add our code. Add a new layer, drag it to the top of the list if it's not already there, and call it `Actions`. This is common practice in Flash – it makes sure you keep all your code in the same place, where it's easy to find.

14. Click on the first frame of the new layer, and open the Actions panel (this may be minimized, just above the Properties panel, or you may need to use Window > Actions). The Actions we add here will be attached to whatever we've highlighted on the Stage or the timeline, so anything we add now will be attached to Frame 1 of the timeline and be run every time the playhead runs past frame 1.

> This may seem a little different to JavaScript, but all we are doing is saying "run this ActionScript when you reach this frame" – no different in essence to saying "run this JavaScript when the page loads", or "run this JavaScript when the user clicks a link".

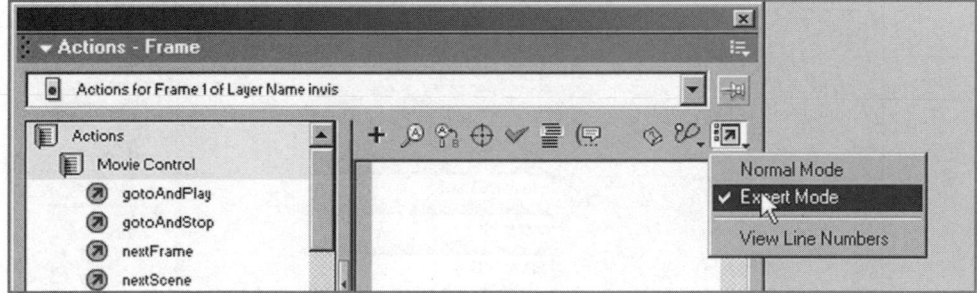

15. At the top right of the Actions panel, click the window menu icon and make sure that Expert mode is selected. This allows us to hand-code script straight into the window, instead of using the drag-and-drop from the menu on the left option.

16. In the window, enter the following;

```
function goClient() {
    getURL("client.html", "_blank");
    getURL("javascript:window.close();", "_self");
}
link.onRelease = goClient;
```

```
function goClient() {
    getURL("client.html", "_blank");
    getURL("javascript:window.close();", "_self");
}
link.onRelease = goClient;
```

You will notice that this looks a lot like JavaScript. In fact, you might even be able to make out what we are doing. First, we define a function called goClient(). This has something called getURL, which seems suspiciously like <a HREF="something" TARGET = "something">, so all the function is doing is loading client.html into a new browser window, and then closing itself by calling javascript as the URL.

The line immediately after the function defines the function as the onRelease event of the button instance link, meaning the code will run when the user releases the button after pressing on it. The dialect may seem a little strange, but the language looks very similar - even down to the way ActionScript uses dot notation when it sets up the event link.onRelease = goClient;.

17. All we need to do now is produce the HTML, so select File > Publish Settings. Flash will create an HTML file based on the name of the FLA unless told otherwise, but we want the HTML file to be called popup.html, because that's what we call it in flashPopUp.html. Make sure you've got the Formats tab showing, uncheck the Use Default Names option right at the bottom, and change the HTML name to popup.html.

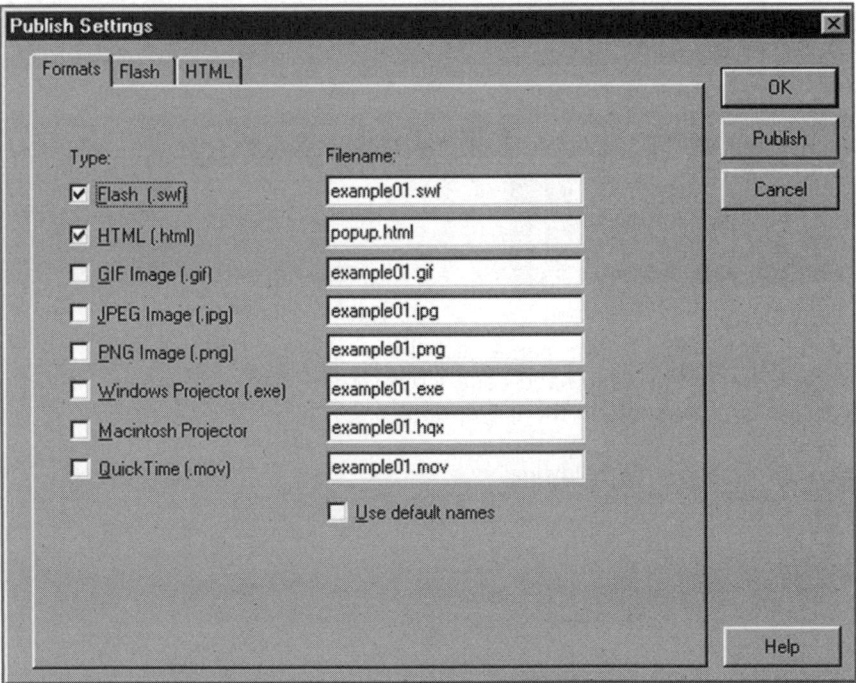

18. Check that you've only got Flash and HTML checked as the export formats, and hit the Publish button.

> The example file for this is included as `example01.html` *in the chapter download if you get stuck.*

19. Open `popup.html` in a text editor. You should see this:

```
<HTML>
<HEAD>
<meta http-equiv=Content-Type content="text/html; charset=ISO-8859-1">
<TITLE>tween2</TITLE>
</HEAD>
<BODY bgcolor="#CCCCCC" >
<!— URL's used in the movie—>
<!— text used in the movie—>
<OBJECT classid="clsid:D27CDB6E-AE6D-11cf-96B8-444553540000"
  codebase="http://download.macromedia.com/pub/shockwave/cabs/flash/
            ➥ swflash.cab#version=6,0,0,0"
 WIDTH="310" HEIGHT="270" id="example01" ALIGN="">
  <PARAM NAME=movie VALUE="example01.swf"> <PARAM NAME=quality VALUE=high>
<PARAM NAME=bgcolor VALUE=#FFFFFF> <EMBED src="example01.swf" quality=high
bgcolor=#FFFFFF WIDTH="310" HEIGHT="270" NAME="example01" ALIGN=""
  TYPE="application/x-shockwave-flash"
PLUGINSPAGE="http://www.macromedia.com/go/getflashplayer"></EMBED>
</OBJECT>
</BODY>
</HTML>
```

20. We need to change the `<body>` tag, as we will see a small gutter around the pop-up if we leave it at default. Change it to;

```
<BODY bgcolor="#FFFFFF" TOPMARGIN="0" LEFTMARGIN="0" BOTTOMMARGIN="0"
➥ RIGHTMARGIN="0" MARGINWIDTH="0" MARGINHEIGHT="0">
```

21. View `flashpopup.html` in a browser. When you click the link, it will open the Flash pop-up. If you click the ad, it will open a new window with `client.html` in it, and then close itself.

> *If you want to test this online, you'll need* `flashpopup.html`, `client.html`, `popup.html`, *and* `example01.swf`.

Replacing HTML with Flash

Many designers and users don't like Flash, because it's a little too brash, and it loses some of the simplicity of HTML. As a designer, you can go for a big Flash site, or you can surreptitiously mix Flash into a predominantly HTML site.

Using frames is a very good way of doing this. Last chapter we had a look at Sham's Painting, so we'll replace the top navigation bar with some Flash. We won't go garish and brash, just the odd spot animation will do it...

Have a look at `example02.fla`. We'll leave you to pore over it, but all we've really done this time is:

- Create normal Flash buttons, with content on the Up and Over states.
- Use File > Import to Import a button sound to go with the edgy text (the sound is exported as part of the SWF).
- Created a keyframe on the Down state of the button, and selected the Sound drop-down menu from the Properties panel to attach the sound to the keyframe. (We set the Sync setting to event, used for short sounds loaded with the SWF.)
- Added an animation to the 'Sham's paintings' test, so that it flickers every now and then.

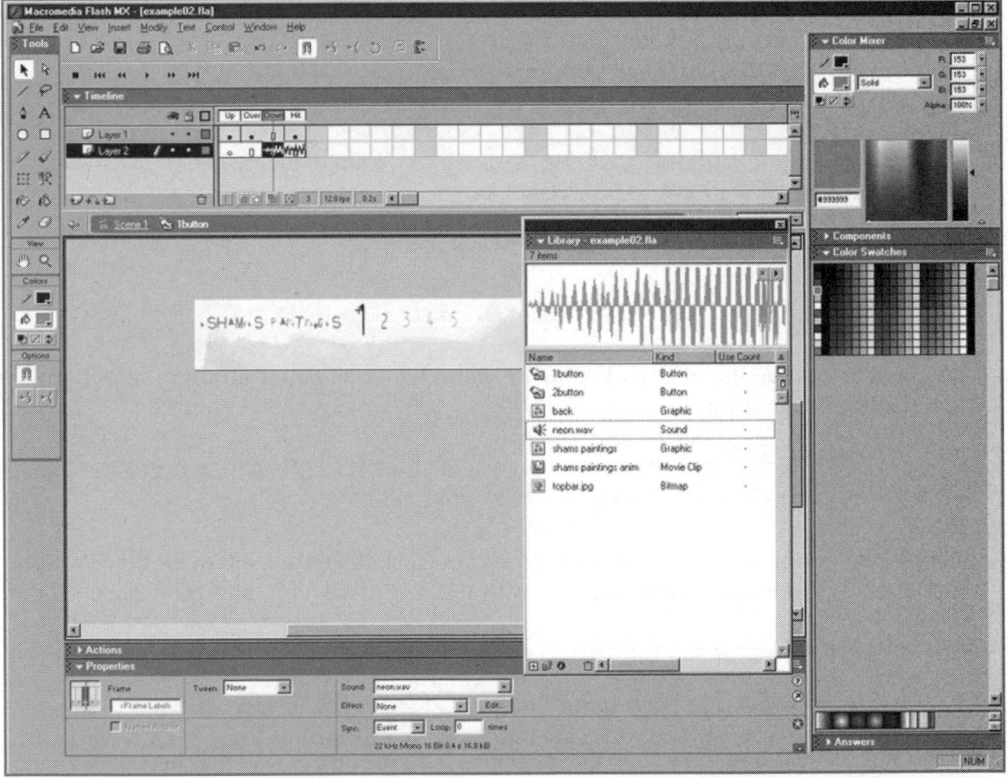

The great thing about the exported files is that there's only two of them: the HTML file, and the 6 KB SWF. No slices, and no separate sound files to upload. That's great news for HTML designers who want to create animation, but are put off by having to create all those slices and manage all those tiny files.

To add this to the **Chapter 11** files is easy: just export the HTML as `topbar.html`, and put it and the SWF file in the same directory as the HTML for *Sham's pictures*.

This book has aimed to give you a rock-solid foundation in all the skills and technologies you need to know to make great websites, but we hope this chapter has given you a glimpse of how you can take this a little bit further...

Getting Your Site Online

It's time to put your site on the Internet, and we have all the tips you need to make the most from your hosting company. We'll cover:

- Domain names and how they work
- Registering a domain name and using web forwarding
- Hosting your site – all the options explored

Now you have built your website, the links are working, the pictures are pretty and the information is sizzling. There is only one problem. You are the only person who can see your work of art. In this chapter we are going to discuss what is involved in getting your site live on the web for the whole world to see.

Whether you want to buy a professional website with advanced features or simply use free space given to you by your ISP, this section has all the information you need.

Overview

Your website currently resides on your hard drive; in order for it to be accessible by the whole world, you will need to transfer the files to a **web server**. A web server is another computer somewhere that is hooked up to the Internet with a constant, super-fast connection. It is all these computers linked together that make up the World Wide Web.

In its simplest terms, you'll need two things – a **domain name** and **web space**. These can be provided by the same company, or different companies. The domain name is the URL of your site, and you need to set this up so that when people type this in your domain host directs them to your site.

The web space you'll need is the actual physical place where you'll store your site files. This will be on an actual computer somewhere as outlined above. Usually bundled with this service are other features such as e-mail.

> *Note that you you can own a domain without taking any web space. If you want to grab your favorite name before someone else does you can register it and host your site later. We'll look at both these in turn.*

Domain name

The **domain name** is what people will type into their browser to bring up your site, e.g. www.mondo.com.pl or www.friendsofed.com. The name is up to you and you can also choose from a range of country-based extensions.

The most common extensions (domains), originally for the US but generally recognized worldwide, are:

- .com   Company
- .net   Internet service
- .org   Non-Profit organization
- .gov   Government Department
- .edu   Educational Institution

There are also many others including country specific ones such as .co.uk for the United Kingdom, .ca for Canada, or .com.pl for Poland.

Choose a name that is short (people don't like to type), is memorable, and is identifiable with your website. One of the problems you will face today is that a lot of the good names are already taken, so you may have to be creative in selecting your name.

> *Your domain can include any letters or numbers, and also the dash symbol (although it cannot start or end with the dash). No other symbols are allowed. It can be between 2 and 67 characters long (including the .com) but the shorter the better.*

To select a name you will have to go to a domain wholesaler site. The process may be different for your country you are living in, but the principle will still be the same. In the last couple of years the government has deregulated the industry and there are now many discount vendors on the web, meaning you can get domains for as cheap as $5-$10.

Shop around for the best price and features. We'll take a walk-through an example in just a few paragraphs time.

Web Forwarding

With web forwarding, which comes in a few guises, you can own a domain (or a number of domains) and have them point to web space elsewhere. For example, you might set up a domain and web space at www.mondowebsite.com, but additionally you might want www.mondowebsite.co.uk and www.mondowebsite.ca as well. You do not need to have three independent sites, just the capacity to forward people who type in your domain to the space you designate.

More often, you might use web forwarding to forward users to free web space provided by your ISP. This is becoming a common feature that ISPs offer, and buying a domain and forwarding it invisibly to your free space can be a very affordable way of managing a professional-looking personal site.

Web forwarding takes two main forms: **redirection** and **cloaking**. Redirection means that people entering www.mondowebsite.com will have their browser instantly sent to another address. Cloaking is when your 'other' address is concealed within an HTML frameset. Without going into the details this means that your domain name www.mondowebsite.com would remain in the browser address bar, making the web forwarding practically invisible. This has the advantage of appearing much more professional.

Registering your name

Finding a registrant can be a tricky process, there are so many to choose from. Keep in mind the services you need now (like e-mail addresses and web-forwarding) and also the services you might need in the future to make your choice one which will serve you in the long-term.

> *Be aware that moving your registration from one company to another can be a costly and time-consuming business. If you come to need services which your registrant cannot offer, you may have to move and it can be very awkward. This is why future-proofing is important. You might also want to check to see if your chosen registrant charges for* **domain transfers***, but note that they may have different policies for transferring* **to** *them and transferring* **away** *from them.*

To be honest, word-of-mouth is arguably the best way to find a good domain/site host. If you know anyone who has a site, ask them what features they've got, and more importantly, about the level of service. Make sure it's right for you, and don't always trust the flashiest banner or the cheapest advertised price. There can sometimes be hidden costs.

Let's take a walk-through a typical process. We'll use as an example Xcalibre.co.uk – the internet company who host friends of ED's popular Flash community at www.phpforflash.com.

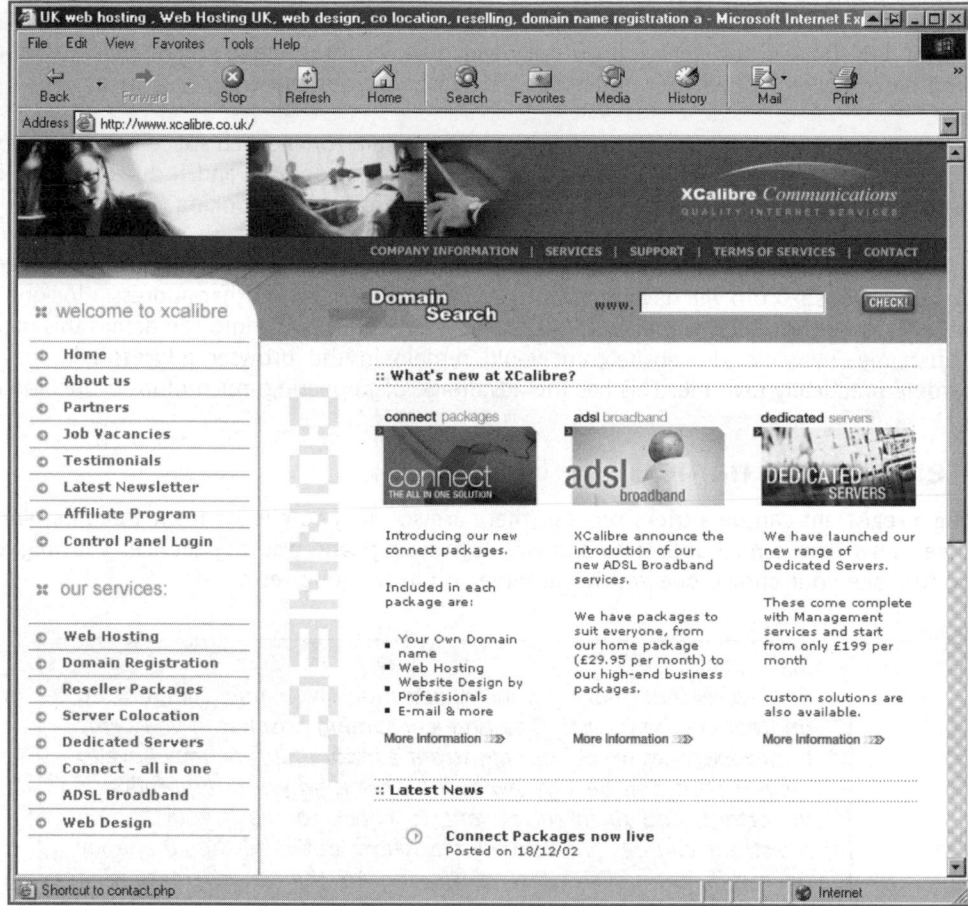

Begin with a search to see if your name is available.

Some sites will allow you to choose an extension at this stage, but in this age of internet saturation, most hosts will instead show you all possible combinations and mark them as available or taken.

Search Results

Please note the new <u>rules</u> for registering me.uk domains

Domain	Status	Cost	Length		
mondowebsite.me.uk	Available	£9.95	2 Years	Add to Order	☐
mondowebsite.biz	Available	£17.50	2 Years	Add to Order	☐
mondowebsite.info	Available	£17.50	2 Years	Add to Order	☐
mondowebsite.co.uk	Available	£9.95	2 Years	Add to Order	☐
mondowebsite.org.uk	Available	£9.95	2 Years	Add to Order	☐
mondowebsite.com	Available	£19.95	2 Years	Add to Order	☐
mondowebsite.net	Available	£19.95	2 Years	Add to Order	☐
mondowebsite.org	Available	£19.95	2 Years	Add to Order	☐
mondowebsite.uk.com	Available	£55.00	2 Years	Add to Order	☐
mondowebsite.ltd.uk	Available	£9.95	2 Years	Add to Order	☐
mondowebsite.plc.uk	Available	£9.95	2 Years	Add to Order	☐
mondowebsite.us.com	Available	£55.00	2 Years	Add to Order	☐
mondowebsite.eu.com	Available	£55.00	2 Years	Add to Order	☐
mondowebsite.br.com	Available	£55.00	2 Years	Add to Order	☐
mondowebsite.uk.net	Available	£55.00	2 Years	Add to Order	☐
mondowebsite.gb.com	Available	£55.00	2 Years	Add to Order	☐
mondowebsite.gb.net	Available	£55.00	2 Years	Add to Order	☐
mondowebsite.de.com	Available	£55.00	2 Years	Add to Order	☐
mondowebsite.ru.com	Available	£55.00	2 Years	Add to Order	☐
mondowebsite.cn.com	Available	£55.00	2 Years	Add to Order	☐
mondowebsite.qc.com	Available	£55.00	2 Years	Add to Order	☐
mondowebsite.no.com	Available	£55.00	2 Years	Add to Order	☐

Next Step!

As you can see we have no competition here and can register as many variations as we wish. The three most popular domains have been highlighted in the screenshot so you can see them clearly in the list.

mondowebsite.com   Available £19.95 2 Years Add to Order ☑

You will possibly be asked if you want to add **web hosting** to your offer. This is where our explanation of web space earlier comes in.

Web hosting

A web hosting account is what you will upload your files to. Your web host is the operator of the computer (the server) that will store your website, and make it available over the Internet to anyone, anywhere in the world.

As mentioned earlier, you might want to limit yourself to a domain and use free space elsewhere for the time being, but for the sake of tutorial let's assume you want to host your site with your domain registrants. There will be a multitude of options presented to you whatever you choose. Here is a rundown of the most important:

:: Hosting Standard		
:: Service	Hosting Standard	Hosting StandardPlus
Websites	1	1
Web Space	50MB	50MB
POP3	5	10
Aliases	✓	✓
Control Panel	✓	✓
Email Forwarding	✓	✓
Full FTP	✓	✓
PHP	✓	✓
SSH	✓	✓
Free Domain Transfers	✓	✓
Access Raw Log Files	✓	✓
Bandwidth	1.0GB/month	2.0GB/month
Dedicated CGI Bin	✓	✓
Preinstalled CGI Scripts	✗	✓
Email Support	✓	✓
Telephone Support	Premium Rate	National Rate
Auto Responders	✓	✓
Web Statistics	normal	enhanced
MYSQL Database	£10.00	✓
WAP Support	✓	✓

How much web space?

This is how much hard drive space they will give you on their server for you to store your files. Most hosts will offer you way more than you will actually need.

Remember that although your original image files were maybe several MB in size, your site has been designed and optimized to be as small and quick to download as possible. This means your final site shouldn't take up very much space at all, but it's always good to have a comfortable amount of extra space for expansion.

> Note that this amount is only the physical space you take up on their server, and **not** anything to do with the number of visitors you are allowed.

How much bandwidth?

Bandwidth is a crucial term in web circles. Bandwidth is the amount of **transfer** you are allowed on your account.

Think of it like when you are downloading a file. If you have a dial-up modem, you can only download so much at a time. You might have several downloads at once, but if one download was taking up all your bandwidth, you'd start finding it difficult to surf at all! Of course, your host has a very high-speed connection. Your bandwidth limit simply expresses how much of that connection you are allowed to use up, and is specified by an amount of transfer in MB.

This is another good reason for keeping your files small. If you have a huge homepage with unoptimized graphics and multimedia, and it weighs in at 500 K, if your bandwidth limit is 1 GB per month (just over 1,000 MB) then after 2,000 visits your site will stop functioning or, more likely, your host will charge you for the excess.

On the other hand if your site is just 50 K then you can have 20,000 visitors!

Bandwidth requirements are completely dependent on file size and traffic. If you have large pages and many visitors, you might need more, but you are unlikely to need more than a standard 1 GB per month for the time being.

> *Check with your prospective host to ask what their charges are and how easy it will be to upgrade to a higher bandwidth account if you need to.*

E-mail

Well, this is pretty essential. You're going to want yourname@mondowebsite.com and possibly more e-mail addresses. There are a few options available.

- POP3 – standing for Point-of-Presence, this is a standard e-mail system whereby your mails are stored on your server, until you come online and download them using Outlook, Outlook Express, Netscape Messenger or the like. You can also send mails by creating them in your client and connecting to the web to send.

- E-mail forwarding – this is where mails to yourname@mondowebsite.com are forwarded to an existing mail address, e.g. yourname@hotmail.com. Note that you cannot send mails which will appear as being from yourname@mondowebsite.com under this set-up.

Assess what your needs are. If this is for a client then you will need to calculate how many distinct addresses are required and what type. Mark up what addresses you can think of, e.g. sales@mondowebsite.com, info@mondowebsite.com, etc, and work it out from there.

Support

You're always going to need some kind of support, even if it's just to report technical problems. Most hosts will offer some kind of support but beware of premium rate numbers, which mean you pay out even just to report problems.

Good e-mail support with reasonably fast responses can be every bit as good as telephone support. Again, assess what you need and make sure you don't overlook this important service.

Dynamic capability

We have just created a **static** site but sites which feature login forms, contact pages, forums and mailing lists require additional technology on the part of the host. You'll probably have heard of ASP, PHP or ColdFusion.

These languages allow your server to interact with your users and with a database, meaning you can store user information and control the pages they see depending on the information they give. You might want to add this kind of functionality in the future, and the good news is tools like **Dreamweaver MX** (which we've mentioned a few times) has all the tools, although that's a book in itself.

> *It is indeed a book in itself, and friends of ED have published Foundation Dreamweaver MX to cover this. As well as the basics of this leading WYSIWYG tool, you'll learn all the advanced Dreamweaver MX techniques, as well as connecting to a database and creating more user-interactive pages using PHP.*

Often you pay for such capabilities, so again it is useful to ask how easily it can be 'bolted on' if you need it in the future. PHP, being an open-source (free) language is often provided without charge and it is one of the most respected and robust server languages available.

Control Panel

Most web hosts will provide you with some kind of control panel, through which you will administer certain areas of your site, and also change e-mail information or passwords. A good control panel makes it extremely easy to manage your site and make updates.

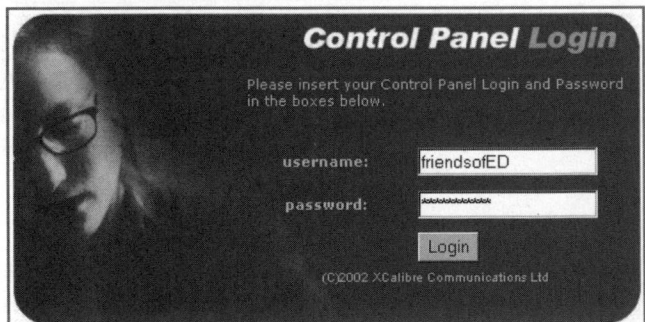

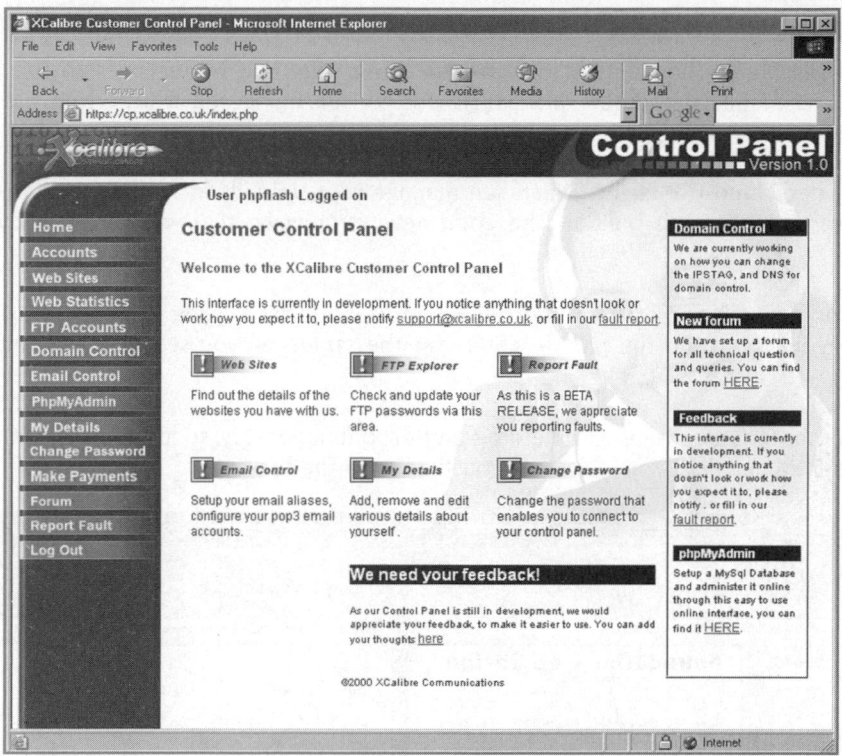

Your control panel might also allow you to upload your files. Otherwise you should ensure you get **FTP access** in order to do this directly. A typical FTP (File Transfer Protocol) address would be ftp.mondowebsite.com and you can use Internet Explorer and Netscape Navigator to upload your files, as we'll see in a few moments.

Sign up!

When you've made your final choices of domain and hosting package, sign up and complete the process. You will have chosen a username and password and these will allow you access to your control panel functions.

> It usually takes between 24 and 48 hours for your domain to be registered and configured.

Uploading your finished website

You should receive full instructions on how to access your site when you sign up, including the FTP address. FTP is a special protocol, like HTTP, but for managing and transferring files rather than just viewing them.

You can get dedicated FTP clients which can manage your uploads for you, and tools like Dreamweaver or FrontPage also have this built in. The good news is however that you can actually do it using your browser.

Try typing in your FTP address into Internet Explorer and (after logging in – File > Login As…) you'll be able to see your space on the remote computer the same way you see files and folders on your own computer.

Like your computer's OS, there's simple drag-and-drop functionality, so it's actually just a case of dragging or copy/pasting your files from your own machine onto the server.

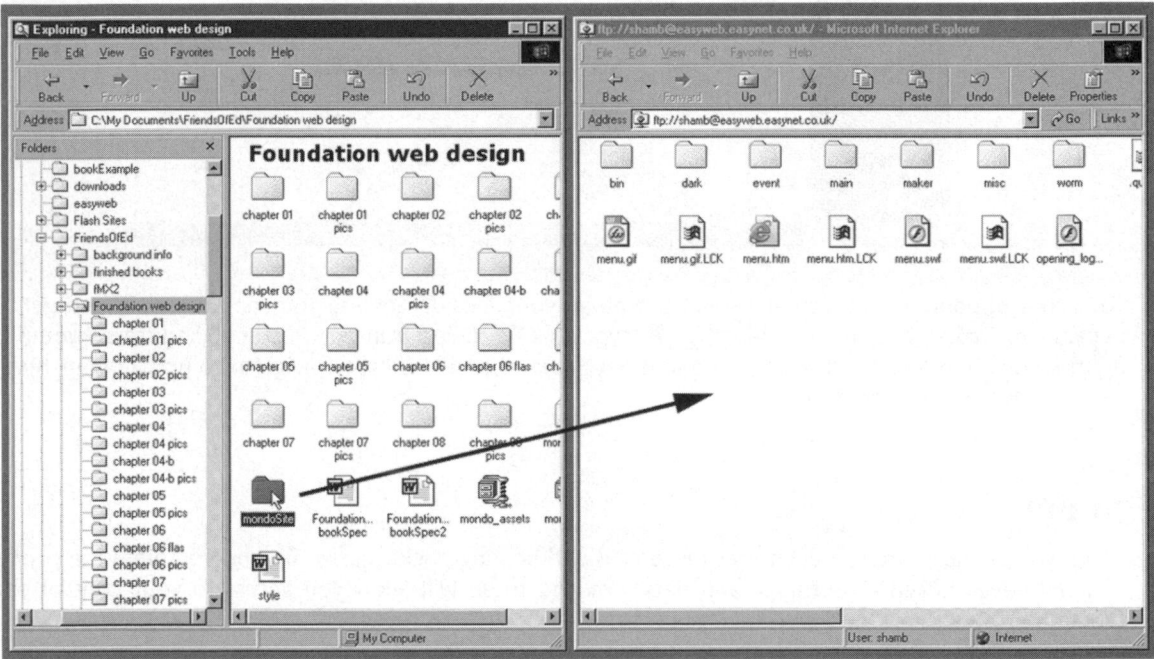

> You'll notice how subfolders in your web space translate to subfolders on your site. For example, a subfolder called images will map to www.mondowebsite.com/images. And if you have created your site with all these folders correctly on your local machine, then you need do nothing to recreate them online except just drag them over!

Once the files are up there, just type your domain name, or a specific page address into your browser to see it all in action, whether it's the case study site Mondo, or your own first web creation. Enjoy and tell all your friends.

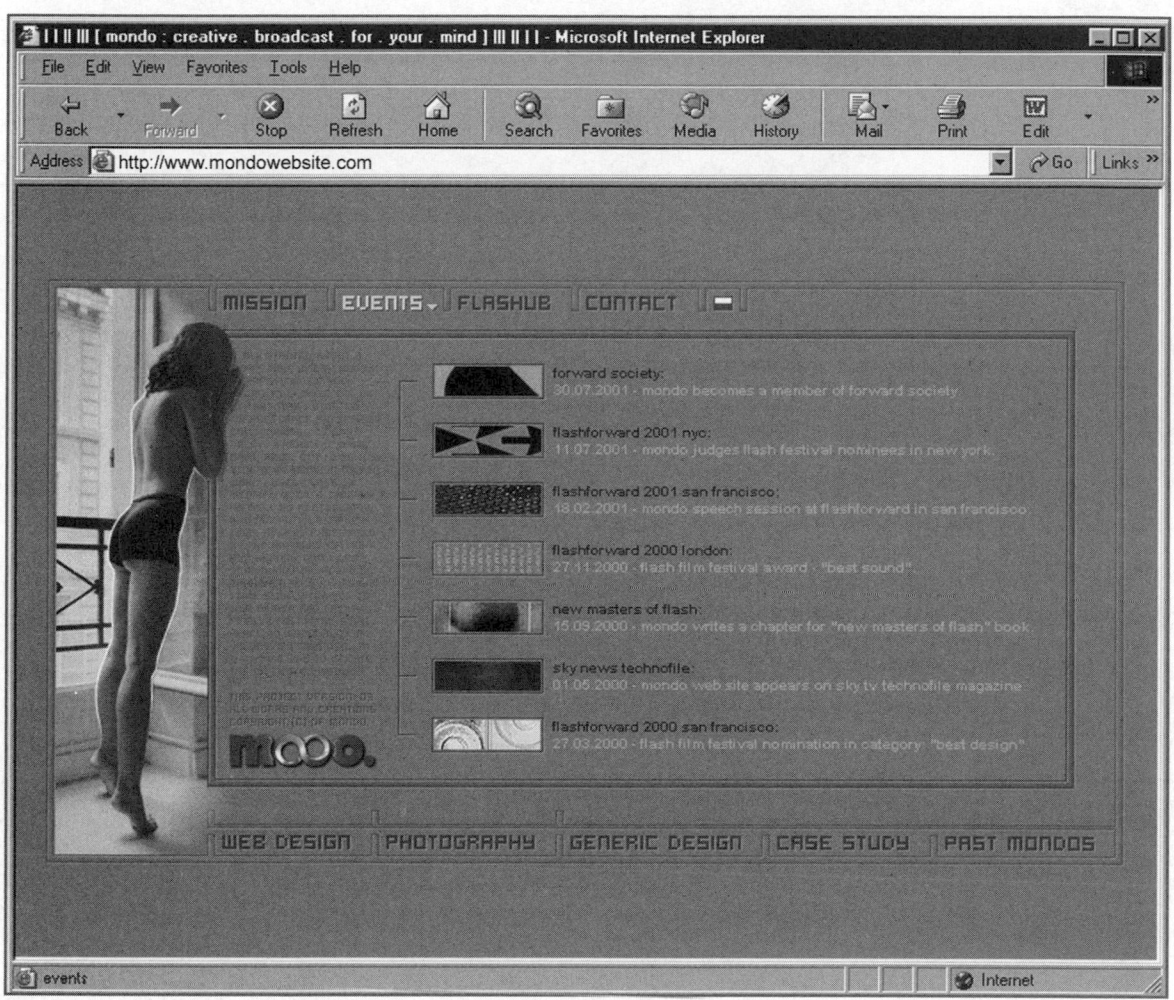

Debugging

The general design intention of HTML is that errors should cause **silent failure**: whenever a browser sees an error, it will try to ignore it and carry on rather than put an error message onto the screen and stop there.

For example, the following HTML will raise no errors, although there are numerous mistakes in it:

```
<html>

<head>
    <script language = "JavaScript">
        document.write("This text is generated by
        JavaScript...")
    </script
</head>


<br><br>
This text is generated by HTML...
<br><br<
This text follows an error in some tags...
</body>

</html>
```

The errors are:
- The </script tag should be needs a closing >
- There is no <body> tag
- The line
<br< should be

If you view the output of the corrected HTML, you would see the output on the right. The listing with errors will give the output on the left.

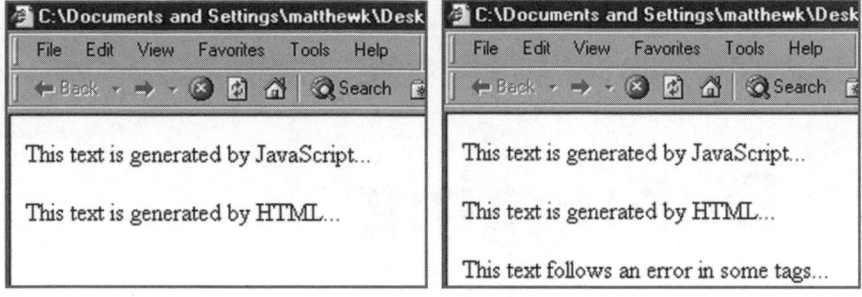

In the incorrect version, the browser can live with the `</script` typo and the lack of a `<body>` tag, but gets confused enough by the `<br><br<` typo to miss out the last sentence of output. This is because it tries to read the line:

```
<br<This text follows an error in some tags...</body>
```

as a single tag, with a `<` at the beginning, carrying on until it sees a `>` to close the tag. It then tries to parse this rather long tag, and fails. The browser ignores this error, resulting in the third sentence disappearing until we fix the HTML.

The fact that the browser ignores errors is actually a good thing, because:

- You can write HTML that Netscape Navigator understands but Internet Explorer doesn't, safe in the knowledge that Internet Explorer will simply ignore it.
- You can add formatting to the HTML so that you can read it (such as splitting code over several lines, and so on), because the browser will simply ignore them if it doesn't understand them as part of HTML.
- If an older browser sees some new tags that it doesn't understand, it will just ignore them.

That's a cool concept, but it starts to cause us problems when we try to include JavaScript in the equation. Errors in JavaScript are significantly more complex than errors in HTML, and because the browser tries to carry on when it hits an error, it can be difficult to find out what is causing the error. Both Netscape Navigator and Internet Explorer know what your scripting errors are – you just need to ask them to tell you...

> *Those seeking amusement may want to browse a few of their favorite sites to see whether they generate any errors. It's surprising how many errors are picked up, especially in supposedly robust sites!*

Internet Explorer for PC

To enable script error reporting in Explorer for PC, select Tools > Internet Options and then select the Advanced tab on the window that appears. Near the top, you will see a set of checkboxes under the heading Browsing. Uncheck Disable Script Debugging and check Display a notification about every script error.

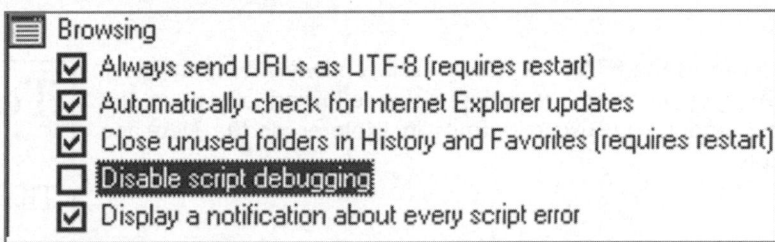

Internet Explorer for Mac

To enable script error reporting in Explorer for Mac, select Preferences on the Explorer menu. Under Web Browser, click Web Content, and in the Active Content area, make sure the Show Scripting Error Alerts option check box is ticked.

Netscape Navigator

To enable script error reporting in Netscape Navigator, simply type Javascript: as the URL. A window called JavaScript Console will open. Error reporting will be active as long as you keep this window open (you can leave it in the background if you wish, just don't close it).

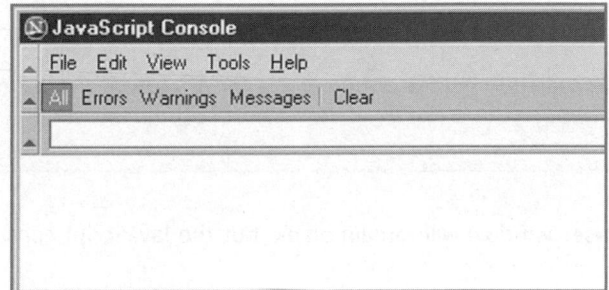

Using the browser to debug a script

The best way to see the debugging features of the browser is to go ahead and try them out with a script containing a known error. The following script has no errors:

```
<html>

<head>
    <script language = "JavaScript">
        document.write("<h2>Test Script</h2>")
        document.write("This is a test");
```

```
            </script>
        </head>

        <body>
        </body>

        </html>
```

If we save this script as the HTML file `debug.html` and view it in a browser with script debugging enabled, we will see the following output in the browser window, and no untoward outputs in Explorer or the Netscape JavaScript console:

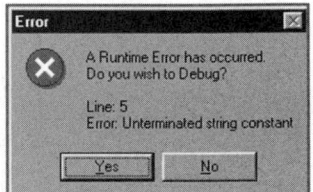

Let's add an error – remove the closing quote on the last `document.write`:

> `document.write(`**`"This is a test`**`);`

In Internet Explorer, the following window will appear to signify that an error has been detected, stating the line number and error description:

> *You may also get the option to use the Microsoft Visual Environment to debug your script if you have Visual Studio installed.*

In Netscape, the browser window will remain blank, but the JavaScript console will display the erroneous line as shown:

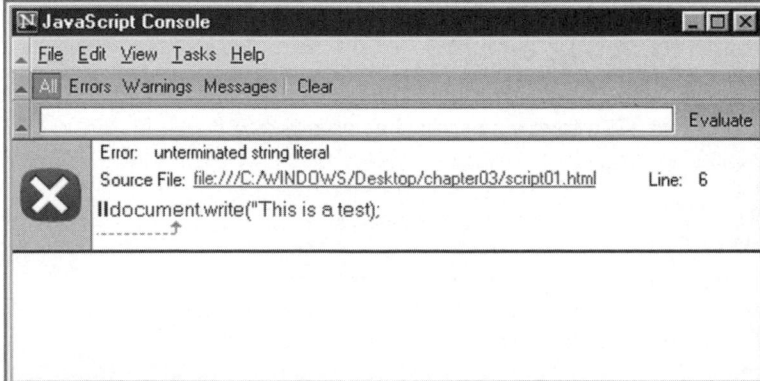

As you can see, the free debugging facilities of Netscape Navigator are far superior to those of Internet Explorer, so it's generally a better idea to use Netscape for your debugging.

One final important point to remember is that script debugging in either browser does not debug errors in your HTML, even if these break the scripts. For example, the following script:

```
<html>

<head>
     <sript language = "JavaScript">
          document.write("<h2>Test Script</h2>")
          document.write("This is a test);
     </script>
</head>

<body>
</body>

</html>
```

...has an error in the first `<script>` tag (`sript` should be `script`). This will render like this:

```
document.write("
```

Test Script

```
") document.write("This is a test);
```

The first `<script>` tag is ignored, so this means that the script itself is now assumed to be plain text. Because the JavaScript parser is not invoked, no errors will appear from it, even though it is obvious that the page is seriously wrong somewhere.

Alternatives

This level of debugging is usually enough for most simple scripts, but if you want to get serious, you can download the *Venkman* JavaScript debugger from:

http://developer.netscape.com/software/jsdebug.html

The debugger is pretty small in size, and should download and install itself in a couple of minutes even on a 56K modem. Once installed, the debugger will be available in Netscape with Tasks > Tools > JavaScript debugger. You may have to close and reopen your browser and restart your computer to complete the installation. The Venkman debugger is beyond the scope of this book, but you can find a set of tutorials at the same URL.

HTML Events

The following table lists the most common events used. It is not meant to be an exhaustive list of events, but instead lists the events you'll most commonly need to use when starting out.

We will look at the following types of events;

- Finding out what the user's mouse pointer is doing via mouse events
- Finding out if the user is using the keyboard via key events
- Finding out when a page is fully loaded into a browser with HTML document events

We have omitted all events that are associated with forms and error checking

Mouse events

We'll look at two types of mouse events: detecting mouse clicks and detecting other mouse states.

Detecting mouse clicks

There are two events that allow you to detect a click; **onClick** and **onDblClick**. The first detects a single-click and the second detects a double-click. The following will output the message 'I have been clicked' if you click on the 'hit me!' link:

```
<html>
<head>
<script language="JavaScript">
function clickFunction(){
```

continues overleaf

```
            document.write('I have been clicked');
            void 0;
      }
      function doubleClickFunction(){
            document.write('I have been double clicked');
            void 0;
      }
      </script>
      </head>

      <body >
      <a href="#" ONCLICK="clickFunction();">hit me!</a>
      </body>
```

Changing the <a> tag to...

```
      <a href="#" ONDBLCLICK="doubleClickFunction();"hit me!</a>
```

...will cause the message 'I have been double-clicked' to appear if you do just that.

> Note that having a click and double-click event in the same tag will mean that the double-click will never be seen in most cases, because the click event will occur on the initial click.

You can add these events to most tags that create clickable content on the screen (including the <body> tag itself, whereby the clickable area becomes the whole document).

Notice that the tag doesn't have to be an <a> link for this (or any other) event to work. In the example above, we have set up links with dummy hrefs of '#', which many beginners would think of first, given that most mouse interaction is related to this tag. We could, however, just as easily make the tag a paragraph for example:

```
      <p ONCLICK="clickFunction();"> hit me!</p>
```

Detecting other mouse states

When you want to detect more than just clicks you need to use the **onMouse** events. They include:

- **onMouseDown** – Detects a mouse press over the content.
- **onMouseMove** – Detects mouse movement over the content. This event will fire continuously if the mouse is continually moving, as long as it stays over the content area.
- **onMouseOut** – Detects when you move out of the content area.
- **onMouseOver** – Detects when you first move over (or 'hover') over the content.
- **onMouseUp** – Detects a mouse release over the content.

The following code will cause a change whenever you start to hover (mouseOver) a paragraph of text:

```html
<html>
<head>
<script language="JavaScript">
function overFunction(){
      document.write('you touched me!');
      void 0;
}
</script>
</head>

<body >
<p ONMOUSEOVER="overFunction();">See what happens when you touch text on
this paragraph...</p>
</body>
</html>
```

The following code will cause the function counter() to run as fast as the browser can handle events, for as long as the mouse is moving over the browser document area. This will cause a count of the number of events triggered on the browser status line (bottom left of the window), and is a good exercise to see how fast the browser can handle events. It's actually pretty slow compared to other application languages (such as the languages video games are written in), because JavaScript is not designed for speed.

```html
<html>
<head>
<script language="JavaScript">
function counter(){
      count = count+1;
      window.status = 'I have run ' + count + ' times so far'
      void 0;
}
count = 0;
</script>
</head>

<body ONMOUSEMOVE="counter();">
<p> move the mouse and watch the status area...</p>
</body>
</html>
```

As well as onClick, there are a number of other events that are *very* similar to the onMouse events. For example, there are two events **onBlur** and **onFocus** that are very similar to onMouseOut and onMouseOver, and for most tags, identical. In general web design, you can almost always get away with only using the onDblClick and the onMouse events listed above.

Detecting keypresses

You can detect what the user is doing with the following events:

- **onKeyDown** – Triggers on a key pressed down
- **onKeyPress** – Triggers on a key being press-released
- **onKeyUp** – Triggers on a key being released

When the user presses a key you will normally see the onKeyDown followed by the onKeyUp. The onKeyUp and onKeyPress events are almost always identical, and occur at the same point; when the user lets go of the key. The only difference between the two occurs in the unlikely situation that the user already has a key pressed down before the page is loaded. In this case, the press-release is not seen, so only the onKeyUp will fire.

Most of the time, you only want to use one of the three key events, and in practice, it's just a case of remembering the name of one of them, because there's not much between them.

Note that you can't actually detect *which* key was used just by using these events (you invariably don't need to anyway), just that a key was used.

The following code shows the onKeyDown event being used...

```
<html>
<head>
<script language="JavaScript">
function keyFunction(){
     document.write('couldn't resist, huh?...');
     void 0;
}
</script>
</head>

<body ONKEYDOWN="keyFunction();">
<br><br><b>DONT PRESS YOUR KEYBOARD OR THIS COMPUTER EXPLODES!</b>
</body>
</html>
```

Keyboard focus

An important issue to bear in mind is that keys are only detected if the browser has keyboard focus. This is a security feature to prevent a hidden browser window surreptitiously reading key presses meant for another browser window. A browser will only be allowed to detect keyboard actions if it is the 'currently selected' window. This means slightly different things on different browsers. It means either:

- The browser window must be active (e.g. its title bar is blue rather than gray in Windows), or
- The browser window must be active and the user has clicked inside it at least once since it become active

HTML document events

There are three events that allow you to act on certain useful triggers during HTML page load. They are:

- **onLoad** – Triggers when the current document is fully loaded
- **onUnload** – Triggers when the current page is about to be discarded and another page loaded
- **onAbort** – Triggers when an image was prevented from loading

The onLoad and onUnload events are used with the <body> tag. The onAbort is used only with the <img> tag, and is triggered when the user hits the browser Stop button whilst an image is in the process of being loaded.

Theevent you need to use most often is the onLoad, and this is to prevent any JavaScript running before the page is fully loaded. This prevents JavaScript assuming buttons, text boxes and other elements are loaded in before they actually are (which would otherwise stop the JavaScript working properly or at all). In most of this chapter, we haven't needed to do this, but for certain pages, you may find that you may need to pause your scripts until the page is in the browser.

The following code shows one way to do this:

```
<html>
<head>
<script language="JavaScript">
function startScripts(){
     window.status = 'start scripts now!'
     void 0;
}
</script>
</head>

<body ONLOAD="startScripts();">
<p> content goes here...</p>
</body>
</html>
```

This simply changes the window status as soon as the page is loaded. The order of the process is:

1. The <head> contents are read but the lines within the function are not executed
2. The page HTML is parsed as per the content between the <body>...</body> tags
3. Finally, when the page is fully parsed and all content is displayed in the browser, the function is actually run via the onLoad event

Layers

A traditional artist is used to drawing on a single surface, such as a piece of paper or canvas. A digital artist can make use of **layers**, which are used to represent multiple surfaces. Think of them as a solid background (the lowest layer), with a stack of glass panes above it. You can paint on one pane (including the lowest) at a time. When viewed from directly above, the painting will look as if it is all painted on a single surface.

The use of layers allows you to work on one layer, and manipulate the contents of that layer without altering other layers. You can also re-arrange the stacking order of the layers, and delete and add layers. If you haven't encountered layers before, try the simple exercise below.

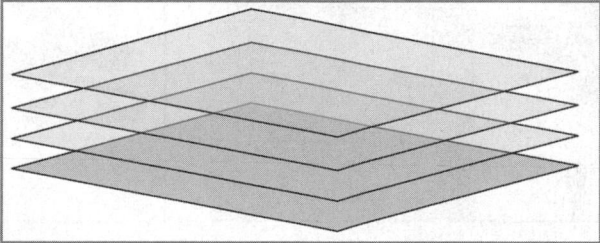

Using layers

1. Create a new file with File > New, and specify dimensions of 500x500.

2. Bring up the layers window with Window > Layers. This contains a thumbnail of each layer in the current stack, showing what you would see if you looked at the layer on its own from above.

As we've seen elsewhere, transparent areas are shown as a checkerboard pattern.

3. In ImageReady, the default layer is called background. In Fireworks, it's simply called layer 1. ImageReady users select the Paintbrush tool, Fireworks users select the Brush tool.

 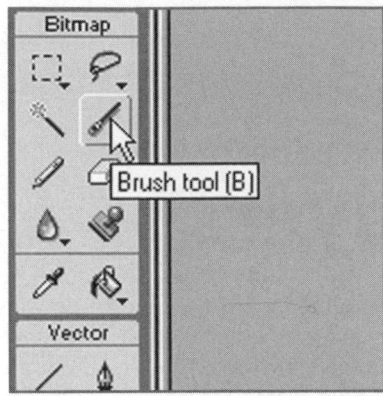

4. Paint a squiggle:

5. To create another layer, ImageReady users need to hit the second icon from the right at the bottom of the window. There is a similar icon on the Fireworks window, but it doesn't do quite the same thing, so you need to use the Layer windows drop-down menu (click on the little arrow on the top right), and select New Layer…

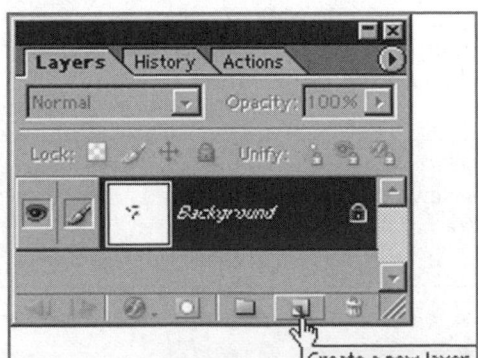 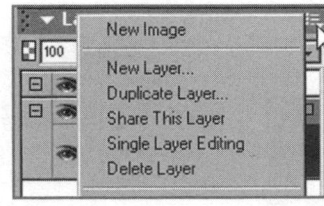

6. With the same brush, but with a different color, draw another squiggle. Because the new layer is both the current layer and the top layer, anything you paint will appear *over* the contents of the previous layer.

 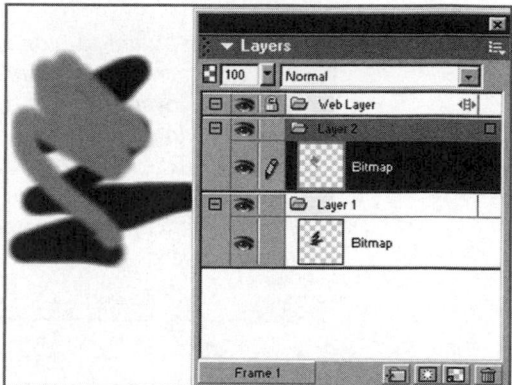

7. If you click on the little eye icon of the new layer, it will toggle the visibility of the layer, and you can see the effect of the different layers.

 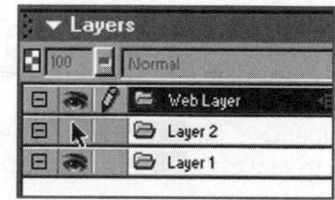

8. Changing the opacity (ImageReady), or alpha (Fireworks) value of the layer can let you see some more subtle blending of the two layers.

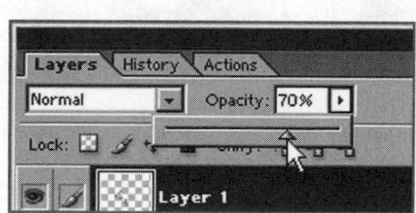 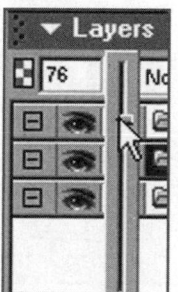

9. You can also use the various tools on one layer or the other. You can use the Eraser tool to remove parts of one layer, for example.

> *If you don't want to hide a layer, but also don't want to draw on it, you can lock one or more layers. To do this in ImageReady, simply select the layer you want to lock, make sure it is currently visible (eye icon showing), and click the black padlock icon (near the top of the window). This locks that layer from change until you unlock it again by clicking the padlock. In Fireworks, click the column immediately to the right of the eye icon. A padlock icon will show, denoting a locked layer.*

10. Create another new layer and use the Type tool (ImageReady) or Text tool (Fireworks) to add some text. The new layer will again appear in front because of the order of the layers.

> *Notice that both applications specify that the new layer contains text. This is because text is created from vectors, whereas the previous work we did involved painting pixels (digital artists usually call work with pixels **painting**, and work with vectors **drawing**). This shows up another use of layers; both applications use them to differentiate between the different types of technology they use to render the final image.*

11. You may accidentally unselect the intended layer now that you have multiple layers, so check the Layers panel to make sure that the changes you make are being applied to the correct layer.

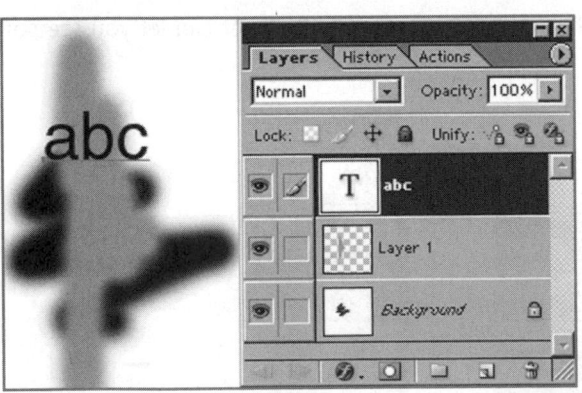
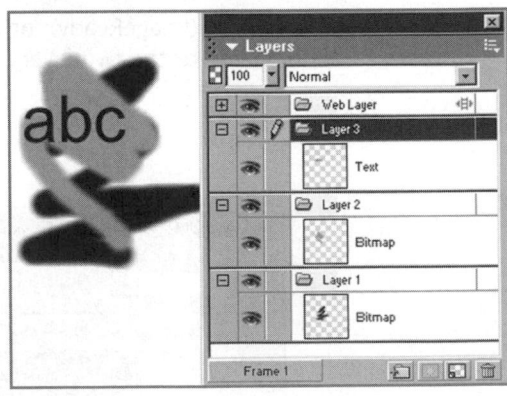

12. Give a couple of your layers more descriptive names by clicking on their titles and entering a new name (you can also delete any of the layers by clicking the trashcan icon at the bottom right of the Layers window). Try moving the layers around in the order as well – just click and drag.

> *Fireworks has a more specialized layer window than ImageReady. It has a* **web layer***, which holds graphics that define how the final exported graphic will look/act on a web page. We look at this in* **Chapter 10***.*

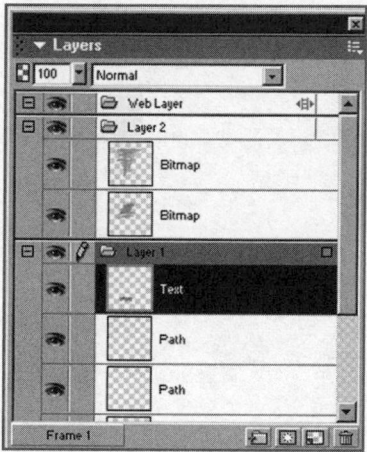

That's about it for layers: they're not a requirement for great images, but they make creating them a whole lot easier!

Index

The index is arranged hierarchically, in alphabetical order, with symbols preceding the letter A. Many second-level entries also occur as first-level entries. This is to ensure that you will find the information you require however you choose to search for it.

friendsof

DESIGNER TO DESIGNER™

friends of ED writes books for you. Any suggestions, or ideas about how you want information given in your ideal book will be studied by our team.

Your comments are valued by friends of ED.

For technical support please contact support@friendsofed.com.

Freephone in USA	800.873.9769
Fax	312.893.8001
UK contact: Tel:	0121.687 4100
Fax:	0121.687.4101

Registration Code: | 416X9VP83XQDO601 |

Foundation Web Design - Registration Card

Name ....

Address ....

City ....State/Region ....

Country ....Postcode/Zip ....

E-mail ....

Profession: design student ☐ freelance designer ☐

part of an agency ☐ inhouse designer ☐

other (please specify) ....

Age: Under 20 ☐ 20-24 ☐ 25-29 ☐ 30-40 ☐ over 40 ☐

Do you use: mac ☐ pc ☐ both ☐

How did you hear about this book?..

Book review (name)..

Advertisement (name) ....

Recommendation ....

Catalog ....

Other ....

Where did you buy this book? ....

Bookstore (name) ....City...........................

Computer Store (name)..

Mail Order...

Other..

How did you rate the overall content of this book?

Excellent ☐ Good ☐

Average ☐ Poor ☐

What applications/technologies do you intend to learn in the near future?..

....

What did you find most useful about this book? ....

....

What did you find the least useful about this book? ....

....

Please add any additional comments ....

....

What other subjects will you buy a computer book on soon?

....

....

What is the best computer book you have used this year?

....

....

Note: This information will only be used to keep you updated about new friends of ED titles and will not be used for any other purpose or passed to any other third party.

ISBN:190434416x

DESIGNER TO DESIGNER™

NB. If you post the bounce back card below in the UK, please send it to:

Arden House,
1102 Warwick Road,
Acocks Green,
Birmingham,UK.
B27 6BH.